The Ethical Life

Fundamental Readings
in Ethics and Moral Problems

RUSS SHAFER-LANDAU

The University of Wisconsin, Madison

New York   Oxford

OXFORD UNIVERSITY PRESS

2010

Oxford University Press, Inc., publishes works that further Oxford University's objective of excellence in research, scholarship, and education.

Oxford   New York
Auckland   Cape Town   Dar es Salaam   Hong Kong   Karachi
Kuala Lumpur   Madrid   Melbourne   Mexico City   Nairobi
New Delhi   Shanghai   Taipei   Toronto

With offices in
Argentina   Austria   Brazil   Chile   Czech Republic   France   Greece
Guatemala   Hungary   Italy   Japan   Poland   Portugal   Singapore
South Korea   Switzerland   Thailand   Turkey   Ukraine   Vietnam

Copyright © 2010 by Oxford University Press, Inc.

Published by Oxford University Press, Inc.
198 Madison Avenue, New York, New York 10016
http://www.oup.com

Oxford is a registered trademark of Oxford University Press.

Library of Congress Cataloging-in-Publication Data
Shafer-Landau, Russ
    The ethical life : fundamental readings in ethics and moral problems / Russ Shafer-Landau.
        p.   cm.
    Includes bibliographical references.
    ISBN 978-0-19-537769-9 (alk. paper)
1. Ethics.   I. Title.
BJ1012.S428 2010
170—dc22   2009019515

Printing Number: 9 8 7 6 5 4 3 2

Printed in the United States of America
on acid-free paper.

CONTENTS

═══ ❧ ═══

ACKNOWLEDGMENTS

It has been a lot of fun putting this book together, but it hasn't always been an easy thing to do. By far the most difficult aspect of the project was the winnowing. Ethics is so large a field, with so much that is provocative and interesting within it—yet books must have their page limits, and those limits often forced me to leave a prized piece behind. It has been a real challenge to offer a representative sampling of subject matter and viewpoints within a book of this size. To the extent that I have met with any success, it is owing in large part to the helpful suggestions and kind critical advice I received from the following philosophers: Jim Anderson, Ralph Baergen, Claudia Card, Tom Carson, Christian Coons, Richard DeGeorge, Neil Delaney, David Detmer, Tyler Doggett, Richard Haynes, Darren Hibbs, John Huss, Carla Johnson, Keith Korcz, Mark LeBar, Hilde Lindeman, Christian Miller, Richard Momeyer, Dave Schmidtz, David Sobel, Stephen Sullivan, Mark van Roojen, Paul Wagner, Kit Wellman, Jason Zinser, and Christopher Zurn. I am very grateful for their assistance.

I would also like to acknowledge the terrific support of my editor at Oxford, Robert Miller, and his crack assistants, Yelena Bromberg and Christina Mancuso, who helped shepherd this book through its various stages. I feel very fortunate to have had a chance to work with Robert on this and other projects over the years, and am, as always, grateful for his advice, constant encouragement, open-mindedness, and inspired good sense.

R.S.L.
Madison, Wisconsin
Autumn 2009

A NOTE ON
THE COMPANION VOLUME

This collection can be used as a self-standing introduction to ethics. It includes readings from each of the major divisions within moral philosophy. With the general introduction, an introduction to each reading, study questions, and all of the supplementary materials available at the book's website, I hope that readers are able to get a very good feel for just how interesting moral philosophy can be.

This collection is designed to serve as a natural partner to *Fundamentals of Ethics* (Oxford University Press), an introduction to moral philosophy that I have written. *Fundamentals* is a textbook, though I hope it is a bit more lively than such a label implies. Both books offer coverage of the good life, the nature of duty and virtue, and the status of morality. The book you have in your hands also offers extensive coverage of many practical ethical problems, such as abortion, the death penalty, famine relief, etc. My hope, of course, is that the two books work neatly in tandem. The theories and positions I present and analyze in *Fundamentals* are here represented by some of their finest defenders. For those who are content to get the view directly from the source, this book should do. But if you would like a moral theory or an ethical position placed in a broader context, its main lines of argument laid out clearly and then critically assessed, then a dip into the companion volume might not be a bad idea.

I am very interested in hearing from readers who are willing to offer me their feedback, both positive and negative. Perhaps you have found some pieces dull or uninspired, or some that were especially exciting and provocative. For teachers who are familiar with this terrain, perhaps you've been disappointed at seeing a beloved piece gone missing, or would like to pass along the success of a given selection in sparking conversation. The easiest way to reach me is by e-mail: *shaferlandau@wisc.edu*. I'd be very pleased to receive your thoughts on how this book might be improved.

HELP FOR
STUDENTS AND INSTRUCTORS

There is a great deal of supplementary material designed to help students and instructors make the most of this book. Within these pages, you will find a set of study questions for each of the 39 readings. In addition, all of the following resources are available at the book's website—*www.oup.com/us/shafer-landau*:

Student Resources

- an overview of the book;
- introductions to each of the book's four main sections;
- further reading for each of the four main sections;
- web links for each of the four main sections; and
- self-quiz questions with answers for each reading.

Instructor Resources are provided on the website, as well as in the *Instructor's Manual* (on CD), which includes:

- essay questions for each section;
- short abstracts of every reading;
- essay and exam questions for every reading;
- multiple-choice questions for every reading;
- wide-ranging essay questions focused on each of the first three main sections; and
- lecture outlines on PowerPoint slides for every reading.

I want to thank my expert research assistant, Justin Horn, for his terrific assistance and initiative in putting these materials together.

INTRODUCTION

M oral philosophy, or ethics—I use the terms interchangeably—is, in its widest application, the study of what we should aspire to in our lives, and of how we should live.

There is no agreed-upon definition of morality, or even of philosophy. We can offer vague (very vague) platitudes, on the order of: philosophy is the love of wisdom; morality is the code that we should live by. It isn't clear to me that we can do *much* better than that. More instructive, I think, is to describe the specific fields within ethics. Through an understanding of these areas, we can better appreciate what moral philosophy is all about.

Nowadays, it is standard to distinguish four different areas of moral philosophy. And (surprise!) the four parts of this book correspond to each of these areas.

The first is known as *value theory*. This is the part of ethics that tries to determine what is valuable in and of itself, what is worth pursuing for its own sake. Is happiness, for instance, the ultimate good? Our first two authors, the Greek philosopher Epicurus and the Englishman John Stuart Mill, certainly think so. But others are skeptical. These include the writer Aldous Huxley, and the late Harvard philosopher Robert Nozick. Perhaps what is most important is simply that we get what we want out of life— even if, unusually, it isn't happiness that we seek? That's what Richard Taylor argues. Yet others (represented here by Jean Kazez) reject this idea, and offer a variety of things (self-determination, moral virtue, happiness, loving relationships, etc.) that are said to be good in their own right.

1

In part 2 we turn to that area of moral philosophy known as *norma-tive ethics*. This large branch of philosophy is devoted to identifying the supreme principle(s) of right action. Many philosophers have sought just a single, fundamental principle that will unify the entire field, that will explain, for instance, why keeping your word, telling the truth, and help-ing the poor are all morally right.

Many important contenders seek to fill this role. Consider, for instance, the golden rule (treat others as you would have them treat you), the divine command theory (acts are right just because God commands them), and ethical egoism (always act so as to best serve your self-interest). Each of these theories advances its own supreme moral rule, which singles out one feature that is meant to explain why every right action is right, and why every immoral action is wrong.

These three theories are fascinating, but they have been largely (though not entirely) rejected by philosophers.[1] I have therefore chosen to focus here on those normative theories that have received much wider support among philosophers. The first of these is *utilitarianism* (defended here by Australian philosopher J.J.C. Smart), which instructs us always to produce the greatest happiness for the greatest number. Utilitarianism focuses on an action's results—Did it yield the greatest happiness of all available actions?—to determine its morality. The German philosopher Immanuel Kant, by contrast, tells us that results are morally irrelevant. Acts are right, he says, just because we can use their guiding principles consistently, without involving ourselves in contradiction. This isn't an easy thought to understand, but the basic idea is pretty simple. The essence of morality, Kant thinks, is fairness and justice. Immorality is a matter of making an exception of yourself, of living by rules that, in some sense, can-not possibly serve as the basis of everyone's actions.

Kant's view shares some features with another important normative ethic, the *social contract theory*. Though this theory was briefly discussed as far back as the ancient Greeks, it was not fully developed until well into the sixteenth century. It was brilliantly developed in the work of Thomas Hobbes, whose book *Leviathan* is excerpted here. The social contract the-ory tells us that morality is essentially a cooperative enterprise, and that the moral rules are those that self-interested people would obey, on the

---

[1] For a survey of the attractions and difficulties of these views, please see the companion volume to this collection, *The Fundamentals of Ethics* (Oxford University Press, 2009).

condition that all others do so as well. Both Kantianism and the social contract theory take the natural ethical question—What if everyone did that?—quite seriously, and both use an answer to this question as a foundation of their normative ethical theory.

Many philosophers have sought a basis for morality in human nature. *Natural law theory* takes this idea most seriously, and in one form or another (there are many varieties), it tries to show that moral action is a matter of acting in a way that respects our nature. Thomas Aquinas is the greatest of the natural lawyers, but owing to the difficulty of his work, I have decided here to provide a contemporary offering by British philosopher Philippa Foot, whose elegant writing may make her distinctive natural law view a bit easier to understand.

Aristotle is next. By many accounts, he is the greatest philosopher who ever lived. He developed the first elaborate version of *virtue ethics*, the view that places the virtues at center stage in ethical inquiry. Virtue theorists reject the idea of a single formula that can provide ethical advice for every occasion. They instead tell us to look to virtuous role models, and imagine what they would do if they were in our shoes. It is tempting to begin ethical thinking by selecting a standard (such as the utilitarian standard), and saying: A virtue is a steady commitment that tends to produce right action, as measured by that standard. Virtue ethicists turn this on its head, and argue that we can understand the nature of right action only by first understanding the virtues.

We then turn to the normative ethical theory offered by British philosopher W. D. Ross, who developed an ethic of *prima facie duties*. Prima facie duties are those that can be outweighed by competing duties. If Ross is right, *every* general duty is like this. We have a standing duty to keep our word, to do justice, to prevent harm, etc. But sometimes these duties conflict with one another. When they do, only one can be our "all-things-considered" duty, the thing we really must do on that particular occasion. The problem, though, is that there is no fixed ranking of the moral principles, and so it can be very difficult to know what to do when they conflict. Sometimes it is more important to prevent harm than to keep our word. Sometimes the reverse is true. And so on, for all conflicts of duty. While Ross thinks that we can know each prima facie moral duty just through careful reflection, things get much more complicated when it comes to knowing what our final, all-things-considered duty is in specific situations.

Some of the most exciting recent work in normative ethics has been done by those who consider morality from the perspective of *feminist ethics.* This is best understood as an approach to ethics, rather than as a single view that is a direct competitor with the normative ethical theories we have briefly looked at thus far. In her selection here, philosopher Hilde Lindemann sketches the distinctive features of a feminist outlook on morality. These include an emphasis on taking the experience of women seriously when developing one's ethical ideas and ideals, and eliminating the many ways in which sexist assumptions creep into traditional philosophizing. Lindemann offers a variety of examples and interesting points as a way of introducing us to the large family of feminist approaches to ethics.

We have thus far canvassed those areas of ethics that deal with the good and the right: value theory, and normative ethics. But there is another part of ethics that takes a step back from these debates, and asks, more generally, about the *status* of moral views in both areas. Philosophers call this branch of moral theory *metaethics*, and it is the focus of part 3.

Metaethics studies such questions as these: Is morality just a convenient fiction? If not, can moral standards be true? Suppose they are. Does their truth depend on personal opinion, social consensus, God's commands, or something else? If there are genuine moral truths, how can we know them? And do they have any authority over us—is it always rational to be moral, or is it sometimes reasonable to take the immoral path?

I have divided the six authors in this part into two camps—those who are skeptical of objective morality, and those who defend it. As I understand it, morality is objective just in case there are some moral standards that apply to us regardless of what any human being believes or cares about.

Opponents of moral objectivity get the first hearing. The Scottish Enlightenment thinker David Hume starts us off. His criticisms of reason's place in ethics have been extremely influential across the past two and a half centuries, and rightly so. Most of today's important critiques of moral objectivity have their ancestors in one or more of the arguments that Hume provided. Hume thought that if moral claims were objectively true, then we should be able to discover our moral duty just by thinking hard about it. But Hume argues that no amount of careful reasoning could do that. And therefore morality cannot be objective.

Hume did not seek to undermine ethics, but rather to offer a diagnosis of its true nature. J. L. Mackie goes further, and argues that all of our moral thinking is based on an error. Mackie believes that moral thought starts from the view that morality is objective. He offers some important arguments to try to show that it isn't. He sees morality as a product of human insecurity and imagination, with no real authority over us. If we all do assume that morality is objective, and if Mackie is right about its being (at best) a useful fiction, then morality really is bankrupt.

Last among the critics of moral objectivity is Gilbert Harman. He argues that ethics and the natural sciences are fundamentally different, in a way that isn't flattering to morality. Science can provide us with an objective picture of reality; ethics cannot, because there is no objective morality. We can verify scientific claims, because the best explanation of our scientific observations is that they have been caused by real objects, out in the world. By contrast, we cannot test our moral beliefs against the world. We have no external check on our moral opinions, no objective moral facts that might cause us to have the moral opinions we do. Consider two competing hypotheses, designed to account for our moral beliefs: (1) we are caused to have the moral beliefs we do because moral facts somehow impress themselves upon us; or (2) our moral views are the product of social influences and agreements. If Harman is correct, then (2) is by far the better explanation.

Then the ethical objectivists get to have their say. Mary Midgley starts us off by arguing against cultural relativism, which is the idea that a society's guiding ideals are the ultimate moral standards. Since different societies have different ideals, there is no universal or objective morality. Midgley invites us to consider the samurai code of testing one's new sword by using it to cleanly carve up an innocent bystander. She argues that relativism is false; if it were true, that would mean that there was nothing immoral about such a killing. She is trying not to disprove relativism once and for all, but rather to show that despite any superficial attractions it may have, our deepest commitments demand that we reject it.

Michael Smith next tries to show how morality can be objective, by arguing that it is made up of those rules that we would all agree to were we calm, cool, collected, and fully informed about the world. There needn't be anything mysterious about objective values on this account. They are the principles that we *would* accept were we fully rational and informed. Thus we can gain moral knowledge by becoming well informed and by reasoning in sophisticated ways. And since we have reason to do what our perfectly ideal counterparts would recommend, this also explains why it is rational to be moral.

One reason that many people deny that ethics is objective is that they fail to see how we can gain moral knowledge if it is. Renford Bambrough's entry tackles this problem head on. Moral rules don't appear to be purely logical ones. Nor do they seem to be scientific principles, known through evidence we gather from our five senses. Hume (and many others) have thought that these two kinds of claims are the only ones that we can know. Bambrough disagrees, and takes us through the most popular of the skeptical arguments, trying to show that none of them is as plausible as it might at first appear.

This concludes the section on metaethics, and with that, the first half of this collection.

No philosopher sees his field exactly the same way others do. My take on what really matters in ethics is bound to be personal and, to some degree, not shared by my fellow practitioners. Still, I have aimed in this volume to respect standard divisions within this large field, and have tried to balance selections from some classic works with some relatively unfamiliar material that strikes me as important and provocative.

Whether beginners or old pros, each of us improves our moral thinking by being exposed to a variety of viewpoints on the deep questions that interest us. The ideal philosophical introduction, therefore, would present at least the main competitors within the various sub-fields that make up ethics, thereby giving newcomers a taste of the different perspectives that have shaped debates within this rich area of philosophy. I hope that I have managed some success on this front, but in at least one case, it would have been clearly impossible to achieve this within a reasonable amount of space.

I am thinking here of the last and largest section of the book, part 4, the one devoted to a variety of *moral problems*. There are far too many interesting moral conundrums to fit them all into a collection of this size. I hope that the topics on offer are compelling, but I recognize that many exciting subjects and insightful articles have been left behind. Short of greatly increasing the size of this collection, I see no way to avoid this, and must hope that the twenty offerings available here are of sufficient interest and importance to do what they are meant to do—inspire you to grapple with their puzzles, thought experiments, and arguments, and to appreciate a bit of the complexity of the moral issues that take center stage in this part of the book. What you have in this section (and all the others) is just a small sampling of possible positions and supporting arguments. The readings throughout this book are designed to whet your appetite, not to sate it.

There is no theoretical unity to this part of the volume. The authors here represent a variety of different theoretical approaches, and some, as you will see, do not argue directly from any normative theory at all.

This might be surprising. For a time-honored picture of how to argue about moral problems is to claim that you must first identify the correct normative theory, take note of the relevant nonmoral facts, and presto!—out comes your moral verdict. This way of arguing actually happens less often than you may think, which is why the more common term for this sort of moral philosophy, *applied ethics*, is a bit misleading. That label implies that all practical moral problems can all be solved in a top-down way, by first selecting the proper normative ethic and then "applying" it—as if that were a straightforward matter of cranking out its implications.

One reason philosophers don't always proceed in this way is because there is still huge disagreement about which normative ethic is the correct one. And so any philosopher who restricted her arguments to applying a single normative theory would be losing a good deal of her audience—specifically, the large segment of it that did not accept her normative ethic. As a result, most philosophers who grapple with real-life moral problems begin not with the grand normative theories, but rather with more concrete principles (keep your word, don't violate patient confidentiality, avoid imposing unnecessary pain, etc.) or examples that we are expected already to accept. Armed with these, the author then tries to show that a commitment to them implies some specific view about the problem at hand.

The topics covered in this last section are of the first importance: famine relief, surrogate motherhood, genetic engineering and cloning, euthanasia, animal rights, environmental duties, abortion, the role of conscience, terrorism, torture, civil disobedience, capital punishment, drug legalization, homosexuality, adultery, and the rights and duties of parents and children. Are there other topics that deserve a place at the table? Absolutely. But these strike me as worthy of our attention, and each of the pieces I have selected presents an interesting set of arguments that deserve careful scrutiny. Some of these pieces do represent pretty direct applications of the normative theories discussed in part 2 of this book. In these cases, you can use the arguments contained here as a way of testing those normative theories. In other cases, as I mention earlier, the arguments will be theoretically more freestanding. In any event, I hope that there will be plenty to inspire your interest, your curiosity, and, occasionally, your outrage. I have found that each of these can be an excellent catalyst to serious philosophical thinking.

PART ONE

Value Theory

The Nature of the Good Life

Letter to Menoeceus

Epicurus

Epicurus (341–270 BCE) was the first of the great hedonists. He argued that pleasure is the fundamental human good, and that the best life is one that is as pleasant as it can be. But his sort of hedonism would be unrecognizable by many nowadays, as Epicurus encouraged moderation and prudence in all things, and counseled us to minimize our indulgence in sensual pleasures. He thought that the most pleasant state was one of emotional tranquillity. Here he explains how to gain such peace of mind: through a moderate lifestyle, coupled with the curative powers of philosophy, which can dispel the false beliefs that lead to so much emotional turmoil. Foremost among these false beliefs is the view that death can harm us.

Epicurus to Menoeceus, greetings:

Let no one be slow to seek wisdom when he is young nor weary in the search of it when he has grown old. For no age is too early or too late for the health of the soul. And to say that the season for studying philosophy has not yet come, or that it is past and gone, is like saying that the season for happiness is not yet or that it is now no more. Therefore, both old and young alike ought to seek wisdom, the former in order that, as age comes over him, he may be young in good things because of the grace of what has been, and the latter in order that, while he is young, he may at the same time be old, because he has no fear of the things which are to come. So we must exercise ourselves in the things which bring happiness, since, if that be present, we have everything, and, if that be absent, all our actions are directed towards attaining it.

Those things which without ceasing I have declared unto you, do them, and exercise yourself in them, holding them to be the elements of right life. First believe that God is a living being immortal and blessed, according to the notion of a god indicated by the common sense of mankind; and so believing, you shall not affirm of him anything that is foreign to his immortality or that is repugnant to his blessedness. Believe about him whatever may uphold both his blessedness and his immortality. For there are gods, and the knowledge of them is manifest; but they are not such as the multitude believe, seeing that men do not steadfastly maintain the notions they form respecting them. Not the man who denies the gods worshipped by the multitude, but he who affirms of the gods what the multitude believes about them is truly impious. For the utterances of the multitude about the gods are not true preconceptions but false assumptions; hence it is that the greatest evils happen to the wicked and the greatest blessings happen to the good from the hand of the gods, seeing that they are always favorable to their own good qualities and take pleasure in men like themselves, but reject as alien whatever is not of their kind.

Accustom yourself to believing that death is nothing to us, for good and evil imply the capacity for sensation, and death is the privation of all sentience; therefore a correct understanding that death is nothing to us makes the mortality of life enjoyable, not by adding to life a limitless time, but by taking away the yearning after immortality. For life has no terrors for him who has thoroughly understood that there are no terrors for him in ceasing to live. Foolish, therefore, is the man who says that he fears death, not because it will pain when it comes, but because it pains in the prospect. Whatever causes no annoyance when it is present, causes only a groundless pain in the expectation. Death, therefore, the most awful of evils, is nothing to us, seeing that, when we are, death is not come, and, when death is come, we are not. It is nothing, then, either to the living or to the dead, for with the living it is not and the dead exist no longer.

But in the world, at one time men shun death as the greatest of all evils, and at another time choose it as a respite from the evils in life. The wise man does not deprecate life nor does he fear the cessation of life. The thought of life is no offense to him, nor is the cessation of life regarded as an evil. And even as men choose of food not merely and simply the larger portion, but the more pleasant, so the wise seek to enjoy the time which is most pleasant and not merely that which is longest. And he who admonishes the young to live well and the old to make a good end speaks foolishly, not merely because of the desirability of life, but because the same exercise at once teaches to live well and to die well. Much worse is he who says that it were good not to be born, but when once one is born to pass quickly through the gates of Hades. For if he truly believes this, why does he not depart from life? It would be easy for him to do so once he were firmly convinced. If he speaks only in jest, his words are foolishness as those who hear him do not believe.

We must remember that the future is neither wholly ours nor wholly not ours, so that neither must we count upon it as quite certain to come nor despair of it as quite certain not to come.

We must also reflect that of desires some are natural, others are groundless; and that of the natural some are necessary as well as natural, and some natural only. And of the necessary desires some are necessary if we are to be happy, some if the body is to be rid of uneasiness, some if we are even to live. He who has a clear and certain understanding of these things will direct every preference and aversion toward securing health of body and tranquillity of mind, seeing that this is the sum and end of a blessed life. For the end of all our actions is to be free from pain and fear, and, when once we have attained all this, the tempest of the soul is laid; seeing that the living creature has no need to go in search of something that is lacking, nor to look for anything else by which the good of the soul and of the body will be fulfilled. When we are pained because of the absence of pleasure, then, and then only, do we feel the need of pleasure. Wherefore we call pleasure the alpha and omega of a blessed life. Pleasure is our first and kindred good. It is the starting-point of every choice and of every aversion, and to it we come back, inasmuch as we make feeling the rule by which to judge of every good thing.

And since pleasure is our first and native good, for that reason we do not choose every pleasure whatsoever, but will often pass over many pleasures when a greater annoyance ensues from them. And often we consider pains superior to pleasures when submission to the pains for a long time brings us as a consequence a greater pleasure. While therefore all pleasure because it is naturally akin to us is good, not all pleasure is should be chosen, just as all pain is an evil and yet not all pain is to be shunned. It is, however, by measuring one against another, and by looking at the conveniences and inconveniences, that all these matters must be judged. Sometimes we treat the good as an evil, and the evil, on the contrary, as a good.

Again, we regard independence of outward things as a great good, not so as in all cases to use little, but so as to be contented with little if we have not much, being honestly persuaded that they have the sweetest enjoyment of luxury who stand least in need of it, and that whatever is natural is easily procured and only the vain and worthless hard to win. Plain fare gives as much pleasure as a costly diet, when once the pain of want has been removed, while bread and water confer the highest possible pleasure when they are brought to hungry lips. To habituate one's self, therefore, to simple and inexpensive diet supplies all that is needful for health, and enables a man to meet the necessary requirements of life without shrinking, and it places us in a better condition when we approach at intervals a costly fare and renders us fearless of fortune.

When we say, then, that pleasure is the end and aim, we do not mean the pleasures of the prodigal or the pleasures of sensuality, as we are understood to do by some through ignorance, prejudice, or willful misrepresentation. By pleasure we mean the absence of pain in the body and of trouble in the soul. It is not an unbroken succession of drinking-bouts and of revelry, not sexual lust, not the enjoyment of the fish and other delicacies of a luxurious table, which produce a pleasant life; it is sober reasoning, searching out the grounds of every choice and avoidance, and banishing those beliefs through which the greatest tumults take possession of the soul. Of all this the beginning and the greatest good is wisdom. Therefore wisdom is a more precious thing even than philosophy; from it spring all the other virtues, for it teaches that we cannot live pleasantly without living wisely, honorably, and justly; nor live wisely, honorably, and justly without living pleasantly. For the virtues have grown into one with a pleasant life, and a pleasant life is inseparable from them.

Who, then, is superior in your judgment to such a man? He holds a holy belief concerning the gods, and is altogether free from the fear of death. He has diligently considered the end fixed by nature, and understands how easily the limit of good things can be reached and attained, and how either the duration or the intensity of evils is but slight. Fate, which some introduce as sovereign over all things, he scorns, affirming rather that some things happen of necessity, others by chance, others through our own agency. For he sees that necessity destroys responsibility and that chance is inconstant; whereas our own actions are autonomous, and it is to them that praise and blame naturally attach. It were better, indeed, to accept the legends of the gods than to bow beneath that yoke of destiny which the natural philosophers have imposed. The one holds out some faint hope that we may escape if we honor the gods, while the necessity of the naturalists is deaf to all entreaties. Nor does he hold chance to be a god, as the world in general does, for in the acts of a god there is no disorder; nor to be a cause, though an uncertain one, for he believes that no good or evil is dispensed by chance to men so as to make life blessed, though it supplies the starting-point of great good and great evil. He believes that the misfortune of the wise is better than the prosperity of the fool. It is better, in short, that what is well judged in action should not owe its successful issue to the aid of chance.

Exercise yourself in these and related precepts day and night, both by yourself and with one who is like-minded; then never, either in waking or in dream, will you be disturbed, but will live as a god among men. For man loses all semblance of mortality by living in the midst of immortal blessings.

Epicurus: Letter to Menoeceus

1) Epicurus claims that "Death is nothing to us." What does he mean by this, and how does he argue for it? Do you find his argument convincing?
2) According to Epicurus, pleasure is "the starting-point of every choice." Is it possible to make decisions based on considerations besides pleasure? Is there ever good reason to do so?
3) Epicurus thinks that pleasure is "our first and kindred good," but he does not recommend indulgence in the pleasures of drinking, fine food, and sex. Why not?
4) What does Epicurus think is the most pleasant sort of life? Do you find the type of life he describes appealing?
5) Epicurus says that a pleasant life is inseparable from the virtues, and that "we cannot live pleasantly without living wisely, honorably, and justly." Do you think he is right about this?

2

Hedonism

John Stuart Mill

....

John Stuart Mill (1806–1873) was one of the great hedonistic thinkers. In this excerpt from his long pamphlet *Utilitarianism* (1863), Mill
defends his complex version of hedonism. Sensitive to criticisms that
it counsels us to pursue a life of brutish pleasure, Mill distinguishes
between higher and lower pleasures, and claims, famously, that it is
better to be Socrates dissatisfied, than a fool satisfied. He also offers
here his much-discussed "proof" of hedonism, by drawing a parallel
between the evidence we have for something's being visible (that all
of us see it) and something's being desirable (that all of us desire it).
He also argues for the claim that we do and can desire nothing but
pleasure, and uses this conjecture as a way of defending the view that
pleasure is the only thing that is always worth pursuing for its own
sake.

....

The creed which accepts, as the foundation of morals, Utility, or the
Greatest-happiness Principle, holds that actions are right in proportion as they tend to promote happiness, wrong as they tend to
produce the reverse of happiness. By happiness is intended pleasure and
the absence of pain; by unhappiness, pain and the privation of pleasure. To
give a clear view of the moral standard set up by the theory, much more
requires to be said; in particular, what things it includes in the ideas of pain
and pleasure, and to what extent this is left an open question. But these

supplementary explanations do not affect the theory of life on which this theory of morality is grounded,—namely, that pleasure, and freedom from pain, are the only things desirable as ends; and that all desirable things (which are as numerous in the utilitarian as in any other scheme) are desirable either for the pleasure inherent in themselves, or as means to the promotion of pleasure and the prevention of pain.

Now, such a theory of life excites in many minds, and among them in some of the most estimable in feeling and purpose, inveterate dislike. To suppose that life has (as they express it) no higher end than pleasure,—no better and nobler object of desire and pursuit,—they designate as utterly mean and groveling; as a doctrine worthy only of swine, to whom the followers of Epicurus were, at a very early period, contemptuously likened: and modern holders of the doctrine are occasionally made the subject of equally polite comparisons by its German, French, and English assailants.

When thus attacked, the Epicureans have always answered, that it is not they, but their accusers, who represent human nature in a degrading light, since the accusation supposes human beings to be capable of no pleasures except those of which swine are capable. If this supposition were true, the charge could not gainsaid, but would then be no longer an imputation; for, if the sources of pleasure were precisely the same to human beings and to swine, the rule of life which is good enough for the one would be good enough for the other. The comparison of the Epicurean life to that of beasts is felt as degrading, precisely because a beast's pleasures do not satisfy a human being's conceptions of happiness. Human beings have faculties more elevated than the animal appetites; and, when once made conscious of them, do not regard any thing as happiness which does not include their gratification. I do not, indeed, consider the Epicureans to have been by any means faultless in drawing out their scheme of consequences from the utilitarian principle. To do this in any sufficient manner, many Stoic as well as Christian elements require to be included. But there is no known Epicurean theory of life which does not assign to the pleasures of the intellect, of the feeling and imagination, and of the moral sentiments, a much higher value as pleasures than to those of mere sensation. It must be admitted, however, that utilitarian writers in general have placed the superiority of mental over bodily pleasures chiefly in the greater permanency, safety, uncostliness, &c., of the former,—that is, in their circumstantial advantages rather than in their intrinsic nature. And, on all these points, utilitarians have fully proved their case; but they might have taken the other, and, as it may be called, higher ground, with entire consistency. It is quite compatible with the principle of utility to recognize the fact, that some *kinds* of pleasure are more desirable and more valuable than others. It would be absurd, that while, in estimating all other things, quality is considered as well as quantity, the estimation of pleasures should be supposed to depend on quantity alone.

If I am asked what I mean by difference of quality in pleasures, or what makes one pleasure more valuable than another, merely as a pleasure, except its being greater in amount, there is but one possible answer. Of two pleasures, if there be one to which all or almost all who have experience of both give a decided preference, irrespective of any feeling of moral obligation to prefer it, that is the more desirable pleasure. If one of the two is, by those who are competently acquainted with both, placed so far above the other that they prefer it, even though knowing it to be attended with a greater amount of discontent, and would not resign it for any quantity of the other pleasure which their nature is capable of, we are justified in ascribing to the preferred enjoyment a superiority in quality, so far outweighing quantity, as to render it, in comparison, of small account.

Now, it is an unquestionable fact, that those who are equally acquainted with and equally capable of appreciating and enjoying both do give a most marked preference to the manner of existence which employs their higher faculties. Few human creatures would consent to be changed into any of the lower animals, for a promise of the fullest allowance of a beast's pleasures: no intelligent human being would consent to be a fool, no instructed person would be an ignoramus, no person of feeling and conscience would be selfish and base, even though they should be persuaded that the fool, the dunce, or the rascal is better satisfied with his lot than they are with theirs. They would not resign what they possess more than he for the most complete satisfaction of all the desires which they have in common with him. If they ever fancy they would, it is only in cases of unhappiness so extreme, that, to escape from it, they would exchange their lot for almost any other, however undesirable in their own eyes. A being of higher faculties requires more to make him happy, is capable probably of more acute suffering, and certainly accessible to it at more points, than one of an inferior type; but, in spite of these liabilities, he can never really wish to sink into what he feels to be a lower grade of existence. We may give what explanation we please of this unwillingness; we may attribute it to pride, a name which is given indiscriminately to some of the most and to some of the least estimable feelings of which mankind are capable; we may refer it to the love of liberty and personal independence,—an appeal to which was with the Stoics one of the most effective means for the inculcation of it; to the love of power, or to the love of excitement, both of which do really enter into and contribute to it: but its most appropriate appellation is a sense of dignity, which all human beings possess in one form or other, and in some, though by no means in exact, proportion to their higher faculties, and which is so essential a part of the happiness of those in whom it is strong, that nothing which conflicts with it could be, otherwise than momentarily, an object of desire to them. Whoever supposes that this preference takes place at a sacrifice of happiness; that the superior being, in any thing like equal circumstances, is not happier than the inferior— confounds the two very different ideas of happiness and content. It is indisputable, that the being whose capacities of enjoyment are low has the greatest chance of having them fully satisfied; and a highly endowed being will always feel that any happiness which he can look for, as the world is constituted, is imperfect. But he can learn to bear its imperfections, if they are at all bearable; and they will not make him envy the being who is indeed unconscious of the imperfections, but only because he feels not at all the good which those imperfections qualify. It is better to be a human being dissatisfied, than a pig satisfied; better to be Socrates dissatisfied, than a fool satisfied. And if the fool or the pig are of a different opinion, it is because they only know their own side of the question. The other party to the comparison knows both sides.

It may be objected, that many who are capable of the higher pleasures, occasionally, under the influence of temptation, postpone them to the lower. But this is quite compatible with a full appreciation of the intrinsic superiority of the higher. Men often, from infirmity of character, make their election for the nearer good, though they know it to be the less valuable, and this no less when the choice is between two bodily pleasures than when it is between bodily and mental. They pursue sensual indulgences to the injury of health, though perfectly aware that health is the greater good. It may be further objected, that many who begin with youthful enthusiasm for everything noble, as they advance in years sink into indolence and selfishness. But I do not believe that those who undergo this very common change voluntarily choose the lower description of pleasures in preference to the higher. I believe, that, before they devote themselves exclusively to the one, they have already become incapable of the other. Capacity for the nobler feelings is in most natures a very tender plant, easily killed, not only by hostile influences, but by mere want of sustenance; and, in the majority of young persons, it speedily dies away if the occupations to which their position in life has devoted them, and the society into which it has thrown them, are not favorable to keeping that higher capacity in exercise. Men lose their high aspirations as they lose their intellectual tastes, because they have not time or opportunity for indulging them; and they addict themselves to inferior pleasures, not because they deliberately prefer them, but because they are either the only ones to which they have access, or the only ones which they are any longer capable of enjoying. It may be questioned whether any one, who has remained equally susceptible to both classes of pleasures, ever knowingly and calmly preferred the lower; though many in all ages have broken down in an ineffectual attempt to combine both.

From this verdict of the only competent judges, I apprehend there can be no appeal. On a question, which is the best worth having of two pleasures, or which of two modes of existence is the most grateful to the feelings, apart from its moral attributes and from its consequences, the judgment of those who are qualified by knowledge of both, or, if they differ, that of the majority among them, must be admitted as final. And there needs be the less hesitation to accept this judgment respecting the quality of pleasures, since there is no other tribunal to be referred to even on the question of quantity. What means are there of determining which is the acutest of two pains, or the intensest of two pleasurable sensations, except the general suffrage of those who are familiar with both? Neither pains nor pleasures are homogeneous, and pain is always heterogeneous with pleasure. What is there to decide whether a particular pleasure is worth purchasing at the cost of particular pain, except the feelings and judgment of the experienced? When, therefore, those feelings and judgment declare the pleasures derived from the higher faculties to be preferable *in kind*, apart from the question of intensity, to those of which the animal nature, disjoined from the higher faculties, is susceptible, they are entitled on this subject to the same regard.

It has already been remarked, that questions of ultimate ends do not admit of proof, in the ordinary acceptation of the term. To be incapable of proof by reasoning is common to all first principles; to the first premises of our knowledge, as well as to those of our conduct. But the former, being matters of fact, may be the subject of a direct appeal to the faculties which judge of fact- namely, our senses, and our internal consciousness. Can an appeal be made to the same faculties on questions of practical ends? Or by what other faculty is cognisance taken of them?

Questions about ends are, in other words, questions what things are desirable. The utilitarian doctrine is, that happiness is desirable, and the only thing desirable, as an end; all other things being only desirable as means to that end. What ought to be required of this doctrine- what conditions is it requisite that the doctrine should fulfil- to make good its claim to be believed?

The only proof capable of being given that an object is visible, is that people actually see it. The only proof that a sound is audible, is that people hear it: and so of the other sources of our experience. In like manner, I apprehend, the sole evidence it is possible to produce that anything is desirable, is that people do actually desire it. If the end which the utilitarian doctrine proposes to itself were not, in theory and in practice, acknowledged to be an end, nothing could ever convince any person that it was so. No reason can be given why the general happiness is desirable, except that each person, so far as he believes it to be attainable, desires his own happiness. This, however, being a fact, we have not only all the proof which the case admits of, but all which it is possible to require, that happiness is a good: that each person's happiness is a good to that person, and the general happiness, therefore, a good to the aggregate of all persons. Happiness has made out its title as one of the ends of conduct, and consequently one of the criteria of morality.

But it has not, by this alone, proved itself to be the sole criterion. To do that, it would seem, by the same rule, necessary to show, not only that people desire happiness, but that they never desire anything else. Now it is palpable that they do desire things which, in common language, are decidedly distinguished from happiness. They desire, for example, virtue, and the absence of vice, no less really than pleasure and the absence of pain. The desire of virtue is not as universal, but it is as authentic a fact, as the desire of happiness. And hence the opponents of the utilitarian standard deem that they have a right to infer that there are other ends of human action besides happiness, and that happiness is not the standard of approbation and disapprobation.

But does the utilitarian doctrine deny that people desire virtue, or maintain that virtue is not a thing to be desired? The very reverse. It maintains not only that virtue is to be desired, but that it is to be desired disinterestedly, for itself. Whatever may be the opinion of utilitarian moralists as to the original conditions by which virtue is made virtue; however they may believe (as they do) that actions and dispositions are only virtuous because they promote another end than virtue; yet this being granted, and it having been decided, from considerations of this description, what is virtuous, they not only place virtue at the very head of the things which are

good as means to the ultimate end, but they also recognise as a psychological fact the possibility of its being, to the individual, a good in itself, without looking to any end beyond it; and hold, that the mind is not in a right
state, not in a state conformable to Utility, not in the state most conducive
to the general happiness, unless it does love virtue in this manner- as a
thing desirable in itself, even although, in the individual instance, it should
not produce those other desirable consequences which it tends to produce,
and on account of which it is held to be virtue. This opinion is not, in the
smallest degree, a departure from the Happiness principle. The ingredients
of happiness are very various, and each of them is desirable in itself, and
not merely when considered as swelling an aggregate. The principle of utility does not mean that any given pleasure, as music, for instance, or any
given exemption from pain, as for example health, is to be looked upon as
means to a collective something termed happiness, and to be desired on
that account. They are desired and desirable in and for themselves; besides
being means, they are a part of the end. Virtue, according to the utilitarian
doctrine, is not naturally and originally part of the end, but it is capable
of becoming so; and in those who love it disinterestedly it has become so,
and is desired and cherished, not as a means to happiness, but as a part of
their happiness.

To illustrate this farther, we may remember that virtue is not the
only thing, originally a means, and which if it were not a means to anything else, would be and remain indifferent, but which by association
with what it is a means to, comes to be desired for itself, and that too
with the utmost intensity. What, for example, shall we say of the love of
money? There is nothing originally more desirable about money than
about any heap of glittering pebbles. Its worth is solely that of the things
which it will buy; the desires for other things than itself, which it is a
means of gratifying. Yet the love of money is not only one of the strongest moving forces of human life, but money is, in many cases, desired in
and for itself; the desire to possess it is often stronger than the desire to
use it, and goes on increasing when all the desires which point to ends
beyond it, to be compassed by it, are falling off. It may, then, be said truly,
that money is desired not for the sake of an end, but as part of the end.
From being a means to happiness, it has come to be itself a principal
ingredient of the individual's conception of happiness. The same may
be said of the majority of the great objects of human life- power, for
example, or fame; except that to each of these there is a certain amount of
immediate pleasure annexed, which has at least the semblance of being

naturally inherent in them; a thing which cannot be said of money. Still, however, the strongest natural attraction, both of power and of fame, is the immense aid they give to the attainment of our other wishes; and it is the strong association thus generated between them and all our objects of desire, which gives to the direct desire of them the intensity it often assumes, so as in some characters to surpass in strength all other desires. In these cases the means have become a part of the end, and a more important part of it than any of the things which they are means to. What was once desired as an instrument for the attainment of happiness, has come to be desired for its own sake. In being desired for its own sake it is, however, desired as part of happiness. The person is made, or thinks he would be made, happy by its mere possession; and is made unhappy by failure to obtain it. The desire of it is not a different thing from the desire of happiness, any more than the love of music, or the desire of health. They are included in happiness. They are some of the elements of which the desire of happiness is made up. Happiness is not an abstract idea, but a concrete whole; and these are some of its parts. And the utilitarian standard sanctions and approves their being so. Life would be a poor thing, very ill provided with sources of happiness, if there were not this provision of nature, by which things originally indifferent, but conducive to, or otherwise associated with, the satisfaction of our primitive desires, become in themselves sources of pleasure more valuable than the primitive pleasures, both in permanency, in the space of human existence that they are capable of covering, and even in intensity.

Virtue, according to the utilitarian conception, is a good of this description. There was no original desire of it, or motive to it, save its conduciveness to pleasure, and especially to protection from pain. But through the association thus formed, it may be felt a good in itself, and desired as such with as great intensity as any other good; and with this difference between it and the love of money, of power, or of fame, that all of these may, and often do, render the individual noxious to the other members of the society to which he belongs, whereas there is nothing which makes him so much a blessing to them as the cultivation of the disinterested love of virtue. And consequently, the utilitarian standard, while it tolerates and approves those other acquired desires, up to the point beyond which they would be more injurious to the general happiness than promotive of it, enjoins and requires the cultivation of the love of virtue up to the greatest strength possible, as being above all things important to the general happiness.

It results from the preceding considerations, that there is in reality nothing desired except happiness. Whatever is desired otherwise than as a means to some end beyond itself, and ultimately to happiness, is desired as itself a part of happiness, and is not desired for itself until it has become so. Those who desire virtue for its own sake, desire it either because the consciousness of it is a pleasure, or because the consciousness of being without it is a pain, or for both reasons united; as in truth the pleasure and pain seldom exist separately, but almost always together, the same person feeling pleasure in the degree of virtue attained, and pain in not having attained more. If one of these gave him no pleasure, and the other no pain, he would not love or desire virtue, or would desire it only for the other benefits which it might produce to himself or to persons whom he cared for. We have now, then, an answer to the question, of what sort of proof the principle of utility is susceptible. If the opinion which I have now stated is psychologically true- if human nature is so constituted as to desire nothing which is not either a part of happiness or a means of happiness, we can have no other proof, and we require no other, that these are the only things desirable. If so, happiness is the sole end of human action, and the promotion of it the test by which to judge of all human conduct; from whence it necessarily follows that it must be the criterion of morality, since a part is included in the whole.

John Stuart Mill: Hedonism

1) Mill claims that "Pleasure, and freedom from pain, are the only things desirable as ends." Are there any examples that can challenge this claim?
2) What does Mill propose as a standard to determine which kinds of pleasure are more valuable than others? Is this a plausible standard?
3) Mill states that it is "Better to be Socrates dissatisfied, than a fool satisfied." What reasons does he give for thinking this?
4) In order to show that an object is visible, it is enough to show that people actually see it. Mill claims, similarly, "The sole evidence it is possible to produce that anything is desirable, is that people do actually desire it." Are visibility and desirability similar in this way?
5) Mill claims that "Each person's happiness is a good to that person." He then concludes from this that "the general happiness" is therefore "a good to the aggregate of all persons." Is this a good argument?

6) According to Mill, "The ingredients of happiness are very various, and each of them is desirable in itself." Does this contradict his earlier claim, given in question 1?

7) At the beginning of this selection, Mill says that pleasure and the absence of pain are the only things desirable as ends. Toward the end he claims that "Happiness is the sole end of human action." Are happiness and pleasure the same thing?

3

Brave New World
Aldous Huxley

In this brief excerpt from Huxley's (1894–1963) dystopian classic, we are presented with a conversation between a character named the Savage, and Mustapha Mond, Resident World Controller for Western Europe. The world they inhabit is one in which the level of contentment is very high: "People are happy; they get what they want, and they never want what they can't get." But this happiness is purchased by medicating the population, restricting their access to fine literature and new ideas, and eliminating all sources of novelty and danger. Misery is done away with, but at what cost?

The Savage argues that happiness is not the most important goal of human life. The best life will include risk and challenges that, when unmet, will lead to grief, and sometimes to tragedy. Both Mond and the Savage recognize that we cannot have everything that we might want—both sustained, guaranteed happiness, and a life of rich and valuable activities that yield such happiness. We must choose. Mond opts for guaranteed happiness, while the Savage argues for the opposite choice.

The room into which the three were ushered was the Controller's study.

'His fordship will be down in a moment.' The Gamma butler left them to themselves.

Helmholtz laughed aloud.

'It's more like a caffeine-solution party than a trial,' he said, and let himself fall into the most luxurious of the pneumatic armchairs. 'Cheer up, Bernard,' he added, catching sight of his friend's green unhappy face. But Bernard would not be cheered; without answering, without even look- ing at Helmholtz, he went and sat down on the most uncomfortable chair in the room, carefully chosen in the obscure hope of somehow deprecating the wrath of the higher powers.

The Savage meanwhile wandered restlessly round the room, peer- ing with a vague superficial inquisitiveness at the books in the shelves, at the sound-track rolls and the reading-machine bobbins in their numbered pigeon-holes. On the table under the window lay a mas- sive volume bound in limp black leather-surrogate, and stamped with large golden Ts. He picked it up and opened it. MY LIFE AND WORK, BY OUR FORD. The book had been published at Detroit by the Society for the Propagation of Fordian Knowledge. Idly he turned the pages, read a sentence here, a paragraph there, and had just come to the conclu- sion that the book didn't interest him, when the door opened, and the Resident World Controller for Western Europe walked briskly into the room.

Mustapha Mond shook hands with all three of them; but it was to the Savage that he addressed himself. 'So you don't much like civilization, Mr Savage,' he said.

The Savage looked at him. He had been prepared to lie, to bluster, to remain sullenly unresponsive; but, reassured by the good-humoured intelligence of the Controller's face, he decided to tell the truth, straight- forwardly. 'No.' He shook his head.

Bernard started and looked horrified. What would the Controller think? To be labelled as the friend of a man who said that he didn't like civilization—said it openly and, of all people, to the Controller—it was terrible. 'But, John,' he began. A look from Mustapha Mond reduced him to an abject silence.

'Of course,' the Savage went on to admit, 'there are some very nice things. All that music in the air, for instance...'

'Sometimes a thousand twangling instruments will hum about my ears, and sometimes voices.'

The Savage's face lit up with a sudden pleasure. 'Have you read it too?' he asked. 'I thought nobody knew about that book here, in England.'

'Almost nobody. I'm one of the very few. It's prohibited, you see. But as I make the laws here, I can also break them. With impunity, Mr Marx,' he added, turning to Bernard. 'Which I'm afraid you *can't* do.'

Bernard sank into a yet more hopeless misery.

'But why is it prohibited?' asked the Savage. In the excitement of meeting a man who had read Shakespeare he had momentarily forgotten everything else.

The Controller shrugged his shoulders. 'Because it's old; that's the chief reason. We haven't any use for old things here.'

'Even when they're beautiful?'

'Particularly when they're beautiful. Beauty's attractive, and we don't want people to be attracted by old things. We want them to like the new ones.'

'But the new ones are so stupid and horrible. Those plays, where there's nothing but helicopters flying about and you *feel* the people kissing.' He made a grimace. 'Goats and monkeys!' Only in Othello's words could he find an adequate vehicle for his contempt and hatred.

'Nice tame animals, anyhow,' the Controller murmured parenthetically.

'Why don't you let them see *Othello* instead?'

'I've told you; it's old. Besides, they couldn't understand it.'

Yes, that was true. He remembered how Helmholtz had laughed at *Romeo and Juliet*. 'Well, then,' he said, after a pause, 'something new that's like *Othello*, and that they could understand.'

'That's what we've all been wanting to write,' said Helmholtz, breaking a long silence.

'And it's what you never will write,' said the Controller. 'Because, if it were really like *Othello* nobody could understand it, however new it might be. And if it were new, it couldn't possibly be like *Othello*.'

'Why not?'

'Yes, why not?' Helmholtz repeated. He too was forgetting the unpleasant realities of the situation. Green with anxiety and apprehension, only Bernard remembered them; the others ignored him. 'Why not?'

'Because our world is not the same as Othello's world. You can't make flivvers without steel—and you can't make tragedies without social instability. The world's stable now. People are happy; they get what they want, and they never want what they can't get. They're well off; they're safe;

they're never ill; they're not afraid of death; they're blissfully ignorant of passion and old age; they're plagued with no mothers or fathers; they've got no wives, or children, or loves to feel strongly about; they're so conditioned that they practically can't help behaving as they ought to behave. And if anything should go wrong, there's *soma*. Which you go and chuck out of the window in the name of liberty, Mr Savage. *Liberty!*' He laughed. 'Expecting Deltas to know what liberty is! And now expecting them to understand *Othello!* My good boy!'

The Savage was silent for a little. 'All the same,' he insisted obstinately, '*Othello's* good, *Othello's* better than those feelies.'

'Of course it is,' the Controller agreed. 'But that's the price we have to pay for stability. You've got to choose between happiness and what people used to call high art. We've sacrificed the high art. We have the feelies and the scent organ instead.'

'But they don't mean anything.'

'They mean themselves; they mean a lot of agreeable sensations to the audience.'

'But they're... they're told by an idiot.'

The Controller laughed. 'You're not being very polite to your friend Mr Watson. One of our most distinguished Emotional Engineers...'

'But he's right,' said Helmholtz gloomily. 'Because it *is* idiotic. Writing when there's nothing to say...'

'Precisely. But that requires the most enormous ingenuity. You're making flivvers out of the absolute minimum of steel—works of art out of practically nothing but pure sensation.'

The Savage shook his head. 'It all seems to me quite horrible.'

'Of course it does. Actual happiness always looks pretty squalid in comparison with the over-compensations for misery. And, of course, stability isn't nearly so spectacular as instability. And being contented has none of the glamour of a good fight against misfortune, none of the picturesqueness of a struggle with temptation, or a fatal overthrow by passion or doubt. Happiness is never grand. [...]

'In a properly organized society like ours, nobody has any opportunities for being noble or heroic. Conditions have got to be thoroughly unstable before the occasion can arise. Where there are wars, where there are divided allegiances, where there are temptations to be resisted, objects of love to be fought for or defended—there, obviously, nobility and heroism have some sense. But there aren't any wars nowadays. The greatest care is taken to prevent you from loving anyone too much. There's no such thing as a divided allegiance; you're so conditioned that you can't help doing what you ought to do. And what you ought to do is on the whole so pleasant, so many of the natural impulses are allowed free play, that there really aren't any temptations to resist. And if ever, by some unlucky chance, anything unpleasant should somehow happen, why, there's always *soma* to give you a holiday from the facts. And there's always *soma* to calm your anger, to reconcile you to your enemies, to make you patient and long-suffering. In the past you could only accomplish these things by making a great effort and after years of hard moral training. Now, you swallow two or three half-gramme tablets, and there you are. Anybody can be virtuous now. You can carry at least half your morality about in a bottle. Christianity without tears—that's what *soma* is.'

'But the tears are necessary. Don't you remember what Othello said? "If after every tempest come such calms, may the winds blow till they have wakened death." There's a story one of the old Indians used to tell us, about the Girl of Mátsaki. The young men who wanted to marry her had to do a morning's hoeing in her garden. It seemed easy; but there were flies and mosquitoes, magic ones. Most of the young men simply couldn't stand the biting and stinging. But the one that could—he got the girl.'

'Charming! But in civilized countries,' said the Controller, 'you can have girls without hoeing for them; and there aren't any flies or mosquitoes to sting you. We got rid of them all centuries ago.'

The Savage nodded, frowning. 'You got rid of them. Yes, that's just like you. Getting rid of everything unpleasant instead of learning to put up with it. Whether 'tis nobler in the mind to suffer the slings and arrows of outrageous fortune, or to take arms against a sea of troubles and by opposing end them. . . . But you don't do either. Neither suffer nor oppose. You just abolish the slings and arrows. It's too easy.' [. . .]

'What you need', the Savage went on, 'is something *with* tears for a change. Nothing costs enough here. [. . .]

'Isn't there something in that?' he asked, looking up at Mustapha Mond. 'Quite apart from God—though of course God would be a reason for it. Isn't there something in living dangerously?'

'There's a great deal in it,' the Controller replied. 'Men and women must have their adrenals stimulated from time to time.'

'What?' questioned the Savage, uncomprehending.

'It's one of the conditions of perfect health. That's why we've made the V.P.S. treatments compulsory.'

'V.P.S.?'

'Violent Passion Surrogate. Regularly once a month. We flood the whole system with adrenalin. It's the complete physiological equivalent of fear and rage. All the tonic effects of murdering Desdemona and being murdered by Othello, without any of the inconveniences.'

'But I like the inconveniences.'

'We don't,' said the Controller. 'We prefer to do things comfortably.'

'But I don't want comfort. I want God, I want poetry, I want real danger, I want freedom, I want goodness. I want sin.'

'In fact,' said Mustapha Mond, 'you're claiming the right to be unhappy.'

'All right, then,' said the Savage defiantly, 'I'm claiming the right to be unhappy.'

'Not to mention the right to grow old and ugly and impotent; the right to have syphilis and cancer; the right to have too little to eat; the right to be lousy; the right to live in constant apprehension of what may happen tomorrow; the right to catch typhoid; the right to be tortured by unspeakable pains of every kind.'

There was a long silence.

'I claim them all,' said the Savage at last.

Mustapha Mond shrugged his shoulders. 'You're welcome,' he said.

Aldous Huxley: Brave New World

1) In this excerpt, the Savage defends "the right to be unhappy." What does he mean by this, and is this a desirable "right" to exercise?

2) The Savage suggests that there is more to life than mere "agreeable sensations" that don't "mean anything." How do you think Mill would respond to this criticism of hedonism?

3) Is an actual adventure more valuable than a "Violent Passion Surrogate"?

4) The Savage gives a list of things he desires besides comfort: "I want God, I want poetry, I want real danger, I want freedom, I want goodness. I want sin." What things (if any) other than pleasure do you desire in your life? Do you desire them only for the pleasure they give you, or for other reasons?

4

The Experience Machine

Robert Nozick

In this brief selection from his book *Anarchy, State and Utopia* (1974), the late Harvard philosopher Robert Nozick (1938–2002) invites us to contemplate a life in which we are placed within a very sophisticated machine that is capable of simulating whatever experiences we find most valuable. Such a life, Nozick argues, cannot be the best life for us, because it fails to make contact with reality. This is meant to show that the good life is not entirely a function of the quality of our inner experiences. Since hedonism measures our well-being in precisely this way, hedonism, says Nozick, must be mistaken.

...Suppose there were an experience machine that would give you any experience you desired. Superduper neuropsychologists could stimulate your brain so that you would think and feel you were writing a great novel, or making a friend, or reading an interesting book. All the time you would be floating in a tank, with electrodes attached to your brain. Should you plug into this machine for life, preprogramming your life's experiences? If you are worried about missing out on desirable experiences, we can suppose that business enterprises have researched thoroughly the lives of many others. You can pick and choose from their large library or smorgasbord of such experiences, selecting your life's experiences for, say, the next two years. After two years have passed, you will have ten minutes or ten hours out of the tank, to select the experiences of your *next* two years. Of course, while in the tank you won't know that you're there; you'll think it's all actually happening. Others can also plug in to have the experiences they want, so there's no need to stay unplugged to serve them. (Ignore problems such as who will service the machines if everybody plugs in.) Would you plug in? *What else can matter to us, other than how our lives feel from the inside?* Nor should you refrain because of the few moments of distress between the moment you've decided and the moment you're plugged. What's a few moments of distress compared to a lifetime of bliss (if that's what you choose), and why feel any distress at all if your decision *is* the best one?

What does matter to us in addition to our experiences? First, we want to *do* certain things, and not just have the experience of doing them. In the case of certain experiences, it is only because first we want to do the actions that we want the experiences of doing them or thinking we've done them. (But *why* do we want to do the activities rather than merely to experience them?) A second reason for not plugging in is that we want to *be* a certain way, to be a certain sort of person. Someone floating in a tank is an indeterminate blob. There is no answer to the question of what a person is like who has long been in the tank. Is he courageous, kind, intelligent, witty, loving? It's not merely that it's difficult to tell; there's no way he is. Plugging into the machine is a kind of suicide. It will seem to some, trapped by a picture, that nothing about what we are like can matter except as it gets reflected in our experiences. But should it be surprising that what *we are* is important to us? Why should we be concerned only with how our time is filled, but not with what we are?

Thirdly, plugging into an experience machine limits us to a man-made reality, to a world no deeper or more important than that which people can construct. There is no *actual* contact with any deeper reality, though the experience of it can be simulated. Many persons desire to leave themselves open to such contact and to a plumbing of deeper significance.[1] This

---

[1] Traditional religious views differ on the *point* of contact with a transcendent reality. Some say that contact yields eternal bliss or Nirvana, but they have not distinguished this sufficiently from merely a *very* long run on the experience machine. Others think it is intrinsically desirable to do the will of a higher being which created us all, though presumably no one would think this if we discovered we had been created as an object of amusement by some superpowerful child from another galaxy or dimension. Still others imagine an eventual merging with a higher reality, leaving unclear its desirability, or where that merging leaves us.

clarifies the intensity of the conflict over psychoactive drugs, which some view as mere local experience machines, and others view as avenues to a deeper reality; what some view as equivalent to surrender to the experience machine, others view as following one of the reasons *not* to surrender!

We learn that something matters to us in addition to experience by imagining an experience machine and then realizing that we would not use it. We can continue to imagine a sequence of machines each designed to fill lacks suggested for the earlier machines. For example, since the experience machine doesn't meet our desire to *be* a certain way, imagine a transformation machine which transforms us into whatever sort of person we'd like to be (compatible with our staying us). Surely one would not use the transformation machine to become as one would wish, and thereupon plug into the experience machine![2] So something matters in addition to one's experiences *and* what one is like. Nor is the reason merely that one's experiences are unconnected with what one is like. For the experience machine might be limited to provide only experiences possible to the sort of person plugged in. Is it that we want to make a difference in the world? Consider then the result machine, which produces in the world any result you would produce and injects your vector input into any joint activity. We shall not pursue here the fascinating details of these or other machines. What is most disturbing about them is their living of our lives for us. Is it misguided to search for *particular* additional functions beyond the competence of machines to do for us? Perhaps what we desire is to live (an active verb) ourselves, in contact with reality. (And this, machines cannot do *for* us.) Without elaborating on the implications of this, which I believe connect surprisingly with issues about free will and causal accounts of knowledge, we need merely note the intricacy of the question of what matters *for people* other than their experiences. Until one finds a satisfactory answer, and determines that this answer does not *also* apply to animals, one cannot

---

[2] Some wouldn't use the transformation machine at all; it seems like *cheating*. But the one-time use of the transformation machine would not remove all challenges; there would still be obstacles for the new us to overcome, a new plateau from which to strive even higher. And is this plateau any the less earned or deserved than that provided by genetic endowment and early childhood environment? But if the transformation machine could be used indefinitely often, so that we could accomplish anything by pushing a button to transform ourselves into someone who could do it easily, there would remain no limits we *need* to strain against or try to transcend. Would there be anything left *to do*? Do some theological views place God outside of time because an omniscient omnipotent being couldn't fill up his days?

reasonably claim that only the felt experiences of animals limit what we may do to them.

Robert Nozick: The Experience Machine

1) Nozick suggests that most people would choose not to plug in to an "experience machine" if given the opportunity. Would you plug in? Why or why not?

2) Hedonists such as Epicurus and Mill claim that pleasure is the only thing worth pursuing for its own sake. If some people would choose not to plug in to the experience machine, does this show that hedonism is false?

3) One reason Nozick gives for not getting into the experience machine is that "We want to *do* certain things, and not just have the experience of doing them." Do some activities have value independently of the experiences they produce? If so, what is an example of such an activity?

4) Nozick claims that "Plugging into the machine is a kind of suicide." What does he mean by this? Do you think he is right?

5

The Meaning of Life

Richard Taylor

....

In this selection from his book *Good and Evil*, philosopher Richard Taylor (1919–2003) argues that life is meaningless, but that this does not undermine our prospects for a good life. He illustrates this claim by invoking the life of the mythical Sisyphus, condemned by the gods to roll a heavy rock up a mountain, forever. There is no ultimate point to Sisyphus's life, and in this, our lives are no different.

However, in a variation on the ancient myth, we can imagine Sisyphus possessed of a good life. All it takes is for the gods to have instilled in him a desire to do exactly what he is doing. Were Sisyphus to acquire a deep love of rock-pushing, his life would be *much* better for him. The same holds in our case. Though nothing we do has any ultimate meaning, we can be quite well off, provided that we get from life what we most care about. For Taylor, satisfying our deepest desires is the key to a good life.

....

The question whether life has any meaning is difficult to interpret, and the more one concentrates his critical faculty on it the more it seems to elude him, or to evaporate as any intelligible question. One wants to turn it aside, as a source of embarrassment, as something that, if it cannot be abolished, should at least be decently covered. And yet I think any reflective person recognizes that the question it raises is important, and that it ought to have a significant answer.

If the idea of meaningfulness is difficult to grasp in this context, so that we are unsure what sort of thing would amount to answering the question, the idea of meaninglessness is perhaps less so. If, then, we can bring before our minds a clear image of meaningless existence, then perhaps we can take a step toward coping with our original question by seeing to what extent our lives, as we actually find them, resemble that image, and draw such lessons as we are able to from the comparison.

Meaningless Existence

A perfect image of meaninglessness, of the kind we are seeking, is found in the ancient myth of Sisyphus. Sisyphus, it will be remembered, betrayed divine secrets to mortals, and for this he was condemned by the gods to roll a stone to the top of a hill, the stone then immediately to roll back down, again to be pushed to the top by Sisyphus, to roll down once more, and so on again and again, *forever*. Now in this we have the picture of meaningless, pointless toil, of a meaningless existence that is absolutely *never* redeemed. It is not even redeemed by a death that, if it were to accomplish nothing more, would at least bring this idiotic cycle to a close. If we were invited to imagine Sisyphus struggling for awhile and accomplishing nothing, perhaps eventually falling from exhaustion, so that we might suppose him then eventually turning to something having some sort of promise, then the meaninglessness of that chapter of his life would not be so stark. It would be a dark and dreadful dream, from which he eventually awakens to sunlight and reality. But he does not awaken, for there is nothing for him to awaken to. His repetitive toil is his life and reality, and it goes on forever, and it is without any meaning whatever. Nothing ever comes of what he is doing, except simply, more of the same. Not by one step, nor by a thousand, nor by ten thousand does he even expiate by the smallest token the sin against the gods that led him into this fate. Nothing comes of it, nothing at all.

This ancient myth has always enchanted men, for countless meanings can be read into it. Some of the ancients apparently thought it symbolized the perpetual rising and setting of the sun, and others the repetitious crashing of the waves upon the shore. Probably the commonest interpretation is that it symbolizes man's eternal struggle and unquenchable spirit, his determination always to try once more in the face of overwhelming discouragement. This interpretation is further supported by that version of the myth according to which Sisyphus was commanded to roll the stone *over* the hill, so that it would finally roll down the other side, but was never quite able to make it.

I am not concerned with rendering or defending any interpretation of this myth, however. I have cited it only for the one element it does unmistakably contain, namely, that of a repetitious, cyclic activity that never comes to anything. We could contrive other images of this that would serve just as well, and no myth-makers are needed to supply the materials of it. Thus, we can imagine two persons transporting a stone—or even a precious gem, it does not matter—back and forth, relay style. One carries it to a near or distant point where it is received by the other; it is returned to its starting point, there to be recovered by the first, and the process is repeated over and over. Except in this relay nothing counts as winning, and nothing brings the contest to any close, each step only leads to a repetition of itself. Or we can imagine two groups of prisoners, one of them engaged in digging a prodigious hole in the ground that is no sooner finished than it is filled in again by the other group, the latter then digging a new hole that is at once filled in by the first group, and so on and on endlessly.

Now what stands out in all such pictures as oppressive and dejecting is not that the beings who enact these roles suffer any torture or pain, for it need not be assumed that they do. Nor is it that their labors are great, for they are no greater than the labors commonly undertaken by most men most of the time. According to the original myth, the stone is so large that Sisyphus never quite gets it to the top and must groan under every step, so that his enormous labor is all for nought. But this is not what appalls. It is not that his great struggle comes to nothing, but that his existence itself is without meaning. Even if we suppose, for example, that the stone is but a pebble that can be carried effortlessly, or that the holes dug by the prisoners are but small ones, not the slightest meaning is introduced into their lives. The stone that Sisyphus moves to the top of the hill, whether we think of it as large or small, still rolls back every time, and the process is repeated forever. Nothing comes of it, and the work is simply pointless. That is the element of the myth that I wish to capture.

Again, it is not the fact that the labors of Sisyphus continue forever that deprives them of meaning. It is, rather, the implication of this: that they come to nothing. The image would not be changed by our supposing him to push a different stone up every time, each to roll down again. But if we supposed that these stones, instead of rolling back to their places as if they had never been moved, were assembled at the top of the hill and there incorporated, say, in a beautiful and enduring temple, then the aspect of meaninglessness would disappear. His labors would then have a point, something would come of them all, and although one could perhaps still say it was not worth it, one could not say that the life of Sisyphus was devoid of meaning altogether. Meaningfulness would at least have made an appearance, and we could see what it was.

That point will need remembering. But in the meantime, let us note another way in which the image of meaninglessness can be altered by making only a very slight change. Let us suppose that the gods, while condemning Sisyphus to the fate just described, at the same time, as an afterthought, waxed perversely merciful by implanting in him a strange and irrational impulse; namely, a compulsive impulse to roll stones. We may if we like, to make this more graphic, suppose they accomplish this by implanting in him some substance that has this effect on his character and drives. I call this perverse, because from our point of view there is clearly no reason why anyone should have a persistent and insatiable desire to do something so pointless as that. Nevertheless, suppose that is Sisyphus' condition. He has but one obsession, which is to roll stones, and it is an obsession that is only for the moment appeased by his rolling them—he no sooner gets a stone rolled to the top of the hill than he is restless to roll up another.

Now it can be seen why this little afterthought of the gods, which I called perverse, was also in fact merciful. For they have by this device managed to give Sisyphus precisely what he wants—by making him want precisely what they inflict on him. However it may appear to us, Sisyphus' fate now does not appear to him as a condemnation, but the very reverse. His one desire in life is to roll stones, and he is absolutely guaranteed its endless fulfillment. Where otherwise he might profoundly have wished surcease, and even welcomed the quiet of death to release him from endless boredom and meaninglessness, his life is now filled with mission and meaning, and he seems to himself to have been given an entry to heaven. Nor need he even fear death, for the gods have promised him an endless opportunity to indulge his single purpose, without concern or frustration. He will be able to roll stones *forever*.

What we need to mark most carefully at this point is that the picture with which we began has not really been changed in the least by adding this supposition. Exactly the same things happen as before. The only change is in Sisyphus' view of them. The picture before was the image of meaningless activity and existence. It was created precisely to be an image of that. It has not lost that meaninglessness, it has now gained not the least shred of meaningfulness. The stones still roll back as before, each phase of Sisyphus' life still exactly resembles all the others, the task is never completed, nothing comes of it, no temple ever begins to rise, and all this cycle of the same pointless thing over and over goes on forever in this picture as in the other. The *only* thing that has happened is this: Sisyphus has been reconciled to it, and indeed more, he has been led to embrace it. Not, however, by reason or persuasion, but by nothing more rational than the potency of a new substance in his veins.

The Meaninglessness of Life

I believe the foregoing provides a fairly clear content to the idea of meaninglessness and, through it, some hint of what meaningfulness, in this sense, might be. Meaninglessness is essentially endless pointlessness, and meaningfulness is therefore the opposite. Activity, and even long, drawn-out and repetitive activity, has a meaning if it has some significant culmination, some more or less lasting end that can be considered to have been the direction and purpose of the activity. But the descriptions so far also provide something else; namely, the suggestion of how an existence that is objectively meaningless, in this sense, can nevertheless acquire a meaning for him whose existence it is.

Now let us ask: Which of these pictures does life in fact resemble? And let us not begin with our own lives, for here both our prejudices and wishes are great, but with the life in general that we share with the rest of creation. We shall find, I think, that it all has a certain pattern, and that this pattern is by now easily recognized.

We can begin anywhere, only saving human existence for our last consideration. We can, for example, begin with any animal. It does not matter where we begin, because the result is going to be exactly the same.

Thus, for example, there are caves in New Zealand, deep and dark, whose floors are quiet pools and whose walls and ceilings are covered with soft light. As one gazes in wonder in the stillness of these caves it seems that the Creator has reproduced there in microcosm the heavens themselves, until one scarcely remembers the enclosing presence of the walls. As one looks more closely, however, the scene is explained. Each dot of light identifies an ugly worm, whose luminous tail is meant to attract insects from the surrounding darkness. As from time to time one of these insects draws near it becomes entangled in a sticky thread lowered by the worm, and is eaten. This goes on month after month, the blind worm lying there in the barren stillness waiting to entrap an occasional bit of nourishment that will only sustain it to another bit of nourishment until....Until what? What great thing awaits all this long and repetitive effort and makes it worthwhile? Really nothing. The larva just transforms itself finally to a tiny winged adult that lacks even mouth parts to feed and lives only a day or two. These adults, as soon as they have mated and laid eggs, are themselves caught in the threads and are devoured by the cannibalist worms, often without having ventured into the day, the only point to their existence having now been fulfilled. This has been going on for millions of years, and to no end other than that the same meaningless cycle may continue for another millions of years.

All living things present essentially the same spectacle. The larva of a certain cicada burrows in the darkness of the earth for seventeen years, through season after season, to emerge finally into the daylight for a brief flight, lay its eggs, and die—this all to repeat itself during the next seventeen years, and so on to eternity. We have already noted, in another connection, the struggles of fish, made only that others may do the same after them and that this cycle, having no other point than itself, may never cease. Some birds span an entire side of the globe each year and then return, only to insure that others may follow the same incredibly long path again and again. One is led to wonder what the point of it all is, with what great triumph this ceaseless effort, repeating itself through millions of years, might finally culminate, and why it should go on and on for so long, accomplishing nothing, getting nowhere. But then one realizes that there is no point to it at all, that it really culminates in nothing, that each of these cycles, so filled with toil, is to be followed only by more of the same. The point of any living thing's life is, evidently, nothing but life itself.

This life of the world thus presents itself to our eyes as a vast machine, feeding on itself, running on and on forever to nothing. And we are part of that life. To be sure, we are not just the same, but the differences are not so great as we like to think; many are merely invented, and none really cancels the kind of meaninglessness that we found in Sisyphus and that we find all around, wherever anything lives. We are conscious of our activity. Our goals, whether in any significant sense we choose them or not, are things of which we are at least partly aware and can therefore in some sense appraise. More significantly, perhaps, men have a history, as other animals do not, such that each generation does not precisely resemble all those before. Still, if we can in imagination disengage our wills from our lives and disregard the deep interest each man has in his own existence, we shall find that they do not so little resemble the existence of Sisyphus. We toil after goals, most of them—indeed every single one of them—of transitory significance and, having gained one of them, we immediately set forth for the next, as if that one had never been, with this next one being essentially more of the same. Look at a busy street any day, and observe the throng going hither and thither. To what? Some office or shop, where the same things will be done today as were done yesterday, and are done now so they may be repeated tomorrow. And if we think that, unlike Sisyphus, these labors do have a point, that they culminate in something lasting and, independently of our own deep interests in them, very worthwhile, then we simply have not considered the thing closely enough. Most such effort is directed only to the establishment and perpetuation of home and family; that is, to the begetting of others who will follow in our steps to do more of the same. Each man's life thus resembles one of Sisyphus' climbs to the summit of his hill, and each day of it one of his steps; the difference is that whereas Sisyphus himself returns to push the stone up again, we leave this to our children. We at one point imagined that the labors of Sisyphus finally culminated in the creation of a temple, but for this to make any difference it had to be a temple that would at least endure, adding beauty to the world for the remainder of time. Our achievements, even though they are often beautiful, are mostly bubbles; and those that do last, like the sandswept pyramids, soon becomes mere curiosities while around them the rest of mankind continues its perpetual toting of rocks, only to see them roll down. Nations are built upon the bones of their founders and pioneers, but only to decay and crumble before long, their rubble then becoming the foundation for others directed to exactly the same fate. The picture of Sisyphus is the picture of existence of the individual man, great or unknown, of nations, of the race of men, and of the very life of the world.

On a country road one sometimes comes upon the ruined hulks of a house and once extensive buildings, all in collapse and spread over with weeds. A curious eye can in imagination reconstruct from what is left a once warm and thriving life, filled with purpose. There was the hearth, where a family once talked, sang, and made plans; there were the rooms, where people loved, and babes were born to a rejoicing mother; there are the musty remains of a sofa, infested with bugs, once bought at a dear price to enhance an ever-growing comfort, beauty, and warmth. Every small piece of junk fills the mind with what once, not long ago, was utterly real, with children's voices, plans made, and enterprises embarked upon.

That is how these stones of Sisyphus were rolled up, and that is how they became incorporated into a beautiful temple, and that temple is what now lies before you. Meanwhile other buildings, institutions, nations, and civilizations spring up all around, only to share the same fate before long. And if the question "What for?" is now asked, the answer is clear: so that just this may go on forever.

The two pictures—of Sisyphus and of our own lives, if we look at them from a distance—are in outline the same and convey to the mind the same image. It is not surprising, then, that men invent ways of denying it, their religions proclaiming a heaven that does not crumble, their hymnals and prayer books declaring a significance to life of which our eyes provide no hint whatever.[1] Even our philosophies portray some permanent and lasting good at which all may aim, from the changeless forms invented by Plato to the beatific vision of St. Thomas and the ideals of permanence contrived by the moderns. When these fail to convince, then earthly ideals such as universal justice and brotherhood are conjured up to take their places and give meaning to man's seemingly endless pilgrimage, some final state that will be ushered in when the last obstacle is removed and the last stone pushed to the hilltop. No one believes, of course, that any such state will be final, or even wants it to be in case it means that human existence would then cease to be a struggle; but in the meantime such ideas serve a very real need.

The Meaning of Life

We noted that Sisyphus' existence would have meaning if there were some point to his labors, if his efforts ever culminated in something that was not just an occasion for fresh labors of the same kind. But that is precisely the meaning it lacks. And human existence resembles his in that respect. Men do achieve things—they scale their towers and raise their stones to their hilltops—but every such accomplishment fades, providing only an occasion for renewed labors of the same kind.

But here we need to note something else that has been mentioned, but its significance not explored, and that is the state of mind and feeling with

---

[1] A popular Christian hymn, sung often at funerals and typical of many hymns, expresses this thought:

> Swift to its close ebbs out life's little day;
> Earth's joys grow dim, its glories pass away;
> Change and decay in all around I see:
> O thou who changest not, abide with me.

which such labors are undertaken. We noted that if Sisyphus had a keen and unappeasable desire to be doing just what he found himself doing, then, although his life would in no way be changed, it would nevertheless have a meaning for him. It would be an irrational one, no doubt, because the desire itself would be only the product of the substance in his veins, and not any that reason could discover, but a meaning nevertheless.

And would it not, in fact, be a meaning incomparably better than the other? For let us examine again the first kind of meaning it could have. Let us suppose that, without having any interest in rolling stones, as such, and finding this, in fact, a galling toil, Sisyphus did nevertheless have a deep interest in raising a temple, one that would be beautiful and lasting. And let us suppose he succeeded in this, that after ages of dreadful toil, all directed at this final result, he did at last complete his temple, such that now he could say his work was done, and he could rest and forever enjoy the result. Now what? What picture now presents itself to our minds? It is precisely the picture of infinite boredom! Of Sisyphus doing nothing ever again, but contemplating what he has already wrought and can no longer add anything to, and contemplating it for an eternity! Now in this picture we have a meaning for Sisyphus' existence, a point for his prodigious labor, because we have put it there; yet, at the same time, that which is really worthwhile seems to have slipped away entirely. Where before we were presented with the nightmare of eternal and pointless activity, we are now confronted with the hell of its eternal absence.

Our second picture, then, wherein we imagined Sisyphus to have had inflicted on him the irrational desire to be doing just what he found himself doing, should not have been dismissed so abruptly. The meaning that picture lacked was no meaning that he or anyone could crave, and the strange meaning it had was perhaps just what we were seeking.

At this point, then, we can reintroduce what has been until now, it is hoped, resolutely pushed aside in an effort to view our lives and human existence with objectivity; namely, our own wills, our deep interest in what we find ourselves doing. If we do this we find that our lives do indeed still resemble that of Sisyphus, but that the meaningfulness they thus lack is precisely the meaningfulness of infinite boredom. At the same time, the strange meaningfulness they possess is that of the inner compulsion to be doing just what we were put here to do, and to go on doing it forever. This is the nearest we may hope to get to heaven, but the redeeming side of that fact is that we do thereby avoid a genuine hell.

If the builders of a great and flourishing ancient civilization could somehow return now to see archaeologists unearthing the trivial remnants of what they had once accomplished with such effort—see the fragments of pots and vases, a few broken statues, and such tokens of another age and greatness—they could indeed ask themselves what the point of it all was, if this is all it finally came to. Yet, it did not seem so to them then, for it was just the building, and not what was finally built, that gave their life meaning. Similarly, if the builders of the ruined home and farm that I described a short while ago could be brought back to see what is left, they would have the same feelings. What we construct in our imaginations as we look over these decayed and rusting pieces would reconstruct itself in their very memories, and certainly with unspeakable sadness. The piece of a sled at our feet would revive in them a warm Christmas. And what rich memories would there be in the broken crib? And the weed-covered remains of a fence would reproduce the scene of a great herd of livestock, so laboriously built up over so many years. What was it all worth, if this is the final result? Yet, again, it did not seem so to them through those many years of struggle and toil, and they did not imagine they were building a Gibraltar. The things to which they bent their backs day after day, realizing one by one their ephemeral plans, were precisely the things in which their wills were deeply involved, precisely the things in which their interests lay, and there was no need then to ask questions. There is no more need of them now—the day was sufficient to itself, and so was the life.

This is surely the way to look at all of life—at one's own life, and each day and moment it contains; of the life of a nation; of the species; of the life of the world; and of everything that breathes. Even the glow worms I described, whose cycles of existence over the millions of years seem so pointless when looked at by us, will seem entirely different to us if we can somehow try to view their existence from within. Their endless activity, which gets nowhere, is just what it is their will to pursue. This is its whole justification and meaning. Nor would it be any salvation to the birds who span the globe every year, back and forth, to have a home made for them in a cage with plenty of food and protection, so that they would not have to migrate any more. It would be their condemnation, for it is the doing that counts for them, and not what they hope to win by it. Flying these prodigious distances, never ending, is what it is in their veins to do, exactly as it was in Sisyphus' veins to roll stones, without end, after the gods had waxed merciful and implanted this in him.

A human being no sooner draws his first breath than he responds to the will that is in him to live. He no more asks whether it will be worthwhile, or whether anything of significance will come of it, than the worms and the birds. The point of his living is simply to be living, in the manner that it is his nature to be living. He goes through his life building his castles, each of these beginning to fade into time as the next is begun; yet, it would be no salvation to rest from all this. It would be a condemnation, and one that would in no way be redeemed were he able to gaze upon the things he has done, even if these were beautiful and absolutely permanent, as they never are. What counts is that one should be able to begin a new task, a new castle, a new bubble. It counts only because it is there to be done and he has the will to do it. The same will be the life of his children, and of theirs; and if the philosopher is apt to see in this a pattern similar to the unending cycles of the existence of Sisyphus, and to despair, then it is indeed because the meaning and point he is seeking is not there—but mercifully so. The meaning of life is from within us, it is not bestowed from without, and it far exceeds in both its beauty and permanence any heaven of which men have ever dreamed or yearned for.

Richard Taylor: The Meaning of Life

1) Taylor suggests that we can understand the idea of meaninglessness by reflecting on the myth of Sisyphus. What is Sisyphus's task, and what makes it a meaningless one?

2) According to Taylor, an activity is meaningful if it has "some more or less lasting end that can be considered to have been the direction and purpose of the activity." Do you think that human lives have this feature? If not, does this make life meaningless?

3) Although Taylor believes that our lives are objectively meaningless, he thinks we can nonetheless *find* meaning in them. How does he think this is possible? Do you agree?

4) Taylor says that if the labors of Sisyphus were to result in a "beautiful and enduring temple," then his life would no longer be meaningless. Yet Taylor thinks that such a life would still be undesirable. Why is this?

5) Taylor claims that individuals find meaning by doing "what it is their will to pursue." If I were to count blades of grass all day because I desired to do so, would this be a meaningful existence?

===== 🐦 =====

6

Necessities

Jean Kazez

....

In this excerpt from her wonderful book on the good life, *The Weight of Things* (2007), Jean Kazez argues for the view that there are a number of basic goods that add value to a life. She thus adopts an objective view of human well-being, according to which certain things make an essential contribution to a good life—even if we don't believe this, or don't value these goods. Here she defends her favored roster of such goods.

One of these is autonomy—the ability to decide for yourself which principles will govern your life, and the ability to follow through on those decisions. She also thinks it essential that a good life improve over time. A life that contains a great amount of good things, but all within one's first decade, followed by a steady decline til death, is not a good life. Also on the list: self-expression, a commitment to morality, and happiness taken in worthwhile activities. Kazez defends each of these claims with interesting examples taken from memoirs and literature.

....

W‍hat kind of evidence would show that something is a fundamental good that's not just relevant to living well, but necessary? There certainly isn't anything like a sure-fire test. We can only aspire to say what seems most reasonable. We certainly should not expect to be able to recognize which are the critical goods in one intuitive flash, without spending time looking at any sort of evidence. It may take you some time before you come to think that happiness or morality, or any other candidate, is fundamentally good. A person could come to think so only after reading a searing biography, or watching a movie, or reflecting on a life experience. At the very least, you would have to sift through examples. We're all familiar with lots of lives and we deem some better than others. If the lives we deem good consistently are lives of—say— eating lots of popcorn, then eating lots of popcorn looks to be a fundamental good with relevance to human well-being. If we deem lives bad when they're lacking popcorn consumption, then that's a reason to view popcorn consumption as a necessity.

Beyond this sort of sifting of cases and discovery of patterns, we learn something from looking at human motivation. Since I'm no more astute a judge of value than anyone else, it pays to think about what people value and how they value it. If many people will stop at nothing to procure popcorn, that's some support for regarding eating popcorn as a necessity. That's not to say that we need to do surveys to show that everyone wants popcorn. The occasional popcorn hater doesn't refute the theory that it's necessary, because desires are manipulable; they're not definitive. But they're certainly a piece of relevant evidence.

HAPPINESS IS A REASONABLE place to begin. Some philosophers have questioned whether feelings of happiness are good at all, let alone fundamentally good. The Stoics, for example, argue that plain physical pleasure adds nothing positive at all to a life that is good because of virtue:

> It is like the light of a lamp eclipsed and obliterated by the rays of the sun; like a drop of honey lost in the vastness of the Aegean sea; a penny added to the riches of Croesus, or a single step on the road from here to India. Such is the value of bodily goods that it is unavoidably eclipsed, overwhelmed and destroyed by the splendour and grandeur of virtue...

Kant takes a kindred stand when he says that the only thing that's good without qualification is the morally good will. If feeling happy is sometimes good, and perhaps even for itself, it's not good at those times when it's enticing us in the wrong direction or rewarding evil deeds.

My intuitions side with the Hedonistic Utilitarians. Happiness is a good thing, always. We don't like to see bad people experience happiness precisely because we do think it's something good, and we want them to have no share of what's good. There's something disturbing about ill-gotten happiness. It's especially creepy to contemplate sadistic pleasure, pleasure that's actually derived from causing others to suffer. But I don't think we can assess whether five minutes of happiness is good or not based on its pedigree. Happiness is good, period.

And it's relevant to how well a life is going. In *Darkness Visible*, William Styron tells the story of a depression that overwhelmed him and nearly drove him to suicide; as the depression lifts, and he has his first moments of non-misery, and then moments of happiness, there's no doubt that his life is going better. You could insist that greater happiness was life-enhancing for him because it paid off in greater creativity or healthier relationships, or some other coin, but that's not what seems to be the case. Think of a time when your own life was not going well. Gradually, you started to be happier. You found your days more pleasant. You enjoyed the company of your friends more. Your boss didn't annoy you as much. You weren't dwelling on worries about the future any more. This change of mood probably improved your life – directly, and because of itself. Happiness, whether it comes about in mysterious ways, in good ways, or in bad ways, is a fundamental good that can directly affect how our lives are going.

If happiness is relevant to the way a life is going, is it also necessary? Without at least some happiness, it does not seem like we can reach the level of even minimally good lives. A person without any happiness at all is unconscious, or continually miserable, or at best in a neutral frame of mind. Of these possibilities, neutrality certainly seems the most appealing, but it's hard to imagine a person constantly in such a state whose life could be judged positively, overall.

HAPPINESS IS CRITICAL, BUT it's not the only critical thing. David Shipler portrays the lives of people struggling to make ends meet in his recent book, *The Working Poor: Invisible in America*. His stories have a recurrent theme: the lack of control that's the cost of poverty. The low-income workers he portrays are deprived of independence, autonomy, self-determination. They have no chance to be the authors of their own lives.

One of his portraits is particularly touching. Caroline works in the women's department at Wal-Mart. She needs to be home with her teen-aged daughter in the evenings, because of her mental retardation and epilepsy, but she's forced to work night shifts. She'd have better hours and make better money as a manager, but—perhaps because she's missing all her teeth—she's repeatedly passed over for promotion. She finally quits the Wal-Mart job, and then one business after another gives her irregular night shifts, until her daughter's teachers become concerned that she's being neglected. Caroline finally loses both her home and her daughter, who goes to live with a relative.

Nobody has perfect control. But there is a level of autonomy beneath which we do not want to fall. Barbara Ehrenreich, in *Nickel and Dimed*, describes the way control is lost even before a person is hired. The job applicant has to take drug tests and fill out phony psychological questionnaires. If hired, the blue-collar worker finds herself being told exactly how every aspect of the job must be performed. In the worst cases, the worker becomes little more than a cog in a machine. Shipler describes a woman in Los Angeles sewing flies into blue jeans at a rate of 767 per hour, on pain of being docked a portion of her hourly wage of $5.75. In the very worst cases, the worker is physically prevented from escaping her thing-like status; she is nearly a slave.

Having more control is one thing, it seems, that would have made Caroline's life better. It would have been a major improvement if she could have controlled her work schedule to accommodate her daughter's needs. Advancing to a managerial position would have increased her control over her daily activities. It would have been some improvement if she had been given the chance to initiate and innovate on the job, instead of having to follow rigidly prescribed routines.

Is autonomy really something we should value in itself?

What I'll say about foolish exercises of autonomy is just what I said about ill-gotten happiness. Autonomy is always, as such, good. What would be *too* counterintuitive would be to say that every increase in autonomy automatically makes a person's life overall better. But we needn't say that. There are other things a life needs besides autonomy, and foolish exercises of autonomy will typically get in the way of the fulfillment of those other needs.

Lack of autonomy tends to be accompanied by unhappiness and greater autonomy by greater happiness. It's difficult, therefore, to disentangle the desire to be more autonomous from the desire to be happier. Still, unless we are utterly determined to construe happiness as the sole motivator in life, the pursuit of autonomy is everywhere to see: it's evident when slaves demand freedom from masters, when teenagers demand more independence from parents, when workers wrestle some control over their hours from managers, when women demand the right to vote.

In contemporary Western culture, there's no doubt that we place a huge premium on personal autonomy. Autonomy is regarded in quite a different way in other settings. Certainly we should avoid drawing a picture of the necessary kinds and amounts of autonomy based on what's in our own backyards. Arranged marriage is alien to us, but does it cut into autonomy excessively? An Indian couple I know tell me how their marriage was arranged in their twenties by thoughtful parents looking out for their best interests; their marriage seems as good as most. On the other hand, in traditional Hindu villages, it's not unusual for parents to arrange the marriage of a girl as young as eight, who is then kept behind the walls of her home until she's old enough to join her husband's household. In this case, unlike the first, there's a disturbing loss of control. In saying so, we're not necessarily holding an alien idea about individual lives over the local one. The local assumption seems really to be that the girl is just a girl, and not entitled to the best life—an idea we are compelled to reject. Her individual interests are regarded as subordinate to the interests of men, or families, or the village as a whole.

Insisting that a good life includes "enough" autonomy seems to particularly conflict with the most traditional Islamic ideas about the good life for women, but again, the contradiction can be read in another way. In Saudi Arabia, women live out their lives in *purdah* hidden in their fathers' or husbands' homes, and behind veils. They depend on male relatives to take them places and are denied the right to vote. As Martha Nussbaum points out in *Women and Human Development*, it's not necessarily true that social arrangements reveal a vision of the best life for a woman; arrangements are often defended because they're thought to be best for society as a whole. The good for individual women doesn't count, or counts for less. By contrast, she supports—persuasively—"a principle of each person as an end."

Surely, though, there are cultures quite unlike our own that really do conceive of what it is for an individual to live well in ways that give less emphasis to autonomy. In Thomas à Kempis's fifteenth-century classic, *The Imitation of Christ*, the advice to the devout is to find someone to obey. Letting someone else run your life is regarded as good, not bad (as long as you attach yourself to the right superior). The ideal of limiting oneself is taken about as far as possible in some of the medieval religious orders. In *Galileo's Daughter*, Dava Sobel describes the religious order where

Galileo—that highly disobedient Catholic—sent his own daughters. In the order of Saint Clare, life was spent within the confines of a convent. The confinement was supposed to facilitate a virtuous life. So Saint Colette explains:

> He Himself deigned and willed to be placed in a sepulchre of stone. And it pleased Him to be so entombed for forty hours. So, my dear Sisters, you follow Him. For after obedience, poverty, and pure chastity, you have holy enclosure to hold on to, enclosure in which you can live for forty years either more or less, and in which you will die.

Imprisonment in the convent was taken to be a good life for the individual sisters, not just a means to some greater collective good.

Stretch our preconceptions as we may, we have to be prepared to say that some views are just wrong. The idea that loss of autonomy is conducive to living the best life is a view that has been superseded by other ideas, even within the monastic tradition, and rightly so.

Happiness, autonomy. Could those be all the necessities there are? "Nowhere Man" must give us pause. He is well endowed with both, but his name is based on the fact that one week he's working at a slaughter-house, but the next week he quits and works at the local animal shelter. Now he's actively involved in Republican politics. Next he's earnestly supporting the Democratic Party. He gets excited about Buddhism and then he's moved on to Jewish Mysticism. "Doesn't have a point of view, knows not where he's going to," as the Beatles song so aptly puts it.

Nowhere Man's problem, on the surface, is that there is no unity or continuity in his life. That sounds like a merely aesthetic criticism (this novel is choppy; it doesn't hang together; the midsection doesn't belong). It seems too abstract to really be relevant to evaluating a life; until, that is, we reframe the problem as a lack of self. We want to be amply endowed with the ingredients covered so far (happiness and autonomy), but we want our way of pursuing them to spring from our "selves."

If we really have a grip on Nowhere Man's problem, we ought to be able to identify instances of it in the real world, and that is harder than one might expect. People's lives can exhibit considerable contrast and variety without anyone suspecting a missing "self." There's no problem with Arnold Schwarzenegger's life, just because he went from action hero in the movies to California governor, or because he's a Republican married into the famously Democratic Kennedy family. It's not the sheer disunity of a life that's bad, but an underlying weak self, a self without any strong preferences. A weak self is indifferent to what, for the rest of us, are big differences. No steady convictions and personal traits control perceptions of what's appealing and what's not. Beyond that, it's hard to say what a strong self is, exactly. But it seems critical to our lives going well. If being autonomous and self-determining are as important as they seem to be, it must be equally important for a person to have a self that does the determining.

A sense of identity tends to make us happy, like the other fundamental goods do. But self and happiness don't always go hand in hand. There's probably some situation in which each of us would choose self over happiness. Some people face that choice as the result of a mental illness. For a person who is profoundly depressed, a treatment of last resort is electroconvulsive therapy, which can result in memory loss. With whole swaths of one's life erased—who your friends were, what you read or wrote, where you traveled, what happened in the world at large—you can become virtually another person. Jonathan Cott reports just this in his memoir *On the Sea of Memory*; he seems to lament having chosen ECT to treat severe depression, longing for a return of self, even a self that was depressed. In *Listening to Prozac*, Peter Kramer worries that the alteration of identity is a quite standard effect of anti-depressants, and wonders whether mood improvement is worth the cost.

Injury to self can be done by medications and memory loss, but the causes are innumerable. Shipler's book sheds light on one of the many ways that people stuck in poverty sometimes come to have problems of "self." Many are victims of sexual abuse who suffer dissociative disorders. In other words, they split off a part of themselves and become mere observers of the abuse. This spares them some of the pain of their victimization, but later they continue to observe as things "happen" to them. They watch themselves neglecting their own children instead of choosing to neglect them or choosing to stop neglecting them.

But problems of self are not just outcomes of poverty. To cite just one literary example, in Zora Neale Hurston's *Their Eyes Were Watching God*, Janie's first two marriages are to well-off men who define the social role she is supposed to play. The way they use her to adorn themselves stops her from finding her own voice. Descending to a lower socio-economic stratum, ironically, she discovers a sense of self. Shipler describes how rich parents neglect children and bestow on them an insidious hunger for attention. They become anxious "people pleasers." A child like this reaches adulthood with a set of traits, interests, and abilities that win Mom and Dad's approval. The adult child winds up with no deep-rooted self at the helm. She casts about, now doing this, now doing that. Even if the thises and thats are good things and produce some happiness, there seems to be something amiss with such a life.

Like autonomy, self-expression is especially prized in contemporary Western societies. But is self merely a Western preoccupation? On the face of it, Buddhist thinking involves a diametrically opposed sense of value. Buddhist sages urge us to lose ourselves, not find ourselves; the very highest thing we can achieve is "no self."

Though Buddhism encourages the realization of no-self, it doesn't encourage us to be like Nowhere Man. I'm inclined to think a Buddhist *doesn't* reject self as I am using the term. What no-self really means is not being rigidly identified with some narrow set of characteristics (I am a female liberal intellectual), not being focused on acquisition, not being egocentric. It is being open, receptive, compassionate.

My intuitions about the critical role of morality agree with the ancients—Plato, Aristotle, and the Stoics—who all regard moral virtue as central to living our lives well. For some of the ancients, the benefit of morality is so significant that morality is the only thing that determines how my life is going. I can't swallow that whole, but morality can, intuitively, make me a better person and my life a better life. It's not always a matter of morality making me happy—though frequently it does. Morality seems to make a direct difference to how well my life is going.

Certainly, there are stories of life getting better because of moral improvement. In Dostoevsky's *Crime and Punishment*, Raskolnikov kills an old woman, struggles to justify himself to himself and his friends, but eventually feels compelled to take responsibility. At the end of the book, he walks up the steps of the police station and confesses, with no particular sensation of pleasure or pain. We know his life is now going better, even before we read the epilogue and find out what happens to him. It's true that his confession has rewards: he's given a lenient sentence because he's admitted to his crime; he's now able to enjoy and reciprocate the love of the devoted and saintly Sonya; and he winds up turning tentatively in the direction of her religious faith. Moments of "infinite happiness" arrive while Raskolnikov serves his term in a Siberian prison camp, and more are assured in the future. But the moment when his life has become better precedes the happiness payoff. The sheer moral improvement at the moment of his confession establishes some life improvement before greater happiness comes along and yields more.

Depending on how morality is understood, it can be easier or harder to see the connection between being moral and living well. The ancient conceptions, with their focus on virtue, are most conducive to seeing the connection. The Aristotelian virtues are sustainers of stability and balance. Being angry at the right time, at the right person, to the right degree, would save a person from being a doormat or a volcano. It's harder to say why a person can make his life go better by sending money to help flood victims on the other side of the world, or by telling the truth in an awkward situation, or by apportioning grades or pay increases fairly. What's the relevance of doing these things for other people to making your own life go well?

Perhaps it comes down to a connection between living well and living among others. If you concern yourself not at all with what you owe to others or with what they need from you, you live in profound isolation. Yes, there are people out there, but in your scheme of things, they're just things – like the rocks in a quarry or the cornstalks in a field. Without morality, you would enjoy, protect, exploit, or destroy others at your pleasure. You would regard yourself as the only one of your kind, the only one whose well-being really matters. If it would be bad to literally be the only one of your kind, the last surviving person, then it's bad to live as if you were. The good of moral behavior toward others, for each of us, is the good of being part of a richer world, in which there are many beings with independent importance.

Morality is good for us because it makes us less alone—it gives me a kind of friendship not just with my *friends* but with everyone. If friendship strikes you as an obvious good, then this explanation will satisfy you. But what if it doesn't? There is this also to say: there is something painfully limited about our lives. You can only live one life—here, not there; now, not in the past or the future; doing this, not that. We break through these limits by identifying with hungry people on the other side of the globe or with the inhabitants of a polluted, over-heated world in the next century. We become (a bit) *them*. Ethical concern is something of a cure for our sense of finitude. It's good to do the right thing because it gives you an expanded life, one that encompasses not just your own feelings and satisfactions and accomplishments, but those of other people (and possibly animals as well).

A list of four necessities—happiness, autonomy, self-expression, and morality—is admirably tidy, but not absurdly restrictive. Each thing on the list is robustly valuable. We certainly act like these things are critically important in our daily lives. Now we enter less certain territory.

Take, to begin with, a woman I will call Constance. She works as a piano teacher, plays Beethoven sonatas splendidly, enjoys going to the symphony. She wears attractive, timeless fashions picked out of the Land's End catalogue and reads the Bible in her spare time. She's a good friend to her neighbors and a generous donor to the American Cancer Society. The problem is that she does exactly these things from the age of 21 to her death at 81. Constance doesn't get better at playing the piano or choose new music. She doesn't grow tired of Land's End fashions. She doesn't get interested in new charities. There is no improvement in any way; there is minimal change. The good she is missing is the good of growth, positive change, progress.

We do seem to value progress itself, and not just the good things that are the outcome of making progress—like greater autonomy, happiness, and accomplishment. Some of the lives we admire most are lives transformed by adversity. Lance Armstrong would impress us if he won the Tour de France over and over again. He impresses us far more because he progressed from cancer survivor to race winner. We're impressed no matter what by a person who is highly autonomous, but we're especially impressed by the great abolitionist Frederick Douglass, who started off as a slave and fought his way to autonomy. Since cancer and slavery are very bad things, and undoubtedly detracted from these two lives, we must accord progress itself a very high value, considering that these lives strike us as being especially good.

We want our lives in some way to go from worse to better. We want that to happen over small stretches and large, in minor ways and in major ways. Moving from worse to better might mean fixing the toaster one morning, or learning salsa dancing in the space of a month, or becoming acquainted with Peru over a summer. Or it could mean becoming a better teacher over a 10-year period, or learning to be more compassionate over a lifetime.

But wouldn't it be better to skip "worse" and go directly to "better"—to have the knowledge, or skills, or activities, or experiences that are "better" from the start? Maybe that would be good for another kind of being. God, in our conception, starts off perfect and stays perfect. Absence of change in a supreme being is no flaw at all. But in us, no progress would be a serious flaw. It's not a fixed toaster, or dancing, or familiarity with Peru that really makes a person's life better. It really is precisely the process of going from broken to fixed, from clumsy to competent, from ignorant to familiar. It's exercising the power to go from worse to better.

In his extraordinary memoir, *Angela's Ashes*, Frank McCourt tells the story of a childhood spent in extreme poverty and heartbreak. He lacks just about every good I've discussed at the beginning of his life, and comes to possess everything as an adult. Is this really a better life than one that starts well and ends well? It certainly is puzzling to say that it is. That would imply that to give our children a shot at the best possible lives, we ought to deliberately put ourselves in dire circumstances. Should we?

It's true that you have a shot at the most extraordinary progress only if you start in the deepest trough. But most people who start in the deepest trough stay there. So, no, we shouldn't seek problems so we can rise to their solutions. If progress is a necessity—and I'm going to say it is, with just a dash of uncertainty—the progress we need is moderate. What we must avoid is complete stagnation. Wherever we start, we should aim higher. It's quite ordinary types of change that we can't do without.

WITH A ROSTER OF good things now in place, let's return for a moment to happiness. Happiness is good wherever it comes from, I've argued, and having some is a necessity. But what if all your happiness comes from valueless sources? Maggie works as a nurse in an intensive care unit. Make her the head nurse so that she has plenty of autonomy. She performs her job impeccably and let's also assume she's a supporter of good causes, perhaps a life-long volunteer at the SPCA. Make it up as you like. She's happy and responsible and she's learned and progressed over time. But here's the hitch. Maggie's happiness comes from Magic Drug. Without it she would find her job grueling, she'd fall into dependent relationships, and she'd hate animals. Magic Drug doesn't just help her derive happiness from her life. It's not like the medication that helped William Styron recover from depression, enabling him to once more derive happiness from his writing and friendships and so on. The source of Maggie's happiness is Magic Drug and nothing else.

Maggie's problem takes plenty of real-world forms. Imagine a person with lots of good in his life, who derives happiness only from gambling. When he's with his lovely wife and children, he's not happy with them, he's happy because he's anticipating the next trip to the casino. (Don't think of this person as an addict, or you'll have trouble believing he has autonomy. No, he's in control of himself. It's just that gambling is his sole source of pleasure.) This strikes me as a blight that stops his life from going entirely well. If he were to stop the gambling and begin to derive satisfaction from spending time with his children (let's say), that would make his life go better.

Happiness is good wherever it comes from, but in addition to wanting happiness, we also want our happiness to come at least substantially from things that have value. The good that Maggie is missing is a funny, subtle sort of thing. There's no one word for it; to have it is to be happy *with* the good things in your life. What we want, beyond happiness and the other things I've discussed, is a link between happiness and the other things. There's no reason for every last drop of our happiness to be derived from valuable things—that would be a rather puritanical expectation—but something's amiss when most of it isn't.

Jean Kazez: Necessities

1) Kazez says that "Happiness is a good thing, always." Do you agree? Is the happiness that a sadistic person gets from torturing someone good? Why or why not?

2) Kazez argues that autonomy is necessary for someone to have a good life. Yet she allows that arranged marriages can turn out as well as freely chosen marriages. Do you think that your life could go well if others made all your decisions for you, provided they did a very good job?

3) What does Kazez think is wrong with the life of "Nowhere Man"? Do you agree with her view that such a life would be undesirable, even if it were filled with happiness?

4) Kazez says that "Ethical concern is something of a cure for our sense of finitude." What does she mean by this? Does she succeed in showing that morality is a necessary part of a good life?

5) Kazez thinks that improvement over time can make a life go better. Which would you prefer: a life of constant happiness, or a life that begins miserably and ends in great achievement and contentment?

6) Is all happiness equally valuable, or does the value of happiness depend on its sources (as Kazez claims)?

PART TWO

Normative Ethics

Theories of Right Conduct

7

Extreme and Restricted Utilitarianism

J.J.C. Smart

J.J.C. Smart here introduces us to two forms of utilitarianism, extreme and restricted, which nowadays go by the name of *act* and *rule utilitarianism*, respectively. Extreme utilitarianism makes the morality of actions depend entirely on their results, requiring us always to do that action, among all available to us at the time, which will yield the greatest overall happiness. Restricted (i.e., rule) utilitarianism, by contrast, assesses the rightness of actions based on whether they adhere to rules that, if embraced by all, would yield optimal happiness.

Smart himself endorses extreme utilitarianism, and presents a criticism of restricted utilitarianism that has been very influential. Suppose that we are faced with a situation in which we must break a moral rule in order to maximize happiness. Since the goal of such rules, from a utilitarian standpoint, is to maximize the world's happiness, the only rational thing to do is to break that rule. And yet restricted utilitarians insist that we honor the rule, even when doing so undermines the ultimate utilitarian goal. That is irrational, says Smart, and gives us decisive reason to prefer the extreme version of utilitarianism.

1

Utilitarianism is the doctrine that the rightness of actions is to be judged by their consequences. What do we mean by "actions" here? Do we mean particular actions or do we mean classes of actions? According to which way we interpret the word "actions" we get two different theories, both of which merit the appellation "utilitarian."

(1) If by "actions" we mean particular individual actions we get the sort of doctrine held by Bentham, Sidgwick, and Moore. According to this doctrine we test individual actions by their consequences, and general rules, like "keep promises," are mere rules of thumb which we use only to avoid the necessity of estimating the probable consequences of our actions at every step. The rightness or wrongness of keeping a promise on a particular occasion depends only on the goodness or badness of the consequences of keeping or of breaking the promise on that particular occasion. Of course part of the consequences of breaking the promise, and a part to which we will normally ascribe decisive importance, will be the weakening of faith in the institution of promising. However, if the goodness of the consequences of breaking the rule is *in toto* greater than the goodness of the consequences of keeping it, then we must break the rule, irrespective of whether the goodness of the consequences of *everybody's* obeying the rule is or is not greater than the consequences of *everybody's* breaking it. To put it shortly, rules do not matter, save *per accidens* as rules of thumb and as *de facto* social institutions with which the utilitarian has to reckon when estimating consequences. I shall call this doctrine "extreme utilitarianism."

(2) A more modest form of utilitarianism has recently become fashionable. The doctrine is to be found in Toulmin's book *The Place of Reason in Ethics*, in Nowell-Smith's *Ethics* (though I think Nowell-Smith has qualms), in John Austin's *Lectures on Jurisprudence* (Lecture II), and even in J. S. Mill, if Urmson's interpretation of him is correct (*Philosophical Quarterly*, vol. 3, pp. 33–9, 1953). Part of its charm is that it appears to resolve the dispute in moral philosophy between intuitionists and utilitarians in a way which is very neat. The above philosophers hold, or seem to hold, that moral rules are more than rules of thumb. In general the rightness of an action is *not* to be tested by evaluating its consequences but only by considering whether or not it falls under a certain rule. Whether the rule is to be considered an acceptable moral rule, is, however, to be decided by considering the consequences of adopting the rule. Broadly, then, actions are

to be tested by rules and rules by consequences. The only cases in which we must test an individual action directly by its consequences are *(a)* when the action comes under two different rules, one of which enjoins it and one of which forbids it, and *(b)* when there is no rule whatever that governs the given case. I shall call this doctrine "restricted utilitarianism."

2

For an extreme utilitarian moral rules are rules of thumb. In practice the extreme utilitarian will mostly guide his conduct by appealing to the rules ("do not lie," "do not break promises," etc.) of common sense morality. This is not because there is anything sacrosanct in the rules themselves but because he can argue that probably he will most often act in an extreme utilitarian way if he does not think as a utilitarian. For one thing, actions have frequently to be done in a hurry. Imagine a man seeing a person drowning. He jumps in and rescues him. There is no time to reason the matter out, but usually this will be the course of action which an extreme utilitarian would recommend if he did reason the matter out. If, however, the man drowning had been drowning in a river near Berchtesgaden in 1938, and if he had had the well known black forelock and moustache of Adolf Hitler, an extreme utilitarian would, if he had time, work out the probability of the man's being the villainous dictator, and if the probability were high enough he would, on extreme utilitarian grounds, leave him to drown. The rescuer, however, has not time. He trusts to his instincts and dives in and rescues the man. And this trusting to instincts and to moral rules can be justified on extreme utilitarian grounds. Furthermore, an extreme utilitarian who knew that the drowning man was Hitler would nevertheless praise the rescuer, not condemn him. For by praising the man he is strengthening a courageous and benevolent disposition of mind, and in general this disposition has great positive utility. (Next time, perhaps, it will be Winston Churchill that the man saves!) We must never forget that an extreme utilitarian may praise actions which he knows to be wrong. Saving Hitler was wrong, but it was a member of a class of actions which are generally right, and the motive to do actions of this class is in general an optimific one. In considering questions of praise and blame it is not the expediency of the praised or blamed action that is at issue, but the expediency of the praise. It can be expedient to praise an inexpedient action and inexpedient to praise an expedient one.

Lack of time is not the only reason why an extreme utilitarian may, on extreme utilitarian principles, trust to rules of common sense morality.

He knows that in particular cases where his own interests are involved his calculations are likely to be biased in his own favor. Suppose that he is unhappily married and is deciding whether to get divorced. He will in all probability greatly exaggerate his own unhappiness (and possibly his wife's) and greatly underestimate the harm done to his children by the break up of the family. He will probably also underestimate the likely harm done by the weakening of the general faith in marriage vows. So probably he will come to the correct extreme utilitarian conclusion if he does not in this instance think as an extreme utilitarian but trusts to common sense morality.

There are many more and subtle points that could be made in connection with the relation between extreme utilitarianism and the morality of common sense. All those that I have just made and many more will be found in Book IV Chapters 3–5 of Sidgwick's *Methods of Ethics*. I think that this book is the best book ever written on ethics, and that these chapters are the best chapters of the book. As they occur so near the end of a very long book they are unduly neglected. I refer the reader, then, to Sidgwick for the classical exposition of the relation between (extreme) utilitarianism and the morality of common sense. One further point raised by Sidgwick in this connection is whether an (extreme) utilitarian ought on (extreme) utilitarian principles to propagate (extreme) utilitarianism among the public. As most people are not very philosophical and not good at empirical calculations, it is probable that they will most often act in an extreme utilitarian way if they do not try to think as extreme utilitarians. We have seen how easy it would be to misapply the extreme utilitarian criterion in the case of divorce. Sidgwick seems to think it quite probable that an extreme utilitarian should not propagate his doctrine too widely. However, the great danger to humanity comes nowadays on the plane of public morality – not private morality. There is a greater danger to humanity from the hydrogen bomb than from an increase of the divorce rate, regrettable though that might be, and there seems no doubt that extreme utilitarianism makes for good sense in international relations. When France walked out of the United Nations because she did not wish Morocco discussed, she said that she was within her rights because Morocco and Algiers are part of her metropolitan territory and nothing to do with UN. This was clearly a legalistic if not superstitious argument. We should not be concerned with the so-called "rights" of France or any other country but with whether the cause of humanity would best be served by discussing Morocco in UN. (I am not saying that the answer to this is "Yes." There are good grounds for supposing that more harm than good would come by such a discussion.) I myself have no hesitation in saying that on extreme utilitarian principles we ought to propagate extreme utilitarianism as widely as possible. But Sidgwick had respectable reasons for suspecting the opposite.

The extreme utilitarian, then, regards moral rules as rules of thumb and as sociological facts that have to be taken into account when deciding what to do, just as facts of any other sort have to be taken into account. But in themselves they do not justify any action.

3

The restricted utilitarian regards moral rules as more than rules of thumb for short-circuiting calculations of consequences. Generally, he argues, consequences are not relevant at all when we are deciding what to do in a particular case. In general, they are relevant only to deciding what rules are good reasons for acting in a certain way in particular cases. This doctrine is possibly a good account of how the modern unreflective twentieth century Englishman often thinks about morality, but surely it is monstrous as an account of how it is most rational to think about morality. Suppose that there is a rule R and that in 99% of cases the best possible results are obtained by acting in accordance with R. Then clearly R is a useful rule of thumb; if we have not time or are not impartial enough to assess the consequences of an action it is an extremely good bet that the thing to do is to act in accordance with R. But is it not monstrous to suppose that if we *have* worked out the consequences and if we have perfect faith in the impartiality of our calculations, and if we *know* that in this instance to break R will have better results than to keep it, we should nevertheless obey the rule? Is it not to erect R into a sort of idol if we keep it when breaking it will prevent, say, some avoidable misery? Is not this a form of superstitious rule-worship (easily explicable psychologically) and not the rational thought of a philosopher?

The point may be made more clearly if we consider Mill's comparison of moral rules to the tables in the nautical almanac (*Utilitarianism*, Everyman Edition, pp. 22–3). This comparison of Mill's is adduced by Urmson as evidence that Mill was a restricted utilitarian, but I do not think that it will bear this interpretation at all. (Though I quite agree with Urmson that many other things said by Mill are in harmony with restricted rather than extreme utilitarianism. Probably Mill had never thought very much about the distinction and was arguing for utilitarianism, restricted or extreme, against other and quite non-utilitarian forms of moral argument.) Mill says: "Nobody argues that the art of navigation is not founded on astronomy, because sailors cannot wait to calculate the Nautical Almanac. Being rational creatures, they go out upon the sea of life with their minds made up on the common questions of right and wrong, as well as on many of the far more difficult questions of wise and foolish.... Whatever we adopt as the fundamental principle of morality, we require subordinate principles to apply it by." Notice that this is, as it stands, only an argument for subordinate principles as rules of thumb. The example of the nautical almanac is misleading because the information given in the almanac is in all cases the same as the information one would get if one made a long and laborious calculation from the original astronomical data on which the almanac is founded. Suppose, however, that astronomy were different. Suppose that the behavior of the sun, moon and planets was very nearly as it is now, but that on rare occasions there were peculiar irregularities and discontinuities, so that the almanac gave us rules of the form "in 99% of cases where the observations are such and such you can deduce that your position is so and so." Furthermore, let us suppose that there were methods which enabled us, by direct and laborious calculation from the original astronomical data, not using the rough and ready tables of the almanac, to get our correct position in 100% of cases. Seafarers might use the almanac because they never had time for the long calculations and they were content with a 99% chance of success in calculating their positions. Would it not be absurd, however, if they *did* make the direct calculation, and finding that it disagreed with the almanac calculation, nevertheless they ignored it and stuck to the almanac conclusion? Of course the case would be altered if there were a high enough probability of making slips in the direct calculation: then we might stick to the almanac result, liable to error though we knew it to be, simply because the direct calculation would be open to error for a different reason, the fallibility of the computer. This would be analogous to the case of the extreme utilitarian who abides by the conventional rule against the dictates of his utilitarian calculations simply because he thinks that his calculations are probably affected by personal bias. But if the navigator were sure of his direct calculations would he not be foolish to abide by his almanac? I conclude, then, that if we change our suppositions about astronomy and the almanac (to which there are no exceptions) to bring the case into line with that of morality (to whose rules there are exceptions), Mill's example loses its appearance of supporting the restricted form of utilitarianism. Let me say once more that I am not here concerned with how ordinary men think about morality but with how they ought to think. We could quite well imagine a race of sailors who acquired a superstitious reverence for their almanac, even though it was only right in 99% of cases, and who indignantly threw overboard any man who mentioned the possibility of a direct calculation. But would this behavior of the sailors be rational?

Let us consider a much discussed sort of case in which the extreme utilitarian might go against the conventional moral rule. I have promised to a friend, dying on a desert island from which I am subsequently rescued, that I will see that his fortune (over which I have control) is given to a jockey club. However, when I am rescued I decide that it would be better to give the money to a hospital, which can do more good with it. It may be argued that I am wrong to give the money to the hospital. But why? *(a)* The hospital can do more good with the money than the jockey club can. *(b)* The present case is unlike most cases of promising in that no one except me knows about the promise. In breaking the promise I am doing so with complete secrecy and am doing nothing to weaken the general faith in promises. That is, a factor, which would normally keep the extreme utilitarian from promise breaking even in otherwise unoptimific cases, does not at present operate. *(c)* There is no doubt a slight weakening in my own character as an habitual promise keeper, and moreover psychological tensions will be set up in me every time I am asked what the man made me promise him to do. For clearly I shall have to say that he made me promise to give the money to the hospital, and, since I am an habitual truth teller, this will go very much against the grain with me. Indeed I am pretty sure that in practice I myself would keep the promise. But we are not discussing what my moral habits would probably make me do; we are discussing what I ought to do. Moreover, we must not forget that even if it would be most rational of me to give the money to the hospital it would also be most rational of you to punish or condemn me if you did, most improbably, find out the truth (e.g. by finding a note washed ashore in a bottle). Furthermore, I would agree that though it was most rational of me to give the money to the hospital it would be most rational of you to condemn me for it. We revert again to Sidgwick's distinction between the utility of the action and the utility of the praise of it.

Many such issues are discussed by A. K. Stout[1] It will be useful to consider one example that he gives. Suppose that during hot weather there is

---

[1] "But Suppose Everybody Did the Same?," *Australasian Journal of Philosophy* vol. 32, pp. 1–29.

an edict that no water must be used for watering gardens. I have a garden and I reason that most people are sure to obey the edict, and that as the amount of water that I use will be by itself negligible no harm will be done if I use the water secretly. So I do use the water, thus producing some lovely flowers which give happiness to various people. Still, you may say, though the action was perhaps optimific, it was unfair and wrong.

There are several matters to consider. Certainly my action should be condemned. We revert once more to Sidgwick's distinction. A right action may be rationally condemned. Furthermore, this sort of offense is normally found out. If I have a wonderful garden when everybody else's is dry and brown there is only one explanation. So if I water my garden I am weakening my respect for law and order, and as this leads to bad results an extreme utilitarian would agree that I was wrong to water the garden. Suppose now that the case is altered and that I can keep the thing secret: there is a secluded part of the garden where I grow flowers which I give away anonymously to a home for old ladies. Are you still so sure that I did the wrong thing by watering my garden? However, this is still a weaker case than that of the hospital and the jockey club. There will be tensions set up within myself: my secret knowledge that I have broken the rule will make it hard for me to exhort others to keep the rule. These psychological ill effects in myself may be not inconsiderable: directly and indirectly they may lead to harm which is at least of the same order as the happiness that the old ladies get from the flowers. You can see that on an extreme utilitarian view there are two sides to the question.

So far I have been considering the duty of an extreme utilitarian in a predominantly non-utilitarian society. I now pass on to a type of case which may be thought to be the trump card of restricted utilitarianism. Consider the rule of the road. It may be said that since all that matters is that everyone should do the same it is indifferent which rule we have, "go on the left hand side" or "go on the right hand side." Hence the only *reason* for going on the left hand side in British countries is that this is the rule. Here the rule does seem to be a reason, in itself, for acting in a certain way. I wish to argue against this. The rule in itself is not a reason for our actions. We would be perfectly justified in going on the right hand side if *(a)* we knew that the rule was to go on the left hand side, and *(b)* we were in a country peopled by super-anarchists who always on principle did the opposite of what they were told. This shows that the rule does not give us a reason for acting so much as an indication of the probable actions of others, which helps us to find out what would be our own most rational course of action. If we are in a country not peopled by anarchists, but by non-anarchist extreme Utilitarians, we expect, other things being equal, that they will keep rules laid down for them. Knowledge of the rule enables us to predict their behavior and to harmonize our own actions with theirs. The rule "keep to the left hand side," then, is not a logical *reason* for action but an anthropological *datum* for planning actions.

I conclude that in every case if there is a rule *R* the keeping of which is in general optimific, but such that in a special sort of circumstances the optimific behavior is to break *R*, then in these circumstances we should break *R*. Of course we must consider all the less obvious effects of breaking *R*, such as reducing people's faith in the moral order, before coming to the conclusion that to break *R* is right: in fact we shall rarely come to such a conclusion. Moral rules, on the extreme utilitarian view, are rules of thumb only, but they are not bad rules of thumb. But if we *do* come to the conclusion that we should break the rule and if we have weighed in the balance our own fallibility and liability to personal bias, what good reason remains for keeping the rule? I can understand "it is optimific" as a reason for action, but why should "it is a member of a class of actions which are usually optimific" or "it is a member of a class of actions which as a class are more optimific than any alternative general class" be a good reason? You might as well say that a person ought to be picked to play for Australia just because all his brothers have been, or that the Australian team should be composed entirely of the Harvey family because this would be better than composing it entirely of any other family. The extreme utilitarian does not appeal to artificial feelings, but only to our feelings of benevolence, and what better feelings can there be to appeal to? Admittedly we can have a pro-attitude to anything, even to rules, but such artificially begotten pro-attitudes smack of superstition. Let us get down to realities, human happiness and misery, and make these the objects of our pro-attitudes and anti-attitudes.

The restricted utilitarian might say that he is talking only of *morality*, not of such things as rules of the road. I am not sure how far this objection, if valid, would affect my argument, but in any case I would reply that as a philosopher I conceive of ethics as the study of how it would be *most rational* to act. If my opponent wishes to restrict the word "morality" to a narrower use he can have the word. The fundamental question is the question of rationality of action *in general*. Similarly if the restricted utilitarian were to appeal to ordinary usage and say "it might be most rational to leave Hitler to drown but it would surely not be *wrong* to rescue him,"

I should again let him have the words "right" and "wrong" and should stick to "rational" and "irrational." We already saw that it would be rational to praise Hitler's rescuer, even though it would have been most rational not to have rescued Hitler. In ordinary language, no doubt, "right" and "wrong" have not only the meaning "most rational to do" and "not most rational to do" but also have the meaning "praiseworthy" and "not praiseworthy." Usually to the utility of an action corresponds utility of praise of it, but as we saw, this is not always so. Moral language could thus do with tidying up, for example by reserving "right" for "most rational" and "good" as an epithet of praise for the motive from which the action sprang. It would be more becoming in a philosopher to try to iron out illogicalities in moral language and to make suggestions for its reform than to use it as a court of appeal whereby to perpetuate confusions.

J.J.C. Smart: Extreme and Restricted Utilitarianism

1) Extreme utilitarians hold that moral rules are "mere rules of thumb," while restricted utilitarians think that the rightness of an action is determined by "whether or not it falls under a certain rule." What exactly is the difference between these two views of moral rules?
2) According to Smart, we should sometimes praise actions we know to be wrong, and condemn actions we know to be right. Why does he think this? Do you agree?
3) Smart claims that restricted utilitarianism amounts to "superstitious rule-worship." What does he mean by this? Do you think he is correct?
4) Extreme utilitarians think that we ought to break our promises whenever doing so will bring about a better outcome than keeping the promise. Are we obligated to keep our promises, even if we could bring about more good by breaking them?
5) In his example of the gardener, Smart suggests that it is sometimes morally acceptable to secretly break the law, even if the law is perfectly just. Do you agree with him?

The Good Will and the Categorical Imperative

Immanuel Kant

....

Immanuel Kant (1724–1804) was the greatest German philosopher who ever lived. In this excerpt from his *Groundwork of the Metaphysics of Morals*, Kant introduces two key elements of his moral philosophy. According to Kant, the first of these, the *good will*, is the only thing possessed of unconditional value: it is valuable in its own right, in every possible circumstance. The good will is the steady commitment to do our duty for its own sake. Our actions possess moral worth if, but only if, they are prompted by the good will.

The second important element is the *categorical imperative*, Kant's term for a requirement of reason that applies to us regardless of what we care about. Moral requirements are categorical imperatives—we must, for instance, sometimes give help to others in need, even if we don't want to, and even if such help gets us nothing that we care about. Kant believed that moral action is rational action. Each of us has a compelling reason to obey morality, even when doing so only frustrates our deepest desires.

Kant here sets out two tests for morally acceptable action. The first says that actions are morally acceptable only when the principles that inspire them can be acted on by everyone consistently. The second requires us to treat humanity always as an end in itself, and never as a mere means. Kant realizes that such formulations are somewhat abstract, and so here offers us a number of illustrations that are meant to help us understand and apply them.

....

From *Groundwork of the Metaphysics of Morals*, trans. Mary Gregor (1998). Reprinted with the permission of Cambridge University Press.

The Good Will

It is impossible to think of anything at all in the world, or indeed even beyond it, that could be considered good without limitation except a **good will**. Understanding, wit, judgment and the like, whatever such *talents* of mind may be called, or courage, resolution, and perseverance in one's plans, as qualities of *temperament*, are undoubtedly good and desirable for many purposes, but they can also be extremely evil and harmful if the will which is to make use of these gifts of nature, and whose distinctive constitution is therefore called *character*, is not good. It is the same with *gifts of fortune*. Power, riches, honor, even health and that complete well-being and satisfaction with one's condition called *happiness*, produce boldness and thereby often arrogance as well unless a good will is present which corrects the influence of these on the mind and, in so doing, also corrects the whole principle of action and brings it into conformity with universal ends—not to mention that an impartial rational spectator can take no delight in seeing the uninterrupted prosperity of a being graced with no feature of a pure and good will, so that a good will seems to constitute the indispensable condition even of worthiness to be happy.

Some qualities are even conducive to this good will itself and can make its work much easier; despite this, however, they have no inner unconditional worth but always presuppose a good will, which limits the esteem one otherwise rightly has for them and does not permit their being taken as absolutely good. Moderation in affects and passions, self-control, and calm reflection are not only good for all sorts of purposes but even seem to constitute a part of the *inner* worth of a person; but they lack much that would be required to declare them good without limitation (however unconditionally they were praised by the ancients); for, without the basic principles of a good will they can become extremely evil, and the coolness of a scoundrel makes him not only far more dangerous but also immediately more abominable in our eyes than we would have taken him to be without it.

A good will is not good because of what it effects or accomplishes, because of its fitness to attain some proposed end, but only because of its volition, that is, it is good in itself and, regarded for itself, is to be valued incomparably higher than all that could merely be brought about by it in favor of some inclination and indeed, if you will, of the sum of all inclinations. Even if, by a special disfavor of fortune or by the niggardly provision of a stepmotherly nature, this will should wholly lack the capacity to carry out its purpose—if with its greatest efforts it should yet achieve nothing and only the good will were left (not, of course, as a mere wish but as the summoning of all means insofar as they are in our control)—then, like a jewel, it would still shine by itself, as something that has its full worth in itself. Usefulness or fruitlessness can neither add anything to this worth nor take anything away from it. Its usefulness would be, as it were, only the setting to enable us to handle it more conveniently in ordinary commerce or to attract to it the attention of those who are not yet expert enough, but not to recommend it to experts or to determine its worth.

We have, then, to explicate the concept of a will that is to be esteemed in itself and that is good apart from any further purpose, as it already dwells in natural sound understanding and needs not so much to be taught as only to be clarified—this concept that always takes first place in estimating the total worth of our actions and constitutes the condition of all the rest. In order to do so, we shall set before ourselves the concept of **duty**, which contains that of a good will though under certain subjective limitations and hindrances, which, however, far from concealing it and making it unrecognizable, rather bring it out by contrast and make it shine forth all the more brightly.

I here pass over all actions that are already recognized as contrary to duty, even though they may be useful for this or that purpose; for in their case the question whether they might have been done *from duty* never arises, since they even conflict with it. I also set aside actions that are really in conformity with duty but to which human beings have *no inclination* immediately and which they still perform because they are impelled to do so through another inclination. For in this case it is easy to distinguish whether an action in conformity with duty is done *from duty* or from a selfseeking purpose. It is much more difficult to note this distinction when an action conforms with duty and the subject has, besides, an *immediate* inclination to it. For example, it certainly conforms with duty that a shopkeeper not overcharge an inexperienced customer, and where there is a good deal of trade a prudent merchant does not overcharge but keeps a fixed general price for everyone, so that a child can buy from him as well as everyone else. People are thus served *honestly*; but this is not nearly enough for us to believe that the merchant acted in this way from duty and basic principles of honesty; his advantage required it; it cannot be assumed here that he had, besides, an immediate inclination toward his customers, so as from love, as it were, to give no one preference over another in the matter of price. Thus the action was done neither from duty nor from immediate inclination but merely for purposes of self-interest.

On the other hand, to preserve one's life is a duty, and besides everyone has an immediate inclination to do so. But on this account the often anxious care that most people take of it still has no inner worth and their maxim has no moral content. They look after their lives *in conformity with duty* but not *from duty*. On the other hand, if adversity and hopeless grief have quite taken away the taste for life; if an unfortunate man, strong of soul and more indignant about his fate than despondent or dejected, wishes for death and yet preserves his life without loving it, not from inclination or fear but from duty, then his maxim has moral content.

To be beneficent where one can is a duty, and besides there are many souls so sympathetically attuned that, without any other motive of vanity or self-interest they find an inner satisfaction in spreading joy around them and can take delight in the satisfaction of others so far as it is their own work. But I assert that in such a case an action of this kind, however it may conform with duty and however amiable it may be, has nevertheless no true moral worth but is on the same footing with other inclinations, for example, the inclination to honor, which, if it fortunately lights upon what is in fact in the common interest and in conformity with duty and hence honorable, deserves praise and encouragement but not esteem; for the maxim lacks moral content, namely that of doing such actions not from inclination but *from duty*. Suppose, then, that the mind of this philanthropist were overclouded by his own grief, which extinguished all sympathy with the fate of others, and that while he still had the means to benefit others in distress their troubles did not move him because he had enough to do with his own; and suppose that now, when no longer incited to it by any inclination, he nevertheless tears himself out of this deadly insensibility and does the action without any inclination, simply from duty; then the action first has its genuine moral worth. Still further: if nature had put little sympathy in the heart of this or that man; if (in other respects an honest man) he is by temperament cold and indifferent to the sufferings of others, perhaps because he himself is provided with the special gift of patience and endurance toward his own sufferings and presupposes the same in every other or even requires it; if nature had not properly fashioned such a man (who would in truth not be its worst product) for a philanthropist, would he not still find within himself a source from which to give himself a far higher worth than what a mere good-natured temperament might have? By all means! It is just then that the worth of character comes out, which is moral and incomparably the highest, namely that he is beneficent not from inclination but from duty.

Thus the moral worth of an action does not lie in the effect expected from it and so too does not lie in any principle of action that needs to borrow its motive from this expected effect. For, all these effects (agreeableness of one's condition, indeed even promotion of others' happiness) could have been also brought about by other causes, so that there would have been no need, for this, of the will of a rational being, in which, however, the highest and unconditional good alone can be found. Hence nothing other than the *representation of the law* in itself, *which can of course occur only in a rational being,* insofar as it and not the hoped-for effect is the determining ground of the will, can constitute the preeminent good we call moral, which is already present in the person himself who acts in accordance with this representation and need not wait upon the effect of his action.

But what kind of law can that be, the representation of which must determine the will, even without regard for the effect expected from it, in order for the will to be called good absolutely and without limitation? Since I have deprived the will of every impulse that could arise for it from obeying some law, nothing is left but the conformity of actions as such with universal law, which alone is to serve the will as its principle, that is, *I ought never to act except in such a way that I could also will that my maxim should become a universal law.* Here mere conformity to law as such, without having as its basis some law determined for certain actions, is what serves the will as its principle, and must so serve it, if duty is not to be every-where an empty delusion and a chimerical concept. Common human reason also agrees completely with this in its practical appraisals and always has this principle before its eyes. Let the question be, for example: may I, when hard pressed, make a promise with the intention not to keep it? Here I easily distinguish two significations the question can have: whether it is prudent or whether it is in conformity with duty to make a false promise. The first can undoubtedly often be the case. I see very well that it is not enough to get out of a present difficulty by means of this subterfuge but that I must reflect carefully whether this lie may later give rise to much greater inconvenience for me than that from which I now extricate myself; and since, with all my supposed *cunning,* the results cannot be so easily foreseen but that once confidence in me is lost this could be far more prejudicial to me than all the troubles I now think to avoid, I must reflect whether the matter might be handled *more prudently* by proceeding on a general maxim and making it a habit to promise nothing except with the intention of keeping it. But it is soon clear to me that such a maxim will still be based only on results feared. To be truthful from duty, however, is something entirely different from being truthful from anxiety about detrimental results, since in the first case the concept of the action in itself already contains a law for me while in the second I must first look about elsewhere to see what effects on me might be combined with it. For, if I deviate from the principle of duty this is quite certainly evil; but if I am unfaithful to my maxim of prudence this can sometimes be very advantageous to me, although it is certainly safer to abide by it. However, to inform myself in the shortest and yet infallible way about the answer to this problem, whether a lying promise is in conformity with duty, I ask myself: would I indeed be content that my maxim (to get myself out of difficulties by a false promise) should hold as a universal law (for myself as well as for others)? and could I indeed say to myself that every one may make a false promise when he finds himself in a difficulty he can get out of in no other way? Then I soon become aware that I could indeed will the lie, but by no means a universal law to lie; for in accordance with such a law there would properly be no promises at all, since it would be futile to avow my will with regard to my future actions to others who would not believe this avowal or, if they rashly did so, would pay me back in like coin; and thus my maxim, as soon as it were made a universal law, would have to destroy itself.

I do not, therefore, need any penetrating acuteness to see what I have to do in order that my volition be morally good. Inexperienced in the course of the world, incapable of being prepared for whatever might come to pass in it, I ask myself only: can you also will that your maxim become a universal law? If not, then it is to be repudiated, and that not because of a disadvantage to you or even to others forthcoming from it but because it cannot fit as a principle into a possible giving of universal law, for which lawgiving reason, however, forces from me immediate respect. Although I do not yet *see* what this respect is based upon (this the philosopher may investigate), I at least understand this much: that it is an estimation of a worth that far outweighs any worth of what is recommended by inclination, and that the necessity of my action from *pure* respect for the practical law is what constitutes duty, to which every other motive must give way because it is the condition of a will good *in itself*, the worth of which surpasses all else.

The Categorical Imperative

Now, all imperatives command either *hypothetically* or *categorically*. The former represent the practical necessity of a possible action as a means to achieving something else that one wills (or that it is at least possible for one to will). The categorical imperative would be that which represented an action as objectively necessary of itself, without reference to another end.

Since every practical law represents a possible action as good and thus as necessary for a subject practically determinable by reason, all imperatives are formulae for the determination of action that is necessary in accordance with the principle of a will which is good in some way. Now, if the action would be good merely as a means *to something else* the imperative is *hypothetical*; if the action is represented as *in itself* good, hence as necessary in a will in itself conforming to reason, as its principle, *then it is categorical.*

There is one imperative that, without being based upon and having as its condition any other purpose to be attained by certain conduct, commands this conduct immediately. This imperative is **categorical**. It has to do not with the matter of the action and what is to result from it, but with the form and the principle from which the action itself follows; and the essential good in the action consists in the disposition, let the result be what it may. This imperative may be called the imperative **of morality**.

When I think of a *hypothetical* imperative in general I do not know beforehand what it will contain; I do not know this until I am given the condition. But when I think of a *categorical* imperative I know at once what it contains. For, since the imperative contains, beyond the law, only the necessity that the maxim[1] be in conformity with this law, while the law contains no condition to which it would be limited, nothing is left with which the maxim of action is to conform but the universality of a law as such; and this conformity alone is what the imperative properly represents as necessary.

There is, therefore, only a single categorical imperative and it is this: *act only in accordance with that maxim through which you can at the same time will that it become a universal law.*

Now, if all imperatives of duty can be derived from this single imperative as from their principle, then, even though we leave it undecided whether what is called duty is not as such an empty concept, we

---

[1] A *maxim* is the subjective principle of acting, and must be distinguished from the *objective* principle, namely the practical law. The former contains the practical rule determined by reason conformably with the conditions of the subject (often his ignorance or also his inclinations), and is therefore the principle in accordance with which the subject *acts*; but the law is the objective principle valid for every rational being, and the principle in accordance with which he *ought to act*, i.e., an imperative.

shall at least be able to show what we think by it and what the concept wants to say.

Since the universality of law in accordance with which effects take place constitutes what is properly called *nature* in the most general sense (as regards its form)—that is, the existence of things insofar as it is determined in accordance with universal laws—the universal imperative of duty can also go as follows: *act as if the maxim of your action were to become by your will a* **universal law of nature**.

We shall now enumerate a few duties in accordance with the usual division of them into duties to ourselves and to other human beings and into perfect and imperfect duties.[2]

1) Someone feels sick of life because of a series of troubles that has grown to the point of despair, but is still so far in possession of his reason that he can ask himself whether it would not be contrary to his duty to himself to take his own life. Now he inquires whether the maxim of his action could indeed become a universal law of nature. His maxim, however, is: from self-love I make it my principle to shorten my life when its longer duration threatens more troubles than it promises agreeableness. The only further question is whether this principle of self-love could become a universal law of nature. It is then seen at once that a nature whose law it would be to destroy life itself by means of the same feeling whose destination is to impel toward the furtherance of life would contradict itself and would therefore not subsist as nature; thus that maxim could not possibly be a law of nature and, accordingly, altogether opposes the supreme principle of all duty.

2) Another finds himself urged by need to borrow money. He well knows that he will not be able to repay it but sees also that nothing will be lent him unless he promises firmly to repay it within a determinate time. He would like to make such a promise, but he still has enough conscience to ask himself: is it not forbidden and contrary to duty to help oneself out of need in such a way? Supposing that he still decided to do so, his maxim of action would go as follows: when I believe myself to be

---

[2] It must be noted here that I reserve the division of duties entirely for a future *Metaphysics of Morals*, so that the division here stands only as one adopted at my discretion (for the sake of arranging my examples). For the rest, I understand here by a perfect duty one that admits no exception in favor of inclination, and then I have not merely external but also internal *perfect duties*; although this is contrary to the use of the word adopted in the schools, I do not intend to justify it here, since for my purpose it makes no difference whether or not it is granted me.

in need of money I shall borrow money and promise to repay it, even though I know that this will never happen. Now this principle of self-love or personal advantage is perhaps quite consistent with my whole future welfare, but the question now is whether it is right. I therefore turn the demand of self-love into a universal law and put the question as follows: how would it be if my maxim became a universal law? I then see at once that it could never hold as a universal law of nature and be consistent with itself, but must necessarily contradict itself. For, the universality of a law that everyone, when he believes himself to be in need, could promise whatever he pleases with the intention of not keeping it would make the promise and the end one might have in it itself impossible, since no one would believe what was promised him but would laugh at all such expressions as vain pretenses.

3) A third finds in himself a talent that by means of some cultivation could make him a human being useful for all sorts of purposes. However, he finds himself in comfortable circumstances and prefers to give himself up to pleasure than to trouble himself with enlarging and improving his fortunate natural predispositions. But he still asks himself whether his maxim of neglecting his natural gifts, besides being consistent with his propensity to amusement, is also consistent with what one calls duty. He now sees that a nature could indeed always subsist with such a universal law, although (as with the South Sea Islanders) the human being should let his talents rust and be concerned with devoting his life merely to idleness, amusement, procreation—in a word, to enjoyment; only he cannot possibly **will** that this become a universal law or be put in us as such by means of natural instinct. For, as a rational being he necessarily wills that all the capacities in him be developed, since they serve him and are given to him for all sorts of possible purposes.

4) Yet a *fourth*, for whom things are going well while he sees that others (whom he could very well help) have to contend with great hardships, thinks: what is it to me? let each be as happy as heaven wills or as he can make himself; I shall take nothing from him nor even envy him; only I do not care to contribute anything to his welfare or to his assistance in need! Now, if such a way of thinking were to become a universal law the human race could admittedly very well subsist, no doubt even better than when everyone prates about sympathy and benevolence and even exerts himself to practice them occasionally, but on the other hand also cheats where he can, sells the right of human beings or otherwise infringes upon it. But although it is possible that a universal law of nature could very well

subsist in accordance with such a maxim, it is still impossible to **will** that such a principle hold everywhere as a law of nature. For, a will that decided this would conflict with itself, since many cases could occur in which one would need the love and sympathy of others and in which, by such a law of nature arisen from his own will, he would rob himself of all hope of the assistance he wishes for himself.

If we now attend to ourselves in any transgression of a duty, we find that we do not really will that our maxim should become a universal law, since that is impossible for us, but that the opposite of our maxim should instead remain a universal law, only we take the liberty of making an *exception* to it for ourselves (or just for this once) to the advantage of our inclination. Consequently, if we weighed all cases from one and the same point of view, namely that of reason, we would find a contradiction in our own will, namely that a certain principle be objectively necessary as a universal law and yet subjectively not hold universally but allow exceptions.

Suppose there were something the *existence of which in itself* has an absolute worth, something which as *an end in itself* could be a ground of determinate laws; then in it, and in it alone, would lie the ground of a possible categorical imperative, that is, of a practical law.

Now I say that the human being and in general every rational being *exists* as an end in itself, *not merely as a means* to be used by this or that will at its discretion; instead he must in all his actions, whether directed to himself or also to other rational beings, always be regarded *at the same time as an end*. All objects of the inclinations have only a conditional worth; for, if there were not inclinations and the needs based on them, their object would be without worth. But the inclinations themselves, as sources of needs, are so far from having an absolute worth, so as to make one wish to have them, that it must instead be the universal wish of every rational being to be altogether free from them. Thus the worth of any object *to be acquired* by our action is always conditional. Beings the existence of which rests not on our will but on nature, if they are beings without reason, still have only a relative worth, as means, and are therefore called *things*, whereas rational beings are called *persons* because their nature already marks them out as an end in itself, that is, as something that may not be used merely as a means, and hence so far limits all choice (and is an object of respect). These, therefore, are not merely subjective ends, the existence of which as an effect of our action has a worth *for us*, but rather *objective ends*, that is, beings the existence of which is in itself an end, and indeed one such that no other end, to which they would serve *merely* as means, can be put in its place, since without it nothing of *absolute worth* would be found anywhere; but if all worth were conditional and therefore contingent, then no supreme practical principle for reason could be found anywhere.

If, then, there is to be a supreme practical principle and, with respect to the human will, a categorical imperative, it must be one such that, from the representation of what is necessarily an end for everyone because it is an *end in itself*, it constitutes an *objective* principle of the will and thus can serve as a universal practical law. The ground of this principle is: *rational nature exists as an end in itself.* The human being necessarily represents his own existence in this way; so far it is thus a *subjective* principle of human actions. But every other rational being also represents his existence in this way consequent on just the same rational ground that also holds for me; thus it is at the same time an *objective* principle from which, as a supreme practical ground, it must be possible to derive all laws of the will. The practical imperative will therefore be the following: *So act that you use humanity, whether in your own person or in the person of any other, always at the same time as an end, never merely as a means.* We shall see whether this can be carried out.

To keep to the preceding examples:

First, as regards the concept of necessary duty to oneself, someone who has suicide in mind will ask himself whether his action can be consistent with the idea of humanity *as an end in itself.* If he destroys himself in order to escape from a trying condition he makes use of a person *merely as a means* to maintain a tolerable condition up to the end of life. A human being, however, is not a thing and hence not something that can be used *merely* as a means, but must in all his actions always be regarded as an end in itself. I cannot, therefore, dispose of a human being in my own person by maiming, damaging or killing him. (I must here pass over a closer determination of this principle that would prevent any misinterpretation, e.g., as to having limbs amputated in order to preserve myself, or putting my life in danger in order to preserve my life, and so forth; that belongs to morals proper.)

Second, as regards necessary duty to others or duty owed them, he who has it in mind to make a false promise to others sees at once that he wants to make use of another human being *merely as a means*, without the other at the same time containing in himself the end. For, he whom I want to use for my purposes by such a promise cannot possibly agree to my way of behaving toward him, and so himself contain the end of this action. This conflict with the principle of other human beings is seen more distinctly if examples of assaults on the freedom and property of others are brought forward. For then it is obvious that he who transgresses the rights of human beings intends to make use of the person of others merely as means, without taking into consideration that, as rational beings, they are always to be valued at the same time as ends, that is, only as beings who must also be able to contain in themselves the end of the very same action.

Third, with respect to contingent (meritorious) duty to oneself, it is not enough that the action does not conflict with humanity in our person as an end in itself; it must also *harmonize with it*. Now there are in humanity predispositions to greater perfection, which belong to the end of nature with respect to humanity in our subject; to neglect these might admittedly be consistent with the *preservation* of humanity as an end in itself but not with the *furtherance* of this end.

Fourth, concerning meritorious duty to others, the natural end that all human beings have is their own happiness. Now, humanity might indeed subsist if no one contributed to the happiness of others but yet did not intentionally withdraw anything from it; but there is still only a negative and not a positive agreement with *humanity as an end in itself* unless everyone also tries, as far as he can, to further the ends of others. For, the ends of a subject who is an end in itself must as far as possible be also *my* ends, if that representation is to have its *full* effect in me.

Immanuel Kant: The Good Will and the Categorical Imperative

1) Kant claims that a good will is the only thing that can be considered "good without limitation." What does he mean by this? Do you find this claim plausible?

2) Unlike hedonists, Kant believes that happiness is not always good. What reasons does he give for thinking this? Do you agree with him?

3) What is the difference between doing something "in conformity with duty" and doing something "from duty"? Is Kant correct in saying that only actions done *from duty* have moral worth?

4) Kant claims to have discovered a *categorical imperative*, a moral requirement that we have reason to follow regardless of what we happen to desire. Can people have reasons for action that are completely independent of their desires?

5) According to Kant, it is morally permissible to act on a particular principle (or "maxim") only if "you can at the same time will that it become a universal law." Do you think this is a good test of whether an action is morally permissible? Can you think of any immoral actions that would pass this test, or any morally permissible actions that would fail it?

6) Kant later gives another formulation of the categorical imperative: "So act that you use humanity, whether in your own person or in the person of any other, always at the same time as an end, never merely as a means." What does it mean to treat someone as an end? Are we always morally required to treat humans in this way?

9

Leviathan

Thomas Hobbes

Thomas Hobbes (1588–1679) is the most brilliant of the modern social contract theorists. His theory, important in both ethics and political philosophy, views the basic moral rules of society as ones that rational people would adopt in order to protect their own interests. Without obedience to such rules, the situation deteriorates into a "war of all against all, in which the life of man is solitary, poor, nasty, brutish and short."

Hobbes was an ethical egoist—someone who thinks that our fundamental duty is to look after our own interests—as well as a social contract theorist. Many commentators have found a tension in this combination. See for yourself whether Hobbes succeeded in justifying the basic moral rules by reference to self-interest.

Among the many interesting features in this excerpt from Hobbes's classic *Leviathan* is his discussion of the fool. The fool is someone who allows that breaking one's promises is unjust, but who thinks that it may sometimes be rational to do so anyway. Hobbes resists this idea. He wants to show that it is always rational to do one's duty—to live by the laws of cooperation that would be accepted by free and rational people. His overall view is motivated by the thought that moral duties must provide each of us with excellent reasons to obey them, and that these reasons must ultimately stem from self-interest. As a result, Hobbes's discussion casts fascinating light on the perennial question of why we should be moral.

Of the Natural Condition of Mankind as Concerning Their Felicity and Misery

Nature hath made men so equal in the faculties of body and mind as that, though there be found one man sometimes manifestly stronger in body or of quicker mind than another, yet when all is reckoned together the difference between man and man is not so considerable as that one man can thereupon claim to himself any benefit to which another may not pretend as well as he. For as to the strength of body, the weakest has strength enough to kill the strongest, either by secret machination or by confederacy with others that are in the same danger with himself.

And as to the faculties of the mind, setting aside the arts grounded upon words, and especially that skill of proceeding upon general and infallible rules, called science, which very few have and but in few things, as being not a native faculty born with us, nor attained, as prudence, while we look after somewhat else, I find yet a greater equality amongst men than that of strength. For prudence is but experience, which equal time equally bestows on all men in those things they equally apply themselves unto. That which may perhaps make such equality incredible is but a vain conceit of one's own wisdom, which almost all men think they have in a greater degree than the vulgar; that is, than all men but themselves, and a few others, whom by fame, or for concurring with themselves, they approve. For such is the nature of men that howsoever they may acknowledge many others to be more witty, or more eloquent or more learned, yet they will hardly believe there be many so wise as themselves; for they see their own wit at hand, and other men's at a distance. But this proveth rather that men are in that point equal, than unequal. For there is not ordinarily a greater sign of the equal distribution of anything than that every man is contented with his share.

From this equality of ability ariseth equality of hope in the attaining of our ends. And therefore if any two men desire the same thing, which nevertheless they cannot both enjoy, they become enemies; and in the way to their end (which is principally their own conservation, and sometimes their delectation only) endeavour to destroy or subdue one another. And from hence it comes to pass that where an invader hath no more to fear than another man's single power, if one plant, sow, build, or possess a convenient seat, others may probably be expected to come prepared with forces united to dispossess and deprive him, not only of the fruit of his labour, but also of his life or liberty. And the invader again is in the like danger of another.

And from this diffidence of one another, there is no way for any man to secure himself so reasonable as anticipation; that is, by force, or wiles, to master the persons of all men he can so long till he see no other power great enough to endanger him: and this is no more than his own conservation requireth, and is generally allowed. Also, because there be some that, taking pleasure in contemplating their own power in the acts of conquest, which they pursue farther than their security requires, if others, that otherwise would be glad to be at ease within modest bounds, should not by invasion increase their power, they would not be able, long time, by standing only on their defence, to subsist. And by consequence, such augmentation of dominion over men being necessary to a man's conservation, it ought to be allowed him.

Again, men have no pleasure (but on the contrary a great deal of grief) in keeping company where there is no power able to overawe them all. For every man looketh that his companion should value him at the same rate he sets upon himself, and upon all signs of contempt or undervaluing naturally endeavours, as far as he dares (which amongst them that have no common power to keep them in quiet is far enough to make them destroy each other), to extort a greater value from his contemners, by damage; and from others, by the example.

So that in the nature of man, we find three principal causes of quarrel. First, competition; secondly, diffidence; thirdly, glory.

The first maketh men invade for gain; the second, for safety; and the third, for reputation. The first use violence, to make themselves masters of other men's persons, wives, children, and cattle; the second, to defend them; the third, for trifles, as a word, a smile, a different opinion, and any other sign of undervalue, either direct in their persons or by reflection in their kindred, their friends, their nation, their profession, or their name.

Hereby it is manifest that during the time men live without a common power to keep them all in awe, they are in that condition which is called war; and such a war as is of every man against every man. For war consisteth not in battle only, or the act of fighting, but in a tract of time, wherein the will to contend by battle is sufficiently known: and therefore the notion of time is to be considered in the nature of war, as it is in the nature of weather. For as the nature of foul weather lieth not in a shower or two of rain, but in an inclination thereto of many days together: so the nature of war consisteth not in actual fighting, but in the known disposition thereto during all the time there is no assurance to the contrary. All other time is peace.

Whatsoever therefore is consequent to a time of war, where every man is enemy to every man, the same consequent to the time wherein men live without other security than what their own strength and their own invention shall furnish them withal. In such condition there is no place for industry, because the fruit thereof is uncertain: and consequently no culture of the earth; no navigation, nor use of the commodities that may be imported by sea; no commodious building; no instruments of moving and removing such things as require much force; no knowledge of the face of the earth; no account of time; no arts; no letters; no society; and which is worst of all, continual fear, and danger of violent death; and the life of man, solitary, poor, nasty, brutish, and short.

It may seem strange to some man that has not well weighed these things that Nature should thus dissociate and render men apt to invade and destroy one another: and he may therefore, not trusting to this inference, made from the passions, desire perhaps to have the same confirmed by experience. Let him therefore consider with himself: when taking a journey, he arms himself and seeks to go well accompanied; when going to sleep, he locks his doors; when even in his house he locks his chests; and this when he knows there be laws and public officers, armed, to revenge all injuries shall be done him; what opinion he has of his fellow subjects, when he rides armed; of his fellow citizens, when he locks his doors; and of his children, and servants, when he locks his chests. Does he not there as much accuse mankind by his actions as I do by my words? But neither of us accuse man's nature in it. The desires, and other passions of man, are in themselves no sin. No more are the actions that proceed from those passions till they know a law that forbids them; which till laws be made they cannot know, nor can any law be made till they have agreed upon the person that shall make it.

It may peradventure be thought there was never such a time nor condition of war as this; and I believe it was never generally so, over all the world: but there are many places where they live so now. For the savage people in many places of America, except the government of small families, the concord whereof dependeth on natural lust, have no government at all, and live at this day in that brutish manner, as I said before. Howsoever, it may be perceived what manner of life there would be, where there were no common power to fear, by the manner of life which men that have formerly lived under a peaceful government use to degenerate into a civil war.

But though there had never been any time wherein particular men were in a condition of war one against another, yet in all times kings and persons of sovereign authority, because of their independency, are in continual jealousies, and in the state and posture of gladiators, having their weapons pointing, and their eyes fixed on one another; that is, their forts, garrisons, and guns upon the frontiers of their kingdoms, and continual spies upon their neighbours, which is a posture of war. But because they uphold thereby the industry of their subjects, there does not follow from it that misery which accompanies the liberty of particular men.

To this war of every man against every man, this also is consequent; that nothing can be unjust. The notions of right and wrong, justice and injustice, have there no place. Where there is no common power, there is no law; where no law, no injustice. Force and fraud are in war the two cardinal virtues. Justice and injustice are none of the faculties neither of the body nor mind. If they were, they might be in a man that were alone in the world, as well as his senses and passions. They are qualities that relate to men in society, not in solitude. It is consequent also to the same condition that there be no propriety, no dominion, no mine and thine distinct; but only that to be every man's that he can get, and for so long as he can keep it. And thus much for the ill condition which man by mere nature is actually placed in; though with a possibility to come out of it, consisting partly in the passions, partly in his reason.

The passions that incline men to peace are: fear of death; desire of such things as are necessary to commodious living; and a hope by their industry to obtain them. And reason suggesteth convenient articles of peace upon which men may be drawn to agreement. These articles are they which otherwise are called the laws of nature, whereof I shall speak more particularly in the two following chapters.

Of the First and Second Natural Laws, and of Contracts

The right of nature, which writers commonly call *jus naturale*, is the liberty each man hath to use his own power as he will himself for the preservation of his own nature; that is to say, of his own life; and consequently, of doing anything which, in his own judgement and reason, he shall conceive to be the aptest means thereunto.

By liberty is understood, according to the proper signification of the word, the absence of external impediments; which impediments may oft take away part of a man's power to do what he would, but cannot hinder him from using the power left him according as his judgement and reason shall dictate to him.

A law of nature, *lex naturalis*, is a precept, or general rule, found out by reason, by which a man is forbidden to do that which is destructive of his life, or taketh away the means of preserving the same, and to omit that by which he thinketh it may be best preserved.

And because the condition of man (as hath been declared in the precedent chapter) is a condition of war of every one against every one, in which case every one is governed by his own reason, and there is nothing he can make use of that may not be a help unto him in preserving his life against his enemies; it followeth that in such a condition every man has a right to every thing, even to one another's body. And therefore, as long as this natural right of every man to every thing endureth, there can be no security to any man, how strong or wise soever he be, of living out the time which nature ordinarily alloweth men to live. And consequently it is a precept, or general rule of reason: that every man ought to endeavour peace, as far as he has hope of obtaining it; and when he cannot obtain it, that he may seek and use all helps and advantages of war. The first branch of which rule containeth the first and fundamental law of nature, which is: to seek peace and follow it. The second, the sum of the right of nature, which is: by all means we can to defend ourselves.

From this fundamental law of nature, by which men are commanded to endeavour peace, is derived this second law: that a man be willing, when others are so too, as far forth as for peace and defence of himself he shall think it necessary, to lay down this right to all things; and be contented with so much liberty against other men as he would allow other men against himself. For as long as every man holdeth this right, of doing anything he liketh; so long are all men in the condition of war. But if other men will not lay down their right, as well as he, then there is no reason for anyone to divest himself of his: for that were to expose himself to prey, which no man is bound to, rather than to dispose himself to peace. This is that law of the gospel: Whatsoever you require that others should do to you, that do ye to them.

Whensoever a man transferreth his right, or renounceth it, it is either in consideration of some right reciprocally transferred to himself, or for some other good he hopeth for thereby. For it is a voluntary act: and of the voluntary acts of every man, the object is some good to himself. And therefore there be some rights which no man can be understood by any words, or other signs, to have abandoned or transferred. As first a man cannot lay down the right of resisting them that assault him by force to take away his life, because he cannot be understood to aim thereby at any good to himself. The same may be said of wounds, and chains, and imprisonment, both because there is no benefit consequent to such patience, as there is to the patience of suffering another to be wounded or imprisoned, as also because a man cannot tell when he seeth men proceed against him by violence whether they intend his death or not. And lastly the motive and end for which this renouncing and transferring of right is introduced is nothing else but the security of a man's person, in his life, and in the means of so preserving life as not to be weary of it. And therefore if a man by words, or other signs, seem to despoil himself of the end for which those signs were intended, he is not to be understood as if he meant it, or that it was his will, but that he was ignorant of how such words and actions were to be interpreted.

The mutual transferring of right is that which men call contract.

Signs of contract are either express or by inference. Express are words spoken with understanding of what they signify: and such words are either of the time present or past; as, I give, I grant, I have given, I have granted, I will that this be yours: or of the future; as, I will give, I will grant, which words of the future are called promise.

Signs by inference are sometimes the consequence of words; sometimes the consequence of silence; sometimes the consequence of actions; sometimes the consequence of forbearing an action: and generally a sign by inference, of any contract, is whatsoever sufficiently argues the will of the contractor.

Words alone, if they be of the time to come, and contain a bare promise, are an insufficient sign of a free gift and therefore not obligatory. For if they be of the time to come, as, tomorrow I will give, they are a sign I have not given yet, and consequently that my right is not transferred, but remaineth till I transfer it by some other act.

If a covenant be made wherein neither of the parties perform presently, but trust one another, in the condition of mere nature (which is a condition of war of every man against every man) upon any reasonable suspicion, it is void: but if there be a common power set over them both, with right and force sufficient to compel performance, it is not void. For he that performeth first has no assurance the other will perform after, because the bonds of words are too weak to bridle men's ambition, avarice, anger, and other passions, without the fear of some coercive power; which in the condition of mere nature, where all men are equal, and judges of the justness of their own fears, cannot possibly be supposed. And therefore he which performeth first does but betray himself to his enemy, contrary to the right he can never abandon of defending his life and means of living.

But in a civil estate, where there a power set up to constrain those that would otherwise violate their faith, that fear is no more reasonable; and for that cause, he which by the covenant is to perform first is obliged so to do.

Of Other Laws of Nature

From that law of nature by which we are obliged to transfer to another such rights as, being retained, hinder the peace of mankind, there followeth a third; which is this: that men perform their covenants made; without which covenants are in vain, and but empty words; and the right of all men to all things remaining, we are still in the condition of war.

And in this law of nature consisteth the fountain and original of justice. For where no covenant hath preceded, there hath no right been transferred, and every man has right to everything and consequently, no action can be unjust. But when a covenant is made, then to break it is unjust and the definition of injustice is no other than the not performance of covenant. And whatsoever is not unjust is just.

But because covenants of mutual trust, where there is a fear of not performance on either part (as hath been said in the former chapter), are invalid, though the original of justice be the making of covenants, yet injustice actually there can be none till the cause of such fear be taken away; which, while men are in the natural condition of war, cannot be done. Therefore before the names of just and unjust can have place, there must be some coercive power to compel men equally to the performance of their covenants, by the terror of some punishment greater than the benefit they expect by the breach of their covenant, and to make good that propriety which by mutual contract men acquire in recompense of the universal right they abandon: and such power there is none before the erection of a Commonwealth. And this is also to be gathered out of the ordinary definition of justice in the Schools, for they say that justice is the constant will of giving to every man his own. And therefore where there is no own, that is, no propriety, there is no injustice; and where there is no coercive power erected, that is, where there is no Commonwealth, there is no propriety, all men having right to all things: therefore where there is no Commonwealth, there nothing is unjust. So that the nature of justice consisteth in keeping of valid covenants, but the validity of covenants begins not but with the constitution of a civil power sufficient to compel men to keep them: and then it is also that propriety begins.

The fool hath said in his heart, there is no such thing as justice, and sometimes also with his tongue, seriously alleging that every man's conservation and contentment being committed to his own care, there could be no reason why every man might not do what he thought conduced thereunto: and therefore also to make, or not make; keep, or not keep, covenants was not against reason when it conduced to one's benefit. He does not therein deny that there be covenants; and that they are sometimes broken, sometimes kept; and that such breach of them may be called injustice, and the observance of them justice: but he questioneth whether injustice, taking away the fear of God (for the same fool hath said in his heart there is no God), not sometimes stand with that reason which dictateth to every man his own good; and particularly then, when it conduceth to such a benefit as shall put a man in a condition to neglect not only the dispraise and revilings, but also the power of other men. The kingdom of God is gotten by violence: but what if it could be gotten by unjust violence? Were it against reason so to get it, when it is impossible to receive hurt by it? And if it be not against reason, it is not against justice: or else justice is not to be approved for good. From such reasoning as this, successful wickedness hath obtained the name of virtue: and some that in all other things have disallowed the violation of faith, yet have allowed it when it is for the getting of a kingdom. And the heathen that believed that Saturn was deposed by his son Jupiter believed nevertheless the same Jupiter to be the avenger of injustice, somewhat like to a piece of law in Coke's Commentaries on Littleton; where he says if the right heir of the crown be attainted of treason, yet the crown shall descend to him, and *eo instante* the attainder be void: from which instances a man will be very prone to infer that when the heir apparent of a kingdom shall kill him that is in possession, though his father, you may call it injustice, or by what other name you will; yet it can never be against reason, seeing all the voluntary actions of men tend to the benefit of themselves; and those actions are most reasonable that conduce most to their ends. This specious reasoning is nevertheless false.

For the question is not of promises mutual, where there is no security of performance on either side, as when there is no civil power erected over the parties promising; for such promises are no covenants: but either where one of the parties has performed already, or where there is a power to make him perform, there is the question whether it be against reason; that is, against the benefit of the other to perform, or not. And I say it is not against reason. For the manifestation whereof we are to consider; first, that when a man doth a thing, which notwithstanding anything can be foreseen and reckoned on tendeth to his own destruction, howsoever some accident, which he could not expect, arriving may turn it to his benefit; yet such events do not make it reasonably or wisely done. Secondly, that in a condition of war, wherein every man to every man, for want of a common power to keep them all in awe, is an enemy, there is no man can hope by his own strength, or wit, to himself from destruction without the help of confederates; where every one expects the same defence by the confederation that any one else does: and therefore he which declares he thinks it reason to deceive those that help him can in reason expect no other means of safety than what can be had from his own single power. He, therefore, that breaketh his covenant, and consequently declareth that he thinks he may with reason do so, cannot be received into any society that unite themselves for peace and defence but by the error of them that receive him; nor when he is received be retained in it without seeing the danger of their error; which errors a man cannot reasonably reckon upon as the means of his security: and therefore if he be left, or cast out of society, he perisheth; and if he live in society, it is by the errors of other men, which he could not foresee nor reckon upon, and consequently against the reason of his preservation; and so, as all men that contribute not to his destruction forbear him only out of ignorance of what is good for themselves.

As for the instance of gaining the secure and perpetual felicity of heaven by any way, it is frivolous; there being but one way imaginable, and that is not breaking, but keeping of covenant.

And for the other instance of attaining sovereignty by rebellion; it is manifest that, though the event follow, yet because it cannot reasonably be expected, but rather the contrary, and because by gaining it so, others are taught to gain the same in like manner, the attempt thereof is against reason. Justice therefore, that is to say, keeping of covenant, is a rule of reason by which we are forbidden to do anything destructive to our life, and consequently a law of nature.

Thomas Hobbes: Leviathan

1) At the beginning of the selection, Hobbes argues that all humans are fundamentally equal. In what ways does Hobbes claim that we are equal? Do you agree with him?

2) Hobbes claims that without a government to enforce law and order, we would find ourselves in a "war...of every man against every man."

What reasons does he give for believing this? Do you think he is right?

3) According to Hobbes, if there were no governments to establish laws, nothing would be just or unjust. Does this seem plausible? Would some actions be unjust, even if there were no authority around to punish those who committed them?

4) Hobbes says, "Of the voluntary acts of every man, the object is some good to himself." Is Hobbes correct in thinking that self-interest is what motivates every voluntary action?

5) Hobbes claims that it is always unjust to violate our covenants (or contracts), provided that there is a government with the power to enforce them. He also claims that any action that does not violate a covenant is just. Can you think of any counterexamples to either of these claims?

6) The "fool" claims that it is rational to unjustly break one's covenants in cases where doing so promotes one's self-interest. How does Hobbes respond to this claim? Do you find Hobbes's replies convincing?

10

Natural Goodness

Philippa Foot

In this excerpt from her book *Natural Goodness* (2001), Philippa Foot argues that we can derive moral norms from so-called natural norms—those that tell us how things ought to be, given insights about their nature. Foot argues that we have no reservations about assessing plants and animals as better or worse members of their species, depending on how well they measure up to natural norms. A deer's nature, for instance, includes, among other things, an ability to run swiftly; a male peacock is, by nature, able to fan its tail in a bright, attractive way. Such natural norms enable us to assess a deer as deficient if it can only hobble along, and a male peacock as doing well if it is, indeed, able to offer an attractive display.

Foot suggests that things are essentially the same when it comes to human beings. The natural norms that apply to us, of course, will not be just the same as those that apply to plants and animals. Still, we can derive standards for how we ought to be, and what we ought to do, based on insights about human nature. This places her latest views within a long tradition of natural law thinkers, who have sought to base morality on features of human nature.

Philippa Foot, from *Natural Goodness* (2001). pp. 26–34, 41–44, 47. By permission of Oxford University Press, Inc.

Natural Norms

Judgements of goodness and badness can have, it seems, a special 'grammar' when the subject belongs to a living thing, whether plant, animal, or human being. This, at least, is what I argue in this book. I think that this special category of goodness is easily overlooked; perhaps because we make so many evaluations of other kinds, as when we assess non-living things in the natural world, such as soil or weather, or again assess artefacts either made by humans as are houses and bridges, or made by animals as are the nests of birds or beavers' dams. But the goodness predicated in these latter cases, like goodness predicated to living things when they are evaluated in a relationship to members of species other than their own, is what I should like to call secondary goodness. It is in this derivative way that we can speak of the goodness of, for example, soil or weather, as such things are related to plants, to animals, or to us. And we also ascribe this secondary goodness to living things, as, for instance, to specimens of plants that grow as we want them to grow, or to horses that carry us as we want to be carried, while artefacts are often named and evaluated by the need or interest that they chiefly serve. By contrast, 'natural' goodness, as I define it, which is attributable only to living things themselves and to their parts, characteristics, and operations, is intrinsic or 'autonomous' goodness in that it depends directly on the relation of an individual to the 'life form' of its species. On barren Mars there is no natural goodness, and even secondary goodness can be attributed to things on that planet only by relating them to our own lives, or to living things existing elsewhere.

My belief is that for all the differences that there are, as we shall see, between the evaluation of plants and animals and their parts and characteristics on the one hand, and the moral evaluation of humans on the other, we shall find that these evaluations share a basic logical structure and status. I want to suggest that moral defect is a form of natural defect not as different as is generally supposed from defect in sub-rational living things. So this is what I shall go on to argue, after a discussion of 'natural goodness' as it is found in sub-rational living things.

Firstly, therefore, I shall explore natural goodness in plants and in animals other than human beings. For help I shall turn to a paper published by Michael Thompson: a paper I admire very much.

Michael Thompson's subject in this paper, which is called 'The Representation of Life', is the description of living things. His thesis is that to understand certain distinctive ways in which we describe individual organisms, we must recognize the logical dependence of these descriptions on the nature of the species to which the individual belongs. Species-dependence is his leitmotif. For this reason he concerns himself with propositions of the form 'S's are F' or 'The S is F', where 'S' holds a place for the name of a species (or 'life form' as he is ready to say for the sake of those who want to give 'species' a technical definition) and 'F' a place for a predicate; so that a representative sentence would be 'Rabbits are herbivores' or 'The rabbit is a herbivore'. He contrasts the logical form of the sentences

> S's are F   (Rabbits are herbivores)
> S's do V   (Rabbits eat grass)

with

> N.N. is F   (Mrs Muff is a rabbit)
> N.N. is doing V   (Mrs Muff is eating grass).

He points out, referring back to an early article by Elizabeth Anscombe, a peculiarity of the *logical form* of the first pair of sentences: that they are logically unquantifiable.[1] They do not speak of an individual rabbit, though the same verbal form can of course be used with that reference, as when the conjurer says to his wife 'The rabbit does not look well'. Nor, of course, do the propositions that interest Michael Thompson predicate something of every member of the species: 'Cats are four-legged but Tibbles may have only three'. Elizabeth Anscombe's original example concerned the number of teeth that human beings have—which is 32, though most human beings have lost quite a few and some never had the full complement. It is arguable that if 'The S is F' (understood in this way) is true then at least some S's must be F. But even if this is so, 'Some S's are F' is clearly not the whole of what such a proposition asserts. Thompson speaks in this context of a 'natural-history account' of the life form or species: of how creatures of this kind live. And he points out, as part of his insistence on the way in which descriptions of individuals depend on the species to which they belong, that without this reference, 'life activities' such as eating or reproducing cannot even be identified in an individual. Eating, for instance, is essentially, conceptually, related to nourishment, and could not be conclusively identified by a story about the taking in, crushing, transforming,

---

[1] Anscombe, "Modern Moral Philosophy," in *Collected Philosophical Papers*, pp. iii, 38.

and spewing out of substances since, for all that, its purpose might be not the maintenance of tissue but, say, skunk-like defence. Mitosis occurs in amoebae and human beings, and is given a uniform description in textbooks: in the first, however, it is reproduction of an individual organism, but in the second not.[2]

Thompson also points out peculiarities of the time references found within such propositions. It is said for instance that certain animals mate at a certain time of the year, and give birth, or lay eggs, so many weeks or months later; but this is 'typically a matter of before and after—"in the spring", "in the fall"...and not of now and then...and when I was young and so forth'.[3] Natural-history sentences, which Thompson also calls 'Aristotelian categoricals', speak of the life cycle of individuals of a given species.[4] In one way, therefore, this is the time-span with which they have to do. In another way, however, a longer time reference is needed, since we must speak of *reproduction*, and the characteristics of a single individual cannot determine what will count as *another of the same*.

It will no doubt be objected here that reproduction is in fact not fixed, since species themselves are subject to change. This is of course important, and it means that Aristotelian categoricals must take account of sub-species adapted to local conditions. The history of a species is not, however, the subject with which Aristotelian categoricals deal. Their truth is truth about a species at a given historical time, and it is only the relative stability of at least the most general features of the different species of living things that makes these propositions possible at all. They tell how a kind of plant or animal, considered at a particular time and in its natural habitat, develops, sustains itself, defends itself, and reproduces. It is only in so far as 'stills' can be made from the moving picture of the evolution of species that we can have a natural history account of the life of a particular kind of living thing. And it is only in so far as we have a 'natural history account' that we can have a 'vital description' of individuals here and now.

Let us now ask how all this is relevant to the normative judgements that we make about plants and animals when we say, for instance, that a plant in our garden is diseased, or not growing properly, or that a certain lioness is a neglectful parent, or a particular rabbit not as reproductive as

---

[2] Thompson, "The Representation of Life" pp. 272–273.
[3] Ibid., p. 282.
[4] Ibid., p. 267.

a rabbit should be. Thompson suggests that the relation between the Aristotelian categorical and the evaluative assessment is very close indeed. In
fact, he says that if we have a true natural-history proposition to the effect
that S's are F, then if a certain individual S—the individual here and now
or then and there—is not F it is therefore not as it should be, but rather
weak, diseased, or in some other way defective.[5] The evaluative assessment is the product of propositions of the two logically different kinds.

Essentially, I think that Thompson is right about this, although I
seem to see a gap in his account of Aristotelian categoricals that has to
be filled in here. For I think he has not said enough to isolate the kind of
proposition that will yield evaluations of individual organisms. His talk
of 'natural-history propositions' was perhaps misleading in that it did
not explicitly separate out what I would like to call the teleological from
the non-teleological attachment of predicates to a subject term that is the
name of a species. Consider, for instance, a sentence such as 'The blue
tit has a round blue patch on its head.' This is superficially like 'The male
peacock has a brightly coloured tail', but in a way of course it is not. For,
on the assumption that colour of head plays no part in the life of the blue
tit, it is in this respect quite unlike the colour of the male peacock's tail:
there would be nothing wrong with the blue tit in my garden *in that* it had
a drab-coloured head; and the peculiarity might or might not accompany
a defect. So how are we to distinguish these two types of propositions? Or
how, again, are we to distinguish the case of leaves rustling when it is windy
from that of flowers opening when the sun comes out? It is natural to say
that the rustling of its leaves plays no part in the life of a tree, whereas pol-
lination is gained by a display of scent and colours in sunshine. But then
we must ask what we mean by 'playing a part in the life' of a living thing.
What counts as 'its life' in this context? And what is 'playing a part'?

There emerges here the special link, mentioned but not explored by
Thompson, between his 'Aristotelian categoricals' and teleology in living
things. Aristotelian categoricals are propositions having to do with the
way that certain features appear or that certain things are done in organisms of a given species either by the whole organism or by their characteristics or parts. But, speaking now for myself rather than for Thompson,
I should say that to obtain the connection between Aristotelian categoricals and evaluation another move must be made. I should say that in plants

---

[5] Ibid., p. 295.

and non-human animals these things all have to do, directly or indirectly, with self-maintenance, as by defence and the obtaining of nourishment, or with the reproduction of the individual, as by the building of nests. This is 'the life' characteristic of the kind of animal with which the categoricals here have to do. What 'plays a part' in this life is that which is causally and teleologically related to it, as putting out roots is related to obtaining nourishment, and attracting insects is related to reproduction in plants.

We start from the fact that there is a basis for the Aristotelian categorical that does not come from the counting of heads. What is this basis? In what was said about the blue tits and the peacocks it was suggested that some but not all general propositions about a species have to do with the teleology of living things of this kind. There is an Aristotelian categorical about the species *peacock* to the effect that the male peacock displays his brilliant tail *in order to* attract a female during the mating season. The display serves this purpose. Let us call such language, purposive language. But be careful here! Where something that S's do is, in this sense, purposive we should beware of slipping over into saying of an individual S that it *has* this purpose when it does this thing. Plants grow upwards in order to get to the light, but it is fanciful to say that that is what my honeysuckle is trying to do or that that is 'its end'. Migrating birds flying off in order to reach the southern insects do not *have* this as their end or purpose even though it could be said to be the end or purpose of the operation. What is crucial to all teleological propositions is the expectation of an answer to the question 'What part does it play in the life cycle of things of the species S?' In other words, 'What is its function?' or 'What good does it do?'

Thus, evaluation of an individual living thing in its own right, with no reference to our interests or desires, is possible where there is intersection of two types of propositions: on the one hand, Aristotelian categoricals (life-form descriptions relating to the species), and on the other, propositions about particular individuals that are the subject of evaluation.

It will be useful to remind ourselves at this point of the elements that came to light in the earlier discussion of 'good' and 'bad' as applied to characteristics and operations of plants and animals.

(a) There was the life cycle, which in those cases consisted roughly of self-maintenance and reproduction.
(b) There was the set of propositions saying *how* for a certain species this was achieved: how nourishment was obtained, how development took place, what defences were available, and how reproduction was secured.

(c) From all this, *norms* were derived, requiring, for instance, a certain degree of swiftness in the deer, night vision in the owl, and cooperative hunting in the wolf.

(d) By the application of these norms to an individual member of the relevant species it (this individual) was judged to be as it should be or, by contrast, to a lesser or greater degree defective in a certain respect.

There are here many details that are not germane to the aim of this book. But something more must be said about the way in which Aristotelian categoricals about the 'how and what' of the life cycle determine normative assessments of individual living things in the here and now or there and then of historical place and time.

As illustration let us consider the Aristotelian categorical stating that the deer is an animal whose form of defence is flight. From this we know that it is a defect, a weakness, in an individual deer if it is slow of foot. Swiftness, as opposed to fierceness or camouflage, is what fits it to escape from its predators. But two remarks must be added about this. In the first place, swiftness does no more than *fit* it to survive: in some circumstances even the greatest speed possible for this type of animal would not be enough. Moreover, by chance it may sometimes be that the fastest deer fleeing from one predator is the very one that gets caught in a trap.[6] Secondly, what is excellence, and what defect, is relative to the natural habitat of the species. Even in a zoo a fleeing animal like a deer that cannot run well is so far forth defective and not as it should be, in spite of the fact that, as this particular individual is by chance placed, this may be no disadvantage for defence or feeding or mating or rearing the young.

Transition to Human Beings

The idea that any features and operations of humans could be evaluated in the same way as those of plants and animals may provoke instant opposition. For to say that this is possible is to imply that some at least of our

---

[6] As it may be the skilful archer who fails to hit a target in the presence of a freak gust of wind. A *maxim* is the subjective principle of acting, and must be distinguished from the *objective* principle, namely the practical law. The former contains the practical rule determined by reason conformably with the conditions of the subject (often his ignorance or also his inclinations), and is therefore the principle in accordance with which the subject *acts*; but the law is the objective principle valid for every rational being, and the principle in accordance with which he *ought to act*, i.e., an imperative.

judgements of goodness and badness in human beings are given truth or falsity by the conditions of human life. And even if it is allowed that certain evaluations of this kind are possible—those vaguely thought of perhaps as 'merely biological'—there is bound to be scepticism about the possibility that 'moral evaluation' could be like this. Surely, it will be urged, we must start afresh when thinking about the subject of moral philosophy. I believe, however, that this is only partly true.

The question remains, however, as to whether once we have made the transition from sub-rational to rational beings we may not need a new theory of evaluation. Surely, my critics will say, it must be so, given the part that the life cycle of a plant or animal rightly played in Michael Thompson's account of the conceptual structure within which the evaluation of properties and operations of individual organisms had a place. For such an evaluation is based on the general relation of this kind of feature to the pattern of life that is the *good of* creatures of this species. But how could we possibly see human good in the same terms? The life cycle of a plant or animal ultimately has to do with what is involved in development, self-sustenance, and reproduction. Are we really going to suggest that human strengths and weaknesses, and even virtues and vices, are to be identified by reference to such 'biological' cycles?

This challenge, ill-conceived as it is in suggesting that the natural-history account of human beings could be explained in terms of a merely animal life, raises a most important and difficult topic. For it is true that in the course of describing 'natural goodness' in plants and animals we have implicitly adverted to the idea of the good of a living thing as well as its goodness in various respects, and the two ideas, though related, are distinct. That this is so can be seen if we think about what it means to benefit a plant or an animal. Very often, to be sure, a living thing is benefited by itself being made better, and there must be a systematic connection between natural goodness and benefit—whether reflexive or other-related as in the case of the stinging bees. But it does not follow that benefit of either kind follows goodness whatever circumstance an individual happens to be in. In our earlier example it was the swiftest deer, ahead of the others, that fell into the hunter's trap; and the properly acting bee that stings a gardener may well bring about the destruction of the nest.

Whether an individual plant or animal actually succeeds in living the life that it is its good to live depends on chance as well as on its own qualities. But its own goodness or defect is conceptually determined by the interaction of natural habitat and natural (species-general) 'strategies' for survival and reproduction. What conceptually determines goodness in a feature or operation is the relation, for the species, of that feature or operation to survival and reproduction, because it is in that that good lies in the botanical and zoological worlds. At that point questions of 'How?' and 'Why?' and 'What for?' come to an end. But clearly this is not true when we come to human beings.

Take reproduction, for instance. Lack of capacity to reproduce is a defect in a human being. But choice of childlessness and even celibacy is not thereby shown to be defective choice, because human good is not the same as plant or animal good. The bearing and rearing of children is not an ultimate good in human life, because other elements of good such as the demands of work to be done may give a man or woman reason to renounce family life. And the great (if often troubling) good of having children has to do with the love and ambition of parents for children, the special role of grandparents, and many other things that simply do not belong to animal life.

Moreover, the good of survival itself is something more complex for human beings than for animals; even for the animals closest to us. The human desire to live is, of course, instinctual, but it often also has to do with a desperate hope that something may yet turn out well in the future. And it seems that the preciousness of the unique memories that each person has is part of what he or she may cling to even in the most terrible of circumstances. In other words, the teleological story goes beyond a reference to survival itself.

The idea of human good is deeply problematic. One may be inclined to think of it as happiness, but much would have to be said before that could be so understood as to be true, and I shall discuss this in a later chapter. Here I want only to recall that Wittgenstein famously said on his deathbed, 'Tell them I have had a wonderful life.' The example should teach us not to be too ready to speak of every good life as 'a happy life': Wittgenstein surely did not have a happy life, being too tormented and self-critical for that.

Thus the idea of a good life for a human being, and the question of its relation to happiness, is each deeply problematic. And, moreover, there is so much diversity in human beings and human cultures that the schema of natural normativity may seem to be inapplicable from the start. Nevertheless, for all the diversities of human life, it is possible to give some quite general account of human necessities, that is, of what is quite generally needed for human good, if only by starting from the negative idea of human deprivation. For then we see at once that human good depends on many characteristics and capacities that are not needed even by animals, never mind by plants. There are, for instance, physical properties such as the kind of larynx that allows of the myriad sounds that make up human language, as well as the kind of hearing that can distinguish them. Moreover, human beings need the mental capacity for learning language; they also need powers of imagination that allow them to understand stories, to join in songs and dances—and to laugh at jokes. Without such things human beings may survive and reproduce themselves, but they are deprived. And what could be more natural than to say on this account that we have introduced the subject of possible human defects; calling them 'natural defects' as we used these terms in the discussion of plant and animal life?

We can see, moreover, that, as with animals, some defects have as we might say 'a reflexive role', in that the deprivation comes primarily to the defective individual; but that there are some that chiefly or at least most directly affect other people. We might think here, for instance, of the failure of maternal affection, or of (non-iterated) 'prisoner's dilemma' cases where each person gains from the action of others but loses through his own. The way of solving the dilemma, however we should understand its details, depends on our human way of thinking. We act within a language that allows us to say 'I owe it to him' or 'I suppose I should play my part' (as we nowadays think, for instance, of taking a bus rather than a car, to reduce traffic on the road, knowing that we ourselves may need to get somewhere urgently by car some other time). There are also human enjoyments such as songs and ceremonials that need cooperative participation. And, further, human societies depend on especially talented individuals playing special roles in a society's life. As some species of animals need a lookout, or as herds of elephants need an old she-elephant to lead them to a watering hole, so human societies need leaders, explorers, and artists. Failure to perform a special role can here be a defect in a man or woman who is not ready to contribute what he or she alone—or best—can give. There is also something wrong with the rest of us if we do not support those of genius, or even special talent, in their work.

In spite of the diversity of human goods—the elements that can make up good human lives—it is therefore possible that the concept of a good human life plays the same part in determining goodness of human characteristics and operations that the concept of flourishing plays in the determination of goodness in plants and animals. So far the conceptual structure seems to be intact. Nor is there any reason to think that it could not be in place even in the evaluations that are nowadays spoken of as the special domain of morality. This special domain—and more generally that of goodness of the will—will be discussed in detail in the next two chapters. But if we ask whether Geach was right to say that human beings need virtues as bees need stings (see Chapter 2), the answer is surely that he was. Men and women need to be industrious and tenacious of purpose not only so as to be able to house, clothe, and feed themselves, but also to pursue human ends having to do with love and friendship. They need the ability to form family ties, friendships, and special relations with neighbours. They also need codes of conduct. And how could they have all these things without virtues such as loyalty, fairness, kindness, and in certain circumstances obedience?

Thus the structure of the derivation is the same whether we derive an evaluation of the roots of a particular tree or the action of a particular human being. The meaning of the words 'good' and 'bad' is not different when used of features of plants on the one hand and humans on the other, but is rather the same as applied, in judgements of natural goodness and defect, in the case of all living things.

Philippa Foot: Natural Goodness

1) What is the difference, according to Foot, between "natural goodness" and "secondary goodness"?
2) Consider the sentence "Cats are four-legged." Foot points out that such a sentence doesn't claim that *all* cats have four legs. Yet it also claims more than the sentence "Some cats are four-legged." What, then, does such a sentence mean?
3) Foot says that a creature is *defective* if it does not possess the traits that "fit it to survive" in its "natural habitat." It follows that a deer is defective if it is unable to run very fast, even if that deer is in a zoo and doesn't need to run from any predators. Is this a plausible claim?
4) What is Foot's objection to the view that a good life is just a happy life? Do you find this objection persuasive?
5) Foot says that the words "good" and "bad" mean the same thing when applied to plants as when applied to humans. What does she mean by this claim? Do you agree with her?

11

Nicomachean Ethics

Aristotle

....

Aristotle (384–322 BCE) was perhaps the greatest philosopher who ever lived. He worked in a variety of philosophical areas (logic, metaphysics, philosophy of mind, epistemology, ethics, rhetoric), and in each field produced work that exerted an influence across many centuries.

His seminal work in moral philosophy is *Nicomachean Ethics*, believed to be a set of carefully recorded lecture notes taken down by Aristotle's students. In this excerpt, from book 2 of the *Nicomachean Ethics*, Aristotle discusses the nature of virtue, its role in a good human life, and its relation to happiness and to "the golden mean." Aristotle's thoughts on the virtues have served as the basis of almost every version of virtue ethics developed in Western philosophy over the past two millennia.

....

Aristotle, from *Nicomachean Ethics* (1998). trans. W.D. Ross. pp. 28–47. By permission of Oxford University Press, Inc.

Moral Virtue

Moral Virtue, How Produced, in What Medium and in What Manner Exhibited

Moral virtue, like the arts, is acquired by repetition of the corresponding acts

VIRTUE, then, being of two kinds, intellectual and moral, intellectual virtue in the main owes both its birth and its growth to teaching (for which reason it requires experience and time), while moral virtue comes about as a result of habit, whence also its name (ἠθική) is one that is formed by a slight variation from the word ἔθος (habit). From this it is also plain that none of the moral virtues arises in us by nature; for nothing that exists by nature can form a habit contrary to its nature. For instance the stone which by nature moves downwards cannot be habituated to move upwards, not even if one tries to train it by throwing it up ten thousand times; nor can fire be habituated to move downwards, nor can anything else that by nature behaves in one way be trained to behave in another. Neither by nature, then, nor contrary to nature do the virtues arise in us; rather we are adapted by nature to receive them, and are made perfect by habit.

Again, of all the things that come to us by nature we first acquire the potentiality and later exhibit the activity (this is plain in the case of the senses; for it was not by often seeing or often hearing that we got these senses, but on the contrary we had them before we used them, and did not come to have them by using them); but the virtues we get by first exercising them, as also happens in the case of the arts as well. For the things we have to learn before we can do them, we learn by doing them, e.g. men become builders by building and lyre-players by playing the lyre; so too we become just by doing just acts, temperate by doing temperate acts, brave by doing brave acts.

These acts cannot be prescribed exactly, but must avoid excess and defect

Since, then, the present inquiry does not aim at theoretical knowledge like the others (for we are inquiring not in order to know what virtue is, but in order to become good, since otherwise our inquiry would have been of no use), we must examine the nature of actions, namely how we ought to do them; for these determine also the nature of the states of character that are produced, as we have said. Now, that we must act according to the right rule is a common principle and must be assumed—it will be discussed later, i.e. both what the right rule is, and how it is related to the other virtues. But this must be agreed upon beforehand, that the whole account of matters of conduct must be given in outline and not precisely, as we said at the very beginning that the accounts we demand must be in accordance with the subject-matter; matters concerned with conduct and questions of what is good for us have no fixity, any more than matters of health. The general account being of this nature, the account of particular cases is yet more lacking in exactness; for they do not fall under any art or precept, but the agents themselves must in each case consider what is appropriate to the occasion, as happens also in the art of medicine or of navigation.

But though our present account is of this nature we must give what help we can. First, then, let us consider this, that it is the nature of such things to be destroyed by defect and excess, as we see in the case of strength and of health (for to gain light on things imperceptible we must use the evidence of sensible things); exercise either excessive or defective destroys the strength, and similarly drink or food which is above or below a certain amount destroys the health, while that which is proportionate both produces and increases and preserves it. So too is it, then, in the case of temperance and courage and the other virtues. For the man who flies from and fears everything and does not stand his ground against anything becomes a coward, and the man who fears nothing at all but goes to meet every danger becomes rash; and similarly the man who indulges in every pleasure and abstains from none becomes self-indulgent, while the man who shuns every pleasure, as boors do, becomes in a way insensible; temperance and courage, then, are destroyed by excess and defect, and preserved by the mean.

But not only are the sources and causes of their origination and growth the same as those of their destruction, but also the sphere of their actualization will be the same; for this is also true of the things which are more evident to sense, e.g. of strength; it is produced by taking much food and undergoing much exertion, and it is the strong man that will be most able to do these things. So too is it with the virtues; by abstaining from pleasures we become temperate, and it is when we have become so that we are most able to abstain from them; and similarly too in the case of courage;

for by being habituated to despise things that are fearful and to stand our ground against them we become brave, and it is when we have become so that we shall be most able to stand our ground against them.

Pleasure in doing virtuous acts is a sign that the virtuous
disposition has been acquired: a variety of considerations
show the essential connexion of moral virtue with
pleasure and pain

We must take as a sign of states of character the pleasure or pain that supervenes upon acts; for the man who abstains from bodily pleasures and delights in this very fact is temperate, while the man who is annoyed at it is self-indulgent, and he who stands his ground against things that are terrible and delights in this or at least is not pained is brave, while the man who is pained is a coward. For moral excellence is concerned with pleasures and pains; it is on account of the pleasure that we do bad things, and on account of the pain that we abstain from noble ones. Hence we ought to have been brought up in a particular way from our very youth, as Plato says, so as both to delight in and to be pained by the things that we ought; this is the right education.

We assume, then, that this kind of excellence tends to do what is best with regard to pleasures and pains, and vice does the contrary.

That virtue, then, is concerned with pleasures and pains, and that by the acts from which it arises it is both increased and, if they are done differently, destroyed, and that the acts from which it arose are those in which it actualizes itself—let this be taken as said.

The actions that produce moral virtue are not good in the same
sense as those that flow from it: the latter must
fulfil certain conditions not necessary in the
case of the arts

The question might be asked, what we mean by saying that we must become just by doing just acts, and temperate by doing temperate acts; for if men do just and temperate acts, they are already just and temperate, exactly as, if they do what is in accordance with the laws of grammar and of music, they are grammarians and musicians.

Or is this not true even of the arts? It is possible to do something that is in accordance with the laws of grammar, either by chance or under the guidance of another. A man will be a grammarian, then, only when he has both said something grammatical and said it grammatically; and this means doing it in accordance with the grammatical knowledge in himself.

Again, the case of the arts and that of the virtues are not similar; for the products of the arts have their goodness in themselves, so that it is enough that they should have a certain character, but if the acts that are in accordance with the virtues have themselves a certain character it does not follow that they are done justly or temperately. The agent also must be in a certain condition when he does them; in the first place he must have knowledge, secondly he must choose the acts, and choose them for their own sakes, and thirdly his action must proceed from a firm and unchangeable character. These are not reckoned in as conditions of the possession of the arts except the bare knowledge; but as a condition of the possession of the virtues knowledge has little or no weight, while the other conditions count not for a little but for everything, i.e. the very conditions which result from often doing just and temperate acts.

Actions, then, are called just and temperate when they are such as the just or the temperate man would do; but it is not the man who does these that is just and temperate, but the man who also does them *as* just and temperate men do them. It is well said, then, that it is by doing just acts that the just man is produced, and by doing temperate acts the temperate man; without doing these no one would have even a prospect of becoming good.

Definition of Moral Virtue
The genus of moral virtue: it is a state of character, not a passion, nor a faculty

Next we must consider what virtue is. Since things that are found in the soul are of three kinds—passions, faculties, states of character—virtue must be one of these. By passions I mean appetite, anger, fear, confidence, envy, joy, friendly feeling, hatred, longing, emulation, pity, and in general the feelings that are accompanied by pleasure or pain; by faculties the things in virtue of which we are said to be capable of feeling these, e.g. of becoming angry or being pained or feeling pity; by states of character the things in virtue of which we stand well or badly with reference to the passions, e.g. with reference to anger we stand badly if we feel it violently or too weakly, and well if we feel it moderately; and similarly with reference to the other passions.

Now neither the virtues nor the vices are *passions*, because we are not called good or bad on the ground of our passions, but are so called on the ground of our virtues and our vices, and because we are neither praised nor blamed for our passions (for the man who feels fear or anger is not praised, nor is the man who simply feels anger blamed, but the man who feels it in a certain way), | but for our virtues and our vices we *are* praised or blamed.

Again, we feel anger and fear without choice, but the virtues are modes of choice or involve choice. Further, in respect of the passions we are said to be moved, but in respect of the virtues and the vices we are said not to be moved but to be disposed in a particular way.

For these reasons also they are not *faculties*; for we are neither called good or bad, nor praised or blamed, for the simple capacity of feeling the passions; again, we have the faculties by nature, but we are not made good or bad by nature; we have spoken of this before.

If, then, the virtues are neither passions nor faculties, all that remains is that they should be *states of character*.

Thus we have stated what virtue is in respect of its genus.

The differentia of moral virtue: it is a disposition to choose the mean

We must, however, not only describe virtue as a state of character, but also say what sort of state it is. We may remark, then, that every virtue or excellence both brings into good condition the thing of which it is the excellence and makes the work of that thing be done well; e.g. the excellence of the eye makes both the eye and its work good; for it is by the excellence of the eye that we see well. Similarly the excellence of the horse makes a horse both good in itself and good at running and at carrying its rider and at awaiting the attack of the enemy. Therefore, if this is true in every case, the virtue of man also will be the state of character which makes a man good and which makes him do his own work well.

How this is to happen we have stated already, but it will be made plain also by the following consideration of the specific nature of virtue. In everything that is continuous and divisible it is possible to take more, less, or an equal amount, and that either in terms of the thing itself or relatively to us; and the equal is an intermediate between excess and defect. By the intermediate in the object I mean that which is equidistant from each of the extremes, which is one and the same for all men; by the intermediate relatively to us that which is neither too much nor too little—and this is not one, nor the same for all. For instance, if ten is many and two is few, six is the intermediate, taken in terms of the object; for it exceeds and is exceeded by an equal amount; this is intermediate according to arithmetical proportion. But the intermediate relatively to us is not to be taken so; if ten pounds are too much for a particular person to eat and two too little, it does not follow that the trainer will order six pounds; for this also is perhaps too much for the person who is to take it, or too little—too little for Milo, too much for the beginner in athletic exercises. The same is true of running and wrestling. Thus a master of any art avoids excess and defect, but seeks the intermediate and chooses this—the intermediate not in the object but relatively to us.

If it is thus, then, that every art does its work well—by looking to the intermediate and judging its works by this standard (so that we often say of good works of art that it is not possible either to take away or to add anything, implying that excess and defect destroy the goodness of works of art, while the mean preserves it; and good artists, as we say, look to this in their work), and if, further, virtue is more exact and better than any art, as nature also is, then virtue must have the quality of aiming at the intermediate. I mean moral virtue; for it is this that is concerned with passions and actions, and in these there is excess, defect, and the intermediate. For instance, both fear and confidence and appetite and anger and pity and in general pleasure and pain may be felt both too much and too little, and in both cases not well; but to feel them at the right times, with reference to the right objects, towards the right people, with the right motive, and in the right way, is what is both intermediate and best, and this is characteristic of virtue. Similarly with regard to actions also there is excess, defect, and the intermediate. Now virtue is concerned with passions and actions, in which excess is a form of failure, and so is defect, while the intermediate is praised and is a form of success; and being praised and being successful are both characteristics of virtue. Therefore virtue is a kind of mean, since, as we have seen, it aims at what is intermediate.

Again, it is possible to fail in many ways (for evil belongs to the class of the unlimited, as the Pythagoreans conjectured, and good to that of the limited), while to succeed is possible only in one way (for which reason also one is easy and the other difficult—to miss the mark easy, to hit it difficult); for these reasons also, then, excess and defect are characteristic of vice, and the mean of virtue;

For men are good in but one way, but bad in many.

Virtue, then, is a state of character concerned with choice, lying in a mean, i.e. the mean relative to us, this being determined by a rational principle, and by that principle by which the man of practical wisdom would determine it. Now it is a mean between two vices, that which depends on excess and that which depends on defect; and again it is a mean because the vices respectively fall short of or exceed what is right in both passions and actions, while virtue both finds and chooses that which is intermediate. Hence in respect of what it is, i.e. the definition which states its essence, virtue is a mean, with regard to what is best and right an extreme.

But not every action nor every passion admits of a mean; for some have names that already imply badness, e.g. spite, shamelessness, envy, and in the case of actions adultery, theft, murder; for all of these and suchlike things imply by their names that they are themselves bad, and not the excesses or deficiencies of them. It is not possible, then, ever to be right with regard to them; one must always be wrong. Nor does goodness or badness with regard to such things depend on committing adultery with the right woman, at the right time, and in the right way, but simply to do any of them is to go wrong. It would be equally absurd, then, to expect that in unjust, cowardly, and voluptuous action there should be a mean, an excess, and a deficiency; for at that rate there would be a mean of excess and of deficiency, an excess of excess, and a deficiency of deficiency. But as there is no excess and deficiency of temperance and courage because what is intermediate is in a sense an extreme, so too of the actions we have mentioned there is no mean nor any excess and deficiency, but however they are done they are wrong; for in general there is neither a mean of excess and deficiency, nor excess and deficiency of a mean.

The above proposition illustrated by reference to particular virtues

We must, however, not only make this general statement, but also apply it to the individual facts. For among statements about conduct those which are general apply more widely, but those which are particular are more true, since conduct has to do with individual cases, and our statements must harmonize with the facts in these cases. We may take these cases from our table. With regard to feelings of fear and confidence courage is the mean; of the people who exceed, he who exceeds in fearlessness has no name (many of the states have no name), while the man who exceeds in confidence is rash, and he who exceeds in fear and falls short in confidence is a coward. With regard to pleasures and pains—not all of them, and not so much with regard to the pains—the mean is temperance, the excess self-indulgence. Persons deficient with regard to the pleasures are not often found; hence such persons also have received no name. But let us call them 'insensible'.

With regard to giving and taking of money the mean is liberality, the excess and the defect prodigality and meanness. In these actions people exceed and fall short in contrary ways; the prodigal exceeds in spending and falls short in taking, while the mean man exceeds in taking and falls short in spending. (At present we are giving a mere outline or summary, and are satisfied with this; later these states will be more exactly determined.) With regard to money there are also other dispositions—a mean, magnificence (for the magnificent man differs from the liberal man; the former deals with large sums, the latter with small ones), an excess, tastelessness and vulgarity, and a deficiency, niggardliness; these differ from the states opposed to liberality, and the mode of their difference will be stated later.

With regard to honour and dishonour the mean is proper pride, the excess is known as a sort of 'empty vanity', and the deficiency is undue humility; and as we said liberality was related to magnificence, differing from it by dealing with small sums, so there is a state similarly related to proper pride, being concerned with small honours while that is concerned with great. For it is possible to desire honour as one ought, and more than one ought, and less, and the man who exceeds in his desires is called ambitious, the man who falls short unambitious, while the intermediate person has no name. The dispositions also are nameless, except that that of the ambitious man is called ambition. Hence the people who are at the extremes lay claim to the middle place; and we ourselves sometimes call the intermediate person ambitious and sometimes unambitious, and sometimes praise the ambitious man and sometimes the unambitious. The reason of our doing this will be stated in what follows; but now let us speak of the remaining states according to the method which has been indicated.

With regard to anger also there is an excess, a deficiency, and a mean. Although they can scarcely be said to have names, yet since we call the intermediate person good-tempered let us call the mean good temper; of the persons at the extremes let the one who exceeds be called irascible, and his vice irascibility, and the man who falls short an unirascible sort of person, and the deficiency unirascibility.

Characteristics of the Extreme and Mean States: Practical Corollaries
The extremes are opposed to each other and to the mean

There are three kinds of disposition, then, two of them vices, involving excess and deficiency respectively, and one a virtue, viz. the mean, and all are in a sense opposed to all; for the extreme states are contrary both to the intermediate state and to each other, and the intermediate to the extremes; as the equal is greater relatively to the less, less relatively to the greater, so the middle states are excessive relatively to the deficiencies, deficient relatively to the excesses, both in passions and in actions. For the brave man appears rash relatively to the coward, and cowardly relatively to the rash man; and similarly the temperate man appears self-indulgent relatively to the insensible man, insensible relatively to the self-indulgent, and the liberal man prodigal relatively to the mean man, mean relatively to the prodigal. Hence also the people at the extremes push the intermediate man each over to the other, and the brave man is called rash by the coward, cowardly by the rash man, and correspondingly in the other cases.

These states being thus opposed to one another, the greatest contrariety is that of the extremes to each other, rather than to the intermediate; for these are further from each other than from the intermediate, as the great is further from the small and the small from the great than both are from the equal. Again, to the intermediate some extremes show a certain likeness, as that of rashness to courage and that of prodigality to liberality; but the extremes show the greatest unlikeness to each other; now contraries are defined as the things that are furthest from each other, so that things that are further apart are more contrary.

To the mean in some cases the deficiency, in some the excess, is more opposed; e.g. it is not rashness, which is an excess, but cowardice, which is a deficiency, that is more opposed to courage, and not insensibility, which is a deficiency, but self-indulgence, which is an excess, that is more opposed to temperance. This happens from two reasons, one being drawn from the thing itself; for because one extreme is nearer and liker to the intermediate, we oppose not this but rather its contrary to the intermediate. E.g., since rashness is thought liker and nearer to courage, and cowardice more unlike, we oppose rather the latter to courage; for things that are further from the intermediate are thought more contrary to it. This, then, is one cause, drawn from the thing itself; another is drawn from ourselves; for the things to which we ourselves more naturally tend seem more contrary to the intermediate. For instance, we ourselves tend more naturally to pleasures, and hence are more easily carried away towards self-indulgence than towards propriety. We describe as contrary to the mean, then, rather the directions in which we more often go to great lengths; and therefore self-indulgence, which is an excess, is the more contrary to temperance.

The mean is hard to attain, and is grasped by perception, not by reasoning

That moral virtue is a mean, then, and in what sense it is so, and that it is a mean between two vices, the one involving excess, the other deficiency, and that it is such because its character is to aim at what is intermediate in passions and in actions, has been sufficiently stated. Hence also it is no easy task to be good. For in everything it is no easy task to find the middle, e.g. to find the middle of a circle is not for everyone but for him who knows; so, too, anyone can get angry—that is easy—or give or spend money; but to do this to the right person, to the right extent, at the right time, with the right motive, and in the right way, *that* is not for everyone, nor is it easy; wherefore goodness is both rare and laudable and noble.

Hence he who aims at the intermediate must first depart from what is the more contrary to it, as Calypso advises—

Hold the ship out beyond that surf and spray.

For of the extremes one is more erroneous, one less so; therefore, since to hit the mean is hard in the extreme, we must as a second best, as people say, take the least of the evils; and this will be done best in the way we describe.

But we must consider the things towards which we ourselves also are easily carried away; for some of us tend to one thing, some to another; and this will be recognizable from the pleasure and the pain we feel. We must drag ourselves away to the contrary extreme; for we shall get into the intermediate state by drawing well away from error, as people do in straightening sticks that are bent.

Now in everything the pleasant or pleasure is most to be guarded against; for we do not judge it impartially. We ought, then, to feel towards pleasure as the elders of the people felt towards Helen, and in all circumstances repeat their saying; for if we dismiss pleasure thus we are less likely to go astray. It is by doing this, then, (to sum the matter up) that we shall best be able to hit the mean.

But this is no doubt difficult, and especially in individual cases; for it is not easy to determine both how and with whom and on what provocation and how long one should be angry; for we too sometimes praise those who fall short and call them good-tempered, but sometimes we praise those who get angry and call them manly. The man, however, who deviates little from goodness is not blamed, whether he do so in the direction of the more or of the less, but only the man who deviates more widely; for *he* does not fail to be noticed. But up to what point and to what extent a man must deviate before he becomes blameworthy it is not easy to determine by reasoning, any more than anything else that is perceived by the senses; such things depend on particular facts, and the decision rests with perception. So much, then, is plain, that the intermediate state is in all things to be praised, but that we must incline sometimes towards the excess, sometimes towards the deficiency; for so shall we most easily hit the mean and what is right.

Aristotle: Nicomachean Ethics

1) Some philosophers have maintained that people are naturally morally good, while others have held that people are naturally wicked. Aristotle takes a middle ground, saying, "Neither by nature, then, nor contrary to nature do the virtues arise in us." Which view do you think is correct, and why?

2) What do you think Aristotle means when he says that "matters concerned with conduct and questions of what is good for us have no fixity"? Do you agree with this statement?

3) What is the difference, according to Aristotle, between performing virtuous actions and being a virtuous person? Do you agree with him that the latter is more valuable?

4) Aristotle says that virtue is a "mean" between extremes. For instance, the virtue of courage consists of the disposition to feel neither too much nor too little fear, but rather some appropriate amount in between. Is this consistent with his claim that some actions (such as stealing or adultery) are always wrong in all circumstances?

5) What advice does Aristotle give regarding how we should go about seeking the mean between extremes? Do you think this is good advice?

12

What Makes Right Acts Right?

W. D. Ross

W. D. Ross (1877–1967) developed a truly novel moral theory in his book *The Right and the Good* (1930), from which this selection is taken. He found something attractive about both utilitarianism and Kantianism, the major theoretical competitors of his day, but found that each had a major flaw. Ross applauded utilitarianism's emphasis on benevolence, but rejected its idea that maximizing goodness is our sole moral duty. Kantianism, on the other hand, preserved the attractive idea that justice is independently important, but erred in claiming that the moral rules that specified such duties were absolute (never to be broken).

Ross created a kind of compromise theory, in which he identified a number of distinct grounds for moral duty (benevolence, fidelity to promises, truth-telling, avoiding harm, gratitude, justice, reparation). Each of these is a basis for a *prima facie duty*—an always-important reason that generates an "all-things-considered" duty, provided that no other reason or set of reasons is weightier in the situation. In other words, it is sometimes acceptable to violate a prima facie duty.

But when? We cannot offer a permanent ranking of these prima facie duties. Sometimes, for instance, it is right to protect the general happiness even if we have to commit an injustice to do so. But at other times, the balance should be struck in the opposite way.

W.D. Ross, "What Makes Right Acts Right?" from *Good and Evil* (1930). pp. 16–32. By permission of Oxford University Press, Inc.

Ross insisted that these prima facie duties are self-evident. Here he offers some very influential (and controversial) remarks on how we can gain moral knowledge, both of the moral principles themselves and of the correct verdicts to reach in particular cases.
....

The point at issue is that to which we now pass, viz. whether there is any general character which makes right acts right, and if so, what it is. Among the main historical attempts to state a single characteristic of all right actions which is the foundation of their rightness are those made by egoism and utilitarianism. But I do not propose to discuss these, not because the subject is unimportant, but because it has been dealt with so often and so well already, and because there has come to be so much agreement among moral philosophers that neither of these theories is satisfactory. A much more attractive theory has been put forward by Professor Moore: that what makes actions right is that they are productive of more *good* than could have been produced by any other action open to the agent.

This theory is in fact the culmination of all the attempts to base rightness on productivity of some sort of result. The first form this attempt takes is the attempt to base rightness on conduciveness to the advantage or pleasure of the agent. This theory comes to grief over the fact, which stares us in the face, that a great part of duty consists in an observance of the rights and a furtherance of the interests of others, whatever the cost to ourselves may be. Plato and others may be right in holding that a regard for the rights of others never in the long run involves a loss of happiness for the agent, that 'the just life profits a man'. But this, even if true, is irrelevant to the rightness of the act. As soon as a man does an action *because* he thinks he will promote his own interests thereby, he is acting not from a sense of its rightness but from self-interest.

To the egoistic theory hedonistic utilitarianism supplies a much-needed amendment. It points out correctly that the fact that a certain pleasure will be enjoyed by the agent is no reason why he ought to bring it into being rather than an equal or greater pleasure to be enjoyed by another, though, human nature being what it is, it makes it not unlikely that he will try to bring it into being. But hedonistic utilitarianism in its turn needs a correction. On reflection it seems clear that pleasure is not the only thing in life that we think good in itself, that for instance we think the possession of a good character, or an intelligent understanding of the world, as good or better. A great advance is made by the substitution of 'productive of the greatest good' for 'productive of the greatest pleasure'.

Not only is this theory more attractive than hedonistic utilitarianism, but its logical relation to that theory is such that the latter could not be true unless it were true, while it might be true though hedonistic utilitarianism were not. It is in fact one of the logical bases of hedonistic utilitarianism. For the view that what produces the maximum pleasure is right has for its bases the views (1) that what produces the maximum good is right, and (2) that pleasure is the only thing good in itself. If, therefore, it can be shown that productivity of the maximum good is not what makes all right actions right, we shall *a fortiori* have refuted hedonistic utilitarianism.

When a plain man fulfils a promise because he thinks he ought to do so, it seems clear that he does so with no thought of its total consequences, still less with any opinion that these are likely to be the best possible. He thinks in fact much more of the past than of the future. What makes him think it right to act in a certain way is the fact that he has promised to do so—that and, usually, nothing more. That his act will produce the best possible consequences is not his reason for calling it right. What lends colour to the theory we are examining, then, is not the actions (which form probably a great majority of our actions) in which some such reflection as 'I have promised' is the only reason we give ourselves for thinking a certain action right, but the exceptional cases in which the consequences of fulfilling a promise (for instance) would be so disastrous to others that we judge it right not to do so. It must of course be admitted that such cases exist. If I have promised to meet a friend at a particular time for some trivial purpose, I should certainly think myself justified in breaking my engagement if by doing so I could prevent a serious accident or bring relief to the victims of one. And the supporters of the view we are examining hold that my thinking so is due to my thinking that I shall bring more good into existence by the one action than by the other. A different account may, however, be given of the matter, an account which will, I believe, show itself to be the true one. It may be said that besides the duty of fulfilling promises I have and recognize a duty of relieving distress, and that when I think it right to do the latter at the cost of not doing the former, it is not because I think I shall produce more good thereby but because I think it the duty which is in the circumstances more of a duty. This account surely corresponds much more closely with what we really think in such a situation. If, so far as I can see, I could bring equal amounts of good into being by fulfilling my promise and by helping some one to whom I had made no promise, I should not hesitate to regard the former as my duty. Yet on the view that what is right is right because it is productive of the most good I should not so regard it.

There are two theories, each in its way simple, that offer a solution of such cases of conscience. One is the view of Kant, that there are certain duties of perfect obligation, such as those of fulfilling promises, of paying debts, of telling the truth, which admit of no exception whatever in favour of duties of imperfect obligation, such as that of relieving distress. The other is the view of, for instance, Professor Moore and Dr. Rashdall, that there is only the duty of producing good, and that all 'conflicts of duties' should be resolved by asking 'by which action will most good be produced?' But it is more important that our theory fit the facts than that it be simple, and the account we have given above corresponds (it seems to me) better than either of the simpler theories with what we really think, viz. that normally promise-keeping, for example, should come before benevolence, but that when and only when the good to be produced by the benevolent act is very great and the promise comparatively trivial, the act of benevolence becomes our duty.

In fact the theory of 'ideal utilitarianism', if I may for brevity refer so to the theory of Professor Moore, seems to simplify unduly our relations to our fellows. It says, in effect, that the only morally significant relation in which my neighbours stand to me is that of being possible beneficiaries by my action. They do stand in this relation to me, and this relation is morally significant. But they may also stand to me in the relation of promisee to promiser, of creditor to debtor, of wife to husband, of child to parent, of friend to friend, of fellow countryman to fellow countryman, and the like; and each of these relations is the foundation of a *prima facie* duty, which is more or less incumbent on me according to the circumstances of the case. When I am in a situation, as perhaps I always am, in which more than one of these *prima facie* duties is incumbent on me, what I have to do is to study the situation as fully as I can until I form the considered opinion (it is never more) that in the circumstances one of them is more incumbent than any other; then I am bound to think that to do this *prima facie* duty is my duty *sans phrase* in the situation.

I suggest '*prima facie* duty' or 'conditional duty' as a brief way of referring to the characteristic (quite distinct from that of being a duty proper) which an act has, in virtue of being of a certain kind (e.g. the keeping of a promise), of being an act which would be a duty proper if it were not at the same time of another kind which is morally significant. Whether an act is a duty proper or actual duty depends on *all* the morally significant kinds it is an instance of.

The phrase '*prima facie* duty' must be apologized for, since (1) it suggests that what we are speaking of is a certain kind of duty, whereas it is in fact not a duty, but something related in a special way to duty. Strictly speaking, we want not a phrase in which duty is qualified by an adjective, but a separate noun. (2) '*Prima' facie* suggests that one is speaking only of an appearance which a moral situation presents at first sight, and which may turn out to be illusory; whereas what I am speaking of is an objective fact involved in the nature of the situation, or more strictly in an element of its nature, though not, as duty proper does, arising from its whole nature.

There is nothing arbitrary about these *prima facie* duties. Each rests on a definite circumstance which cannot seriously be held to be without moral significance. Of *prima facie* duties I suggest, without claiming completeness or finality for it, the following division.

1. Some duties rest on previous acts of my own. These duties seem to include two kinds.
    A. Those resting on a promise or what may fairly be called an implicit promise, such as the implicit undertaking not to tell lies which seems to be implied in the act of entering into conversation (at any rate by civilized men), or of writing books that purport to be history and not fiction. These may be called the duties of fidelity.
    B. Those resting on a previous wrongful act. These may be called the duties of reparation.
2. Some rest on previous acts of other men, i.e. services done by them to me. These may be loosely described as the duties of gratitude.
3. Some rest on the fact or possibility of a distribution of pleasure or happiness (or of the means thereto) which is not in accordance with the merit of the persons concerned; in such cases there arises a duty to upset or prevent such a distribution. These are the duties of justice.
4. Some rest on the mere fact that there are beings in the world whose condition we can make better in respect of virtue, or of intelligence, or of pleasure. These are the duties of beneficence.

5. Some rest on the fact that we can improve our own condition in respect of virtue or of intelligence. These are the duties of self-improvement.
6. I think that we should distinguish from (4) the duties that may be summed up under the title of 'not injuring others'. No doubt to injure others is incidentally to fail to do them good; but it seems to me clear that non-maleficence is apprehended as a duty distinct from that of beneficence, and as a duty of a more stringent character.

The essential defect of the 'ideal utilitarian' theory is that it ignores, or at least does not do full justice to, the highly personal character of duty. If the only duty is to produce the maximum of good, the question who is to have the good—whether it is myself, or my benefactor, or a person to whom I have made a promise to confer that good on him, or a mere fellow man to whom I stand in no such special relation—should make no difference to my having a duty to produce that good. But we are all in fact sure that it makes a vast difference.

If the objection be made, that this catalogue of the main types of duty is an unsystematic one resting on no logical principle, it may be replied, first, that it makes no claim to being ultimate. It is a *prima facie* classification of the duties which reflection on our moral convictions seems actually to reveal. And if these convictions are, as I would claim that they are, of the nature of knowledge, and if I have not misstated them, the list will be a list of authentic conditional duties, correct as far as it goes though not necessarily complete. The list of *goods* put forward by the rival theory is reached by exactly the same method—the only sound one in the circumstances—viz. that of direct reflection on what we really think. Loyalty to the facts is worth more than a symmetrical architectonic or a hastily reached simplicity. If further reflection discovers a perfect logical basis for this or for a better classification, so much the better.

It may, again, be objected that our theory that there are these various and often conflicting types of *prima facie* duty leaves us with no principle upon which to discern what is our actual duty in particular circumstances. But this objection is not one which the rival theory is in a position to bring forward. For when we have to choose between the production of two heterogeneous goods, say knowledge and pleasure, the 'ideal utilitarian' theory can only fall back on an opinion, for which no logical basis can be offered, that one of the goods is the greater; and this is no better than a similar opinion that one of two duties is the more urgent. And again, when we consider the infinite variety of the effects of our actions in the way of pleasure, it must surely be admitted that the claim which *hedonism* sometimes makes, that it offers a readily applicable criterion of right conduct, is quite illusory.

I am unwilling, however, to content myself with an *argumentum ad hominem*, and I would contend that in principle there is no reason to anticipate that every act that is our duty is so for one and the same reason. Why should two sets of circumstances, or one set of circumstances, not possess different characteristics, any one of which makes a certain act our *prima facie* duty? When I ask what it is that makes me in certain cases sure that I have a *prima facie* duty to do so and so, I find that it lies in the fact that I have made a promise; when I ask the same question in another case, I find the answer lies in the fact that I have done a wrong. And if on reflection I find (as I think I do) that neither of these reasons is reducible to the other, I must not on any *a priori* ground assume that such a reduction is possible.

It is necessary to say something by way of clearing up the relation between *prima facie* duties and the actual or absolute duty to do one particular act in particular circumstances. If, as almost all moralists except Kant are agreed, and as most plain men think, it is sometimes right to tell a lie or to break a promise, it must be maintained that there is a difference between *prima facie* duty and actual or absolute duty. When we think ourselves justified in breaking, and indeed morally obliged to break, a promise in order to relieve some one's distress, we do not for a moment cease to recognize a *prima facie* duty to keep our promise, and this leads us to feel, not indeed shame or repentance, but certainly compunction, for behaving as we do; we recognize, further, that it is our duty to make up somehow to the promisee for the breaking of the promise. We have to distinguish from the characteristic of being our duty that of tending to be our duty. Any act that we do contains various elements in virtue of which it falls under various categories. In virtue of being the breaking of a promise, for instance, it tends to be wrong; in virtue of being an instance of relieving distress it tends to be right.

Something should be said of the relation between our apprehension of the *prima facie* rightness of certain types of act and our mental attitude towards particular acts. It is proper to use the word 'apprehension' in the former case and not in the latter. That an act, *qua* fulfilling a promise, or *qua* effecting a just distribution of good, or *qua* returning services rendered, or *qua* promoting the good of others, or *qua* promoting the virtue or insight of the agent, is *prima facie* right, is self-evident; not in the sense that it is evident from beginning of our lives, or as soon as we attend to the proposition for the first time, but in the sense that when we have reached sufficient mental maturity and have given sufficient attention to the proposition it is evident without any need of proof, or of evidence beyond itself. It is self-evident just as a mathematical axiom, or the validity of a form of inference, is evident. The moral order expressed in these propositions is just as much part of the fundamental nature of the universe (and, we may add, of any possible universe in which there were moral agents at all) as is the spatial or numerical structure expressed in the axioms of geometry or arithmetic. In our confidence that these propositions are true there is involved the same trust in our reason that is involved in our confidence in mathematics; and we should have no justification for trusting it in the latter sphere and distrusting it in the former. In both cases we are dealing with propositions that cannot be proved, but that just as certainly need no proof.

Our judgements about our actual duty in concrete situations have none of the certainty that attaches to our recognition of the general principles of duty. A statement is certain, i.e. is an expression of knowledge, only in one or other of two cases: when it is either self-evident, or a valid conclusion from self-evident premises. And our judgements about our particular duties have neither of these characters. (1) They are not self-evident. Where a possible act is seen to have two characteristics, in virtue of one of which it is *prima facie* right, and in virtue of the other *prima-facie* wrong, we are (I think) well aware that we are not certain whether we ought or ought not to do it; that whether we do it or not, we are taking a moral risk. We come in the long run, after consideration, to think one duty more pressing than the other, but we do not feel certain that it is so. And though we do not always recognize that a possible act has two such characteristics, and though there may be cases in which it has not, we are never certain that any particular possible act has not, and therefore never certain that it is right, nor certain that it is wrong. For, to go no further in the analysis, it is enough to point out that any particular act will in all probability in the course of time contribute to the bringing about of good or of evil for many human beings, and thus have a *prima facie* rightness or wrongness of which we know nothing. (2) Again, our judgements about our particular duties are not logical conclusions from self-evident premises. The only possible premises would be the general principles stating their *prima facie* rightness or wrongness *qua* having the different characteristics they do have; and even if we could (as we cannot) apprehend the extent to which an act will tend on the one hand, for example, to bring about advantages for our benefactors, and on the other hand to bring about disadvantages for fellow men who are not our benefactors, there is no principle by which we can draw the conclusion that it is on the whole right or on the whole wrong. In this respect the judgement as to the rightness of a particular act is just like the judgement as to the beauty of a particular natural object or work of art. A poem is, for instance, in respect of certain qualities beautiful and in respect of certain others not beautiful; and our judgement as to the degree of beauty it possesses on the whole is never reached by logical reasoning from the apprehension of its particular beauties or particular defects. Both in this and in the moral case we have more or less probable opinions which are not logically justified conclusions from the general principles that are recognized as self-evident.

There is therefore much truth in the description of the right act as a fortunate act. If we cannot be certain that it is right, it is our good fortune if the act we do is the right act. This consideration does not, however, make the doing of our duty a mere matter of chance. There is a parallel here between the doing of duty and the doing of what will be to our personal advantage. We never *know* what act will in the long run be to our advantage. Yet it is certain that we are more likely in general to secure our advantage if we estimate to the best of our ability the probable tendencies of our actions in this respect, than if we act on caprice. And similarly we are more likely to do our duty if we reflect to the best of our ability on the *prima facie* rightness or wrongness of various possible acts in virtue of the characteristics we perceive them to have, than if we act without reflection. With this greater likelihood we must be content.

The general principles of duty are obviously not self-evident from the beginning of our lives. How do they come to be so? The answer is, that they come to be self-evident to us just as mathematical axioms do. We find by experience that this couple of matches and that couple make four matches, that this couple of balls on a wire and that couple make four balls: and by reflection on these and similar discoveries we come to see that it is of the nature of two and to make four. In a precisely similar way, we see the *prima facie* rightness of an act which would be the fulfilment of a particular promise, and of another which would be the fulfilment of another promise, and when we have reached sufficient maturity to think in general terms, we apprehend *prima facie* rightness to belong to the nature of any fulfilment of promise. What comes first in time is the apprehension of the self-evident *prima facie* rightness of an individual act of a particular type. From this we come by reflection to apprehend the self-evident general principle of *prima facie* duty. From this, too, perhaps along with the apprehension of the self-evident *prima facie* rightness of the same act in virtue of its having another characteristic as well, and perhaps in spite of the apprehension of its *prima facie* wrongness in virtue of its having some third characteristic, we come to believe something not self-evident at all, but an object of probable opinion, viz. that this particular act is (not *prima facie* but) actually right.

In what has preceded, a good deal of use has been made of 'what we really think' about moral questions; a certain theory has been rejected because it does not agree with what we really think. It might be said that this is in principle wrong; that we should not be content to expound what our present moral consciousness tells us but should aim at a criticism of our existing moral consciousness in the light of theory. Now I do not doubt that the moral consciousness of men has in detail undergone a good deal of modification as regards the things we think right, at the hands of moral theory. But if we are told, for instance, that we should give up our view that there is a special obligatoriness attaching to the keeping of promises because it is self-evident that the only duty is to produce as much good as possible, we have to ask ourselves whether we really, when we reflect, are convinced that this is self-evident, and whether we really can get rid of our view that promise-keeping has a bindingness independent of productiveness of maximum good. In my own experience I find that I cannot, in spite of a very genuine attempt to do so; and I venture to think that most people will find the same.

I would maintain, in fact, that what we are apt to describe as 'what we think' about moral questions contains a considerable amount that we do not think but know, and that this forms the standard by reference to which the truth of any moral theory has to be tested, instead of having itself to be tested by reference to any theory. I hope that I have in what precedes indicated what in my view these elements of knowledge are that are involved in our ordinary moral consciousness.

It would be a mistake to found a natural science on 'what we really think', i.e. on what reasonably thoughtful and well educated people think about the subjects of the science before they have studied them scientifically. For such opinions are interpretations, and often misinterpretations, of sense-experience; and the man of science must appeal from these to sense-experience itself, which furnishes his real data. In ethics no such appeal is possible. We have no more direct way of access to the facts about rightness and goodness and about what things are right or good, than by thinking about them; the moral convictions of thoughtful and well-educated people are the data of ethics just as sense-perceptions are the data of a natural science. Just as some of the latter have to be rejected as illusory, so have some of the former; but as the latter are rejected only when they are in conflict with other more accurate sense-perceptions, the former are rejected only when they are in conflict with other convictions which stand better the test of reflection. The existing body of moral convictions of the best people is the cumulative product of the moral reflection of many generations, which has developed an extremely delicate power of appreciation of moral distinctions; and this the theorist cannot afford to treat with anything other than the greatest respect. The verdicts of the moral consciousness of the best people are the foundation on which he must build; though he must first compare them with one another and eliminate any contradictions they may contain.

W. D. Ross: What Makes Right Acts Right?

1) Ross begins by considering the view that the right action is the one that is "productive of more *good* than could have been produced by any other action open to the agent." What objections does he offer to this view? Do you think they are good ones?

2) Ross also considers Kant's view, according to which there are certain moral rules that must be followed without exception. What does Ross think is wrong with this theory? Do you agree with his criticism?

3) What does Ross mean by "prima facie duties," and how do these differ from "duties proper"? How does he think we should use our knowledge of prima facie duties to determine what our duty is in a particular situation?

4) How does Ross think we come to know prima facie duties? Do you find his view plausible?

5) What reasons does Ross give for his claim that we can never be certain about what the right thing to do is in a particular situation? Do you agree with him about this?

6) Ross claims that "the moral convictions of thoughtful and well-educated people are the data of ethics just as sense-perceptions are the data of a natural science." Is beginning with our own moral convictions the best way of doing ethics, or do you think there is a better way?

13

What Is Feminist Ethics?

Hilde Lindemann

Hilde Lindemann offers us a brief overview of feminist ethics in this selection. She first discusses the nature of feminism, and identifies some of the various ways that people have defined it. Lindemann argues against thinking of feminism as focused primarily on equality, women, or the differences between the sexes. She instead invites us to think of feminism as based on considerations of gender—specifically, considerations to do with the lesser degree of power that women have, largely the world over, as compared with men.

Lindemann proceeds to discuss the sex/gender distinction, and to identify the central tasks of feminist ethics: to understand, criticize, and correct the inaccurate gender assumptions that underlie our moral thinking and behavior. An important approach of most feminists is a kind of skepticism about the ability to distinguish political commitments from intellectual ones. Lindemann concludes by discussing this skepticism and its implications for feminist thought.

A few years ago, a dentist in Ohio was convicted of having sex with his female patients while they were under anesthesia. I haven't been able to discover whether he had to pay a fine or do jail time, but I do

Hilde Lindemann, "What is Feminist Ethics?" from *An Invitation to Feminist Ethics* (2004). pp. 2–3, 6–16. Reproduced with the permission of The McGraw-Hill Companies.

remember that the judge ordered him to take a course in ethics. And I recall thinking how odd that order was. Let's suppose, as the judge apparently did, that the dentist really and truly didn't know it was wrong to have sex with anesthetized patients (this will tax your imagination, but try to suppose it anyway). Can we expect—again, as the judge apparently did—that on completing the ethics course, the dentist would be a better, finer man?

Hardly. If studying ethics could make you good, then the people who have advanced academic degrees in the subject would be paragons of moral uprightness. I can't speak for all of them, of course, but though the ones I know are nice enough, they're no more moral than anyone else. Ethics doesn't improve your character. Its *subject* is morality, but its relationship to morality is that of a scholarly study to the thing being studied. In that respect, the relationship is a little like the relationship between grammar and language.

Let's explore that analogy. People who speak fluent English don't have to stop and think about the correctness of the sentence "He gave it to *her*." But here's a harder one. Should you say, "He gave it to *her* who must be obeyed?" or "He gave it to *she* who must be obeyed?" To sort this out, it helps to know a little grammar—the systematic, scholarly description of the structure of the language and the rules for speaking and writing in it. According to those rules, the object of the preposition "to" is the entire clause that comes after it, and the subject of that clause is "she." So, even though it sounds peculiar, the correct answer is "He gave it to she who must be obeyed."

In a roughly similar vein, morally competent adults don't have to stop and think about whether it's wrong to have sex with one's anesthetized patients. But if you want to understand whether it's wrong to have large signs in bars telling pregnant women not to drink, or to sort out the conditions under which it's all right to tell a lie, it helps to know a little ethics. The analogy between grammar and ethics isn't exact, of course. For one thing, there's considerably more agreement about what language is than about what morality is. For another, grammarians are concerned only with the structure of language, not with the meaning or usage of particular words. In both cases, however, the same point can be made: You already have to know quite a lot about how to behave—linguistically or morally— before there's much point in studying either grammar or ethics.

What Is Feminism?

What, then, is feminism? As a social and political movement with a long, intermittent history, feminism has repeatedly come into public awareness, generated change, and then disappeared again. As an eclectic body of theory, feminism entered colleges and universities in the early 1970s as a part of the women's studies movement, contributing to scholarship in every academic discipline, though probably most heavily in the arts, social sciences, literature, and the humanities in general. Feminist ethics is a part of the body of theory that is being developed primarily in colleges and universities.

Many people in the United States think of feminism as a movement that aims to make women the social equals of men, and this impression has been reinforced by references to feminism and feminists in the newspapers, on television, and in the movies. But bell hooks has pointed out in *Feminist Theory from Margin to Center* (1984, 18–19) that this way of defining feminism raises some serious problems. Which men do women want to be equal to? Women who are socially well off wouldn't get much advantage from being the equals of the men who are poor and lower class, particularly if they aren't white. Hooks's point is that there are no women and men in the abstract. They are poor, black, young, Latino/a, old, gay, able-bodied, upper class, down on their luck, Native American, straight, and all the rest of it. When a woman doesn't think about this, it's probably because she doesn't have to. And that's usually a sign that her own social position is privileged. In fact, privilege often means that there's something uncomfortable going on that others have to pay attention to but you don't. So, when hooks asks which men women want to be equal to, she's reminding us that there's an unconscious presumption of privilege built right in to this sort of demand for equality.

There's a second problem with the equality definition. Even if we could figure out which men are the ones to whom women should be equal, that way of putting it suggests that the point of feminism is somehow to get women to measure up to what (at least some) men already are. Men remain the point of reference; theirs are the lives that women would naturally want. If the first problem with the equality definition is "Equal to *which* men?" the second problem could be put as "Why equal to *any* men?" Reforming a system in which men are the point of reference by allowing women to perform as their equals "forces women to focus on men and address men's conceptions of women rather than creating and developing women's values about themselves," as Sarah Lucia Hoagland puts it in *Lesbian Ethics* (1988, 57). For that reason, Hoagland and some other feminists believe that feminism is first and foremost about women.

But characterizing feminism as about women has its problems too. What, after all, is a woman? In her 1949 book, *The Second Sex*, the French feminist philosopher Simone de Beauvoir famously observed, "One is not born, but becomes a woman. No biological, psychological, or economic fate determines the figure that the human female presents in society: it is civilization as a whole that produces this creature, intermediate between male and eunuch, which is described as feminine" (Beauvoir 1949, 301). Her point is that while plenty of human beings are born female, 'woman' is not a natural fact about them—it's a social invention. According to that invention, which is widespread in "civilization as a whole," man represents the positive, typical human being, while woman represents only the negative, the not-man. She is the Other against whom man defines himself—he is all the things that she is not. And she exists only in relation to him. In a later essay called "One Is Not Born a Woman," the lesbian author and theorist Monique Wittig (1981, 49) adds that because women belong to men sexually as well as in every other way, women are necessarily heterosexual. For that reason, she argued, lesbians aren't women.

But, you are probably thinking, everybody knows what a woman is, and lesbians certainly *are* women. And you're right. These French feminists aren't denying that there's a perfectly ordinary use of the word *woman* by which it means exactly what you think it means. But they're explaining what this comes down to, if you look at it from a particular point of view. Their answer to the question "What is a woman?" is that women are different from men. But they don't mean this as a trite observation. They're saying that 'woman' refers to *nothing but* difference from men, so that apart from men, women aren't anything. 'Man' is the positive term, 'woman' is the negative one, just like 'light' is the positive term and 'dark' is nothing but the absence of light.

A later generation of feminists have agreed with Beauvoir and Wittig that women are different from men, but rather than seeing that difference as simply negative, they put it in positive terms, affirming feminine qualities as a source of personal strength and pride. For example, the philosopher Virginia Held thinks that women's moral experience as mothers, attentively nurturing their children, may serve as a better model for social relations than the contract model that the free market provides. The poet Adrienne Rich celebrated women's passionate nature (as opposed, in stereotype, to the rational nature of men), regarding the emotions as morally valuable rather than as signs of weakness.

But defining feminism as about the positive differences between men and women creates yet another set of problems. In her 1987 *Feminism*

Unmodified, the feminist legal theorist Catharine A. MacKinnon points out that this kind of difference, as such, is a symmetrical relationship: If I am different from you, then you are different from me in exactly the same respects and to exactly the same degree. "Men's differences from women are equal to women's differences from men," she writes. "There is an *equality* there. Yet the sexes are not socially equal" (MacKinnon 1987, 37). No amount of attention to the differences between men and women explains why men, as a group, are more socially powerful, valued, advantaged, or free than women. For that, you have to see differences as counting in certain ways, and certain differences being created precisely because they give men *power* over women.

Although feminists disagree about this, my own view is that feminism isn't—at least not directly—about equality, and it isn't about women, and it isn't about difference. It's about power. Specifically, it's about the social pattern, widespread across cultures and history, that distributes power asymmetrically to favor men over women. This asymmetry has been given many names, including the subjugation of women, sexism, male dominance, patriarchy, systemic misogyny, phallocracy, and the oppression of women. A number of feminist theorists simply call it gender, and throughout this book, I will too.

What Is Gender?

Most people think their gender is a natural fact about them, like their hair and eye color: "Jones is 5 foot 8, has red hair, and is a man." But gender is a *norm*, not a fact. It's a prescription for how people are supposed to act; what they must or must not wear; how they're supposed to sit, walk, or stand; what kind of person they're supposed to marry; what sorts of things they're supposed to be interested in or good at; and what they're entitled to. And because it's an *effective* norm, it creates the differences between men and women in these areas.

Gender doesn't just tell women to behave one way and men another, though. It's a *power* relation, so it tells men that they're entitled to things that women aren't supposed to have, and it tells women that they are supposed to defer to men and serve them. It says, for example, that men are supposed to occupy positions of religious authority and women are supposed to run the church suppers. It says that mothers are supposed to take care of their children but fathers have more important things to do. And it says that the things associated with femininity are supposed to take a back seat to the things that are coded masculine. Think of the many tax dollars allocated to the military as compared with the few tax dollars allocated to the arts. Think about how kindergarten teachers are paid as compared to how stockbrokers are paid. And think about how many presidents of the United States have been women. Gender operates through social institutions (like marriage and the law) and practices (like education and medicine) by disproportionately conferring entitlements and the control of resources on men, while disproportionately assigning women to subordinate positions in the service of men's interests.

To make this power relation seem perfectly natural—like the fact that plants grow up instead of down, or that human beings grow old and die—gender constructs its norms for behavior around what is supposed to be the natural biological distinction between the sexes. According to this distinction, people who have penises and testicles, XY chromosomes, and beards as adults belong to the male sex, while people who have clitorises and ovaries, XX chromosomes, and breasts as adults belong to the female sex, and those are the only sexes there are. Gender, then, is the complicated set of cultural meanings that are constructed around the two sexes. Your sex is either male or female, and your gender—either masculine, or feminine—corresponds socially to your sex.

As a matter of fact, though, sex isn't quite so simple. Some people with XY chromosomes don't have penises and never develop beards, because they don't have the receptors that allow them to make use of the male hormones that their testicles produce. Are they male or female? Other people have ambiguous genitals or internal reproductive structures that don't correspond in the usual manner to their external genitalia. How should we classify them? People with Turner's syndrome have XO chromosomes instead of XX. People with Klinefelter's syndrome have three sex chromosomes: XXY. Nature is a good bit looser in its categories than the simple male/female distinction acknowledges. Most human beings can certainly be classified as one sex or the other, but a considerable number of them fall somewhere in between.

The powerful norm of gender doesn't acknowledge the existence of the in-betweens, though. When, for example, have you ever filled out an application for a job or a driver's license or a passport that gave you a choice other than M or F? Instead, by basing its distinction between masculine and feminine on the existence of two and only two sexes, gender makes the inequality of power between men and women appear natural and therefore legitimate.

Gender, then, is about power. But it's not about the power of just one group over another. Gender always interacts with other social markers— such as race, class, level of education, sexual orientation, age, religion, physical and mental health, and ethnicity—to distribute power unevenly among women positioned differently in the various social orders, and it does the same to men. A man's social status, for example, can have a great deal to do with the extent to which he's even perceived as a man. There's a wonderful passage in the English travel writer Frances Trollope's *Domestic Manners of the Americans* (1831), in which she describes the exaggerated delicacy of middle-class young ladies she met in Kentucky and Ohio. They wouldn't dream of sitting in a chair that was still warm from contact with a gentleman's bottom, but thought nothing of getting laced into their corsets in front of a male house slave. The slave, it's clear, didn't count as a man—not in the relevant sense, anyway. Gender is the force that makes it matter whether you are male or female, but it always works hand in glove with all the other things about you that matter at the same time. It's one power relation intertwined with others in a complex social system that distinguishes your betters from your inferiors in all kinds of ways and for all kinds of purposes.

Power and Morality

If feminism is about gender, and gender is the name for a social system that distributes power unequally between men and women, then you'd expect feminist ethicists to try to *understand, criticize,* and *correct* how gender operates within our moral beliefs and practices. And they do just that. In the first place, they challenge, on moral grounds, the powers men have over women, and they claim for women, again on moral grounds, the powers that gender denies them. As the moral reasons for opposing gender are similar to the moral reasons for opposing power systems based on social markers other than gender, feminist ethicists also offer moral arguments against systems based on class, race, physical or mental ability, sexuality, and age. And because all these systems, including gender, are powerful enough to *conceal* many of the forces that keep them in place, it's often necessary to make the forces visible by explicitly identifying—and condemning—the various ugly ways they allow some people to treat others. This is a central task for feminist ethics.

Feminist ethicists also produce theory about the moral meaning of various kinds of *legitimate* relations of unequal power, including relationships of dependency and vulnerability, relationships of trust, and relationships based on something other than choice. Parent–child relationships, for example, are necessarily unequal and for the most part unchosen. Parents can't help having power over their children, and while they may have chosen to have children, most don't choose to have the particular children they do, nor do children choose their parents. This raises questions about the responsible use of parental power and the nature of involuntary obligations, and these are topics for feminist ethics. Similarly, when you trust someone, that person has power over you. Whom should you trust, for what purposes, and when is trust not warranted? What's involved in being trustworthy, and what must be done to repair breaches of trust? These too are questions for feminist ethics.

Third, feminist ethicists look at the various forms of power that are required for morality to operate properly at all. How do we learn right from wrong in the first place? We usually learn it from our parents, whose power to permit and forbid, praise and punish, is essential to our moral training. For whom or what are we ethically responsible? Often this depends on the kind of power we have over the person or thing in question. If, for instance, someone is particularly vulnerable to harm because of something I've done, I might well have special duties toward that person. Powerful social institutions—medicine, religion, government, and the market, to take just a few examples—typically dictate what is morally required of us and to whom we are morally answerable. Relations of power set the terms for who must answer to whom, who has authority over whom, and who gets excused from certain kinds of accountability to whom. But because so many of these power relations are illegitimate, in that they're instances of gender, racism, or other kinds of bigotry, figuring out which ones are morally justified is a task for feminist ethics.

Description and Prescription

So far it sounds as if feminist ethics devotes considerable attention to *description*—as if feminist ethicists were like poets or painters who want to show you something about reality that you might otherwise have missed. And indeed, many feminist ethicists emphasize the importance of understanding how social power actually works, rather than concentrating solely on how it ought to work. But why, you might ask, should ethicists worry about how power operates within societies? Isn't it up to sociologists and political scientists to describe how things *are*, while ethicists concentrate on how things *ought* to be?

As the philosopher Margaret Urban Walker has pointed out in *Moral Contexts*, there is a tradition in Western philosophy, going all the way back to Plato, to the effect that morality is something ideal and that ethics, being the study of morality, properly examines only that ideal. According to this tradition, notions of right and wrong as they are found in the world are unreliable and shadowy manifestations of something lying outside of human experience—something to which we ought to aspire but can't hope to reach. Plato's Idea of the Good, in fact, is precisely not of this earth, and only the gods could truly know it. Christian ethics incorporates Platonism into its insistence that earthly existence is fraught with sin and error and that heaven is our real home. Kant too insists that moral judgments transcend the histories and circumstances of people's actual lives, and most moral philosophers of the twentieth century have likewise shown little interest in how people really live and what it's like for them to live that way. "They think," remarks Walker (2001), "that there is little to be learned from what is about what ought to be" (3).

In Chapter Four [omitted here—ed.] we'll take a closer look at what goes wrong when ethics is done that way, but let me just point out here that if you don't know how things are, your prescriptions for how things ought to be won't have much practical effect. Imagine trying to sail a ship without knowing anything about the tides or where the hidden rocks and shoals lie. You might have a very fine idea of where you are trying to go, but if you don't know the waters, at best you are likely to go off course, and at worst you'll end up going down with all your shipmates. If, as many feminists have noted, a crucial fact about human selves is that they are always embedded in a vast web of relationships, then the forces at play within those relationships must be understood. It's knowing how people are situated with respect to these forces, what they are going through as they are subjected to them, and what life is like in the face of them, that lets us decide which of the forces are morally justified. Careful description of how things are is a crucial part of feminist methodology, because the power that puts certain groups of people at risk of physical harm, denies them full access to the good things their society has to offer, or treats them as if they were useful only for other people's purposes is often hidden and hard to see. If this power isn't seen, it's likely to remain in place, doing untold amounts of damage to great numbers of people.

All the same, feminist ethics is *normative* as well as descriptive. It's fundamentally about how things ought to be, while description plays the crucial but secondary role of helping us to figure that out. Normative language is the language of "ought" instead of "is," the language of "worth" and "value," "right" and "wrong," "good" and "bad." Feminist ethicists differ on a number of normative issues, but as the philosopher Alison Jaggar (1991) has famously put it, they all share two moral commitments: "that the subordination of women is morally wrong and that the moral experience of women is worthy of respect" (95). The first commitment—that women's interests ought not systematically to be set in the service of men's—can be understood as a moral challenge to power under the guise of gender. The second commitment—that women's experience must be taken seriously—can be understood as a call to acknowledge how that power operates. These twin commitments are the two normative legs on which any feminist ethics stands.

Morality and Politics

If the idealization of morality goes back over two thousand years in Western thought, a newer tradition, only a couple of centuries old, has split off morality from politics. According to this tradition, which can be traced to Kant and some other Enlightenment philosophers, morality concerns the relations between persons, whereas politics concerns the relations among nation-states, or between a state and its citizens. So, as Iris Marion Young (1990) puts it, ethicists have tended to focus on intentional actions by individual persons, conceiving of moral life as "conscious, deliberate, a rational weighing of alternatives," whereas political philosophers have focused on impersonal governmental systems, studying "laws, policies, the large-scale distribution of social goods, countable quantities like votes and taxes" (149).

For feminists, though, the line between ethics and political theory isn't quite so bright as this tradition makes out. It's not always easy to tell where feminist ethics leaves off and feminist political theory begins. There are two reasons for this. In the first place, while ethics certainly concerns personal behavior, there is a long-standing insistence on the part of feminists that the personal *is* political. In a 1970 essay called "The Personal Is Political," the political activist Carol Hanisch observed that "personal problems are political problems. There are no personal solutions at this time" (204–205). What Hanisch meant is that even the most private areas of everyday life, including such intensely personal areas as sex, can function to maintain abusive power systems like gender. If a heterosexual woman believes, for example, that contraception is primarily her responsibility because she'll have to take care of the baby if she gets pregnant, she is propping up a system that lets men evade responsibility not only for pregnancy, but for their own offspring as well. Conversely, while unjust social arrangements such as gender and race invade every aspect of people's personal lives, "there are no personal solutions," either when Hanisch wrote those words or now, because to shift dominant understandings of how certain groups may be treated, and what other groups are entitled to expect of them, requires concerted political action, not just personal good intentions.

The second reason why it's hard to separate feminist ethics from feminist politics is that feminists typically subject the ethical theory they produce to critical political scrutiny, not only to keep untoward political biases out, but also to make sure that the work accurately reflects their feminist politics. Many nonfeminist ethicists, on the other hand, don't acknowledge that their work reflects their politics, because they don't think it should. Their aim, by and large, has been to develop ideal moral theory that applies to all people, regardless of their social position or experience of life, and to do that objectively, without favoritism, requires them to leave their own personal politics behind. The trouble, though, is that they aren't really leaving their own personal politics behind. They're merely refusing to notice that their politics is inevitably built right in to their theories. (This is an instance of Lindemann's ad hoc rule Number 22: Just because you think you are doing something doesn't mean you're actually doing it.) Feminists, by contrast, are generally skeptical of the idealism nonfeminists favor, and they're equally doubtful that objectivity can be achieved by stripping away what's distinctive about people's experiences or commitments. Believing that it's no wiser to shed one's political allegiances in the service of ethics than it would be to shed one's moral allegiances, feminists prefer to be transparent about their politics as a way of keeping their ethics intellectually honest.

Hilde Lindemann: What Is Feminist Ethics?

1) Near the beginning of her piece, Lindemann claims that "studying ethics doesn't improve your character." Do you think she is right about this? If so, what is the point of studying ethics?
2) What problems does Lindemann raise for the view that feminism is fundamentally about equality between men and women? Can these problems be overcome, or must we admit that feminism is concerned with equality?

3) What is the difference between sex and gender? Why does Lindemann think that gender is essentially about power? Do you think she is right about this?
4) Lindemann claims that feminist ethics is "*normative* as well as descriptive." What does she mean by this? In what ways is feminist ethics more descriptive than other approaches to ethics? Do you see this as a strength or a weakness?
5) What is meant by the slogan "the personal is political"? Do you agree with the slogan?
6) Lindemann claims that one should not set aside one's political views when thinking about ethical issues. What reasons does she give for thinking this? Do you agree with her?

For Further Reading

Baier, Annette. 1994. *Moral Prejudices: Essays on Ethics.* Cambridge, MA: Harvard University Press.

Beauvoir, Simone de. 1949 [1974]. *The Second Sex.* Trans. and ed. H. M. Parshley. New York: Modern Library.

Hanisch, Carol. 1970. "The Personal Is Political." In *Notes from the Second Year.* New York: Radical Feminism.

Hoagland, Sarah Lucia. 1988. *Lesbian Ethics: Toward New Value.* Palo Alto, CA: Institute of Lesbian Studies.

Hooks, Bell. 1984. *Feminist Theory from Margin to Center.* Boston: South End Press.

Jaggar, Alison. 1991. "Feminist Ethics: Projects, Problems, Prospects." In *Feminist Ethics*, ed. Claudia Card. Lawrence: University Press of Kansas.

MacKinnon, Catharine A. 1987. *Feminism Unmodified.* Cambridge, MA: Harvard University Press.

Plumwood, Val. 2002. *Environmental Culture: The Ecological Crisis of Reason.* London: Routledge.

Walker, Margaret Urban. 2001. "Seeing Power in Morality: A Proposal for Feminist Naturalism in Ethics." In *Feminists Doing Ethics*, ed. Peggy DesAutels and Joanne Waugh. Lanham, MD: Rowman & Littlefield.

——. 2003. *Moral Contexts.* Lanham, MD: Rowman & Littlefield.

Wittig, Monique. 1981. "One Is Not Born a Woman." *Feminist Issues* 1, no. 2.

Young, Iris Marion. 1990. *Justice and the Politics of Difference.* Princeton, NJ: Princeton University Press.

PART THREE

Metaethics

The Status of Morality

14

Moral Distinctions Not Derived from Reason

David Hume

David Hume (1711–1776) sought to offer a wholly naturalistic account of the nature and origins of morality. He rejected the idea of eternal moral truths, graspable by reason alone. He thought that morality is essentially a way of organizing our emotional responses to a value-free world. In this excerpt from his first masterpiece, *A Treatise of Human Nature* (1737), Hume offers several influential arguments against moral rationalism—the idea that reason is the basis of morality, our primary means of gaining moral knowledge, and the source of moral motivation. Also included here is perhaps his most famous claim about morality, namely, that one cannot derive an *ought* from an *is*. According to Hume, it is impossible to substantiate a claim about what ought to be done, or ought to be the case, solely from claims about how the world actually is. Since reason is confined to telling us what is the case, it cannot, by itself, supply us with advice about our duty, or about which ideals we should aspire to.

I t has been observed, that nothing is ever present to the mind but its perceptions; and that all the actions of seeing, hearing, judging, loving, hating, and thinking, fall under this denomination. The mind can never exert itself in any action which we may not comprehend under the term of *perception*; and consequently that term is no less applicable to those judgments by which we distinguish moral good and evil, than to every other operation of the mind. To approve of one character, to condemn another, are only so many different perceptions.

Now, as perceptions resolve themselves into two kinds, viz. *impressions* and *ideas*, this distinction gives rise to a question, with which we shall open up our present inquiry concerning morals, *whether it is by means of our ideas or impressions we distinguish betwixt vice and virtue, and pronounce an action blamable or praise-worthy?* This will immediately cut off all loose discourses and declamations, and reduce us to something precise and exact on the present subject.

Those who affirm that virtue is nothing but a conformity to reason; that there are eternal fitnesses and unfitnesses of things, which are the same to every rational being that considers them; that the immutable measure of right and wrong impose an obligation, not only on human creatures, but also on the Deity himself: all these systems concur in the opinion, that morality, like truth, is discerned merely by ideas, and by their juxtaposition and comparison. In order, therefore, to judge of these systems, we need only consider whether it be possible from reason alone, to distinguish betwixt moral good and evil, or whether there must concur some other principles to enable us to make that distinction.

If morality had naturally no influence on human passions and actions, it were in vain to take such pains to inculcate it; and nothing would be more fruitless than that multitude of rules and precepts with which all moralists abound. Philosophy is commonly divided into *speculative* and *practical*; and as morality is always comprehended under the latter division, it is supposed to influence our passions and actions, and to go beyond the calm and indolent judgments of the understanding. And this is confirmed by common experience, which informs us that men are often governed by their duties, and are deterred from some actions by the opinion of injustice, and impelled to others by that of obligation.

Since morals, therefore, have an influence on the actions and affections, it follows that they cannot be derived from reason; and that because reason alone, as we have already proved, can never have any such influence. Morals excite passions, and produce or prevent actions. Reason of itself is utterly impotent in this particular. The rules of morality, therefore, are not conclusions of our reason.

No one, I believe, will deny the justness of this inference; nor is there any other means of evading it, than by denying that principle on which it is founded. As long as it is allowed, that reason has no influence on our passions and actions, it is in vain to pretend that morality is discovered only by a deduction of reason. An active principle can never be founded on an inactive; and if reason be inactive in itself, it must remain so in all its shapes and appearances, whether it exerts itself in natural or moral subjects, whether it considers the powers of external bodies, or the actions of rational beings.

It would be tedious to repeat all the arguments by which I have proved that reason is perfectly inert, and can never either prevent or produce any action or affection. It will be easy to recollect what has been said upon that subject. I shall only recall on this occasion one of these arguments, which I shall endeavour to render still more conclusive, and more applicable to the present subject.

Reason is the discovery of truth or falsehood. Truth or falsehood consists in an agreement or disagreement either to the *real* relations of ideas, or to *real* existence and matter of fact. Whatever therefore is not susceptible of this agreement or disagreement, is incapable of being true or false, and can never be an object of our reason. Now, it is evident our passions, volitions, and actions, are not susceptible of any such agreement or disagreement; being original facts and realities, complete in themselves, and implying no reference to other passions, volitions, and actions. It is impossible, therefore, they can be pronounced either true or false, and be either contrary or conformable to reason.

This argument is of double advantage to our present purpose. For it proves *directly*, that actions do not derive their merit from a conformity to reason, nor their blame from a contrariety to it; and it proves the same truth more *indirectly*, by showing us, that as reason can never immediately prevent or produce any action by contradicting or approving of it, it cannot be the source of moral good and evil, which are found to have that influence. Actions may be laudable or blamable; but they cannot be reasonable or unreasonable: laudable or blamable, therefore, are not the same with reasonable or unreasonable. The merit and demerit of actions frequently contradict, and sometimes control our natural propensities. But reason has no such influence. Moral distinctions, therefore, are not the offspring of reason. Reason is wholly inactive, and can never be the source of so active a principle as conscience, or a sense of morals.

But perhaps it may be said, that though no will or action can be immediately contradictory to reason, yet we may find such a contradiction in some of the attendants of the actions, that is, in its causes or effects. The action may cause a judgment, or may be *obliquely* caused by one, when the judgment concurs with a passion; and by an abusive way of speaking, which philosophy will scarce allow of, the same contrariety may, upon that account, be ascribed to the action. How far this truth or falsehood may be the source of morals, it will now be proper to consider.

It has been observed that reason, in a strict and philosophical sense, can have an influence on our conduct only after two ways: either when it excites a passion, by informing us of the existence of something which is a proper object of it; or when it discovers the connection of causes and effects, so as to afford us means of exerting any passion. These are the only kinds of judgment which can accompany our actions, or can be said to produce them in any manner; and it must be allowed, that these judgments may often be false and erroneous. A person may be affected with passion, by supposing a pain or pleasure to lie in an object which has no tendency to produce either of these sensations, or which produces the contrary to what is imagined. A person may also take false measures for the attaining of his end, and may retard, by his foolish conduct, instead of forwarding the execution of any object. These false judgments may be thought to affect the passions and actions, which are connected with them, and may be said to render them unreasonable, in a figurative and improper way of speaking. But though this be acknowledged, it is easy to observe, that these errors are so far from being the source of all immorality, that they are commonly very innocent, and draw no manner of guilt upon the person who is so unfortunate as to fall into them. They extend not beyond a mistake of *fact*, which moralists have not generally supposed criminal, as being perfectly involuntary. I am more to be lamented than blamed, if I am mistaken with regard to the influence of objects in producing pain or pleasure, or if I know not the proper means of satisfying my desires. No one can ever regard such errors as a defect in my moral character. A fruit, for instance, that is really disagreeable, appears to me at a distance, and, through mistake, I fancy it to be pleasant and delicious. Here is one error. I choose certain means of reaching this fruit, which are not proper for my end. Here is a second error; nor is there any third one, which can ever possibly enter into our reasonings concerning actions. I ask, therefore, if a man in this situation, and guilty of these two errors, is to be regarded as vicious and criminal, however unavoidable they might have been? Or if it be possible to imagine that such errors are the sources of all immorality?

And here it may be proper to observe, that if moral distinctions be derived from the truth or falsehood of those judgments, they must take place wherever we form the judgments; nor will there be any difference, whether the question be concerning an apple or a kingdom, or whether the error be avoidable or unavoidable.

For as the very essence of morality is supposed to consist in an agreement or disagreement to reason, the other circumstances are entirely arbitrary, and can never either bestow on any action the character of virtuous or vicious, or deprive it of that character. To which we may add, that this agreement or disagreement, not admitting of degrees, all virtues and vices would of course be equal.

Should it be pretended, that though a mistake of *fact* be not criminal, yet a mistake of *right* often is; and that this may be the source of immorality: I would answer, that it is impossible such a mistake can ever be the original source of immorality, since it supposes a real right and wrong; that is, a real distinction in morals, independent of these judgments. A mistake, therefore, of right, may become a species of immorality; but it is only a secondary one, and is founded on some other antecedent to it.

As to those judgments which are the *effects* of our actions, and which, when false, give occasion to pronounce the actions contrary to truth and reason; we may observe, that our actions never cause any judgment, either true or false, in ourselves, and that it is only on others they have such an influence. It is certain that an action, on many occasions, may give rise to false conclusions in others; and that a person, who, through a window, sees any lewd behaviour of mine with my neighbour's wife, may be so simple as to imagine she is certainly my own. In this respect my action resembles somewhat a lie or falsehood; only with this difference, which is material, that I perform not the action with any intention of giving rise to a false judgment in another, but merely to satisfy my lust and passion. It causes, however, a mistake and false judgment by accident; and the falsehood of its effects may be ascribed, by some odd figurative way of speaking, to the action itself. But still I can see no pretext of reason for asserting, that the tendency to cause such an error is the first spring or original source of all immorality.

Thus, upon the whole, it is impossible that the distinction betwixt moral good and evil can be made by reason; since that distinction has an influence upon our actions, of which reason alone is incapable. Reason and judgment may, indeed, be the mediate cause of an action, by prompting or by directing a passion; but it is not pretended that a judgment of this kind, either in its truth or falsehood, is attended with virtue or vice. And as to the judgments, which are caused by our judgments, they can still less bestow those moral qualities on the actions which are their causes.

But, to be more particular, and to show that those eternal immutable fitnesses and unfitnesses of things cannot be defended by sound philosophy, we may weigh the following considerations.

If the thought and understanding were alone capable of fixing the boundaries of right and wrong, the character of virtuous and vicious either must lie in some relations of objects, or must be a matter of fact which is discovered by our reasoning. This consequence is evident. As the operations of human understanding divide themselves into two kinds, the comparing of ideas, and the inferring of matter of fact, were virtue discovered by the understanding, it must be an object of one of these operations; nor is there any third operation of the understanding which can discover it. There has been an opinion very industriously propagated by certain philosophers, that morality is susceptible of demonstration; and though no one has ever been able to advance a single step in those demonstrations, yet it is taken for granted that this science may be brought to an equal certainty with geometry or algebra. Upon this supposition, vice and virtue must consist in some relations; since it is allowed on all hands, that no matter of fact is capable of being demonstrated. Let us therefore begin with examining this hypothesis, and endeavour, if possible, to fix those moral qualities which have been so long the objects of our fruitless researches; point out distinctly the relations which constitute morality or obligation, that we may know wherein they consist, and after what manner we must judge of them.

If you assert that vice and virtue consist in relations susceptible of certainty and demonstration, you must confine yourself to those *four* relations which alone admit of that degree of evidence; and in that case you run into absurdities from which you will never be able to extricate yourself. For as you make the very essence of morality to lie in the relations, and as there is no one of these relations but what is applicable, not only to an irrational but also to an inanimate object, it follows that even such objects must be susceptible of merit or demerit. *Resemblance, contrariety, degrees in quality*, and *proportions in quantity and number*; all these relations belong as properly to matter as to our actions, passions, and volitions. It is unquestionable, therefore, that morality lies not in any of these relations, nor the sense of it in their discovery.

Should it be asserted, that the sense of morality consists in the discovery of some relation distinct from these, and that our enumeration was not complete when we comprehended all demonstrable relations under four general heads; to this I know not what to reply, till some one be so good as to point out to me this new relation. It is impossible to refute a system which has never yet been explained. In such a manner of fighting in the dark, a man loses his blows in the air, and often places them where the enemy is not present.

I must therefore, on this occasion, rest contented with requiring the two following conditions of any one that would undertake to clear up this system. *First*, as moral good and evil belong only to the actions of the mind, and are derived from our situation with regard to external objects, the relations from which these moral distinctions arise must lie only betwixt internal actions and external objects, and must not be applicable either to internal actions, compared among themselves, or to external objects, when placed in opposition to other external objects. For as morality is supposed to attend certain relations, if these relations could belong to internal actions considered singly, it would follow, that we might be guilty of crimes in ourselves, and independent of our situation with respect to the universe; and in like manner, if these moral relations could be applied to external objects, it would follow that even inanimate beings would be susceptible of moral beauty and deformity. Now, it seems difficult to imagine that any relation can be discovered betwixt our passions, volitions, and actions, compared to external objects, which relation might not belong either to these passions and volitions, or to these external objects, compared among *themselves*.

But it will be still more difficult to fulfil the *second* condition, requisite to justify this system. According to the principles of those who maintain an abstract rational difference betwixt moral good and evil, and a natural fitness and unfitness of things, it is not only supposed, that these relations, being eternal and immutable, are the same, when considered by every rational creature, but their *effects* are also supposed to be necessarily the same; and it is concluded they have no less, or rather a greater, influence in directing the will of the Deity, than in governing the rational and virtuous of our own species. These two particulars are evidently distinct. It is one thing to know virtue, and another to conform the will to it. In order, therefore, to prove that the measures of right and wrong are eternal laws, *obligatory* on every rational mind, it is not sufficient to show the relations upon which they are founded: we must also point out the connection betwixt the relation and the will; and must prove that this connection is so necessary, that in every well-disposed mind, it must take place and have its influence; though the difference betwixt these minds be in other respects immense and infinite. Now, besides what I have already proved, that even in human nature no relation can ever alone produce any action; besides this, I say, it has been shown, in treating of the understanding, that there is no connection of cause and effect, such as this is supposed to be, which is discoverable otherwise than by experience, and of which we can pretend to have any security by the simple consideration of the objects. All beings in the universe, considered in themselves, appear entirely loose and independent of each other. It is only by experience we learn their influence and connection; and this influence we ought never to extend beyond experience.

Thus it will be impossible to fulfil the *first* condition required to the system of eternal rational measures of right and wrong; because it is impossible to show those relations, upon which such a distinction may be founded: and it is as impossible to fulfil the *second* condition: because we cannot prove *a priori*, that these relations, if they really existed and were perceived, would be universally forcible and obligatory.

Nor does this reasoning only prove, that morality consists not in any relations that are the objects of science; but if examined, will prove with equal certainty, that it consists not in any *matter of fact*, which can be discovered by the understanding. This is the *second* part of our argument; and if it can be made evident, we may conclude that morality is not an object of reason. But can there be any difficulty in proving that vice and virtue are not matters of fact, whose existence we can infer by reason? Take any action allowed to be vicious; wilful murder, for instance. Examine it in all lights, and see if you can find that matter of fact, or real existence, which you call *vice*. In whichever way you take it, you find only certain passions, motives, volitions, and thoughts. There is no other matter of fact in the case. The vice entirely escapes you, as long as you consider the object. You never can find it, till you turn your reflection into your own breast, and find a sentiment of disapprobation, which arises in you, towards this action. Here is a matter of fact; but it is the object of feeling, not of reason. It lies in yourself, not in the object. So that when you pronounce any action or character to be vicious, you mean nothing, but that from the constitution of your nature you have a feeling or sentiment of blame from the contemplation of it. Vice and virtue, therefore, may be compared to sounds, colours, heat, and cold, which, according to modern philosophy, are not qualities in objects, but perceptions in the mind: and this discovery in morals, like that other in physics, is to be regarded as a considerable advancement of the speculative sciences; though, like that too, it has little or no influence on practice. Nothing can be more real, or concern us more, than our own sentiments of pleasure and uneasiness; and if these be favourable to virtue, and unfavourable to vice, no more can be requisite to the regulation of our conduct and behaviour.

I cannot forbear adding to these reasonings an observation, which may, perhaps, be found of some importance. In every system of morality which I have hitherto met with, I have always remarked, that the author proceeds for some time in the ordinary way of reasoning, and establishes the being of a God, or makes observations concerning human affairs; when of a sudden I am surprised to find, that instead of the usual copulations of propositions, *is*, and *is not*, I meet with no proposition that is not connected with an *ought*, or an *ought not*. This change is imperceptible; but is, however, of the last consequence. For as this *ought*, or *ought not*, expresses some new relation or affirmation, it is necessary that it should be observed and explained; and at the same time that a reason should be given, for what seems altogether inconceivable, how this new relation can be a deduction from others, which are entirely different from it. But as authors do not commonly use this precaution, I shall presume to recommend it to the readers; and am persuaded, that this small attention would subvert all the vulgar systems of morality, and let us see that the distinction of vice and virtue is not founded merely on the relations of objects, nor is perceived by reason.

David Hume: Moral Distinctions Not Derived from Reason

1) According to Hume, "reason has no influence on our actions and passions." What does Hume mean by this? Do you think he is right?
2) Hume claims that the rules of morality "are not conclusions of our reason." How does he argue for this? Do you find his argument convincing?
3) Hume admits that "false judgments" may influence our behavior, but argues that the truth of our judgments does not determine whether actions are morally right or wrong. What is his argument for thinking this?
4) According to Hume, to say that an action is wrong is equivalent to saying that "from the constitution of your nature you have a feeling or sentiment of blame from the contemplation of it." Is this a plausible account of what we mean when we say that an action is wrong? Does

this imply that different actions are wrong for different people, depending on how they feel?

5) Hume claims it is "inconceivable" that we can deduce claims about what *ought* to be the case from claims about what *is* the case. What exactly does he mean by this? Do you think there are any counterexamples to this claim?

15

The Subjectivity of Values

J. L. Mackie

J. L. Mackie (1917–1981), who taught for many years at Oxford University, regarded all ethical views as bankrupt. In this excerpt from his book *Ethics: Inventing Right and Wrong* (1977), Mackie outlines the basic ideas and the central motivating arguments for his *error theory*—the view that all positive moral claims are mistaken. All moral talk, as Mackie sees it, is based on a false assumption: that there are objective moral values. This fundamental error infects the entire system of morality. The foundations are corrupt, and so the entire moral edifice must come tumbling down.

Mackie offers a number of important arguments to substantiate his critique of morality. The argument from relativity claims that the extent of moral disagreement is best explained by the claim that there are no objective values. The argument from queerness contends that objective moral values would be objectionably different from any other kind of thing in the universe, possessed of strange powers that are best rejected. Mackie concludes with his account of why so many people, for so long, have fallen into error by succumbing to the temptation to think of morality as objective.

Moral Scepticism

There are no objective values. This is a bald statement of the thesis of this chapter, but before arguing for it I shall try to clarify and restrict it in ways that may meet some objections and prevent some misunderstanding.

The claim that values are not objective, are not part of the fabric of the world, is meant to include not only moral goodness, which might be most naturally equated with moral value, but also other things that could be more loosely called moral values or disvalues—rightness and wrongness, duty, obligation, an action's being rotten and contemptible, and so on. It also includes non-moral values, notably aesthetic ones, beauty and various kinds of artistic merit. I shall not discuss these explicitly, but clearly much the same considerations apply to aesthetic and to moral values, and there would be at least some initial implausibility in a view that gave the one a different status from the other.

The claim to objectivity, however ingrained in our language and thought, is not self-validating. It can and should be questioned. But the denial of objective values will have to be put forward not as the result of an analytic approach, but as an 'error theory', a theory that although most people in making moral judgements implicitly claim, among other things, to be pointing to something objectively prescriptive, these claims are all false. It is this that makes the name 'moral scepticism' appropriate.

But since this is an error theory, since it goes against assumptions ingrained in our thought and built into some of the ways in which language is used, since it conflicts with what is sometimes called common sense, it needs very solid support. It is not something we can accept lightly or casually and then quietly pass on. If we are to adopt this view, we must argue explicitly for it. Traditionally it has been supported by arguments of two main kinds, which I shall call the argument from relativity and the argument from queerness.

The Argument from Relativity

The argument from relativity has as its premiss the well-known variation in moral codes from one society to another and from one period to another, and also the differences in moral beliefs between different groups and classes within a complex community. Such variation is in itself merely a truth of descriptive morality, a fact of anthropology which entails neither first order nor second order ethical views. Yet it may indirectly support second order subjectivism: radical differences between first order moral judgements make it difficult to treat those judgements as apprehensions of objective truths. But it is not the mere occurrence of disagreements that tells against the objectivity of values. Disagreement on questions in history or biology or cosmology does not show that there are no objective issues in these fields for investigators to disagree about. But such scientific disagreement results from speculative inferences or explanatory hypotheses based on inadequate evidence, and it is hardly plausible to interpret moral disagreement in the same way. Disagreement about moral codes seems to reflect people's adherence to and participation in different ways of life. The causal connection seems to be mainly that way round: it is that people approve of monogamy because they participate in a monogamous way of life rather than that they participate in a monogamous way of life because they approve of monogamy. Of course, the standards may be an idealization of the way of life from which they arise: the monogamy in which people participate may be less complete, less rigid, than that of which it leads them to approve. This is not to say that moral judgements are purely conventional. Of course there have been and are moral heretics and moral reformers, people who have turned against the established rules and practices of their own communities for moral reasons, and often for moral reasons that we would endorse. But this can usually be understood as the extension, in ways which, though new and unconventional, seemed to them to be required for consistency, of rules to which they already adhered as arising out of an existing way of life. In short, the argument from relativity has some force simply because the actual variations in the moral codes are more readily explained by the hypothesis that they reflect ways of life than by the hypothesis that they express perceptions, most of them seriously inadequate and badly distorted, of objective values.

But there is a well-known counter to this argument from relativity, namely to say that the items for which objective validity is in the first place to be claimed are not specific moral rules or codes but very general basic principles which are recognized at least implicitly to some extent in all society—such principles as provide the foundations of what Sidgwick has called different methods of ethics: the principle of universalizability, perhaps, or the rule that one ought to conform to the specific rules of any way of life in which one takes part, from which one profits, and on which one relies, or some utilitarian principle of doing what tends, or seems likely, to promote the general happiness. It is easy to show that such general principles, married with differing concrete circumstances, different existing social patterns or different preferences, will beget different specific moral rules; and there is some plausibility in the claim that the specific rules thus generated will vary from community to community or from group to group in close agreement with the actual variations in accepted codes.

The argument from relativity can be only partly countered in this way. To take this line the moral objectivist has to stay that it is only in these principles that the objective moral character attaches immediately to its descriptively specified ground or subject: other moral judgements are objectively valid or true, but only derivatively and contingently—if things had been otherwise, quite different sorts of actions would have been right. And despite the prominence in recent philosophical ethics of universalization, utilitarian principles, and the like, these are very far from constituting the whole of what is actually affirmed as basic in ordinary moral thought. Much of this is concerned rather with what Hare calls "ideals" or, less kindly, 'fanaticism'. That is, people judge that some things are good or right, and others are bad or wrong, not because—or at any rate not only because—they exemplify some general principle for which widespread implicit acceptance could be claimed, but because something about those things arouses certain responses immediately in them, though they would arouse radically and irresolvably different responses in others. 'Moral sense' or 'intuition' is an initially more plausible description of what supplies many of our basic moral judgements than 'reason'. With regard to all these starting points of moral thinking the argument from relativity remains in full force.

The Argument from Queerness

Even more important, however, and certainly more generally applicable, is the argument from queerness. This has two parts, one metaphysical, the other epistemological. If there were objective values, then they would be entities or qualities or relations of a very strange sort, utterly different from anything else in the universe. Correspondingly, if we were aware of them, it would have to be by some special faculty of moral perception or intuition, utterly different from our ordinary ways of knowing everything else. These points were recognized by Moore when he spoke of non-natural qualities, and by the intuitionists in their talk about a 'faculty of moral intuition'. Intuitionism has long been out of favour, and it is indeed easy to point out its implausibilities. What is not so often stressed, but is more important, is that the central thesis of intuitionism is one to which any objectivist view of values is in the end committed: intuitionism merely makes unpalatably plain what other forms of objectivism wrap up. Of course the suggestion that moral judgements are made or moral problems solved by just sitting down and having an ethical intuition is a travesty of actual moral thinking. But, however complex the real process, it will require (if it is to yield authoritatively prescriptive conclusions) some input of this distinctive sort, either premises or forms of argument or both. When we ask the awkward question, how we can be aware of this authoritative prescriptivity, of the truth of these distinctively ethical premises or of the cogency of this distinctively ethical pattern of reasoning, none of our ordinary accounts of sensory perception or introspection or the framing and confirming of explanatory hypotheses or inference or logical construction or conceptual analysis, or any combination of these, will provide a satisfactory answer; 'a special sort of intuition' is a lame answer, but it is the one to which the clear-headed objectivist is compelled to resort.

Indeed, the best move for the moral objectivist is not to evade this issue, but to look for companions in guilt. For example, Richard Price argues that it is not moral knowledge alone that such an empiricism as those of Locke and Hume is unable to account for, but also our knowledge and even our ideas of essence, number, identity, diversity, solidity, inertia, substance, the necessary existence and infinite extension of time and space, necessity and possibility in general, power, and causation. If the understanding, which Price defines as the faculty within us that discerns truth, is also a source of new simple ideas of so many other sorts, may it not also be a power of immediately perceiving right and wrong, which yet are real characters of actions?

This is an important counter to the argument from queerness. The only adequate reply to it would be to show how, on empiricist foundations, we can construct an account of the ideas and beliefs and knowledge that we have of all these matters. I cannot even begin to do that here, though I have undertaken some parts of the task elsewhere. I can only state my belief that satisfactory accounts of most of these can be given in empirical terms. If some supposed metaphysical necessities or essences resist such treatment, then they too should be included, along with objective values, among the targets of the argument from queerness.

This queerness does not consist simply in the fact that ethical statements are 'unverifiable'. Although logical positivism with its verifiability theory of descriptive meaning gave an impetus to non-cognitive accounts of ethics, it is not only logical positivists but also empiricists of a much more liberal sort who should find objective values hard to accommodate. Indeed, I would not only reject the verifiability principle but also deny the conclusion commonly drawn from it, that moral judgements lack descriptive meaning. The assertion that there are objective values or intrinsically prescriptive entities or features of some kind, which ordinary moral judgements presuppose, is, I hold, not meaningless but false.

Plato's Forms give a dramatic picture of what objective values would have to be. The Form of the Good is such that knowledge of it provides the knower with both a direction and an overriding motive; something's being good both tells the person who knows this to pursue it and makes him pursue it. An objective good would be sought by anyone who was acquainted with it, not because of any contingent fact that this person, or every person, is so constituted that he desires this end, but just because the end has to-be-pursuedness somehow built into it. Similarly, if there were objective principles of right and wrong, any wrong (possible) course of action would have not-to-be-doneness somehow built into it. Or we should have something like Clarke's necessary relations of fitness between situations and actions, so that a situation would have a demand for such-and-such an action somehow built into it.

The need for an argument of this sort can be brought out by reflection on Hume's argument that 'reason' – in which at this stage he includes all sorts of knowing as well as reasoning – can never be an 'influencing motive of the will'. Someone might object that Hume has argued unfairly from the lack of influencing power (not contingent upon desires) in ordinary objects of knowledge and ordinary reasoning, and might maintain that values differ from natural objects precisely in their power, when known, automatically to influence the will. To this Hume could, and would need to, reply that this objection involves the postulating of value-entities or value-features of quite a different order from anything else with which we are acquainted, and of a corresponding faculty with which to detect them. That is, he would have to supplement his explicit argument with what I have called the argument from queerness.

Another way of bringing out this queerness is to ask, about anything that is supposed to have some objective moral quality, how this is linked with its natural features. What is the connection between the natural fact that an action is a piece of deliberate cruelty – say, causing pain just for fun – and the moral fact that it is wrong? It cannot be an entailment, a logical or semantic necessity. Yet it is not merely that the two features occur together. The wrongness must somehow be 'consequential' or 'supervenient'; it is wrong because it is a piece of deliberate cruelty. But just what *in the world* is signified by this 'because'? And how do we know the relation that it signifies, if this is something more than such actions being socially condemned, and condemned by us too, perhaps through our having absorbed attitudes from our social environment? It is not even sufficient to postulate a faculty which 'sees' the wrongness: something must be postulated which can see at once the natural features that constitute the cruelty, and the wrongness, and the mysterious consequential link between the two. Alternatively, the intuition required might be the perception that wrongness is a higher order property belonging to certain natural properties; but what is this belonging of properties to other properties, and how can we discern it? How much simpler and more comprehensible the situation would be if we could replace the moral quality with some sort of subjective response which could be causally related to the detection of the natural features on which the supposed quality is said to be consequential.

It may be thought that the argument from queerness is given an unfair start if we thus relate it to what are admittedly among the wilder products of philosophical fancy—Platonic Forms, non-natural qualities, self-evident relations of fitness, faculties of intuition, and the like. Is it equally forceful if applied to the terms in which everyday moral judgements are more likely to be expressed—though still, as has been argued in the original work, with a claim to objectivity—'you must do this', 'you can't do that', 'obligation', 'unjust', 'rotten', 'disgraceful', 'mean', or talk about good reasons for or against possible actions? Admittedly not; but that is because the objective prescriptivity, the element a claim for whose authoritativeness is embedded in ordinary moral thought and language, is not yet isolated in these forms of speech, but is presented along with relations to desires and feelings, reasoning about the means to desired ends, inter-personal demands, the injustice which consists in the violation of what are in the context the accepted standards of merit, the psychological constituents of meanness, and so on. There is nothing queer about any of these, and under cover of them the claim for moral authority may pass unnoticed. But if I am right in arguing that it is ordinarily there, and is therefore very likely to be incorporated almost automatically in philosophical accounts of ethics which systematize our ordinary thought even in such apparently innocent terms as these, it needs to be examined, and for this purpose it needs to be isolated and exposed as it is by the less cautious philosophical reconstructions.

Patterns of Objectification

Considerations of these kinds suggest that it is in the end less paradoxical to reject than to retain the common-sense belief in the objectivity of moral values, provided that we can explain how this belief, if it is false, has become established and is so resistant to criticisms. This proviso is not difficult to satisfy.

On a subjectivist view, the supposedly objective values will be based in fact upon attitudes which the person has who takes himself to be recognizing and responding to those values. If we admit what Hume calls the mind's 'propensity to spread itself on external objects', we can understand the supposed objectivity of moral qualities as arising from what we can call the projection or objectification of moral attitudes. This would be analogous to what is called the 'pathetic fallacy', the tendency to read our feelings into their objects. If a fungus, say, fills us with disgust, we may be inclined to ascribe to the fungus itself a non-natural quality of foulness. But in moral contexts there is more than this propensity at work. Moral attitudes themselves are at least partly social in origin: socially established—and socially necessary—patterns of behaviour put pressure on individuals, and each individual tends to internalize these pressures and to join in requiring these patterns of behaviour of himself and of others. The attitudes that are objectified into moral values have indeed an external source, though not the one assigned to them by the belief in their absolute authority. Moreover, there are motives that would support objectification. We need morality to regulate interpersonal relations, to control some of the ways in which people behave towards one another, often in opposition to contrary inclinations. We therefore want our moral judgements to be authoritative for other agents as well as for ourselves: objective validity would give them the authority required. Aesthetic values are logically in the same position as moral ones; much the same metaphysical and epistemological considerations apply to them. But aesthetic values are less strongly objectified than moral ones; their subjective status, and an 'error theory' with regard to such claims to objectivity as are incorporated in aesthetic judgements, will be more readily accepted, just because the motives for their objectification are less compelling.

But it would be misleading to think of the objectification of moral values as primarily the projection of feelings, as in the pathetic fallacy. More important are wants and demands. As Hobbes says, 'whatsoever is the object of any man's Appetite or Desire, that is it, which he for his part calleth *Good*'; and certainly both the adjective 'good' and the noun 'goods' are used in non-moral contexts of things because they are such as to satisfy desires. We get the notion of something's being objectively good, or having intrinsic value, by reversing the direction of dependence here, by making the desire depend upon the goodness, instead of the goodness on the desire. And this is aided by the fact that the desired thing will indeed have features that make it desired, that enable it to arouse a desire or that make it such as to satisfy some desire that is already there. It is fairly easy to confuse the way in which a thing's desirability is indeed objective with its having in our sense objective value. The fact that the word 'good' serves as one of our main moral terms is a trace of this pattern of objectification.

J. L. Mackie: The Subjectivity of Values

1) Why does Mackie refer to his view as an "error theory"? What is the "error" that Mackie takes himself to be pointing out?

2) Mackie cites widespread disagreement about morality as evidence for his view that there are no objective moral values. Yet he admits that the existence of scientific disagreement does not suggest that there are no objective scientific truths. Why does Mackie think that ethics is different from science in this regard? Do you think he is right about this?

3) One might object to Mackie's argument from disagreement by noting that some moral prohibitions (against killing innocent people, against adultery, etc.) are widely shared across cultures. Does this show that there is something wrong with the argument from disagreement? How do you think Mackie would respond to such an objection?

4) Mackie claims that objective values, if they existed, would be entities "of a very strange sort, utterly different from anything else in the universe." What feature of moral values would make them so strange? Do you agree with Mackie that the "queerness" of moral properties is a good reason to deny their existence?

5) Mackie suggests that his view is "simpler and more comprehensible" than accepting objective values. In what ways is his view simpler? Is this a good reason to reject the existence of objective values?

6) Mackie thinks that for his error theory to succeed, he must explain how people come to think that there are objective moral values in the first place. How does he attempt to do so? Do you think he is successful?

16

Ethics and Observation

Gilbert Harman

In this brief selection from his book *The Nature of Morality* (1977), Gilbert Harman argues that there is a fundamental difference between the claims of ethics and those of the natural sciences. We can verify scientific claims by testing them against the world. We can't do this with moral claims. The reason is that moral facts appear to cause nothing, and without any causal power, it is impossible to detect their presence. This leaves us no choice but to test our moral views exclusively by seeing how well they relate to other beliefs we already hold. But since those further moral beliefs are also unable to be scientifically confirmed, there is no reason to think that moral beliefs can record some independent reality, in the way that true scientific beliefs report facts about the natural world.

Harman's arguments have generated a substantial amount of attention, focusing our thoughts as they do on what seems to be a fundamental difference between scientific claims and moral claims. If there is a moral reality out there, awaiting our discovery, then we should, says Harman, be able to find out about it in the same way we learn about the natural world that science describes. But we can't do that. In a part of the book that is omitted here, Harman relies on the arguments from this selection to support his moral relativism, which insists that morality is a matter of social agreements, with no objective basis.

Gilbert Harman, "Ethics and Observation" from *The Nature of Morality* (1977), pp. 3–10. By permission of Oxford University Press, Inc.

Harman's arguments have been very influential in shaping debates within metaethics over the past few decades. Many have found his ideas compelling. Others have sought to show that ethics is really a kind of natural science, its claims testable "against the world," and so subject to scientific confirmation. Still others have been content to deny that ethics is any kind of science, but have then proceeded to argue that ethics is none the worse for this difference.

....

The Basic Issue

Can moral principles be tested and confirmed in the way scientific principles can? Consider the principle that, if you are given a choice between five people alive and one dead or five people dead and one alive, you should always choose to have five people alive and one dead rather than the other way round. We can easily imagine examples that appear to confirm this principle. Here is one:

> You are a doctor in a hospital's emergency room when six accident victims are brought in. All six are in danger of dying but one is much worse off than the others. You can just barely save that person if you devote all of your resources to him and let the others die. Alternatively, you can save the other five if you are willing to ignore the most seriously injured person.

It would seem that in this case you, the doctor, would be right to save the five and let the other person die. So this example, taken by itself, confirms the principle under consideration. Next, consider the following case.

> You have five patients in the hospital who are dying, each in need of a separate organ. One needs a kidney, another a lung, a third a heart, and so forth. You can save all five if you take a single healthy person and remove his heart, lungs, kidneys, and so forth, to distribute to these five patients. Just such a healthy person is in room 306. He is in the hospital for routine tests. Having seen his test results, you know that he is perfectly healthy and of the right tissue compatibility. If you do nothing, he will survive without incident; the other patients will die, however. The other five patients can be saved only if the person

in Room 306 is cut up and his organs distributed. In that case, there would be one dead but five saved.

The principle in question tells us that you should cut up the patient in Room 306. But in this case, surely you must not sacrifice this innocent bystander, even to save the five other patients. Here a moral principle has been tested and disconfirmed in what may seem to be a surprising way.

This, of course, was a "thought experiment." We did not really compare a hypothesis with the world. We compared an explicit principle with our feelings about certain imagined examples. In the same way, a physicist performs thought experiments in order to compare explicit hypotheses with his "sense" of what should happen in certain situations, a "sense" that he has acquired as a result of his long working familiarity with current theory. But scientific hypotheses can also be tested in real experiments, out in the world.

Can moral principles be tested in the same way, out in the world? You can observe someone do something, but can you ever perceive the rightness or wrongness of what he does? If you round a corner and see a group of young hoodlums pour gasoline on a cat and ignite it, you do not need to *conclude* that what they are doing is wrong; you do not need to figure anything out; you can *see* that it is wrong. But is your reaction due to the actual wrongness of what you see or is it simply a reflection of your moral "sense," a "sense" that you have acquired perhaps as a result of your moral upbringing?

Observation

The issue is complicated. There are no pure observations. Observations are always "theory laden." What you perceive depends to some extent on the theory you hold, consciously or unconsciously. You see some children pour gasoline on a cat and ignite it. To really see that, you have to possess a great deal of knowledge, know about a considerable number of objects, know about people: that people pass through the life stages infant, baby, child, adolescent, adult. You must know what flesh and blood animals are, and in particular, cats. You must have some idea of life. You must know what gasoline is, what burning is, and much more. In one sense, what you "see" is a pattern of light on your retina, a shifting array of splotches, although, even that is theory, and you could never adequately describe what you see in that sense. In another sense, you see what you do because of the theories you hold. Change those theories and you would see something else, given the same pattern of light.

Similarly, if you hold a moral view, whether it is held consciously or unconsciously, you will be able to perceive rightness or wrongness, goodness or badness, justice or injustice. There is no difference in this respect between moral propositions and other theoretical propositions. If there is a difference, it must be found elsewhere.

Observation depends on theory because perception involves forming a belief as a fairly direct result of observing something; you can form a belief only if you understand the relevant concepts and a concept is what it is by virtue of its role in some theory or system of beliefs. To recognize a child as a child is to employ, consciously or unconsciously, a concept that is defined by its place in a framework of the stages of human life. Similarly, burning is an empty concept apart from its theoretical connections to the concepts of heat, destruction, smoke, and fire.

Moral concepts—Right and Wrong, Good and Bad, Justice and Injustice—also have a place in your theory or system of beliefs and are the concepts they are because of their context. If we say that observation has occurred whenever an opinion is a direct result of perception, we must allow that there is moral observation, because such an opinion can be a moral opinion as easily as any other sort. In this sense, observation may be used to confirm or disconfirm moral theories. The observational opinions that, in this sense, you find yourself with can be in either agreement or conflict with your consciously explicit moral principles. When they are in conflict, you must choose between your explicit theory and observation. In ethics, as in science, you sometimes opt for theory, and say that you made an error in observation or were biased or whatever, or you sometimes opt for observation, and modify your theory.

In other words, in both science and ethics, general principles are invoked to explain particular cases and, therefore, in both science and ethics, the general principles you accept can be tested by appealing to particular judgments that certain things are right or wrong, just or unjust, and so forth; and these judgments are analogous to direct perceptual judgments about facts.

Observational Evidence

Nevertheless, observation plays a role in science that it does not seem to play in ethics. The difference is that you need to make assumptions about certain physical facts to explain the occurrence of the observations that support a scientific theory, but you do not seem to need to make assumptions about any moral facts to explain the occurrence of the so-called moral observations I have been talking about. In the moral case, it would seem that you need only make assumptions about the psychology or moral sensibility of the person making the moral observation. In the scientific case, theory is tested against the world.

The point is subtle but important. Consider a physicist making an observation to test a scientific theory. Seeing a vapor trail in a cloud chamber, he thinks, "There goes a proton." Let us suppose that this is an observation in the relevant sense, namely, an immediate judgment made in response to the situation without any conscious reasoning having taken place. Let us also suppose that his observation confirms his theory, a theory that helps give meaning to the very term "proton" as it occurs in his observational judgment. Such a confirmation rests on inferring an explanation. He can count his making the observation as confirming evidence for his theory only to the extent that it is reasonable to explain his making the observation by assuming that, not only is he in a certain psychological "set," given the theory he accepts and his beliefs about the experimental apparatus, but furthermore, there really was a proton going through the cloud chamber, causing the vapor trail, which he saw as a proton. (This is evidence for the theory to the extent that the theory can explain the proton's being there better than competing theories can.) But, if his having made that observation could have been equally well explained by his psychological set alone, without the need for any assumption about a proton, then the observation would not have been evidence for the existence of that proton and therefore would not have been evidence for the theory. His making the observation supports the theory only because, in order to explain his making the observation, it is reasonable to assume something about the world over and above the assumptions made about the observer's psychology. In particular, it is reasonable to assume that there was a proton going through the cloud chamber, causing the vapor trail.

Compare this case with one in which you make a moral judgment immediately and without conscious reasoning, say, that the children are wrong to set the cat on fire or that the doctor would be wrong to cut up one healthy patient to save five dying patients. In order to explain your making the first of these judgments, it would be reasonable to assume, perhaps, that the children really are pouring gasoline on a cat and you are seeing them do it. But, in neither case is there any obvious reason to assume anything about "moral facts," such as that it really is wrong to set the cat on fire or to cut up the patient in Room 306. Indeed, an assumption about moral facts would seem to be totally irrelevant to the explanation of your making the judgment you make. It would seem that all we need assume is that you have certain more or less well articulated moral principles that are reflected in the judgments you make, based on your moral sensibility. It seems to be completely irrelevant to our explanation whether your intuitive immediate judgment is true or false.

The observation of an event can provide observational evidence for or against a scientific theory in the sense that the truth of that observation can be relevant to a reasonable explanation of why that observation was made. A moral observation does not seem, in the same sense, to be observational evidence for or against any moral theory, since the truth or falsity of the moral observation seems to be completely irrelevant to any reasonable explanation of why that observation was made. The fact that an observation of an event was made at the time it was made is evidence not only about the observer but also about the physical facts. The fact that you made a particular moral observation when you did does not seem to be evidence about moral facts, only evidence about you and your moral sensibility. Facts about protons can affect what you observe, since a proton passing through the cloud chamber can cause a vapor trail that reflects light to your eye in a way that, given your scientific training and psychological set, leads you to judge that what you see is a proton. But there does not seem to be any way in which the actual rightness or wrongness of a given situation can have any effect on your perceptual apparatus. In this respect, ethics seems to differ from science.

In considering whether moral principles can help explain observations, it is therefore important to note an ambiguity in the word "observation." You see the children set the cat on fire and immediately think, "That's wrong." In one sense, your observation is that what the children are doing is wrong. In another sense, your observation is your thinking that thought. Moral observations might explain observations in the first sense but not in the second sense. Certain moral principles might help to explain why it was *wrong* of the children to set the cat on fire, but moral principles seem to be of no help in explaining *your thinking* that that is wrong. In the first sense of "observation," moral principles can be tested by observation— "That this act is wrong is evidence that causing unnecessary suffering is wrong." But in the second sense of "observation," moral principles cannot clearly be tested by observation, since they do not appear to help explain observations in this second sense of "observation." Moral principles do not seem to help explain your observing what you observe.

Of course, if you are already given the moral principle that it is wrong to cause unnecessary suffering, you can take your seeing the children setting the cat on fire as observational evidence that they are doing something wrong. Similarly, you can suppose that your seeing the vapor trail is observational evidence that a proton is going through the cloud chamber, if you are given the relevant physical theory. But there is an important apparent difference between the two cases. In the scientific case, your making that observation is itself evidence for the physical theory because the physical theory explains the proton, which explains the trail, which explains your observation. In the moral case, your making your observation does not seem to be evidence for the relevant moral principle because that principle does not seem to help explain your observation. The explanatory chain from principle to observation seems to be broken in morality. The moral principle may "explain" why it is wrong for the children to set the cat on fire. But the wrongness of that act does not appear to help explain the act, which you observe, itself. The explanatory chain appears to be broken in such a way that neither the moral principle nor the wrongness of the act can help explain why you observe what you observe.

A qualification may seem to be needed here. Perhaps the children perversely set the cat on fire simply "because it is wrong." Here it may seem at first that the actual wrongness of the act does help explain why they do it and therefore indirectly helps explain why you observe what you observe just as a physical theory, by explaining why the proton is producing a vapor trail, indirectly helps explain why the observer observes what he observes. But on reflection we must agree that this is probably an illusion. What explains the children's act is not clearly the actual wrongness of the act but, rather, their belief that the act is wrong. The actual rightness or wrongness of their act seems to have nothing to do with why they do it.

Observational evidence plays a part in science it does not appear to play in ethics, because scientific principles can be justified ultimately by their role in explaining observations, in the second sense of observation—by their explanatory role. Apparently, moral principles cannot be justified in the same way. It appears to be true that there can be no explanatory chain between moral principles and particular observings in the way that there can be such a chain between scientific principles and particular observings. Conceived as an explanatory theory, morality, unlike science, seems to be cut off from observation.

Not that every legitimate scientific hypothesis is susceptible to direct observational testing. Certain hypotheses about "black holes" in space cannot be directly tested, for example, because no signal is emitted from within a black hole. The connection with observation in such a case is indirect. And there are many similar examples. Nevertheless, seen in the large, there is the apparent difference between science and ethics we have noted. The scientific realm is accessible to observation in a way the moral realm is not.

Ethics and Mathematics

Perhaps ethics is to be compared, not with physics, but with mathematics. Perhaps such a moral principle as "You ought to keep your promises" is confirmed or disconfirmed in the way (whatever it is) in which such a mathematical principle as "$5 + 7 = 12$" is. Observation does not seem to play the role in mathematics it plays in physics. We do not and cannot perceive numbers, for example, since we cannot be in causal contact with them. We do not even understand what it would be like to be in causal contact with the number 12, say. Relations among numbers cannot have any more of an effect on our perceptual apparatus than moral facts can.

Observation, however, *is* relevant to mathematics. In explaining the observations that support a physical theory, scientists typically appeal to mathematical principles. On the other hand, one never seems to need to appeal in this way to moral principles. Since an observation is evidence for what best explains it, and since mathematics often figures in the explanations of scientific observations, there is indirect observational evidence for mathematics. There does not seem to be observational evidence, even indirectly, for basic moral principles. In explaining why certain observations have been made, we never seem to use purely moral assumptions. In this respect, then, ethics appears to differ not only from physics but also from mathematics.

Gilbert Harman: Ethics and Observation

1) According to Harman, "Observations are always 'theory laden.'" What does he mean by this? Do you think he is correct?
2) Harman claims that ethics differs from science in that "you do not seem to need to make assumptions about any moral facts to explain the occurrence of the so-called moral observations." How does Harman think we can explain moral observations? Is his explanation a good one?

3) Harman says that the rightness or wrongness of actions cannot "have any effect on your perceptual apparatus." Can moral features (such as rightness or wrongness) ever cause anything? If not, is this good reason to conclude that they do not exist?

4) It might be suggested that ethics is similar to mathematics in that neither can be empirically confirmed. What is Harman's argument against this suggestion? How does our evidence for mathematical claims differ from our evidence for ethical claims?

5) Suppose that we accept Harman's assertion that ethical claims cannot be tested by observation. What should we conclude from this? Does this show that moral principles cannot be objectively true?

=== ❧ ===

17

Trying Out One's New Sword

Mary Midgley

....

In this paper, Mary Midgley argues against a popular form of relativism, according to which all moral standards are local, possessed of no universal authority or applicability. She offers her criticisms by inviting us to reflect on certain cases, and showing us that some of our deepest beliefs strongly clash with the implications of moral relativism. This does not force us to reject relativism, of course—our commonsense beliefs may have to go. But Midgley thinks that when we work our way through these cases, we will see that relativism offers no good basis for abandoning our deeply held moral convictions. As she sees things, it is moral relativism that must, in the end, be abandoned.

....

All of us are, more or less, in trouble today about trying to understand cultures strange to us. We hear constantly of alien customs. We see changes in our lifetime which would have astonished our parents. I want to discuss here one very short way of dealing with this difficulty, a drastic way which many people now theoretically favour. It consists in simply denying that we can ever understand any culture except our own well enough to make judgements about it. Those who recommend this hold that the world is sharply divided into separate societies, sealed units, each with its own system of thought. They feel that the respect and toler-ance due from one system to another forbids us ever to take up a critical position to any other culture. Moral judgement, they suggest, is a kind of coinage valid only in its country of origin.

I shall call this position "moral isolationism". I shall suggest that it is certainly not forced upon us, and indeed that it makes no sense at all. People usually take it up because they think it is a respectful attitude to other cultures. In fact, however, it is not respectful. Nobody can respect what is entirely unintelligible to them. To respect someone, we have to know enough about him to make a *favourable* judgement, however gen-eral and tentative. And we do understand people in other cultures to this extent. Otherwise a great mass of our most valuable thinking would be paralysed.

To show this, I shall take a remote example, because we shall probably find it easier to think calmly about it than we should with a contempo-rary one, such as female circumcision in Africa or the Chinese Cultural Revolution. The principles involved will still be the same. My example is this. There is, it seems, a verb in classical Japanese which means "to try out one's new sword on a chance wayfarer". (The word is *tsujigiri*, literally "crossroads-cut".) A samurai sword had to be tried out because, if it was to work properly, it had to slice through someone at a single blow, from the shoulder to the opposite flank. Otherwise, the warrior bungled his stroke. This could injure his honour, offend his ancestors, and even let down his emperor. So tests were needed, and wayfarers had to be expended. Any wayfarer would do—provided, of course, that he was not another Samurai. Scientists will recognize a familiar problem about the rights of experimen-tal subjects.

Now when we hear of a custom like this, we may well reflect that we simply do not understand it; and therefore are not qualified to criticize it at all, because we are not members of that culture. But we are not members of any other culture either, except our own. So we extend the principle to cover all extraneous cultures, and we seem therefore to be moral isolation-ists. But this is, as we shall see, an impossible position. Let us ask what it would involve.

We must ask first: Does the isolating barrier work both ways? Are people in other cultures equally unable to criticize *us*? This question struck me sharply when I read a remark in *The Guardian* by an anthropologist about a South American Indian who had been taken into a Brazilian town for an operation, which saved his life. When he came back to his village, he made several highly critical remarks about the white Brazilians' way of life. They may very well have been justified. But the interesting point was that the anthropologist called these remarks "a damning indictment of Western civilization". Now the Indian had been in that town about two weeks. Was he in a position to deliver a damning indictment? Would we ourselves be qualified to deliver such an indictment on the Samurai, provided we could spend two weeks in ancient Japan? What do we really think about this?

My own impression is that we believe that outsiders can, in principle, deliver perfectly good indictments—only, it usually takes more than two weeks to make them damning. Understanding has degrees. It is not a slap-dash yes-or-no matter. Intelligent outsiders can progress in it, and in some ways will be at an advantage over the locals. But if this is so, it must clearly apply to ourselves as much as anybody else.

Our next question is this: Does the isolating barrier between cultures block praise as well as blame? If I want to say that the Samurai culture has many virtues, or to praise the South American Indians, am I pre-vented from doing *that* by my outside status? Now, we certainly do need to praise other societies in this way. But it is hardly possible that we could praise them effectively if we could not, in principle, criticize them. Our praise would be worthless if it rested on no definite grounds, if it did not flow from some understanding. Certainly we may need to praise things which we do not *fully* understand. We say "there's something very good here, but I can't quite make out what it is yet". This happens when we want to learn from strangers. And we can learn from strangers. But to do this we have to distinguish between those strangers who are worth learning from and those who are not. Can we then judge which is which?

This brings us to our third question: What is involved in judging? Now plainly there is no question here of sitting on a bench in a red robe and sentencing people. Judging simply means forming an opinion, and express-ing it if it is called for. Is there anything wrong about this? Naturally, we ought to avoid forming—and expressing—*crude* opinions, like that of a simple-minded missionary, who might dismiss the whole Samurai culture as entirely bad, because non-Christian. But this is a different objection. The trouble with crude opinions is that they are crude, whoever forms them, not that they are formed by the wrong people. Anthropologists, after all, are outsiders quite as much as missionaries. Moral isolationism forbids us to form *any* opinions on these matters. Its ground for doing so is that we don't understand them. But there is much that we don't understand in our own culture too. This brings us to our last question: If we can't judge other cultures, can we really judge our own? Our efforts to do so will be much damaged if we are really deprived of our opinions about other societies, because these provide the range of comparison, the spectrum of alternatives against which we set what we want to understand. We would have to stop using the mirror which anthropology so helpfully holds up to us.

In short, moral isolationism would lay down a general ban on moral reasoning. Essentially, this is the programme of immoralism, and it carries a distressing logical difficulty. Immoralists like Nietzsche are actually just a rather specialized sect of moralists. They can no more afford to put moralizing out of business than smugglers can afford to abolish customs regulations. The power of moral judgement is, in fact, not a luxury, not a perverse indulgence of the self-righteous. It is a necessity. When we judge something to be bad or good, better or worse than something else, we are taking it as an example to aim at or avoid. Without opinions of this sort, we would have no framework of comparison for our own policy, no chance of profiting by other people's insights or mistakes. In this vacuum, we could form no judgements on our own actions.

Now it would be odd if Homo sapiens had really got himself into a position as bad as this—a position where his main evolutionary asset, his brain, was so little use to him. None of us is going to accept this sceptical diagnosis. We cannot do so, because our involvement in moral isolationism does not flow from apathy, but from a rather acute concern about human hypocrisy and other forms of wickedness. But we polarize that concern around a few selected moral truths. We are rightly angry with those who despise, oppress or steamroll other cultures. We think that doing these things is actually *wrong*. But this is itself a moral judgement. We could not condemn oppression and insolence if we thought that all our condemnation were just a trivial local quirk of our own culture. We could still less do it if we tried to stop judging altogether.

Real moral scepticism, in fact, could lead only to inaction, to our losing all interest in moral questions, most of all in those which concern other societies. When we discus these things, it becomes instantly clear how far we are from doing this. Suppose, for instance, that I criticize the bisecting Samurai, that I say his behaviour is brutal. What will usually happen next is that someone will protest, will say that I have no right to make criticisms like that of another culture. But it is most unlikely that he will use this move to end the discussion of the subject. Instead, he will justify the Samurai. He will try to fill in the background, to make me understand the custom, by explaining the exalted ideals of discipline and devotion which produced it. He will probably talk of the lower value which the ancient Japanese placed on individual life generally. He may well suggest that this is a healthier attitude than our own obsession with security. He may add, too, that the wayfarers did not seriously mind being bisected, that in principle they accepted the whole arrangement.

Now an objector who talks like this is implying that it *is* possible to understand alien customs. That is just what he is trying to make me do. And he implies, too, that if I do succeed in understanding them, I shall do something better than giving up judging them. He expects me to change my present judgement to a truer one—namely, one that is favourable. And the standards I must use to do this cannot just be Samurai standards. They have to be ones current in my own culture. Ideals like discipline and devotion will not move anybody unless he himself accepts them. As it happens, neither discipline nor devotion is very popular in the West at present. Anyone who appeals to them may well have to do some more arguing to make *them* acceptable, before he can use them to explain the Samurai. But if he does succeed here, he will have persuaded us, not just that there was something to be said for them in ancient Japan, but that there would be here as well.

Isolating barriers simply cannot arise here. If we accept something as a serious moral truth about one culture, we can't refuse to apply it—in however different an outward form—to other cultures as well, wherever circumstances admit it. If we refuse to do this, we just are not taking the other culture seriously. This becomes clear if we look at the last argument used by my objector—that of justification by consent of the victim. It is suggested that sudden bisection is quite in order, *provided* that it takes place between consenting adults. I cannot now discuss how conclusive this justification is. What I am pointing out is simply that it can only work if we believe that *consent* can make such a transaction respectable—and this is a thoroughly modern and Western idea. It would probably never occur to a Samurai; if it did, it would surprise him very much. It is *our* standard. In applying it, too, we are likely to make another typically Western demand. We shall ask for good factual evidence that the wayfarers actually do have this rather surprising taste—that they are really willing to be bisected. In applying Western standards in this way, we are not being confused or irrelevant. We are asking the questions which arise *from where we stand*, questions which we can see the sense of. We do this because asking questions which you can't see the sense of is humbug. Certainly we can extend our questioning by imaginative effort. We can come to understand other societies better. By doing so, we may make their questions our own, or we may see that they are really forms of the questions which we are asking already. This is not impossible. It is just very hard work. The obstacles which often prevent it are simply those of ordinary ignorance, laziness and prejudice.

If there were really an isolating barrier, of course, our own culture could never have been formed. It is no sealed box, but a fertile jungle of different influences—Greek, Jewish, Roman, Norse, Celtic and so forth, into which further influences are still pouring—American, Indian, Japanese, Jamaican, you name it. The moral isolationist's picture of separate unmixable cultures is quite unreal. People who talk about British history usually stress the value of this fertilizing mix, no doubt rightly. But this is not just an odd fact about Britain. Except for the very smallest and most remote, all cultures are formed out of many streams. All have the problem of digesting and assimilating things which, at the start, they do not understand. All have the choice of learning something from this challenge, or, alternatively, of refusing to learn, and fighting it mindlessly instead.

This universal predicament has been obscured by the fact that anthropologists used to concentrate largely on very small and remote cultures, which did not seem to have this problem. These tiny societies, which had often forgotten their own history, made neat, self-contained subjects for study. No doubt it was valuable to emphasize their remoteness, their extreme strangeness, their independence of our cultural tradition. This emphasis was, I think, the root of moral isolationism. But, as the tribal studies themselves showed, even there the anthropologists were able to interpret what they saw and make judgements—often favourable—about the tribesmen. And the tribesmen, too, were quite equal to making judgements about the anthropologists—and about the tourists and Coca-Cola salesmen who followed them. Both sets of judgements, no doubt, were somewhat hasty, both have been refined in the light of further experience. A similar transaction between us and the Samurai might take even longer. But that is no reason at all for deeming it impossible. Morally as well as physically, there is only one world, and we all have to live in it.

Mary Midgley: Trying Out One's New Sword

1) What does Midgley mean by "moral isolationism"? Do you think moral isolationism is a widely held view in our society today?

2) How does Midgley argue for her claim that "moral isolationism would lay down a general ban on moral reasoning"? Do you think she is right about this?

3) What "logical difficulty" does Midgley think moral isolationism faces? Can the moral isolationist respond convincingly to this difficulty?

4) Moral isolationism is often motivated by the thought that we should be tolerant and respectful of other cultures. Yet Midgley argues that these concerns actually require us to *reject* moral isolationism. What are her reasons for thinking this? Are they good ones?

5) At the end of her essay, Midgley mentions that our culture today has been influenced by many different cultural traditions. What problems does this raise for moral isolationism?

18

Realism

Michael Smith

....

Michael Smith presents the outlines of a view known to philosophers as *moral realism*. Realism claims that moral judgments can be true independently of what anyone happens to believe of them. Smith endorses this conception of morality, but recognizes that there are many objections to be answered. One of the most important of these is based on the idea that moral facts must somehow be able to motivate us, in part by providing us reasons for action. And yet how we are motivated, and what reasons we have, seem to be subjective, not objective, matters. Our motives and reasons seem to depend on what we care about—and yet the content of morality, if it really is objective, is not going to depend on what we want.

Smith seeks to show that the objectivity of morality is compatible with these motivational and reason-giving requirements. He does this by defending the view that moral duties are those that we would all agree to, were we each fully informed and perfectly rational. Moral rules originate in agreement that stems from judgments made from an ideal perspective.

If Smith is correct, then morality is objective—its standards are those that ideal judges would agree on. We can each be mistaken about our moral duty, because we can fail to have all the needed information to make a decision, or fail to be fully rational (or both). And moral duties will supply us with reasons for action, even if we don't care about

---

Michael Smith, "Realism" from *Ethics* (1994), ed. Peter Singer, pp. 170–176. By permission of Oxford University Press, Inc.

doing our duty. They supply us with such reasons because our more enlightened selves would endorse these duties, and we have reason to follow the advice of our fully informed, perfectly rational counterparts. And we will be moved to do our duty, provided that we are rational. Someone who is rational will act on the best reasons that apply to her, and these, says Smith, are moral reasons that stem from what we would agree to if were judging things from the best possible vantage point. In this way, Smith offers an account of morality that can explain why it is objective, why it provides us reason to obey it, and why it will motivate rational people.

....

Most of us take moral appraisal pretty much for granted. To the extent that we worry, we simply worry about *getting it right*. Philosophers too worry about getting the answers to moral questions right. However, traditionally, they have also been worried about the whole business of moral appraisal itself. The problem they have grappled with emerges when we focus on two distinctive features of moral practice; for, surprisingly, these features pull against each other, threatening to make the very idea of morality look altogether incoherent.

The first feature is implicit in our concern to get the answers to moral questions *right*, for this concern presupposes that there are correct answers to moral questions to be had, and thus that there exists a domain of distinctively *moral* facts. Moreover, we seem to think that these facts have a particular character, for the only relevant determinant of the rightness of an act would seem to be the circumstances in which that action takes place. Agents whose circumstances are identical face the same moral choice: if they perform the same act then either they both act rightly or they both act wrongly.

Something like this conception of moral facts seems to explain our pre-occupation with moral argument. Since we are all in the same boat, so, it seems, we think that a conversation in which agents carefully muster and assess each other's reasons for and against their moral opinions is the best way to discover what the moral facts are. If the participants are open-minded and thinking clearly then we seem to think that such an argument should result in a *convergence* in moral opinion—a convergence upon the truth.

We may summarise this first feature of moral practice as follows: we seem to think that moral questions have correct answers, that these answers are made correct by objective moral facts, that these facts are determined by circumstances, and that, by arguing, we can discover what these facts are. The term "objective" here simply signifies the possibility of a convergence in moral views of the kind just mentioned.

Consider now the second feature. Suppose we reflect and decide that we did the wrong thing in (say) refusing to give to famine relief. It seems we come to think we failed to do something for which there was a good reason. And this has motivational implications. For now imagine the situation if we refuse again when next the opportunity arises. We will have refused to do what we think we have good reason to do, and this will occasion serious puzzlement. An explanation of some sort will need to be forthcoming (perhaps weakness of will or irrationality of some other kind). Why? Because, other things being equal, having a moral opinion seems to require having a corresponding reason, and therefore motivation, to act accordingly.

These two distinctive features of moral practice—the *objectivity* and the *practicality* of moral judgement—are widely thought to have both metaphysical and psychological implications. However, and unfortunately, these implications are the exact opposite of each other. In order to see why, we need to pause for a moment to reflect on the nature of human psychology.

According to the standard picture of human psychology—a picture we owe to David Hume—there are two main kinds of psychological state. On the one hand there are beliefs, states that purport to represent the way the world is. Since our beliefs purport to represent the world, they are subject to rational criticism: specifically, they are assessable in terms of truth and falsehood. And on the other hand there are also desires, states that represent how the world is to be. Desires are unlike beliefs in that they do not even purport to represent the way the world is. They are therefore not assessable in terms of truth and falsehood. Indeed, according to the standard picture, our desires are not subject to any sort of rational criticism at all. The fact that we have a certain desire is, with a proviso to be mentioned presently, simply a fact about ourselves to be acknowledged. In themselves, desires are all on a par, rationally neutral.

This is important, for it suggests that though facts about the world may rightly affect our beliefs, such facts should, again with a proviso to be mentioned presently, have no rational impact upon our desires. They may of course, have some *non*-rational impact. Seeing a spider, I may be overcome with a morbid fear and desire never to be near one. However this is not a change in my desires mandated by reason. It is a *non*-rational change in my desires.

Now for the proviso. Suppose, contrary to the example just given, I acquire an aversion to spiders because I come to believe, falsely, that they have an unpleasant odour. This is certainly an irrational aversion. However, this is not contrary to the spirit of the standard picture. For my aversion is *based on* a further desire and belief: my desire not to smell that unpleasant odour and my belief that that odour is given off by spiders. Since I can be rationally criticised for having the belief, as it is false, so I can be rationally criticised for having the aversion it helps to produce. The proviso is thus fairly minor: desires are subject to rational criticism, but only insofar as they are based on irrational beliefs. Desires that do not have this feature are not subject to rational criticism at all.

According to the standard picture, then, there are two kinds of psychological state—beliefs and desires—utterly distinct and different from each other. This picture is important because it provides us with a model for understanding human action. A human action is the product of these two forces: a desire representing the way the world is to be and a belief telling us how the world is, and thus how it has to be changed, so as to make it that way.

We said earlier that the objectivity and the practicality of moral judgement have both metaphysical and psychological implications. We can now say what they are. Consider first the objectivity of moral judgement: the idea that there are moral facts, determined by circumstances, and that, by arguing, we can discover what these objective moral facts are. This implies, metaphysically, that amongst the various facts there are in the world there aren't just facts about (say) the consequences of our actions on the well-being of sentient creatures, there are also distinctively *moral* facts: facts about the rightness and wrongness of our actions having these consequences. And, psychologically, the implication is thus that when we make a moral judgement we express our *beliefs* about the way these moral facts are. Our moral beliefs are representations of the way the world is *morally*.

Given the standard picture of human psychology, there is a further psychological implication. For whether or not people who have a certain moral belief desire to act accordingly must now be seen as a further and entirely separate question. They may happen to have a corresponding desire, they may not. However, either way, they cannot be rationally criticised.

But now consider the second feature, the practicality of moral judgement, the idea that to have a moral opinion simply *is*, contrary to what has just been said, to have a corresponding reason, and thus motivation, to act accordingly. Psychologically, since making a moral judgement entails having a certain desire, and no recognition of a fact about the world could rationally compel us to have one desire rather than another, this seems to imply that our judgement must really simply *be* an expression of that desire. And this psychological implication has a metaphysical counterpart. For, contrary to initial appearance, it seems that when we judge it right to give to famine relief (say), we *are not* responding to any moral fact. In judging it right to give to famine relief, we are really simply expressing our desire that people give to famine relief. It is as if we were yelling "Hooray for giving to famine relief!"—no mention of a moral fact there, in fact, no factual claim at all.

We are now in a position to see why philosophers have been worried about the whole business of moral appraisal. The problem is that the *objectivity* and the *practicality* of moral judgement pull in quite opposite directions from each other. The objectivity of moral judgement suggests that there are moral facts, determined by circumstances, and that our moral judgements express our beliefs about what these facts are. But though this is presupposed by moral argument, it leaves it entirely mysterious how or why having a moral view has special links with what we are motivated to do. And the practicality of moral judgement suggests just the opposite, that our moral judgements express our desires. While this seems presupposed in the link between moral judgement and motivation, it leaves it entirely mysterious how or why moral judgements can be the subject of moral argument.

The very idea of morality may therefore be incoherent, for what is required to make sense of a moral judgement is a queer sort of fact about the universe: a fact whose recognition necessarily impacts upon our desires. But the standard picture of human psychology tells us that there are no such facts. Nothing could be everything a moral judgement purports to be—or so the standard picture tells us.

At long last we are in a position to see what this essay is about. For *moral realism* is simply the metaphysical view that there exist moral facts. The psychological counterpart to realism is cognitivism, the view that moral judgements express our beliefs about what these moral facts are.

Moral realism thus contrasts with two alternative metaphysical views: *irrealism* and *moral nihilism*. According to the irrealists, there are no moral facts, but neither are moral facts required to make sense of moral practice. We can happily acknowledge that our moral judgements simply express our desires about how people behave. This is non-cognitivism, the psychological counterpart to irrealism. By contrast, according to the moral nihilists, the irrealists are right that there are no moral facts, but wrong about what is required to make sense of moral practice. Without moral facts moral practice is all a sham, much like religious practice without belief in God.

Which, then, should we believe: realism, irrealism or nihilism? I favour realism. Let me say why. We have assumed from the outset that judgements of right and wrong are judgements about our reasons for action. But though these judgements seem to concern a realm of facts about our reasons, what casts doubt on this is the standard picture of human psychology. For it tells us that, since judgements about our reasons have motivational implications, so they must really simply be expressions of our desires. It seems to me that here we see the real devil of the piece: the standard picture of human psychology's tacit conflation of *reasons* with *motives*. Seeing why this is so enables us to see why we may legitimately talk about our *beliefs* about the reasons we have, and why having such beliefs makes it rational to have corresponding desires; why such beliefs have motivational implications.

Imagine giving the baby a bath. As you do, it begins to scream uncontrollably. Nothing you do seems to help. As you watch, you are overcome with a desire to drown it in the bathwater. You are *motivated* to drown the baby. Does this entail that you have a *reason* to drown the baby? Commonsense tells us that, since this desire is not *worth* satisfying, it does not provide you with such a reason; that, in this case, you are motivated to do something you have *no* reason to do. But can the standard picture agree with commonsense on this score? No, it cannot. For your desire to drown the baby need be based on no false belief, and, as such, the standard picture tells us it is beyond rational criticism. There is no sense in which it is not worth satisfying—or so the standard picture tells us. But this is surely wrong.

The problem is that the standard picture gives no special privilege to what we would want if we were 'cool, calm, and collected'. Yet commonsense tells us that not being cool, calm, and collected may lead to all sorts of irrational emotional outbursts. Having those desires that we would have if we were cool, calm, and collected thus seems to be an *independent* rational ideal. When cool, calm, and collected, you would want that the baby isn't drowned, no matter how much it screams, and no matter how overcome you may be, in your uncool, uncalm, and uncollected state, with a desire to drown it. This is why you have no reason to drown the baby. It seems to me that this insight is the key to reconciling the objectivity with the practicality of moral judgement.

Judgements of right and wrong express our beliefs about our reasons. But what sort of fact is a fact about our reasons? The preceding discussion suggests that they are not facts about what we *actually* desire, as the standard picture would have it, but are rather facts about what we *would* desire if we were in certain idealised conditions of reflection: if, say, we were well informed, cool, calm, and collected.

According to this account, then, I have a reason to give to famine relief in my particular circumstances just in case, if I were in such idealised conditions of reflection, I would desire that, even when in my particular circumstances, I give to famine relief. Now this sort of fact may certainly be the object of a belief. And moreover having such a belief—a belief about our reasons—certainly seems to rationally require of us that we have corresponding desires.

In order to see this, suppose I believe I would desire to give to famine relief if I were cool, calm, and collected but, being uncool, uncalm, and uncollected, I don't desire to give to famine relief. Am I rationally criticizable for not having the desire? I surely am. After all, from my own point of view my beliefs and desires form a more coherent, and thus a rationally preferable, package if I do in fact desire what I believe I would desire if I were cool, calm, and collected. This is because, since it is an independent rational ideal to have the desires I would have if I were cool, calm, and collected so, from my own point of view, if I believe that I would have a certain desire under such conditions and yet fail to have it, my beliefs and desires fail to meet this ideal. To believe that I would desire to give to famine relief if I were cool, calm, and collected and yet fail to desire to give to famine relief is thus to manifest a commonly recognizable species of rational failure.

If this is right then, contrary to the standard picture, a broader class of desires may be rationally criticized. The desires of those who fail to desire to do what they believe they have reason to do can be rationally criticized even though they may not be based on any false belief. And, if this is right, then the standard picture is wrong to suggest that a judgement with motivational implications must really be the expression of a desire. For a judgement about an agent's reasons has motivational implications— the rational agent is motivated accordingly—and yet it is the expression of a belief.

Have we said enough to solve the problem facing the moral realist? Not yet. Moral judgements aren't *just* judgements about the reasons we have. They are judgements about the reasons we have *where those reasons are determined entirely by our circumstances*. People in the same circumstances face the same moral choice: if they do the same then either they both act rightly (they both do what they have reason to do) or they both act wrongly (they both do what they have reason not to do). Does the account of reasons we have given support this?

Suppose our circumstances are identical. Is it right for each of us to give to famine relief? According to the story just told, it is right that I give to famine relief just in case I have a reason to do so, and I have such a reason just in case, if I were in idealised conditions of reflection—well informed, cool, calm, and collected—I would desire to give to famine relief. And the same is true of you. If our circumstances are the same then, supposedly, we should both have such a reason or both lack such a reason. But do we?

The question is whether, if we were well informed, cool, calm, and collected, we would all *converge* in the desires we have. Would we converge or would there always be the possibility of some non-rationally-explicable difference in our desires *even under such conditions*? The standard picture of human psychology now returns to center-stage. For it tells us that there is always the possibility of some non-rationally-explicable difference in our desires *even under such idealised conditions of reflection*. This is the residue of the standard picture's conception of desire as a psychological state that is beyond rational criticism.

If there is such a possibility then the realist's attempt to reconcile the objectivity and the practicality of moral judgement simply fails. For we are forced to accept that there is a *fundamental relativity* in the reasons we have. What we have reason to do is relative to what we would desire under idealised conditions of reflection, and this may differ from person to person. It is not wholly determined by our circumstances, as moral facts are supposed to be.

Many philosophers believe that there is always such a possibility; that our reasons are fundamentally relative. But this seems unwarranted to me. For it seems to me that moral practice is itself the forum in which we will *discover* whether there is a fundamental relativity in our reasons.

After all, in moral practice we attempt to change people's moral beliefs by engaging them in rational argument: i.e. by getting their beliefs to approximate those they would have under more idealised conditions of reflection. And sometimes we succeed. When we succeed, other things being equal, we succeed in changing their desires. How, then, can we say in advance that this procedure will never result in a massive *convergence* in moral beliefs? And, if it did result in a massive convergence in our moral beliefs—and thus in our desires—then why not say that this convergence would itself be best explained by the fact that the beliefs and desires that emerge have some *privileged* rational status? Something like such a convergence on certain mathematical judgements in mathematical practice lies behind our conviction that those claims enjoy a privileged rational status. So why not think that a like convergence in moral practice would show that those moral judgements and concerns enjoy the same privileged rational status? At this point, the standard picture's insistence that there is a fundamental relativity in our reasons begins to sound all too much like a hollow dogma.

The kind of moral realism described here endorses a conception of moral facts that is a far cry from the picture noted at the outset: moral facts as queer facts about the universe whose recognition necessarily impacts upon our desires. The realist has eschewed queer facts about the universe in favour of a more 'subjectivist' conception of moral facts. The realist's point, however, is that such a conception of moral facts may make them subjective only in the innocuous sense that they are facts about our reasons: i.e. facts about what we would *want* under certain idealised conditions of reflection. For wants are, admittedly, states enjoyed by subjects. But moral facts remain objective insofar as they are facts about what *we*, not just *you* or *I*, would want under such conditions. The existence of a moral fact—say, the rightness of giving to famine relief in certain circumstances—requires that, under idealised conditions of reflection, rational creatures would *converge* upon a desire to give to famine relief in such circumstances.

Of course, it must be said that moral argument has not yet produced the sort of convergence in our desires that would make the idea of a moral fact—a fact about the reasons we have entirely determined by our circumstances—look plausible. But neither has moral argument had much of a history in times in which we can engage in free reflection unhampered by a false biology (the Aristotelian tradition) or a false belief in God (the Judeo-Christian tradition). It remains to be seen whether sustained moral argument can elicit the requisite convergence in our moral beliefs, and corresponding desires, to make the idea of a moral fact look plausible. The kind of moral realism described here holds out the hope that it will. Only time will tell.

Michael Smith: Realism

1) Smith claims that "objectivity" is "a distinctive feature of moral practice." What exactly does he mean by *objectivity*? Do you agree that it is a standard feature of everyday moral practice?

2) Smith says that "practicality" is a second distinctive feature of morality. What does he mean by *practicality*? Do you agree that this is also a standard feature of moral practice?

3) According to the "standard picture of human psychology" Smith presents, desires cannot be rationally criticized, with one exception. What is the exception? Allowing for this exception, does this picture of human psychology seem correct?

4) Smith suggests that "the very idea of morality may be incoherent," because morality seems to involve believing in "a queer sort of fact." What sort of fact is Smith referring to? Is this sort of fact so strange that we should deny its existence?

5) What are the differences between the three metaphysical views Smith presents: moral realism, irrealism, and moral nihilism? Which view do you think is most plausible, and why?

6) Smith thinks it is important to distinguish between *motives* and *reasons*. What does he think is the difference between the two? Do you find his account of reasons convincing? Why or why not?

7) According to Smith's theory, moral facts exist only if we would all have the same desires in ideal conditions. Why does Smith's theory require this convergence? Is it plausible to think that we would converge in this way?

19

Proof

Renford Bambrough

....

In this excerpt from his book *Moral Scepticism and Moral Knowledge*
(1979), Renford Bambrough (1926–1999) tries to undermine the
most common arguments aimed at showing that we can never have
moral knowledge. He also offers a positive argument designed to vin-
dicate the existence of moral knowledge.

Bambrough's positive argument is quite simple. We know that a
child about to undergo a very painful operation ought to be given an
anesthetic. Therefore, as Bambrough sees it, we have at least one piece
of moral knowledge. And of course we have many others—cases in
which we can't help but believe that certain actions would be morally
required, or morally forbidden.

Bambrough then considers some classic objections to the possibility of moral knowledge. Four of these deserve special mention.
First, moral disagreement appears to be far greater than scientific disagreement, and this discrepancy is to be explained by the (alleged) fact
that morality is not objective, and so cannot yield moral knowledge.
The second objection is that our moral opinions are simply products of our environment and upbringing, and thus cannot be reliable.
The third is that moral claims are not statements of fact, but rather
expressions of feelings, and so cannot be true, and therefore cannot be
known. The last is that there are no recognized methods for resolving

---

moral disputes, and the absence of such methods prevents us from gaining moral knowledge. Bambrough argues that each of these objections is mistaken.

....

I t is well known that recent philosophy, under the leadership of Moore and Wittgenstein, has defended common sense and common language against what seem to many contemporary philosophers to be the paradoxes, the obscurities and the mystifications of earlier metaphysical philosophers. The spirit of this work is shown by the titles of two of the most famous of Moore's papers: 'A Defence of Common Sense' and 'Proof of an External World'. It can be more fully but still briefly described by saying something about Moore's defence of the commonsense belief that there are external material objects. His proof of an external world consists essentially in holding up his hands and saying, 'Here are two hands; therefore there are at least two material objects.' He argues that no proposition that could plausibly be alleged as a reason in favour of doubting the truth of the proposition that I have two hands can possibly be more certainly true than that proposition itself. If a philosopher produces an argument against my claim to *know* that I have two hands, I can therefore be sure in advance that *either* at least one of the premises of argument is false, *or* there is a mistake in the reasoning by which he purports to derive from his premises the conclusion that I do not know that I have two hands.

Many contemporary philosophers accept Moore's proof of an external world. Many contemporary philosophers reject the claim that we have moral knowledge. There are some contemporary philosophers who both accept Moore's proof of an external world and reject the claim that we have moral knowledge. The position of these philosophers is self-contradictory. If we can show by Moore's argument that there is an external world, then we can show *by parity of reasoning*, by an exactly analogous argument, that we have moral knowledge, that there are some propositions of morals which are *certainly* true, and which we *know* to be true.

My proof that we have moral knowledge consists essentially in saying, 'We know that this child, who is about to undergo what would otherwise be painful surgery, should be given an anaesthetic before the operation. Therefore we know at least one moral proposition to be true.' I argue that no proposition that could plausibly be alleged as a reason in favour of doubting the truth of the proposition that the child should be given an anaesthetic can possibly be more certainly true than that proposition itself. If a philosopher produces an argument against my claim to *know* that the child should be given an anaesthetic, I can therefore be sure in advance that *either* at least one of the premises of his argument is false, *or* there is a mistake in the reasoning by which he purports to derive from his premises the conclusion that I do not know that the child should be given an anaesthetic.

When Moore proves that there is an external world he is defending a commonsense belief. When I prove that we have moral knowledge I am defending a commonsense belief. The contemporary philosophers who both accept Moore's proof of an external world and reject the claim that we have moral knowledge defend common sense in one field and attack common sense in another field. They hold fast to common sense when they speak of our knowledge of the external world, and depart from common sense when they speak of morality.

The commonsense view is that we *know* that stealing is wrong, that promise-keeping is right, that unselfishness is good, that cruelty is bad. Common language uses in moral contexts the whole range of expressions that it also uses in non-moral contexts when it is concerned with knowledge and ignorance, truth and falsehood, reason and unreason, questions and answers. We speak as naturally of a child's not knowing the difference between right and wrong as we do of his not knowing the difference between right and left. We say that we do not know what to do as naturally as we say that we do not know what is the case. We say that a man's moral views are unreasonable as naturally as we say that his views on a matter of fact are unreasonable. In moral contexts, just as naturally as in non-moral contexts, we speak of thinking, wondering, asking; of beliefs, opinions, convictions, arguments, conclusions; of dilemmas, problems, solutions; of perplexity, confusion, consistency and inconsistency, of errors and mistakes, of teaching, learning, training, showing, proving, finding out, understanding, realising, recognising and coming to see.

Those who reject the commonsense account of moral knowledge, like those who reject the commonsense account of our knowledge of the external world, do of course offer arguments in favour of their rejection. In both cases those who reject the commonsense account offer very much the same arguments whether or not they recognise that the account they are rejecting is in fact the commonsense account. If we now look at the arguments that can be offered against the commonsense account of moral knowledge we shall be able to see whether they are sufficiently similar to the arguments that can be offered against the commonsense account of our knowledge of the external world to enable us to sustain our charge of inconsistency against a philosopher who attacks common sense in one field and defends it in the other. (We may note in passing that many philosophers in the past have committed the converse form of the same *prima facie* inconsistency: they have rejected the commonsense account of our knowledge of the external world but have accepted the commonsense account of moral knowledge.)

'Moral disagreement is more widespread, more radical and more persistent than disagreement about matters of fact.'

I have two main comments to make on this suggestion: the first is that it is almost certainly untrue, and the second is that it is quite certainly irrelevant.

The objection loses much of its plausibility as soon as we insist on comparing the comparable. We are usually invited to contrast our admirably close agreement that there is a glass of water on the table with the depth, vigour and tenacity of our disagreements about capital punishment, abortion, birth control and nuclear disarmament. But this game may be played by two or more players. A sufficient reply in kind is to contrast our general agreement that this child should have an anaesthetic with the strength and warmth of the disagreements between cosmologists and radio astronomers about the interpretation of certain radioastronomical observations. If the moral sceptic then reminds us of Christian Science we can offer him in exchange the Flat Earth Society.

But this is a side issue. Even if it is true that moral disagreement is more acute and more persistent than other forms of disagreement, it does not follow that moral knowledge is impossible. However long and violent a dispute may be, and however few or many heads may be counted on this side or on that, it remains possible that one party to the dispute is right and the others wrong. Galileo was right when he contradicted the cardinals; and so was Wilberforce when he rebuked the slave-owners.

There is a more direct and decisive way of showing the irrelevance of the argument from persistent disagreement. The question of whether a given type of enquiry is objective is the question whether it is *logically capable* of reaching knowledge, and is therefore an *a priori*, logical question. The question of how much agreement or disagreement there is between those who actually engage in that enquiry is a question of psychological or sociological fact. It follows that the question about the actual extent of agreement or disagreement has no bearing on the question of the objectivity of the enquiry. If this were not so, the objectivity of every enquiry might wax and wane through the centuries as men become more or less disputatious or more or less proficient in the arts of persuasion.

'Our moral opinions are conditioned by our environment and upbringing.'

It is under this heading that we are reminded of the variegated customs and beliefs of Hottentots, Eskimos, Polynesians and American Indians, which do indeed differ widely from each other and from our own. But this objection is really a special case of the general argument from disagreement, and it can be answered on the same lines. The beliefs of the Hottentots and the Polynesians about straightforwardly factual matters differ widely from our own, but that does not tempt us to say that science is subjective. It is true that most of those who are born and bred in the stately homes of England have a different outlook on life from that of the Welsh miner or the Highland crofter, but it is also true that all these classes of people differ widely in their factual beliefs, and not least in their factual beliefs about themselves and each other.

The moral sceptic's favourite examples are often presented as though they settled the issue beyond further argument.

(1) Herodotus reports that within the Persian Empire there were some tribes that buried their dead and some that burned them. Each group thought that the other's practice was barbarous. But (a) they agreed that respect must be shown to the dead; (b) they lived under very different climatic conditions; (c) we can now see that they were guilty of moral myopia in setting such store by what happened, for good or bad reasons, to be their own particular practice. Moral progress in this field has consisted in coming to recognise that burying-versus-burning is not an issue on which it is necessary for the whole of mankind to have a single, fixed, universal standpoint, regardless of variations of conditions in time and place.

(2) Some societies practice polygamous marriage. Others favour monogamy. Here again there need be no absolute and unvarying rule. In societies where women heavily outnumber men, institutions may be appropriate which would be out of place in societies where the numbers of men and women are roughly equal. The moralist who insists that monogamy

is right, regardless of circumstances, is like the inhabitant of the Northern Hemisphere who insists that it is always and everywhere cold at Christmas, or the inhabitant of the Southern Hemisphere who cannot believe that it is ever or anywhere cold at Christmas.

(3) Some societies do not disapprove of what we condemn as 'stealing'. In such societies, anybody may take from anybody else's house anything he may need or want. This case serves further to illustrate that circumstances objectively alter cases, that relativity is not only compatible with, but actually required by, the objective and rational determination of questions of right and wrong. I can maintain that Bill Sykes is a rogue, and that prudence requires me to lock all my doors and windows against him, without being committed to holding that if an Eskimo takes whalemeat from the unlocked igloo of another Eskimo, then one of them is a knave and the other a fool. It is not that we disapprove of stealing and that the Eskimos do not, but that their circumstances differ so much from ours as to call for new consideration and a different judgement, which may be that in their situation stealing is innocent, or that in their situation there is no private property and therefore no possibility of *stealing* at all.

(4) Some tribes leave their elderly and useless members to die in the forest. Others, including our own, provide old-age pensions and geriatric hospitals. But we should have to reconsider our arrangements if we found that the care of the aged involved for us the consequences that it might involve for a nomadic and pastoral people: general starvation because the old could not keep pace with the necessary movement to new pastures; children and domestic animals a prey to wild beasts; a life burdensome to all and destined to end with the early extinction of the tribe.

'When I say that something is good or bad or right or wrong I commit myself, and reveal something of my attitudes and feelings.'

This is quite true, but it is equally and analogously true that when I say that something is true or false, or even that something is red or round, I also commit myself and reveal something of my *beliefs*. Emotivist and imperativist philosophers have sometimes failed to draw a clear enough distinction between what is said or meant by a particular form of expression and what is implied or suggested by it, and even those who have distinguished clearly and correctly between meaning and implication in the case of moral propositions have often failed to see that exactly the same distinction can be drawn in the case of non-moral propositions. If I say 'this is good' and then add 'but I do not approve of it', I certainly behave oddly enough to owe you an explanation; but I behave equally oddly and owe you a comparable explanation if I say 'that is true, but I don't believe it.' If it is held that I contradict myself in the first case, it must be allowed that I contradict myself in the second case. If it is claimed that I do not contradict myself in the second case, then it must be allowed that I do not contradict myself in the first case. If this point can be used as an argument against the objectivity of morals, then it can also be used as an argument against the objectivity of science, logic, and of every other branch of enquiry.

The parallel between *approve* and *believe* and between *good* and *true* is so close that it provides a useful test of the paradoxes of subjectivism and emotivism. The emotivist puts the cart before the horse in trying to explain goodness in terms of approval, just as he would if he tried to explain truth in terms of belief. Belief cannot be explained without introducing the notion of truth, and approval cannot be explained without introducing the notion of goodness. To believe is (roughly) to hold to be true, and to approve is (equally roughly) to hold to be good. Hence it is as unsatisfactory to try to reduce goodness to approval, or to approval plus some other component, as it would be to try to reduce truth to belief, or to belief plus some other component.

If we are to give a correct account of the logical character of morality we must preserve the distinction between appearance and reality, between seeming and really being, that we clearly and admittedly have to preserve if we are to give a correct account of truth and belief. Just as we do and must hope that what we believe (what seems to us to be true) is in fact true, so we must hope that what we approve (what seems to us to be good) is in fact good.

I can say of another, 'He thinks it is raining, but it is not,' and of myself, 'I thought it was raining, but it was not.' I can also say of another, 'He thinks it is good, but it is not,' and of myself, 'I thought it was good, but it was not.'

'A dispute which is purely moral is inconclusive in principle. The specifically moral element in moral disputes is one which cannot be resolved by investigation and reflection.'

This objection brings into the open an assumption that is made at least implicitly by most of those who use Hume's remark as a subjectivist weapon: the assumption that whatever is a logical or factual dispute, or a mixture of logical and factual disputes, is necessarily *not* a moral dispute; that nothing is a moral dispute unless it is *purely* moral in the sense that it is a dispute between parties who agree on *all* the relevant factual and logical questions. But the *purely moral* dispute envisaged by this assumption is a pure fiction. The search for the 'specifically moral element' in moral disputes is a wild-goose chase, and is the result of the initial confusion of supposing that no feature of moral reasoning is *really* a feature of moral reasoning, or is *characteristic* of moral reasoning, unless it is peculiar to moral reasoning. It is as if one insisted that a ginger cake could be fully characterised, and could only be characterised, by saying that there is ginger in it. It is true that ginger is the peculiar ingredient of a ginger cake as contrasted with other cakes, but no cake can be made entirely of ginger, and the ingredients that are combined with ginger to make ginger cakes are the same as those that are combined with chocolate, lemon, orange or vanilla to make other kinds of cakes; and ginger itself, when combined with other ingredients and treated in other ways, goes into the making of ginger puddings, ginger biscuits and ginger beer.

To the question 'What is the place of reason in ethics?' why should we not answer: 'The place of reason in ethics is exactly what it is in other enquiries, to enable us to find out the relevant facts and to make our judgements mutually consistent, to expose factual errors and detect logical inconsistencies'? This might seem to imply that there are some moral judgements which will serve as starting points for any moral enquiry, and will not themselves be proved, as others may be proved by being derived from them or disproved by being shown to be incompatible with them, and also to imply that we cannot engage in moral argument with a man with whom we agree on *no* moral question. In so far as these implications are correct they apply to all enquiry, and not only to moral enquiry; and they do not, when correctly construed, constitute any objection to the rationality and objectivity of morality or of any other mode of enquiry. They seem to make difficulties for moral objectivity only when they are associated with a picture of rationality which, though it has always been powerful in the minds of philosophers, can be shown to be an unacceptable caricature.

Here again the moral sceptic is partial and selective in his use of an argument of indefinitely wide scope: if it were true that a man must accept unprovable moral premises before I could prove to him that there is such a thing as moral knowledge it would equally be true that a man must accept an unprovable material object proposition before Moore could prove to him that there is an external world. Similarly, if a moral conclusion can be proved only to a man who accepts unprovable moral premises then a physical conclusion can be proved only to a man who accepts unprovable physical premises.

'There are recognised methods for settling factual and logical disputes, but there are no recognised methods for settling moral disputes.'

This is either false, or true but irrelevant, according to how it is understood. Too often those who make this complaint are arguing in a circle, since they will count nothing as a recognised method of argument unless it is a recognised method of logical or scientific argument. If we adopt this interpretation, then it is true that there are no recognised methods of moral argument, but the lack of such methods does not affect the claim that morality is objective. One department of enquiry has not been shown to be no true department of enquiry when all that has been shown is that it cannot be carried on by exactly the methods that are appropriate to some other department of enquiry. We know without the help of the sceptic that morality is not identical with logic or science.

But in its most straightforward sense the claim is simply false. There *are* recognised methods of moral argument. Whenever we say 'How would you like it if somebody did this to you?' or 'How would it be if we all acted like this?' we are arguing according to recognised and established methods, and are in fact appealing to the consistency requirement to which I have already referred. It is true that such appeals are often ineffective, but it is also true that well-founded logical or scientific arguments often fail to convince those to whom they are addressed. If the present objection is pursued beyond this point it turns into the argument from radical disagreement.

The moral sceptic is even more inclined to exaggerate the amount of disagreement that there is about methods of moral argument than he is inclined to exaggerate the amount of disagreement in moral belief as such. One reason for this is that he concentrates his attention on the admittedly striking and important fact that there is an enormous amount of immoral *conduct*. But most of those who *behave* immorally appeal to the very same methods of moral argument as those who condemn their immoral conduct. Hitler broke many promises, but he did not explicitly hold that promise-breaking as such and in general was permissible. When others broke their promises to him he complained with the same force and in the same terms as those with whom he himself had failed to keep faith. And whenever he broke a promise he tried to *justify* his breach by claiming that other obligations overrode the duty to keep the promise. He did not simply deny that it was his duty to keep promises. He thus entered into the very process of argument by which it is possible to condemn so many of his own actions. He was *inconsistent* in requiring of other nations and their leaders standards of conduct to which he himself did not conform, and in failing to produce *convincing reasons* for his own departures from the agreed standards.

Renford Bambrough: Proof

1) G.E. Moore famously "proved" the existence of an external world by pointing out that he had hands. Bambrough claims that his own proof of the existence of moral knowledge is similar to Moore's argument. Are the two arguments really similar? If we accept Moore's argument, must we accept Bambrough's?

2) Bambrough says that it is "almost certainly untrue" that there is more moral disagreement than scientific disagreement. Do you agree with him?

3) Contrary to Mackie, Bambrough claims that moral disagreement "has no bearing on the question of the objectivity of the inquiry." What is Bambrough's argument for this? Do you think it is a good one? How might someone like Mackie respond?

4) Some have noted that our moral views are heavily conditioned by our environment, and take this to be a good reason to reject the possibility of moral knowledge. Bambrough claims that this is merely "a special case of the general argument from disagreement." Is he right?

5) Hume claimed that moral statements are expressions of our attitudes of approval or disapproval, and thus are not subject to rational criticism. How does Bambrough respond to this claim? Do you find his reply convincing?

6) Throughout the article, Bambrough points out a number of similarities between scientific claims and moral claims. He argues that if we are not

skeptical about scientific knowledge, we should not be skeptical about moral knowledge. Are there any differences between morality and science that would justify being skeptical about one but not the other?

7) By what methods does Bambrough think we can settle moral disputes? Do you think we can gain moral knowledge using the methods he mentions?

PART FOUR

Moral Problems

20

The Singer Solution to World Poverty

Peter Singer

Peter Singer argues that our ordinary patterns of spending money on ourselves are immoral. Such spending involves the purchase of many things that are not essential to preserving our lives or health. The money we spend on fancy dinners, new clothes, or vacations could instead be sent to relief agencies that save people's lives. We don't know our potential beneficiaries, but that is morally irrelevant. Our decision not to spend money to save their lives is morally inexcusable.

Singer offers us a series of fascinating examples in which people have the opportunity to prevent an innocent person's death but fail to do so. We regard the person in each example as having done something extremely immoral. Singer argues that we who spend money on inessential personal pleasures are no better.

But what if most of the people we know are also failing to give anything to famine relief or aid agencies? That doesn't let us off the hook—it just means that they are also behaving in a deeply immoral way.

Perhaps the money sent overseas will not do as much good as advertised? Singer mentions some very reliable aid agencies (and provides contact information) that will not squander your money. For a couple hundred dollars, you can save a child's life, or purchase a few new additions to your wardrobe. If Singer is right, then choosing to spend that money on yourself means knowingly allowing an innocent person to die. Given the relatively small sacrifice you would be making if you sent that money overseas, and given the great benefit you would be providing if you did, morality gives you no choice. World poverty can largely be solved if we in the wealthier nations did our moral duty and gave much more than we currently do to those in greatest need.

....

In the Brazilian film "Central Station," Dora is a retired schoolteacher who makes ends meet by sitting at the station writing letters for illiterate people. Suddenly she has an opportunity to pocket $1,000. All she has to do is persuade a homeless 9-year-old boy to follow her to an address she has been given. (She is told he will be adopted by wealthy foreigners.) She delivers the boy, gets the money, spends some of it on a television set, and settles down to enjoy her new acquisition. Her neighbor spoils the fun, however, by telling her that the boy was too old to be adopted—he will be killed and his organs sold for transplantation. Perhaps Dora knew this all along, but after her neighbor's plain speaking, she spends a troubled night. In the morning Dora resolves to take the boy back.

Suppose Dora had told her neighbor that it is a tough world, other people have nice new TV's too, and if selling the kid is the only way she can get one, well, he was only a street kid. She would then have become, in the eyes of the audience, a monster. She redeems herself only by being prepared to bear considerable risks to save the boy.

At the end of the movie, in cinemas in the affluent nations of the world, people who would have been quick to condemn Dora if she had not rescued the boy go home to places far more comfortable than her apartment. In fact, the average family in the United States spends almost one-third of its income on things that are no more necessary to them than Dora's new TV was to her. Going out to nice restaurants, buying new clothes because the old ones are no longer stylish, vacationing at beach resorts—so much of our income is spent on things not essential to the preservation of our lives and health. Donated to one of a number of charitable agencies, that money could mean the difference between life and death for children in need.

All of which raises a question: In the end, what is the ethical distinction between a Brazilian who sells a homeless child to organ peddlers and an American who already has a TV and upgrades to a better one—knowing

202 The Ethical Life

that the money could be donated to an organization that would use it to save the lives of kids in need?

Of course, there are several differences between the two situations that could support different moral judgments about them. For one thing, to be able to consign a child to death when he is standing right in front of you takes a chilling kind of heartlessness; it is much easier to ignore an appeal for money to help children you will never meet. Yet for a utilitarian philosopher like myself—that is, one who judges whether acts are right or wrong by their consequences—if the upshot of the American's failure to donate the money is that one more kid dies on the streets of a Brazilian city, then it is, in some sense, just as bad as selling the kid to the organ peddlers. But one doesn't need to embrace my utilitarian ethic to see that, at the very least, there is a troubling incongruity in being so quick to condemn Dora for taking the child to the organ peddlers while, at the same time, not regarding the American consumer's behavior as raising a serious moral issue.

In his 1996 book, *Living High and Letting Die*, the New York University philosopher Peter Unger presented an ingenious series of imaginary examples designed to probe our intuitions about whether it is wrong to live well without giving substantial amounts of money to help people who are hungry, malnourished or dying from easily treatable illnesses like diarrhea. Here's my paraphrase of one of these examples:

Bob is close to retirement. He has invested most of his savings in a very rare and valuable old car, a Bugatti, which he has not been able to insure. The Bugatti is his pride and joy. In addition to the pleasure he gets from driving and caring for his car, Bob knows that its rising market value means that he will always be able to sell it and live comfortably after retirement. One day when Bob is out for a drive, he parks the Bugatti near the end of a railway siding and goes for a walk up the track. As he does so, he sees that a runaway train, with no one aboard, is running down the railway track. Looking farther down the track, he sees the small figure of a child very likely to be killed by the runaway train. He can't stop the train and the child is too far away to warn of the danger, but he can throw a switch that will divert the train down the siding where his Bugatti is parked. Then nobody will be killed—but the train will destroy his Bugatti. Thinking of his joy in owning the car and the financial security it represents, Bob decides not to throw the switch. The child is killed. For many years to come, Bob enjoys owning his Bugatti and the financial security it represents.

Bob's conduct, most of us will immediately respond, was gravely wrong. Unger agrees. But then he reminds us that we, too, have opportunities to save the lives of children. We can give to organizations like UNICEF or Oxfam America. How much would we have to give one of these organizations to have a high probability of saving the life of a child threatened by easily preventable diseases? (I do not believe that children are more worth saving than adults, but since no one can argue that children have brought their poverty on themselves, focusing on them simplifies the issues.) Unger called up some experts and used the information they provided to offer some plausible estimates that include the cost of raising money, administrative expenses and the cost of delivering aid where it is most needed. By his calculation, $200 in donations would help a sickly 2-year-old transform into a healthy 6-year-old—offering safe passage through childhood's most dangerous years. To show how practical philosophical argument can be, Unger even tells his readers that they can easily donate funds by using their credit card and calling one of these toll-free numbers: (800) 367-5437 for Unicef; (800) 693-2687 for Oxfam America. [http://supportunicef. org/forms/whichcountry2.html for Unicef and http://www.oxfam.org/ eng/donate.htm for Oxfam—PS]

Now you, too, have the information you need to save a child's life. How should you judge yourself if you don't do it? Think again about Bob and his Bugatti. Unlike Dora, Bob did not have to look into the eyes of the child he was sacrificing for his own material comfort. The child was a complete stranger to him and too far away to relate to in an intimate, personal way. Unlike Dora, too, he did not mislead the child or initiate the chain of events imperiling him. In all these respects, Bob's situation resembles that of people able but unwilling to donate to overseas aid and differs from Dora's situation.

If you still think that it was very wrong of Bob not to throw the switch that would have diverted the train and saved the child's life, then it is hard to see how you could deny that it is also very wrong not to send money to one of the organizations listed above. Unless, that is, there is some morally important difference between the two situations that I have overlooked.

Is it the practical uncertainties about whether aid will really reach the people who need it? Nobody who knows the world of overseas aid can doubt that such uncertainties exist. But Unger's figure of $200 to save a child's life was reached after he had made conservative assumptions about the proportion of the money donated that will actually reach its target.

One genuine difference between Bob and those who can afford to donate to overseas aid organizations but don't is that only Bob can save the child on the tracks, whereas there are hundreds of millions of people who can give $200 to overseas aid organizations. The problem is that most of them aren't doing it. Does this mean that it is all right for you not to do it?

Suppose that there were more owners of priceless vintage cars—Carol, Dave, Emma, Fred, and so on, down to Ziggy—all in exactly the same situation as Bob, with their own siding and their own switch, all sacrificing the child in order to preserve their own cherished car. Would that make it all right for Bob to do the same? To answer this question affirmatively is to endorse follow-the-crowd ethics—the kind of ethics that led many Germans to look away when the Nazi atrocities were being committed. We do not excuse them because others were behaving no better.

We seem to lack a sound basis for drawing a clear moral line between Bob's situation and that of any reader of this article with $200 to spare who does not donate it to an overseas aid agency. These readers seem to be acting at least as badly as Bob was acting when he chose to let the runaway train hurtle toward the unsuspecting child. In the light of this conclusion, I trust that many readers will reach for the phone and donate that $200. Perhaps you should do it before reading further.

Now that you have distinguished yourself morally from people who put their vintage cars ahead of a child's life, how about treating yourself and your partner to dinner at your favorite restaurant? But wait. The money you will spend at the restaurant could also help save the lives of children overseas! True, you weren't planning to blow $200 tonight, but if you were to give up dining out just for one month, you would easily save that amount. And what is one month's dining out, compared to a child's life? There's the rub. Since there are a lot of desperately needy children in the world, there will always be another child whose life you could save for another $200. Are you therefore obliged to keep giving until you have nothing left? At what point can you stop?

Hypothetical examples can easily become farcical. Consider Bob. How far past losing the Bugatti should he go? Imagine that Bob had got his foot stuck in the track of the siding, and if he diverted the train, then before it rammed the car it would also amputate his big toe. Should he still throw the switch? What if it would amputate his foot? His entire leg?

As absurd as the Bugatti scenario gets when pushed to extremes, the point it raises is a serious one: only when the sacrifices become very significant indeed would most people be prepared to say that Bob does nothing wrong when he decides not to throw the switch. Of course, most people could be wrong; we can't decide moral issues by taking opinion polls. But consider for yourself the level of sacrifice that you would demand of Bob, and then think about how much money you would have to give away in order to make a sacrifice that is roughly equal to that. It's almost certainly much, much more than $200. For most middle-class Americans, it could easily be more like $200,000.

Isn't it counterproductive to ask people to do so much? Don't we run the risk that many will shrug their shoulders and say that morality, so conceived, is fine for saints but not for them? I accept that we are unlikely to see, in the near or even medium-term future, a world in which it is normal for wealthy Americans to give the bulk of their wealth to strangers. When it comes to praising or blaming people for what they do, we tend to use a standard that is relative to some conception of normal behavior. Comfortably off Americans who give, say, 10 percent of their income to overseas aid organizations are so far ahead of most of their equally comfortable fellow citizens that I wouldn't go out of my way to chastise them for not doing more. Nevertheless, they should be doing much more, and they are in no position to criticize Bob for failing to make the much greater sacrifice of his Bugatti.

At this point various objections may crop up. Someone may say: "If every citizen living in the affluent nations contributed his or her share I wouldn't have to make such a drastic sacrifice, because long before such levels were reached, the resources would have been there to save the lives of all those children dying from lack of food or medical care. So why should I give more than my fair share?" Another, related, objection is that the Government ought to increase its overseas aid allocations, since that would spread the burden more equitably across all taxpayers.

Yet the question of how much we ought to give is a matter to be decided in the real world—and that, sadly, is a world in which we know that most people do not, and in the immediate future will not, give substantial amounts to overseas aid agencies. We know, too, that at least in the next year, the United States Government is not going to meet even the very modest United Nations-recommended target of 0.7 percent of gross national product; at the moment it lags far below that, at 0.09 percent, not even half of Japan's 0.22 percent or a tenth of Denmark's 0.97 percent. Thus, we know that the money we can give beyond that theoretical "fair share" is still going to save lives that would otherwise be lost. While the idea that no one need do more than his or her fair share is a powerful one, should it prevail if we know that others are not doing their fair share and that children will die preventable deaths unless we do more than our fair share? That would be taking fairness too far.

Thus, this ground for limiting how much we ought to give also fails. In the world as it is now, I can see no escape from the conclusion that each one of us with wealth surplus to his or her essential needs should be giving most of it to help people suffering from poverty so dire as to be life-threatening. That's right: I'm saying that you shouldn't buy that new car, take that cruise, redecorate the house or get that pricey new suit. After all, a $1,000 suit could save five children's lives.

So how does my philosophy break down in dollars and cents? An American household with an income of $50,000 spends around $30,000 annually on necessities, according to the Conference Board, a nonprofit economic research organization. Therefore, for a household bringing in $50,000 a year, donations to help the world's poor should be as close as possible to $20,000. The $30,000 required for necessities holds for higher incomes as well. So a household making $100,000 could cut a yearly check for $70,000. Again, the formula is simple: whatever money you're spending on luxuries not necessities, should be given away.

Now, evolutionary psychologists tell us that human nature just isn't sufficiently altruistic to make it plausible that many people will sacrifice so much for strangers. On the facts of human nature, they might be right, but they would be wrong to draw a moral conclusion from those facts. If it is the case that we ought to do things that, predictably, most of us won't do, then let's face that fact head-on. Then, if we value the life of a child more than going to fancy restaurants, the next time we dine out we will know that we could have done something better with our money. If that makes living a morally decent life extremely arduous, well, then that is the way things are. If we don't do it, then we should at least know that we are failing to live a morally decent life—not because it is good to wallow in guilt but because knowing where we should be going is the first step toward heading in that direction.

When Bob first grasped the dilemma that faced him as he stood by that railway switch, he must have thought how extraordinarily unlucky he was to be placed in a situation in which he must choose between the life of an innocent child and the sacrifice of most of his savings. But he was not unlucky at all. We are all in that situation.

Peter Singer: The Singer Solution to World Poverty

1) Was it morally wrong of Bob to refrain from throwing the switch, thus allowing the child to die? Is there any moral difference between Bob's decision and the decision of well-off people to spend money on luxuries rather than the alleviation of poverty?

2) One difference between the case of Bob and the case of someone not giving to charity is that Bob is the only person in a position to prevent the child's death, while many people are in a position to give to charity. Why doesn't Singer think that this is a morally relevant difference? Do you agree with him?

3) How much of our income does Singer think we are morally required to give away? Do you find his standard reasonable?

4) How does Singer respond to the objection that his theory is too demanding, and that people will never make the sacrifices he suggests? Do you find his response convincing?

5) One might respond to Singer's proposals by claiming that instead of individuals contributing money to alleviate world poverty, governments should be responsible for handling such efforts. Why doesn't Singer think that this undermines his view that middle-class people should give large percentages of their income to charity?

21

Paid Surrogacy: Arguments and Responses

Heidi Malm

···

In this article, Heidi Malm presents a variety of arguments against paid surrogate motherhood arrangements, and explains why she thinks that every one of them fails. One argument claims that such contracts involve the selling of babies, and are immoral for that reason. Malm accepts the idea that selling a human being is immoral, but denies that surrogate motherhood contracts do this.

Another argument is that paying a woman to bear one's child is, in effect, to rent out her womb, and so to treat the surrogate mother as a merely commercial object. Malm denies that such contracts amount to any kind of rental of a woman's body, and argues instead that they offer compensation for a difficult service rendered—compensation that, crucially, respects the woman's right to use her body as she sees fit.

A further objection to surrogacy arrangements is that they are exploitative, and prey on poorer women, who provide such services only because they have no other viable economic options. Malm replies that many surrogates are not economically impoverished, and, of those who are, we do not serve their interests by prohibiting what may be their only way to escape poverty.

Malm concludes with consideration of two further arguments— neither of which, she thinks, are strong enough to undermine the general presumption that we ought to be free to do with our bodies whatever

Heidi Malm, "Paid Surrogacy: Arguments and Responses" from *Public Affairs Quarterly* 3 (1989), pp. 57–64.

we like, so long as we violate no one else's rights. Since Malm does not think that surrogacy contracts violate anyone's rights, such arrangements should (as she sees it) be regarded as morally acceptable.

....

I n a society that prizes individual liberty, the burden of proof rests on those who want to prohibit, or otherwise restrict, surrogate motherhood arrangements. This paper examines five arguments intended to show that *paid* surrogacy arrangements ought to be prohibited. The arguments are primarily ethical in nature, as opposed to legal, and deontological as opposed to consequentialist. After finding none of the arguments successful, I consider the view that while paid surrogacy arrangements are morally permissible, they ought not be legally enforceable. I argue that even this view is problematic.

I. Selling Babies

When ruling on the recent Baby "M" case, chief justice Robert N. Wilenz wrote for the New Jersey Supreme Court:

> We find no offense to our present laws where a woman voluntarily and without payment agrees to act as a 'surrogate' mother, provided that she is not subject to a binding agreement to surrender her child ... *this is the sale of a child*, or, at the very least, the sale of a mother's right to her child, the only mitigating factor being that one of the purchasers is the father. Almost every evil that prompted the prohibition of the payment of money in connection with adoption exists here. (*In re Baby "M,"* N.J. Supreme Court, No. A-39, Feb. 3, 1988; emphasis added.)

This passage contains the central premise of what is perhaps the strongest argument against paid surrogate motherhood arrangements (henceforth called "contracted child-bearing arrangements"),[1] namely, that the payments made in these arrangements constitute the buying and selling of a baby. If this is correct, then we have strong moral grounds—Kantian notions of respect for persons (as well as adequate legal grounds—our current laws against baby-selling)—for prohibiting

---

[1] The term "surrogate mother" is misleading. In typical cases (those not involving embryo transfer) the so-called "surrogate mother" is both the genetic mother of the child and the birth-mother of the child. The only "mother" role she does not (intend to) fulfill is the social one.

such arrangements. The argument may be stated as follows: (1) It is morally wrong to treat persons (including babies) as objects of commerce. (2) Contracted child-bearing arrangements treat babies as objects of commerce. (3) Therefore, contracted child-bearing arrangements are morally objectionable.

Let us grant the truth of premise (1) and focus our attention on premise (2). Are we committed to viewing the payments made in contracted child-bearing arrangements as payments *for the baby*? A proponent may deny that we are, claiming that the payments are for the woman's services. They are, that is, compensation for the efforts and risks of bearing a child (for example, for not drinking coffee or alcohol for nine months, for not engaging in potentially dangerous activities, for the risks involved in giving birth, for the loss of earnings from other sources, and for the effort it may take to return her body to the condition it was in prior to pregnancy). This is not a patently unreasonable claim. Thus a critic of contracted child-bearing arrangements must provide an argument showing that it is unreasonable, if she is to object to these arrangements on the grounds that they involve the buying and selling of babies.

One such argument is suggested in the following passage by Sara Ketchum. She suggests the claim that if the payments made are merely for the woman's services, then the "customers" of contracted child-bearing arrangements may not get what they want, which is custody of the child:

> The "surrogate" or contracting mother is, after all, the mother. In an ordinary custody decision, a genetic father who pays the biological mother of the child to take care of the child does not thereby gain exclusive custody of the child, nor does his financial contribution establish him as the primary caretaker for purposes of determining custody. (Ketchum 1987, p. 3.)

Let us grant that my paying you for your efforts and risks of bearing a child will not *thereby* gain me exclusive custody of the child. This is supported by the case Ketchum cites (in which a father's financial contribution does not establish him as the sole caretaker), and by a case in which the person making the payments is not related to the child (for example, Albert pays Betty to bear a child whose genetic parents would be Betty and Carl). The relevant question is whether it follows from this that the payments made in contracted child-bearing arrangements cannot reasonable be viewed as payments for the woman's services that they must be for the baby itself (or at least for rights to the baby). To see that it does not, consider following case:

Diane and Erick have, respectively, healthy ova and healthy sperm. Diane's uterus, however, has been damaged in a way that prevents her from carrying a child to term. Diane and Erick thus seek the help of Francine, who *is* able to carry a child, and agree to pay her $10,000 to carry to term a conceptus that results from the in vitro fertilization of Diane's ovum with Erick's sperm.

In this case I think it is quite reasonable to maintain that the payments to Francine were payments for her services. If Diane and Erick have custodial rights to the child (and it seems to me that they do) then their rights are a function of their being the child's genetic parents; they did not purchase the rights, nor the baby itself, from Francine. Now consider the following modified version of the above case:

Diane does not have healthy ova but Gloria does. Gloria donates one of her ova to Diane and Erick, and it is then fertilized, in vitro, with Erick's sperm. The conceptus is implanted in Francine who is paid $10,000 to carry the child to term.

Again, I think it is quite reasonable to view the payments to Francine as payments for her services. They were not for the baby itself.

The point of these cases is to show that in cases in which the woman bearing the child is not the genetic mother of the child, it is reasonable to view the payments to her as payments for her services. But if it is reasonable in these cases, then it is also reasonable in cases in which the woman bearing the child *is* the genetic mother of the child. For she may be, as did Gloria, donating an ovum (or waiving her claims to custody, as I discuss in section IV), and may be, as did Francine, accepting payments for her efforts and risks of carrying the child to term. Thus even though my paying you for your efforts and risks of bearing a child does not *thereby* gain me exclusive custody of the child (I may gain that custody in other ways), it is nonetheless reasonable to view the payments made in contracted child-bearing arrangements as payments for the woman's services. Given this, we cannot prohibit these arrangements out of hand on the gounds that they involve the buying and selling of babies.

II. Selling Bodies

A second argument against contracted child-bearing arrangements parallels the first. It is captured in the popular notion of "renting a womb" and asserts: To pay a woman to bear a child for another is to treat her body as an object of commerce. But to treat a woman's body as an object of commerce is, as Ketchum argues, to treat her as

> less than an end (or as less than a person)....To make a person or a person's body an object of commerce is to treat the person as part of another's domain, particularly if the sale of A to B gives B rights to A or to A's body...(Ketchum 1987, p.9.)

Let us grant that if contracted child-bearing arrangements do treat women's bodies as objects of commerce—as things that may be bought, sold, or rented—then they ought to be prohibited. The problem with the argument is that it fails to distinguish between (a) my paying you for *you* to use your body in a way that benefits me, and (b) my paying you for *me* to use your body in a way that benefits me. The difference is important, for it determines whether my payments to you give me a right to your body, and thus whether they treat your body as an object of commerce and you as "less than a person." To illustrate the difference, suppose that you own a lawnmower. (I do not mean to suggest that women's bodies are on a par with machines.) If I need to have my lawn mowed then I might (a) pay you for *me* to use your lawnmower to mow my lawn, in which case I can be said to *rent* your lawnmower from you, or (b) pay you for *you* to use your lawnmower to mow my lawn, in which case I do not rent your lawnmower from you but pay you for your services. In the former case I acquire a right to your lawnmower (the right to use it for a limited period of time). In the latter case I do not. The right I have here is at most a right to insist that *you* do with your lawnmower what you said you would. But that is not a right to your lawnmower.

When we apply this distinction to the issue of contracted child-bearing arrangements we see that there is no need to view the payments to the woman as payments that consititute the *rental* of her body. The customer does not acquire a space over which he then has control. He may not paint it blue, keep a coin in it, or do whatever else he pleases as long as he does not cause permanent damage. Instead, the woman is being paid for *her* to use *her* body in a way that benefits him—she is being compensated for her services. But this does not treat her body as an object of commerce—as something that can be bought, sold or rented—any more than does my paying a surgeon to perform an operation, a cabby to drive a car, or a model to pose for a drawing. My payments to the surgeon do not give me a right to her arm, make her an object of my domain, nor deny that there is a person there. Indeed, it seems that recognizing that persons can enter into agreements to use their own bodies in ways that benefit others reaffirms their status as persons—as agents—rather than denies it. In short, then, we cannot prohibit contracted child-bearing arrangements on the grounds that they treat women's bodies as commerce and thus treat women as less than persons.

III. Exploitation

A third argument against contracted child-bearing arrangements asserts that the opportunity to be paid for one's services in bearing a child will exploit poor women. They may feel compelled to enter into these arrangements when they would prefer not to do so. Thus we ought to prohibit the arrangements in order to protect poor women form exploitation.

There are four partial responses to this argument which, taken together, seem to me to provide adequate grounds for rejecting the argument. First, there is at least some evidence that the opportunity to be paid for one's services in bearing a child has not in fact, and in general, been exploitive of poor women. Statistics indicate that the "average surrogate mother is white, attended two years of college, married young, and has all the children she and her husband want."[2] These are not the characteristics of the group we envision when we express concerns about protecting the poor from exploitation.[3]

Second, though the opportunity to be paid for one's services in bearing a child may come to exploit poor women as the arrangements increase in popularity, the same can be said of any opportunity to be paid for one's services. But we do not serve the interests of poor women in general if, in the efforts to protect them from exploitation, we prohibited them the means of escaping poverty.

Third, our concern about exploitation seems to presuppose that the act of bearing a child for another is so detestable, so degrading, that few women would enter into these arrangements were they not forced to do so out of economic necessity. But the statistics mentioned above suggest that this is not the case. Moreover, some women enjoy being pregnant and

---

[2] Radin, 1988, p. 1930. The statistics are from "Surrogate Motherhood: A Practice That's Still Undergoing Birth Pangs," *Los Angeles Times*, March 22, 1987, sec. 6, at. 12, col. 2.

[3] It is also worth noting that the offer to bear a child for another (and be compensated for one's efforts and risks in doing so) is not unjustly coercive, in the sense that it does not leave the woman worse off than she would have been had the offer not been made. (For contrast, consider a gunman's "Your money or your life" offer, which does leave the recipient worse off.)

may view their act as altruistic: They are doing for another what that other cannot do for him or herself, and thereby allowing that other to know the joys (and pains) of raising an offspring.

Finally, if our aim is to protect those women who *do* view bearing a child for another as degrading, but nonetheless feel compelled to do so out of economic necessity, then we can protect those women by putting restrictions on who can *enter into* contracted child-bearing arrangements—we need not prohibit the arrangements entirely. Of course, one might object that such restrictions would be unfair, because they would prohibit poor women from doing something that other women were allowed to do, but that would suggest that the restrictions would be denying the poor women a good, rather than protecting them from a harm, which in turn would suggest that the initial concerns about exploitation were misguided.

IV. Transferring Rights

A fourth argument turns our attention away from the monetary aspect of contracted child-bearing arrangements and towards the nature of parental custodial rights. It can be stated most clearly if we assume that the customer would be the genetic father of the child, and that the woman being paid to bear the child would be the genetic mother. The argument is as follows.

Even if the father does not purchase the mother's custodial right from her, he still must acquire that right if he is to achieve his aim of exclusive custody. But viewing parental custodial rights as something that can be *transferred* from one to another (if not outright sold), presupposes that the custodial relationship between parent and child is a *property*relationship—and that is morally objectionable. On the other hand, if we view parental custodial rights more plausibly as "rights to maintain a relationship" then we will be unlikely to think of them as something one can transfer. Ketchum writes:

> We have good reasons for allowing birth-mothers to relinquish their children because otherwise we would be forcing children into the care of people who either do not want them or feel themselves unable to care for them. However, that custody is waivable in this way does not entail that it is saleable or even transferrable....If a mother's right is a right to maintain a relationship, it is implausible to treat it as transferrable; having the option of terminating a relationship with A does not entail having the option of deciding who A will relate to next. (Ketchum 1987, p. 8.)

The suggestion that we view parental custodial rights as rights to maintain a relationship is, I think, a good one. The problem with the argument is that there is nothing in the nature of contracted child-bearing arrangements that requires that custody be transferred rather than waived. In order for one parent to gain exclusive custody of a child, it is not the case that that parent must *acquire* the other parent's parental custodial right, such that he or she now has *two* custodial rights—two rights to maintain a relationship—when before he or she had only one. One parent may obtain exclusive custody of a child merely by the other parent's *waiving* his or her custodial right. The one parent would then have exclusive custody because he or she is then the only parent *with* a custodial right. But his or her right to maintain a relationship has not somehow doubled in size. (This is supported by the fact that a judge is not required to find a parent with exclusive custody *twice* as unfit as a parent who shares custody before she would be justified in removing the child from that parent's care. Indeed, we may think it should be just the reverse.) Thus unless we are willing to assume that the genetic mother of a child is the only parent with a custodial right to the child (an interesting twist on Aristotelian biology), we cannot prohibit contracted child-bearing arrangements on the grounds that they require the transfer of parental custodial rights and thus treat children as property.

V. The Needs of Others

The last argument I will address focuses on the needs of persons not principally involved in contracted child-bearing arrangements, namely, children awaiting adoption. Margaret Radin writes:

> There is a danger that unwanted children might remain parentless even if only unpaid surrogacy is allowed, because those seeking children will turn less frequently to adoption.... Thus the prohibition of all surrogacy might be grounded on a concern for unwanted children and their chances in life. (Radin 1988, p. 1931.)

Ketchum augments this view by noting that while there may be a shortage of "healthy white infants" available for adoption,

> there are children living in orphanages in third world countries about whom it is hard to believe they would not be better off being adopted by an American couple...It is just possible that they would be more likely to be adopted if contracted motherhood were less available. (Ketchum 1987, p. 13.)

Though I share Radin's and Ketchum's concern for these children, and recognize the need to find homes for them, I have strong reservations about allowing this need to count as grounds for prohibiting contracted child-bearing arrangements. If the need to find homes for hard to place children provides grounds for not allowing an *infertile* couple to have and raise a child genetically related to at least one of them, then it also provides grounds—and just as strong grounds—for not allowing a *fertile* couple to have and raise a child genetically related to at least one of them. Yet few of us would tolerate—much less advocate—a government which could legitimately say to a fertile couple "I am sorry, we cannot allow you to have and raise a child genetically related to at least one of you because there are too many other children who need homes."

VI. Conclusion

I have considered and rejected five arguments in favor of prohibiting contracted child-bearing arrangements. I would like to conclude by raising a concern about the more moderate view that while contracted child-bearing arrangements are morally permissible, they ought not to be legally enforceable.

Presumably, the grounds in favor of this view are that it would allow persons to enter into contracted child-bearing arrangements while protecting women from the harm of being obliged to waive their custodial right to child with whom they have bonded. So far so good. Yet if we are to protect the women who *do* bond with the child during pregnancy, without risking harm to those who do not, then the arrangements will have to be cancellable only by the woman. For we would not protect the latter group of women (nor the women in general) were the customers allowed to say, midstream, "I'm sorry, I've changed my mind, you keep the child and I'll keep my money."

Now the concern I have about this view is the picture it paints in which the only interest the man has at stake is his money. It suggests that if the woman cancels the arrangement, then the man keeps his money and everything is *status quo*. But, of course, everything may not be status quo. For if the woman carries the child to term then the man has in existence a child—a son or daughter—which, given some courts current presumption against joint custody, and *de facto* presumption in favor of awarding sole custody to the mother, is a child about whom he is not likely to have custody. This is quite different from never having a child at all. I do not mean to suggest that the interests of the father outweigh those of the mother, but only that when passing legislation we need to be aware that both parties have important non-monetary interests at stake.

Heidi Malm: Paid Surrogacy: Arguments and Responses

1) One standard criticism of paid surrogacy arrangements is that they amount to "baby selling," or at least the selling of custody rights. How does Malm argue against this criticism? Do you find her argument convincing?

2) What is the difference, according to Malm, between renting a person's body and paying a person for her services? Which category do you think contracted child-bearing arrangements fall into?

3) Malm has a number of responses to the worry that surrogacy arrangements have the potential to exploit poor women. Does she successfully rebut this worry?

4) Malm argues that surrogate mothers do not *transfer* their custody rights to others, but merely *waive* them. One might object that paying another person to waive her custody rights is still morally problematic. Do you think this is a good objection? How would Malm respond to such a criticism?

5) While Malm admits that prohibiting contracted child-bearing arrangements might have the positive consequence of increasing the adoption rate of needy children, she denies that this justifies prohibiting such arrangements. Why does she think this? Do you agree with her?

Bibliographic Appendix

Ketchum, Sara, "Selling Babies and Selling Bodies: Surrogate Motherhood and the Problem of Commodification." Presented at the Pacific Division Meetings of the American Philosophical Association, Portland Oregon, March 1987.

Radin, Mararet, "Market Inalienability," *Harvard Law Review*, vol. 100 (1988), pp. 1849–1937.

22

Playing God: Genes, Clones, and Luck

Ronald Dworkin

. . . .

In this excerpt from his book *Sovereign Virtue* (2000), philosopher and legal scholar Ronald Dworkin considers a number of recent arguments that have been advanced to try to show that certain kinds of genetic engineering, and cloning, are immoral. The three arguments Dworkin discusses are based on the dangers posed by current technology; on the potential injustice suffered by those too poor to afford genetic enhancements; and on the need to maintain diversity within the human gene pool. Dworkin believes that each of these arguments is unsuccessful, and proceeds to identify what he thinks is our deepest fear about genetic engineering and cloning: that such technologies amount to human beings "playing God." Dworkin then explores what such a charge amounts to, and argues that it, too, fails to undermine the morality of cloning and genetic engineering.

. . . .

A. Why Not

The most arresting of the possibilities geneticists are now exploring would give scientists and doctors the power to choose which human beings

"Playing God: Genes, Clones, and Luck," reprinted by permission of the publisher from SOVEREIGN VIRTUE by Ronald Dworkin, pp. 437–446, Cambridge, Mass.: Harvard University Press, Copyright 2000 by Ronald Dworkin. First appeared for a meeting of the Twenty-first Century Foundation.

there will be. People gained that power long ago, in a broad and clumsy way, when they came to understood that allowing certain people rather than others to mate would have consequences for the kind of children they produced. Eugenics, which was supported by George Bernard Shaw and Oliver Wendell Holmes as well as Adolf Hitler, was modeled on that simple insight. But genetic science now holds out the possibility, at least as comprehensible fantasy, of creating particular human beings who have been designed, one by one, according to a detailed blueprint, or of changing existing human beings, either as fetuses or later, to create people with chosen genetic properties.

Even the fantasy of this, when the technology was first described, was greeted with shock and indignation, and that shock crystallized when scientists in Scotland cloned an adult sheep, and other scientists and publicists speculated that the technique could be used to clone human beings. Committees hurriedly appointed by governments and international bodies all immediately denounced the very idea. President Clinton ruled that federal funds could not be used to finance research into human cloning, and the United States Senate considered forbidding, through preposterously over-broad and panicky legislation, any and all such research. The possibility of comprehensive genetic engineering—altering a zygote's genetic composition to produce a battery of desired physical, mental, and emotional propensities—has also aroused great fear and revulsion, and any success in engineering mammals, comparable to the creation of the sheep, Dolly, would undoubtedly provoke a similar official response. (In this discussion I shall often use the word "engineering" to include both comprehensive genetic alteration and human cloning, the latter being treated as a special case of the former. Of course engineering and cloning are very different techniques, but many of the social and moral issues they raise are the same.)

The rhetoric of the European Parliament is not untypical of the reaction that prospects of genetic engineering have produced. In its "resolution on the cloning of the human embryo," that body declared its "firm conviction that the cloning of human beings, whether on an experimental basis, in the context of fertility treatments, preimplantation diagnosis, for tissue transplantation, or for any other purpose whatsoever, is unethical, morally repugnant, contrary to respect for the person, and a grave violation of fundamental human rights which can not under any circumstances be justified or accepted." How might we justify, or even explain, this blunderbuss reaction? We might explore three grounds of objection that are frequently mentioned. First, genetic research is said to pose great danger, and extreme caution is therefore urged. If human cloning or other comprehensive genetic engineering is possible at all, research into it or attempts at it might result in an unacceptable number of miscarriages or in the birth of an unacceptable number of deformed children, for example. Second, some people resist research into genetic engineering on grounds of social justice. Cloning, if available, is bound to be hideously expensive for a long time, and hence would be available only to rich people who would want, out of vanity, to clone themselves, increasing the unfair advantages of wealth. (Opponents horrified by the prospect of cloning have cited the specter of thousands of Rupert Murdochs or Donald Trumps.) Third, much of the hostile reaction has been generated by a detached and reasonably familiar aesthetic value. Engineering, if available, might well be used to perpetuate now desired traits of height, intelligence, color and personality, and the world would be robbed of the variety that seems essential to novelty, originality and fascination. We must discuss each of these supposed justifications for a ban on research and development, but in my own view they do not separately or together explain the dogmatic strength of the reaction I described.

Security

It is unclear how far the Dolly precedent should be relied on in predicting the likely results of experimentation into human cloning. On the one hand, technical skill will presumably improve; on the other, human cloning may prove exponentially more difficult than cloning sheep. Several hundred attempts were necessary to produce one sheep, but, as I understand it, the rest were lost through early miscarriage, and no deformed but viable sheep was produced. Nor is there much reason to think that either cloning or engineering would produce germline damage threatening generations of deformity, or deformity that would not appear for generations. In any case, however, these dangers are not enough, on their own, to justify forbidding the further research that could refine our appreciation of them, and perhaps our ability to forestall or reduce whichever threats are in fact genuine. True, the sudden appearance of Dr. Seed, in the headlines and on the screen, promising to clone anyone for a high price, was enough to terrify anyone. But regulation can rein him in, along with the thousands of other cloning cowboys who would be bound to appear, without closing down research altogether. If we are assessing the risks of damage that experimentation or testing might produce, moreover, we must also take into account the hope that advancing and refining the techniques of genetic engineering will vastly decrease the number of defects and deformities with which people are now born or into which they inexorably grow. The balance of risk might well be thought to tilt in favor of experimentation.

Justice

We can easily imagine genetic engineering's becoming a perquisite of the rich, and therefore as exacerbating the already savage injustice of both prosperous and impoverished societies. But these techniques have uses beyond vanity, and these uses may justify research and trials, even if we decide that vanity is an inappropriate and forbidden motive. We noticed, earlier, the important medical gains that have already been achieved through selective engineering, and more comprehensive engineering can confidently be expected to expand these enormously. Cloning may prove to have particularly dramatic medical benefits. Parents of a desperately sick child might want another child, whom they would love as much as any other, but whose blood or marrow might save the life of the sick child from which it was cloned. Cloning individual human stem cells to produce a particular organ for transplant, rather than an entire organism, might have even more evident benefits. A reengineered and then heavily cloned cell, taken from a cancer patient, might prove to be a cure for that cancer when the clones were reintroduced. We must also count benefits beyond the narrowly medical. Childless couples, for example, or single women or single men might wish to procreate through cloning, which they might think better than the alternatives available. Or they may have no alternative at all.

Perhaps we could regulate engineering to screen out all but approved motives. If this is possible, does justice demand it, even if we assume that there are no other objections to it? I do not believe so. We should not...seek to improve equality by leveling down, and, as in the case of more orthodox genetic medicine, techniques available for a time only to the very rich often produce discoveries of much more general value for everyone. The remedy for injustice is redistribution, not denial of benefits to some with no corresponding gain to others.

Aesthetics

We already have clones—genetically identical multiple births (which have increased as a result of infertility treatment) produce clones—and the history of genetically identical children shows that identical genes do not produce identical phenotypes. We may have underestimated nature in years past, but nurture remains important too, and the reaction to the prospect of engineering has underestimated its importance in turn. Nevertheless, people do fear that if we replace the genetic "lottery" with engineered reproduction, the welcome diversity of human types will be progressively replaced with uniformity dictated by vogue. To some degree, of course, greater uniformity is unambiguously desirable: there is no value, aesthetic or otherwise, in the fact that some people are doomed to a disfigured and short life. But it is widely believed better that, within limits, people look different and act differently in ways that might well be the consequence of different alleles. This thought appeals to a derivative value: that it is better for everyone to live in a world of differences. But it might also be seen as appealing to a detached value: many people think that diversity is a value in itself, so that it would remain valuable even if, for some reason, people came to prefer uniformity.

What is not plain, however, is how far engineering, even if it were freely and inexpensively available, would actually threaten desirable diversity. Presumably all parents, if given a choice, would wish their children to have the level of intelligence and other skills that we now regard as normal, or even that we now believe superior. But we cannot regard that as undesirable: it is, after all, the object of education, ordinary as well as remedial, to improve intelligence and skill levels across the board. Do we have good reason to fear that if parents had the choice they would often prefer cloning one of them—or cloning a third person—to sexual reproduction that produces a child bearing the genes of both? Or that they would choose cloning for reasons other than to exclude damaging alleles, or because they were incapable of sexual reproduction? That seems unlikely. Do we have reason to fear (as many people do fear) that parents will engineer a reproductive zygote in order to make it a male rather than a female child, for example? It is true that in certain communities—in northern India, for example—male children are apparently preferred to female ones. But that preference seems so sensitive to economic circumstances, as well as to shifting cultural prejudices, that it offers no reason for thinking that the world will suddenly be swamped with a generation dominated by males. Selective abortion for sex has been available, as a result of amniocentesis and liberal abortion laws, for some time now, and no such general trend seems to have been established. In any case, we would not be justified in stopping experimentation on the basis of such thin speculation.

The fear, however, goes beyond a fear of sexual asymmetry: it is a fear that one phenotype—say, blond, conventionally good-looking, nonaggressive, tall, musically talented, and witty—will come to dominate a culture in which that phenotype is particularly valued. We should pause to notice the scientific assumptions embedded in that fear: it supposes not only that comprehensive genetic design is possible, but that the various properties of the preferred phenotype can be assembled in the same person through that design, as if each property were the product of a single allele whose possession made the property at least very highly likely, and that could be specified, and would have that consequence, independently of the specification of or phenotypic expression of other alleles. Each of those assumptions seems improbable, and their combination highly so. It seems much more likely that even parents with state of the art engineering at their disposal would have fewer combinations to choose from, and more risks to run about the impact of nurture and experience, and that they would make these choices differently in response to the very differences among them that we now celebrate. The later impact of differing personal choices by their offspring themselves, perhaps in search of individuality, would enlarge on those differences.

The basic motivational assumptions behind the fear seem equally as dubious as the scientific assumptions, moreover. Most people delight in the mysteries of reproduction—that value is, after all, at the root of the very objection we are considering—and many, and perhaps the great bulk, of people would forgo engineering, beyond trying to eliminate obvious defects and handicaps, as distasteful. If all this is right, the aesthetic objection is overblown or, at best, premature. We would need much more information, of a kind that could be produced only through research and experimentation, before we could even judge the assumptions on which the objection is founded, and it would therefore seem irrational to rely on that objection to prevent that research.

B. Playing God

The arguments and objections we have so far been canvassing do not provide what T. S. Eliot called an "objective correlative" for the immediate and largely sustained revulsion that I described. People feel some deeper, less articulate ground for that revulsion, even if they have not or perhaps cannot fully articulate that ground, but can express it only in heated and logically inappropriate language, like the bizarre reference to "fundamental human rights" in the European Parliament resolution I quoted earlier.

We will not adequately appreciate the real power of the political and social resistance to further research into genetic engineering, or the genuine moral and ethical issues that such research presents, until we have better understood that deeper ground, and we might begin with another familiar piece of rhetoric. It is wrong, people say, particularly after more familiar objections have been found wanting, to play God.

Playing God is thought wrong in itself, quite apart from any bad consequences it will or may have for any identifiable human being. Nevertheless it is deeply unclear what the injunction really means—unclear what playing God is, and what, exactly, is wrong with it. It can't mean that it is always wrong for human beings to attempt to resist natural catastrophes, or to improve upon the hand that nature has dealt them. People do that—always have done that—all the time. What is the difference, after all, between inventing penicillin and using engineered and cloned genes to cure even more terrifying diseases than penicillin cures? What is the difference between setting your child strenuous exercises to reduce his weight or increase his strength and altering his genes, while an embryo, with the same end in view?

These are not rhetorical questions. We must try to answer them, but we must begin at some distance from them, in the overall structure of our moral and ethical experience. For that structure depends, crucially, on a fundamental distinction between what we are responsible for doing or deciding, individually or collectively, and what is given to us, as a background against which we act or decide, but which we are powerless to change. For the Greeks, this was a distinction between themselves and their fate or destiny, which was in the hands or the laps of the gods. For people, even today, who are religious in a conventional way, it is a distinction between how God designed the world, including our natural condition in it, and the scope of the free will he also created. More sophisticated people use the language of science to the same effect: for them the fundamental distinction falls between what nature, including evolution, has created, by way of particles and energy and genes, and what we do in that world and with those genes. For everyone, the distinction, however they describe it, draws a line between who and what we are, for which either a divine will or no one but a blind process is responsible, and what we do with that inheritance, for which we are indeed, separately or together, responsible.

That crucial boundary between chance and choice is the spine of our ethics and our morality, and any serious shift in that boundary is seriously dislocating. Our sense of a life well lived, for example, is fundamentally shaped by supposed givens about the upper limits of human life span. If people could suddenly be expected to live ten times as long as we now do, we would have to recreate the whole range of our opinions about what an attractive kind of life would be, and also our opinions about what activities that carry some risk of accidental death for others, like driving, are morally permissible. History already offers, in our own time, less dramatic but nevertheless profound examples of how scientific change radically dislocates values. People's settled convictions about the responsibilities of leaders to protect their own soldiers in war, at any cost, changed when scientists split the atom and vastly increased the carnage that those convictions could justify. People's settled convictions about euthanasia and suicide changed when deathbed medicine dramatically increased a doctor's power to extend life beyond the point at which that life had any meaning for the patient. In each case a period of moral stability was replaced by moral insecurity, and it is revealing that in both episodes people reached for the expression "playing God," in one case to accuse the scientists who had dramatically increased our powers over nature by cracking what had been thought fundamental in God's design, and in the other to criticize dying patients for taking upon themselves a decision that the past limits of medicine had made it easy to treat as God's alone.

My hypothesis is that genetic science has suddenly made us aware of the possibility of a similar though far greater pending moral dislocation. We dread the prospect of people designing other people because that possibility in itself shifts—much more dramatically than in these other examples—the chance/choice boundary that structures our values as whole, and such a shift threatens, not to offend any of our present values, derivative or detached, but, on the contrary, to make a great part of these suddenly obsolete. Our physical being—the brain and body that furnishes each person's material substrate—has long been the absolute paradigm of what is both devastatingly important to us and, in its initial condition, beyond our power to alter and therefore beyond the scope of our responsibility, either individual or collective. The popularity of the term "genetic lottery" itself shows the centrality of our conviction that what we most basically *are* is a matter of chance not choice. I do not mean that genetic continuity provides the key to the technical philosophical problem of personal identity, though some philosophers have indeed thought this. I mean to make a psychological point: people think that the very essence of the distinction between what God or nature provides, and what they are responsible for making of or with that provision, is to be defined physically, in terms of what is in "the genes" or, in a metaphor reflecting an older science, "the blood."

If we were to take seriously the possibility we are now exploring—that scientists really have gained the capacity to create a human being having any phenotype that they or their prospective parents choose—then we could chart the destruction of settled moral and ethical attitudes starting at almost any point. We use the chance/choice distinction not simply in our assignments of responsibility for situations or events, for example, but in our assessments of pride, including pride in what nature has given us. It is a striking phenomenon, now, that people take pride in physical attributes or skills they did not choose or create, like physical appearance or strength, but not when these can be seen to be the results of the efforts of others in which they played no part. A woman who puts herself in the hands of a cosmetic surgeon may rejoice in the result but can take no pride in it; certainly not the pride she would have taken if she had been born into the same beauty. What would happen to pride in our physical attributes, or even what we made of them, if these were the inexorable results not of a nature in whose pride we are allowed, as it were, to share, but of the decision of our parents and their hired geneticists?

But the most dramatic use of the fundamental chance/choice distinction is in the assignment of personal and collective responsibility, and it is here that the danger of moral insecurity seems greatest. We now accept the condition in which we were born as a parameter of our responsibility—we must make the best of it that we can—but not as itself a potential arena of blame, except in those special cases, themselves of relatively recent discovery, in which some-one's behavior altered his embryonic development, through smoking, for example, or drugs. Otherwise, though we may curse fate for how we are...we may blame no one else. The same distinction holds, at least for most people, and for many reflective moral philosophers, for social responsibility as well. We feel a greater responsibility to compensate victims of industrial accidents and of racial prejudice, as in both cases victims, though in different ways, of society generally, than we feel to compensate those born with genetic defects or those injured by lightning or in those other ways that lawyers and insurance companies call "acts of God." How would all this change if everyone was as he is through the decisions of others, including the decision of some parents not to intervene but to let nature take its course?

Change it must. But how and why? Once again, these questions are not rhetorical. I do not know the answers, and can hardly guess at them. But that is the point. The terror many of us feel at the thought of genetic engineering is not a fear of what is wrong; it is rather a fear of losing our grip on what is wrong. We are not entitled—it would be a serious confusion—to think that even the most dramatic shifts in the chance/choice boundary somehow challenge morality itself: that there will one day be no more wrong or right. But we are entitled to worry that our settled convictions will, in large numbers, be undermined, that we will be in a kind of moral free-fall, that we will have to think again against a new background and with uncertain results. Playing God is playing with fire.

Suppose that this hypothesis, at least as it might be corrected and improved, makes sense, and accounts for the powerful surd in people's emotional reaction to genetic engineering that is not accounted for by the more discrete grounds we first examined. Have we then discovered not only an explanation but a justification for the objection, a reading of "don't play God" that shows why, at least in this instance, we shouldn't? I think not. We would have discovered a challenge that we must take up rather than a reason for turning back. For our hypothesis implies no *value*—derivative or detached—at all. It reveals only reasons why our contemporary values, of both kinds, may be wrong or at least ill considered. If we are to be morally and ethically responsible, there can be no turning back once we find, as we have found, that some of the most basic presuppositions of these values are mistaken. Playing God is indeed playing with fire. But that is what we mortals have done since Prometheus, the patron saint of dangerous discovery. We play with fire and take the consequences, because the alternative is cowardice in the face of the unknown.

Ronald Dworkin: Playing God: Genes, Clones, and Luck

1) Some people worry that attempts to clone or genetically engineer human beings could result in miscarriages or in deformed humans. How does Dworkin respond to this worry? Is his response adequate?

2) Suppose a rich couple wants to genetically engineer their child to be smarter and more athletic than average. Does Dworkin think that it would be unjust for them to do so? Do you? Why or why not?

3) What is the aesthetic objection to cloning and genetic engineering? Why does Dworkin think it fails? Do you agree with him?

4) What is the "chance/choice boundary" and why does Dworkin think it is so important to our moral thought?

5) How does Dworkin interpret the claim that we ought not to "play God"? Do concerns about "playing God" give us good reason to prohibit genetic engineering?

23

The Morality of Euthanasia

James Rachels

James Rachels (1941–2003) argues that active euthanasia is sometimes morally permissible. Active euthanasia occurs when someone (typically a medical professional) takes action to deliberately end a patient's life, at the patient's request, for the patient's own good. Rachels argues that considerations of mercy play a vital role in justifying active euthanasia in many cases.

He first considers a utilitarian argument on behalf of active euthanasia, but finds problems with utilitarianism that are weighty enough to undermine this argument. However, Rachels believes that a different version can succeed. In this one, Rachels claims that any action that promotes the best interests of all concerned, and that violates no rights, is morally acceptable. Since, he claims, active euthanasia sometimes satisfies this description, it is sometimes morally acceptable.

The single most powerful argument in support of euthanasia is the argument from mercy. It is also an exceptionally simple argument, at least in its main idea, which makes one uncomplicated point. Terminally ill patients sometimes suffer pain so horrible that it is beyond the comprehension of those who have not actually experienced it. Their

From "Euthanasia," in Tom Beauchamp, ed., *Matters of Life and Death*, Second Edition (1986), pp. 49–52 (McGraw-Hill Publishers).

suffering can be so terrible that we do not like even to read about it or think about it; we recoil even from the descriptions of such agony. The argument from mercy says euthanasia is justified because it provides an end to *that*.

The great Irish satirist Jonathan Swift took eight years to die, while, in the words of Joseph Fletcher, "His mind crumbled to pieces." At times the pain in his blinded eyes was so intense he had to be restrained from tearing them out with his own hands. Knives and other potential instruments of suicide had to be kept from him. For the last three years of his life, he could do nothing but sit and drool: and when he finally died it was only after convulsions that lasted thirty-six hours.

Swift died in 1745. Since then, doctors have learned how to eliminate much of the pain that accompanies terminal illness, but the victory has been far from complete. So, here is a more modern example.

Stewart Alsop was a respected journalist who died in 1975 of a rare form of cancer. Before he died, he wrote movingly of his experiences as a terminal patient. Although he had not thought much about euthanasia before, he came to approve of it after rooming briefly with someone he called Jack:

> The third night that I roomed with Jack in our tiny double room in the solid-tumor ward of the cancer clinic of the National Institutes of Health in Bethesda, Md., a terrible thought occurred to me.
>
> Jack had a melanoma in his belly, a malignant solid tumor that the doctors guessed was about the size of a softball. The cancer had started a few months before with a small tumor in his left shoulder, and there had been several operations since. The doctors planned to remove the softball-sized tumor, but they knew Jack would soon die. The cancer had metastasized—it had spread beyond control.
>
> Jack was good-looking, about 28, and brave. He was in constant pain, and his doctor had prescribed an intravenous shot of a synthetic opiate—a pain-killer, or analgesic—every four hours. His wife spent many of the daylight hours with him, and she would sit or lie on his bed and pat him all over, as one pats a child, only more methodically, and this seemed to help control the pain. But at night, when his pretty wife had left (wives cannot stay overnight at the NIH clinic) and darkness fell, the pain would attack without pity.
>
> At the prescribed hour, a nurse would give Jack a shot of the synthetic analgesic, and this would control the pain for perhaps two hours or a bit more. Then he would begin to moan, or whimper, very low, as though he didn't want to wake me. Then he would begin to howl, like a dog.

When this happened, either he or I would ring for a nurse, and ask for a pain-killer. She would give him some codeine or the like by mouth, but it never did any real good—it affected him no more than half an aspirin might affect a man who had just broken his arm. Always the nurse would explain as encouragingly as she could that there was not long to go before the next intravenous shot—"Only about 50 minutes now." And always poor Jack's whimpers and howls would become more loud and frequent until at last the blessed relief came.

The third night of this routine the terrible thought occurred to me. "If Jack were a dog," I thought, "what would be done with him?" The answer was obvious: the pound, and chloroform. No human being with a spark of pity could let a living thing suffer so, to no good end.

The NIH clinic is, of course, one of the most modern and best-equipped hospitals we have. Jack's suffering was not the result of poor treatment in some backward rural facility; it was the inevitable product of his disease, which medical science was powerless to prevent.

I have quoted Alsop at length not for the sake of indulging in gory details but to give a clear idea of the kind of suffering we are talking about. We should not gloss over these facts with euphemistic language or squeamishly avert our eyes from them. For only by keeping them firmly and vividly in mind can we appreciate the full force of the argument from mercy: If a person prefers—and even begs for—death as the only alternative to lingering on *in this kind of torment*, only to die anyway after a while, then surely it is not immoral to help this person die sooner. As Alsop put it, "No human being with a spark of pity could let a living thing suffer so, to no good end."

The Utilitarian Version of the Argument

In connection with this argument, the utilitarians deserve special mention. They argued that actions and social policies should be judged right or wrong *exclusively* according to whether they cause happiness or misery; and they argued that when judged by this standard, euthanasia turns out to be morally acceptable. The utilitarian argument may be elaborated as follows:

(1) Any action or social policy is morally right if it serves to increase the amount of happiness in the world or to decrease the amount of misery. Conversely, an action or social policy is morally wrong if it serves to decrease happiness or to increase misery.

(2) The policy of killing, at their own request, hopelessly ill patients who are suffering great pain would decrease the amount of misery in the world. (An example could be Alsop's friend Jack.)

(3) Therefore, such a policy would be morally right.

The first premise of this argument, (1), states the Principle of Utility, which is the basic utilitarian assumption. Today most philosophers think that this principle is wrong, because they think that the promotion of happiness and the avoidance of misery are not the *only* morally important things. Happiness, they say, is only one among many values that should be promoted: freedom, justice, and a respect for people's rights are also important. To take one example: people *might* be happier if there were no freedom of religion, for if everyone adhered to the same religious beliefs, there would be greater harmony among people. There would be no unhappiness caused within families by Jewish girls marrying Catholic boys, and so forth. Moreover, if people were brainwashed well enough, no one would mind not having freedom of choice. Thus happiness would be increased. But, the argument continues, even if happiness *could* be increased this way, it would not be right to deny people freedom of religion, because people have a right to make their own choices. Therefore, the first premise of the utilitarian argument is unacceptable.

There is a related difficulty for utilitarianism, which connects more directly with the topic of euthanasia. Suppose a person is leading a miserable life—full of more unhappiness than happiness—but does *not* want to die. This person thinks that a miserable life is better than none at all. Now I assume that we would all agree that the person should not be killed; that would be plain, unjustifiable murder. Yet it *would* decrease the amount of misery in the world if we killed this person—it would lead to an increase in the balance of happiness over unhappiness—and so it is hard to see how, on strictly utilitarian grounds, it could be wrong. Again, the Principle of Utility seems to be an inadequate guide for determining right and wrong. So we are on shaky ground if we rely on *this* version of the argument from mercy for a defense of euthanasia.

Doing What Is in Everyone's Best Interests

Although the foregoing utilitarian argument is faulty, it is nevertheless based on a sound idea. For even if the promotion of happiness and avoidance of misery are not the *only* morally important things, they are still very important. So, when an action or a social policy would decrease misery, that is *a* very strong reason in its favor. In the cases of voluntary euthanasia we are now considering, great suffering is eliminated, and since the patient requests it, there is no question of violating individual rights. That is why, regardless of the difficulties of the Principle of Utility, the utilitarian version of the argument still retains considerable force.

I want now to present a somewhat different version of the argument from mercy, which is inspired by utilitarianism but which avoids the difficulties of the foregoing version by not making the Principle of Utility a premise of the argument. I believe that the following argument is sound and proves that active euthanasia *can* be justified:

(1) If an action promotes the best interests of *everyone* concerned and violates *no one's* rights, then that action is morally acceptable.

(2) In at least some cases, active euthanasia promotes the best interests of everyone concerned and violates no one's rights.

(3) Therefore, in at least some cases, active euthanasia is morally acceptable.

It would have been in everyone's best interests if active euthanasia had been employed in the case of Stewart Alsop's friend Jack. First, and most important, it would have been in Jack's own interests, since it would have provided him with an easier, better death, without pain. (Who among us would choose Jack's death, if we had a choice, rather than a quick painless death?) Second, it would have been in the best interests of Jack's wife. Her misery, helplessly watching him suffer, must have been almost unbearable. Third, the hospital staff's best interests would have been served, since if Jack's dying had not been prolonged, they could have turned their attention to other patients whom they could have helped. Fourth, other patients would have benefited, since medical resources would no longer have been used in the sad, pointless maintenance of Jack's physical existence. Finally, if Jack himself requested to be killed, the act would not have violated his rights. Considering all this, how can active euthanasia in this case be wrong? How can it be wrong to do an action that is merciful, that benefits everyone concerned, and that violates no one's rights?

James Rachels: The Morality of Euthanasia

1) Would someone in circumstances like Jack's be better off dead? That is, would dying quickly and painlessly be in his best interest?

2) What are Rachels's objections to the principle of utility? Do you find them convincing?

3) How does Rachels's second argument differ from the utilitarian argument? Do you agree with Rachels that it is a stronger argument?

4) Rachels claims that euthanasia cannot be said to violate anyone's rights, given that the patient requests it. Do you find this claim plausible? Is it possible to do something that violates someone's rights even if he or she consents to it?

5) Rachels claims that (in some cases) active euthanasia promotes the interests of everyone concerned. If our society were to allow active euthanasia, would this be harmful to anyone's interests? Why or why not?

24
===== ~ =====

The Survival Lottery
John Harris

....

In this paper, John Harris invites us to consider the merits of a special sort of organ transplant scheme, which he calls the survival lottery. Each year, many thousands of people die because of organ failure and the lack of a suitable donor organ. Harris proposes that we remedy this situation by instituting a lottery among (almost) all citizens. Whenever two or more people are in need of a vital organ, we pick a citizen at random to be vivisected (dissected while alive—though presumably under anesthesia!), so that his or her organs can be distributed to those who need them to survive.

We don't do this with any sort of punitive intent, but rather in order to minimize the number of people who die, through no fault of their own, because of organ failure. True, the organ donor being killed is wholly innocent. But then so are those who are dying for lack of a donor organ.

Harris is well aware that the lottery sounds like outright murder, and he devotes the bulk of the article to presenting, and then countering, a great many objections to it. He acknowledges that there may be problems with making such a system feasible in practice. If these problems could be ironed out, however, Harris thinks that rational and morally enlightened people would endorse this proposal for their own society.

....

John Harris, "The Survival Lottery", *Philosophy* (1975), pp. 81–87. Reprinted with the permission of Cambridge University Press.

Let us suppose that organ transplant procedures have been perfected; in such circumstances if two dying patients could be saved by organ transplants then, if surgeons have the requisite organs in stock and no other needy patients, but nevertheless allow their patients to die, we would be inclined to say, and be justified in saying, that the patients died because the doctors refused to save them. But if there are no spare organs in stock and none otherwise available, the doctors have no choice, they cannot save their patients and so must let them die. In this case we would be disinclined to say that the doctors are in any sense the cause of their patients' deaths. But let us further suppose that the two dying patients, Y and Z, are not happy about being left to die. They might argue that it is not strictly true that there are no organs which could be used to save them. Y needs a new heart and Z new lungs. They point out that if just one healthy person were to be killed his organs could be removed and both of them be saved. We and the doctors would probably be alike in thinking that such a step, while technically possible, would be out of the question. We would not say that the doctors were killing their patients if they refused to prey upon the healthy to save the sick. And because this sort of surgical Robin Hoodery is out of the question we can tell Y and Z that they cannot be saved, and that when they die they will have died of natural causes and not of the neglect of their doctors. Y and Z do not however agree, they insist that if the doctors fail to kill a healthy man and use his organs to save them, then the doctors will be responsible for their deaths.

Many philosophers have for various reasons believed that we must not kill even if by doing so we could save life. They believe that there is a moral difference between killing and letting die. On this view, to kill A so that Y and Z might live is ruled out because we have a strict obligation not to kill but a duty of some lesser kind to save life. A. H. Clough's dictum "Thou shalt not kill but need'st not strive officiously to keep alive" expresses bluntly this point of view. The dying Y and Z may be excused for not being much impressed by Clough's dictum. They agree that it is wrong to kill the innocent and are prepared to agree to an absolute prohibition against so doing. They do not agree, however, that A is more innocent than they are. Y and Z might go on to point out that the currently acknowledged right of the innocent not to be killed, even where their deaths might give life to others, is just a decision to prefer the lives of the fortunate to those of the unfortunate. A is innocent in the sense that he has done nothing to deserve death, but Y and Z are also innocent in this sense. Why should they be the ones to die simply because they are so unlucky as to have diseased organs? Why, they might argue, should their living or dying be left to chance when in so many other areas of human life we believe that we have an obligation to ensure the survival of the maximum number of lives possible?

Y and Z argue that if a doctor refuses to treat a patient, with the result that the patient dies, he has killed that patient as sure as shooting, and that, in exactly the same way, if the doctors refuse Y and Z the transplants that they need, then their refusal will kill Y and Z, again as sure as shooting. The doctors, and indeed the society which supports their inaction, cannot defend themselves by arguing that they are neither expected, nor required by law or convention, to kill so that lives may be saved (indeed, quite the reverse) since this is just an appeal to custom or authority. A man who does his own moral thinking must decide whether, in these circumstances, he ought to save two lives at the cost of one, or one life at the cost of two. The fact that so called "third parties" have never before been brought into such calculations, have never before been thought of as being involved, is not an argument against their now becoming so. There are of course, good arguments against allowing doctors simply to haul passers-by off the streets whenever they have a couple of patients in need of new organs. And the harmful side-effects of such a practice in terms of terror and distress to the victims, the witnesses and society generally, would give us further reasons for dismissing the idea. Y and Z realize this and have a proposal, which they will shortly produce, which would largely meet objections to placing such power in the hands of doctors and eliminate at least some of the harmful side-effects.

In the unlikely event of their feeling obliged to reply to the reproaches of Y and Z, the doctors might offer the following argument: they might maintain that a man is only responsible for the death of someone whose life he might have saved, if, in all the circumstances of the case, he ought to have saved the man by the means available. This is why a doctor might be a murderer if he simply refused or neglected to treat a patient who would die without treatment, but not if he could only save the patient by doing something he ought in no circumstances to do—kill the innocent. Y and Z readily agree that a man ought not to do what he ought not to do, but they point out that if the doctors, and for that matter society at large, ought on balance to kill one man if two can thereby be saved, then failure to do so will involve responsibility for the consequent deaths. The fact that Y's and Z's proposal involves killing the innocent cannot be a reason for refusing to consider their proposal, for this would just be a refusal to face the question at issue and so avoid having to make a decision as to what ought to be done in circumstances like these. It is Y's and Z's claim that failure to adopt their plan will also involve killing the innocent, rather more of the innocent than the proposed alternative.

To back up this last point, to remove the arbitrariness of permitting doctors to select their donors from among the chance passers-by outside hospitals, and the tremendous power this would place in doctors' hands, to mitigate worries about side-effects and lastly to appease those who wonder why poor old A should be singled out for sacrifice, Y and Z put forward the following scheme: they propose that everyone be given a sort of lottery number. Whenever doctors have two or more dying patients who could be saved by transplants, and no suitable organs have come to hand through "natural" deaths, they can ask a central computer to supply a suitable donor. The computer will then pick the number of a suitable donor at random and he will be killed so that the lives of two or more others may be saved. No doubt if the scheme were ever to be implemented a suitable euphemism for "killed" would be employed. Perhaps we would begin to talk about citizens being called upon to "give life" to others. With the refinement of transplant procedures such a scheme could offer the chance of saving large numbers of lives that are now lost. Indeed, even taking into account the loss of the lives of donors, the numbers of untimely deaths each year might be dramatically reduced, so much so that everyone's chance of living to a ripe old age might be increased. If this were to be the consequence of the adoption of such a scheme, and it might well be, it could not be dismissed lightly. It might of course be objected that it is likely that more old people will need transplants to prolong their lives than will the young, and so the scheme would inevitably lead to a society dominated by the old. But if such a society is thought objectionable, there is no reason to suppose that a program could not be designed for the computer that would ensure the maintenance of whatever is considered to be an optimum age distribution throughout the population.

Suppose that inter-planetary travel revealed a world of people like ourselves, but who organized their society according to this scheme. No one was considered to have an absolute right to life or freedom from interference, but everything was always done to ensure that as many people as possible would enjoy long and happy lives. In such a world a man who attempted to escape when his number was up or who resisted on the grounds that no one had a right to take his life, might well be regarded as a murderer. We might or might not prefer to live in such a world, but the morality of its inhabitants would surely be one that we could respect. It would not be obviously more barbaric or cruel or immoral than our own.

Y and Z are willing to concede one exception to the universal application of their scheme. They realize that it would be unfair to allow people who have brought their misfortune on themselves to benefit from the lottery. There would clearly be something unjust about killing the abstemious B so that W (whose heavy smoking has given him lung cancer) and X (whose drinking has destroyed his liver) should be preserved to over-indulge again.

What objections could be made to the lottery scheme? A first straw to clutch at would be the desire for security. Under such a scheme we would never know when we would hear *them* knocking at the door. Every post might bring a sentence of death, every sound in the night might be the sound of boots on the stairs. But, as we have seen, the chances of actually being called upon to make the ultimate sacrifice might be slimmer than is the present risk of being killed on the roads, and most of us do not lie trembling a-bed, appalled at the prospect of being dispatched on the morrow. The truth is that lives might well be more secure under such a scheme.

If we respect individuality and see every human being as unique in his own way, we might want to reject a society in which it appeared that individuals were seen merely as interchangeable units in a structure, the value of which lies in its having as many healthy units as possible. But of course Y and Z would want to know why A's individuality was more worthy of respect than theirs.

Another plausible objection is the natural reluctance to play God with men's lives, the feeling that it is wrong to make any attempt to re-allot the life opportunities that fate has determined, that the deaths of Y and Z would be "natural," whereas the death of anyone killed to save them would have been perpetrated by men. But if we are able to change things, then to elect not to do so is also to determine what will happen in the world.

Neither does the alleged moral differences between killing and letting die afford a respectable way of rejecting the claims of Y and Z. For if we really want to counter proponents of the lottery, if we really want to answer Y and Z and not just put them off, we cannot do so by saying that the lottery involves killing and object to it for that reason, because to do so would, as we have seen, just beg the question as to whether the failure to save as many people as possible might not also amount to killing.

To opt for the society which Y and Z propose would be then to adopt a society in which saintliness would be mandatory. Each of us would have to recognize a binding obligation to give up his own life for others when called upon to do so. In such a society anyone who reneged upon this duty would be a murderer. The most promising objection to such a society, and indeed to any principle which required us to kill A in order to save Y and Z, is, I suspect, that we are committed to the right of self-defence. If I can kill A to save Y and Z then he can kill me to save P and Q, and it is only if I am prepared to agree to this that I will opt for the lottery or be prepared to agree to a man's being killed if doing so would save the lives of more than one other man. Of course there is something paradoxical about basing objections to the lottery scheme on the right of self-defence since, *ex hyposthesi*, each person would have a better chance of living to a ripe old age if the lottery scheme were to be implemented. None the less, the feeling that no man should be required to lay down his life for others makes many people shy away from such a scheme, even though it might be rational to accept it on prudential grounds, and perhaps even mandatory on utilitarian grounds. Again, Y and Z would reply that the right of self-defence must extend to them as much as to anyone else; and while it is true that they can only live if another man is killed, they would claim that it is also true that if they are left to die, then someone who lives on does so over their dead bodies.

It might be argued that the institution of the survival lottery has not gone far to mitigate the harmful side-effects in terms of terror and distress to victims, witnesses and society generally, that would be occasioned by doctors simply snatching passers-by off the streets and disorganizing them for the benefit of the unfortunate. Donors would after all still have to be procured, and this process, however it was carried out, would still be likely to prove distressing to all concerned. The lottery scheme would eliminate the arbitrariness of leaving the life and death decisions to the doctors, and remove the possibility of such terrible power falling into the hands of any individuals, but the terror and distress would remain. The effect of having to apprehend presumably unwilling victims would give us pause. Perhaps only a long period of education or propaganda could remove our abhorrence. What this abhorrence reveals about the rights and wrongs of the situation is however more difficult to assess. We might be inclined to say that only monsters could ignore the promptings of conscience so far as to operate the lottery scheme. But the promptings of conscience are not necessarily the most reliable guide. In the present case Y and Z would argue that such promptings are mere squeamishness, an over-nice self-indulgence that costs lives. Death, Y and Z would remind us, is a distressing experience whenever and to whomever it occurs, so the less it occurs the better. Fewer victims and witnesses will be distressed as part of the side-effects of the lottery scheme than would suffer as part of the side-effects of not instituting it.

Lastly, a more limited objection might be made, not to the idea of killing to save lives, but to the involvement of "third parties." Why, so the objection goes, should we not give X's heart to Y or Y's lungs to X, the same number of lives being thereby preserved and no one else's life set at risk? Y's and Z's reply to this objection differs from their previous line of argument. To amend their plan so that the involvement of so called "third parties" is ruled out would, Y and Z claim, violate their right to equal concern and respect with the rest of society. They argue that such a proposal would amount to treating the unfortunate who need new organs as a class within society whose lives are considered to be of less value than those of its more fortunate members. What possible justification could there be for singling out one group of people whom we would be justified in using as donors but not another? The idea in the mind of those who would propose such a step must be something like the following: since Y and Z cannot survive, since they are going to die in any event, there is no harm in putting their names into the lottery, for the chances of their dying cannot thereby be increased and will in fact almost certainly be reduced. But this is just to ignore everything that Y and Z have been saying. For if their lottery scheme is adopted they are not going to die anyway—their chances of dying are no greater and no less than those of any other participant in the lottery whose number may come up. This ground for confining selection of donors to the unfortunate therefore disappears. Any other ground must discriminate against Y and Z as members of a class whose lives are less worthy of respect than those of the rest of society.

It might more plausibly be argued that the dying who cannot themselves be saved by transplants, or by any other means at all, should be the priority selection group for the computer programme. But how far off must death be for a man to be classified as "dying"? Those so classified might argue that their last few days or weeks of life are as valuable to them (if not more valuable) than the possibly longer span remaining to others. The problem of narrowing down the class of possible donors without discriminating unfairly against some sub-class of society is, I suspect, insoluble.

Such is the case for the survival lottery. Utilitarians ought to be in favour of it, and absolutists cannot object to it on the ground that it involves killing the innocent, for it is Y's and Z's case that any alternative must also involve killing the innocent. If the absolutist wishes to maintain his objection he must point to some morally relevant difference between positive and negative killing. This challenge opens the door to a large topic with a whole library of literature, but Y and Z are dying and do not have time to explore it exhaustively. In their own case the most likely candidate for some feature which might make this moral difference is the malevolent intent of Y and Z themselves. An absolutist might well argue that while no one intends the deaths of Y and Z, no one necessarily wishes them dead, or aims at their demise for any reason, they do mean to kill A (or have him killed). But Y and Z can reply that the death of A is no part of their plan, they merely wish to use a couple of his organs, and if he cannot live without them…*tant pis!* None would be more delighted than Y and Z if artificial organs would do as well, and so render the lottery scheme otiose.

One form of absolutist argument perhaps remains. This involves taking an Orwellian stand on some principle of common decency. The argument would then be that even to enter into the sort of "macabre" calculations that Y and Z propose displays a blunted sensibility, a corrupted and vitiated mind. Forms of this argument have recently been advanced by Noam Chomsky (*American Power and the New Mandarins*) and Stuart Hampshire (*Morality and Pessimism*). The indefatigable Y and Z would of course deny that their calculations are in any sense "macabre," and would present them as the most humane course available in the circumstances. Moreover they would claim that the Orwellian stand on decency is the product of a closed mind, and not susceptible to rational argument. Any reasoned defence of such a principle must appeal to notions like respect for human life, as Hampshire's argument in fact does, and these Y and Z could make conformable to their own position.

Can Y and Z be answered? Perhaps only by relying on moral intuition, on the insistence that we do feel there is something wrong with the survival lottery and our confidence that this feeling is prompted by some morally relevant difference between our bringing about the death of A and our bringing about the deaths of Y and Z. Whether we could retain this confidence in our intuitions if we were to be confronted by a society in which the survival lottery operated, was accepted by all, and was seen to save many lives that would otherwise have been lost, it would be interesting to know.

There would of course be great practical difficulties in the way of implementing the lottery. In so many cases it would be agonizingly difficult to decide whether or not a person had brought his misfortune on himself. There are numerous ways in which a person may contribute to his predicament, and the task of deciding how far, or how decisively, a person is himself responsible for his fate would be formidable. And in those cases where we can be confident that a person is innocent of responsibility for his predicament, can we acquire this confidence in time to save him? The lottery scheme would be a powerful weapon in the hands of someone willing and able to misuse it. Could we ever feel certain the lottery was safe from unscrupulous computer programmers? Perhaps we should be thankful that such practical difficulties make the survival lottery an unlikely consequence of the perfection of transplants. Or perhaps we should be appalled.

It may be that we would want to tell Y and Z that the difficulties and dangers of their scheme would be too great a price to pay for its benefits. It is as well to be clear, however, that there is also a high, perhaps an even higher, price to be paid for the rejection of the scheme. That price is the lives of Y and Z and many like them, and we delude ourselves if we suppose that the reason why we reject their plan is that we accept the sixth commandment.

John Harris: The Survival Lottery

1) What exactly is a survival lottery, and how would it work? Do you think it would be morally permissible to institute one?
2) Some people might object to Harris's proposal by claiming that it is never morally permissible to kill innocent people. Why doesn't Harris think this is a good objection? Do you find his criticisms of this objection convincing?
3) Another objection to the survival lottery claims that any such policy would cause widespread terror, since anyone could be selected to have his or her organs harvested. Is this a good objection? How does Harris respond?
4) Harris allows one exception to the universal application of the survival lottery. What is the exception? Do you agree that these individuals should be excluded from the lottery?

5) Some might think that instituting a survival lottery amounts to "playing God." What does it mean to "play God"? Is it always wrong to do so?

6) What "practical difficulties" does Harris think we would face if we tried to institute a survival lottery? Could these difficulties be overcome?

≡═ ❧ ═≡

25

Unsanctifying Human Life

Peter Singer

....

Many people think that human life (and only human life) is somehow sacred. They believe that human life has a value different in kind, and certainly in degree, from that of all other animals. Peter Singer disagrees.

Using a number of cases to illustrate the widespread commitment to a doctrine of the sanctity of human life, Singer argues that there is nothing uniquely valuable about being human. He thinks that the lives of some nonhuman animals are as valuable as those of some humans. When human beings suffer serious brain damage, for instance, or from very severe retardation, their mental lives may be no more complex than those of many nonhuman animals. Singer argues that our treatment of others should depend on their capacities, rather than on species membership. If we are unwilling to perform very harmful experiments upon fellow human beings, no matter their mental capacities, then we should be equally reluctant, says Singer, to perform such experiments upon nonhuman animals. The same goes for prematurely killing and eating them.

Singer argues that discrimination on the basis of species membership—what he terms "speciesism"—is wrong for precisely the same reason that racism or sexism is wrong. These last two kinds of injustice fasten upon morally irrelevant characteristics to demote whole groups of people to second-class status. Singer argues that those who treat animals as if they had such status, solely because they are not a member of our species, are committing a similar kind of injustice.

....

P eople often say that life is sacred. They almost never mean what they say. They do not mean, as their words seem to imply, that *all* life is sacred. If they did, killing a pig, or for that matter, pulling up a cabbage, would be as contrary to their doctrine as infanticide. So when, in the context of medical ethics, people talk of the sanctity of life, it is the sanctity of *human* life that they really mean. It is this doctrine that I shall be discussing from now on.

In discussing the doctrine of the sanctity of human life, I shall not take the term "sanctity" in any specifically religious sense. Although I think that the doctrine does have a religious origin, and I shall say more about this shortly, it is now part of a broadly secular ethic, and it is as part of this secular ethic that it is most influential today. Not all those who talk about "the sanctity of life" are religious, and of those that are religious, in many cases their affirmation of the sanctity of life is independent of their religious views. In the secular context in which problems of medical ethics are usually discussed today, those who talk of the sanctity of human life are trying to say, essentially, that human life has some very special value; and a crucial implication of this assertion is the idea that there is a radical difference between the value of a human life and the value of the life of some other animal—a difference not merely in degree, but of quality or kind.

It is this idea, the idea that *human* life as such has unique value, that I shall criticize. Before I do so, however, I want to demonstrate how deep-seated and pervasive this idea of the unique value of human life is, and how far this idea is sometimes taken in our own society, and within the field of medicine. To demonstrate this, I offer two instances from different areas of medicine.

First, as an example of the value attributed to human life, I summarize a case history from Anthony Shaw's recent article, "Dilemmas of 'Informed Consent' in Children".[1]

> A baby was born with Down's syndrome (mongolism), intestinal obstruction, and a congenital heart condition. The mother, believing that the retarded infant would be impossible for her to care for adequately, refused to consent to surgery to remove the intestinal obstruction. Without surgery, of course, the baby would soon die. Thereupon a local child-welfare agency, invoking a state child-abuse stature, obtained a court order directly that surgery be performed. After a complicated course of surgery and thousands of dollars worth of medical

---

[1] Anthony Shaw, "Dilemmas of Informed Consent' in Children," *New England Journal of Medicine*, vol. 289, no. 17 (1973).

care, the infant was returned to her mother. In addition to her mental retardation, the baby's physical growth and development remained markedly retarded because of her severe cardiac disease. A follow-up enquiry eighteen months after the baby's birth revealed that the mother felt more than ever that she had been done an injustice.

This case, then, shows how much some people are prepared to do in order to ensure that a human infant lives, irrespective of the actual or potential mental capacities of the infant, its physical condition, or the wishes of the mother.

While some doctors are struggling to preserve life in cases of this sort, others are using their medical training in another way: They design and carry out experiments on non-human animals. I will give an example of the kind of work that is quite frequently done, because its nature is not as well known as it ought to be. This particular experiment was carried out at the University of Michigan Medical School, and funded by the National Research Council and the U.S. Public Health Service. The description which follows is drawn from the researchers' own account, which they published in the journal *Psychopharmacologia*:[2]

> The researchers confined sixty-four monkeys in small cubicles. These monkeys were then given unlimited access to a variety of drugs, through tubes implanted in their arms. They could control the intake by pressing a lever. In some cases, after the monkeys had become addicted, supplies were abruptly cut off. Of the monkeys that had become addicted to morphine, three were "observed to die in convulsions" while others found dead in the morning were "presumed to have died in convulsions." Monkeys that had taken large amounts of cocaine inflicted severe wounds upon themselves, including biting off their fingers and toes, before dying convulsive deaths. Amphetamines caused one monkey to "pluck all of the hair off his arms and abdomen." In general, the experimenters found that "The manifestations of toxicity...were similar to the well-known toxicities of these drugs in man." They noted that experiments on animals with addictive drugs had been going on in their laboratory for "the last 20 years."

I know that it is not pleasant to think about experiments of this nature; but since they are a real part of medicine, they should not be ignored. In fact

---

[2] G. Deneau, T. Yanagita and M. Seevers, "Self-Administration of Psychoactive Substances by the Monkey," *Psychopharmacologia*, vol. 16, pp. 30–48.

this experiment is by no means exceptional, and is perhaps no worse than the routine testing of new drugs, foodstuffs, and cosmetics, which results in the poisoning of millions of animals annually in the United States. Nor, for that matter, is the case of the mongoloid infant exceptional, apart from the fact that it was necessary to invoke the law; more commonly, the doctors would have obtained the mother's signature, though how often that signature implies genuine 'informed consent' is another matter.

The question that arises from consideration of these two kinds of cases is simply this: can it be right to make great efforts to save the life of a mongoloid human infant, when the mother does not want the infant to live, and at the same time not be wrong to kill, slowly and painfully, a number of monkeys?

One obvious defense of the addiction experiment that might be offered is that by means of such experiments, results are obtained which lead to the elimination of more suffering than is caused by the experiments themselves. In fact, this is usually not the case. Certainly in the experiment I described, no startling new discoveries were made, and any connection with the alleviation of suffering seems very tenuous. But anyway, this defense is irrelevant to the comparison I am drawing between the way we treat humans and other animals. We would not forcibly addict mongoloid infants to drugs and then allow them to die in convulsions even if we did believe that useful knowledge could thus be obtained. Why do we think it wrong to treat members of our own species in the same way that we treat other species?

Can it ever be right to treat one kind of being in a way that we would not treat another kind? Of course it can, if the beings differ in relevant respects. Which respects are relevant will depend on the treatment in question. We could defend a decision to teach young members of our own species to read, without making the same effort on behalf of young dogs, on the grounds that the two kinds of being differ in their capacity to benefit from these efforts. This difference is obviously relevant to the particular proposal. On the other hand, anyone who proposed teaching some humans to read, but not others, on the grounds that people whose racial origin is different from his own should not be encouraged to read, would be discriminating on an arbitrary basis, since race as such has nothing to do with the extent to which a person can benefit from being able to read.

Now what is the position when we compare severely and irreparably retarded human infants with non-human animals like pigs and dogs, monkeys and apes? I think we are forced to conclude that in at least some cases the human infant does not possess any characteristics or capacities that are not also possessed, to an equal or higher degree, by many non-human animals. This is true of such capacities as the capacity to feel pain, to act intentionally, to solve problems, to communicate with and relate to other beings; and such characteristics as self-awareness, a sense of one's own existence over time, concern for other beings, and curiosity. In all these respects adult members of the species I have mentioned equal or surpass many retarded infant members of our own species; moreover some of these non-humans surpass anything that some human infants might eventually achieve even with intensive care and assistance. (In case anyone should be uncertain about this, may I remind you that chimpanzees have now been taught to communicate by means of American Sign Language, the standard language used by deaf people in this country, and have mastered vocabularies of well over a hundred signs, including signs which indicate that they possess self-awareness, and the concept of time.)

So when we decide to treat one being—the severely and irreparably retarded infant—in one way, and the other being—the pig, monkey, or whatever—in another way, there seems to be no difference between the two that we can appeal to in defense of our discrimination. There is, of course, the fact that one being is, biologically, a member of our own species, while the others are members of other species. This difference, however, cannot justify different treatment, except perhaps in very special circumstances; for it is precisely the kind of arbitrary difference that the most crude and overt kind of racist tries to use to justify racial discrimination. Just as a person's race is, in itself, nearly always irrelevant to the question of how that person should be treated, so a being's species is, in itself, nearly always irrelevant. If we are prepared to discriminate against a being simply because it is not a member of our own species, although it has capacities equal or superior to those of a member of our own species, how can we object to the racist discriminating against those who are not of his own race, although they have capacities equal or superior to those of members of his own race?

I said a moment ago that a difference of species cannot justify different treatment except perhaps in very special circumstances. It may be worth mentioning the circumstances I have in mind. If we had discovered a new drug which we thought might be a very powerful aid in the treatment of serious diseases, we might feel that it should be tested in some way before being used on normal humans, in order to see if it had dangerous side-effects. Assuming that there was no reliable way of testing it except on a living, sentient creature, should we test it on a severely and irreparably retarded human infant, or on some other animal, like a monkey? Here, if the capacities of the beings are equal, I think we might be justified in saying that the biological species of the being was relevant. Since many drugs affect different species in unpredictably different ways, we would probably achieve our goal sooner by testing the drug on the retarded member of our own species than on the monkey; this would mean that we would have to use less subjects for our experiment, and so inflict less suffering all told. This seems to be a reasonable ground for preferring to use the human infant, rather than the monkey, if we have already decided to test the drug on one or other of the two. So discrimination on the basis of species, in the rare cases in which it is justified, seems to go *against* our present practices, rather than in favor of them. (Even here, it ought to be said, we would not really be discriminating on the basis of species *as such*, but rather using the species of the being as an indication of further possible unknown differences between them.)

The doctrine of the sanctity of human life, as it is normally understood, has as its core a discrimination on the basis of species and nothing else. Those who espouse the doctrine make no distinction, in their opposition to killing, between normal humans who have developed to a point at which they surpass anything that other animals can achieve, or humans in a condition of hopeless senility, or human fetuses, or infant humans, or severely brain-damaged humans. Yet those who use the sanctity of life doctrine as a ground for opposition to killing any human being show little or no concern over the vast amount of quite unnecessary killing of non-human animals that goes on in our society, despite the fact that, as I have said, many of these other animals equal or surpass, on any test that I can imagine to be relevant, humans in all the categories I have just mentioned, except for normal humans beyond the age of infancy. It is significant to note, too, that even if we allow the relevance of a being's potential (and there are serious objections to so doing) there are still human beings, whose life is allegedly sacrosanct, who cannot be distinguished from other animals in respect of their potential.

A doctrine which went by the name of "the sanctity of human life" would not necessarily have to be a speciesist doctrine. The term "human" is not, strictly, a biological term, and it is a mistake to assume that "human being" refers to precisely the same beings as are designated by the biological idea of "member of the species *homo sapiens.*" "Human," according to the Oxford English Dictionary, means "of, belonging to, or characteristic of man"; or in a slightly different sense, "having or showing the qualities or attributes proper to or distinctive of man." If the advocates of the "sanctity of human life" doctrine were to take this definition seriously, they would find their views radically transformed. According to the definition, whether we class a being as "human" will depend on what qualities or attributes we think characteristic of, proper to, or distinctive of man (and I assume that by "man," the dictionary here means men and women, mankind as a whole). So we would then have to try to draw up a list of these qualities or attributes. This list would probably include some or all of the capacities and characteristics that I mentioned earlier, when comparing retarded infants and monkeys, but to decide which properties were necessary and which sufficient would be difficult. Let us say, though, just to take an example, that we decide that what is characteristic or distinctive of men and women is a capacity for self-awareness or self-consciousness. Then we will not count severely retarded infants as human beings, even though they are clearly members of *homo sapiens*; at the same time we might decide, after examining the abilities displayed by apes, dolphins, and perhaps some other mammals, to count these beings as human beings.

In any case, if we follow the dictionary definition of "human," one point seems certain, whatever criteria we eventually select as distinctive of men and women: severely and irreparably retarded *homo sapiens* infants would be in the same category as a great many members of other species. This seems true, anyway, so long as we stay within the secular context that I have been assuming throughout this discussion. If we allow appeals to religious doctrines, based on special revelations, other conclusions might be possible....

Is the only problem with the doctrine of the sanctity of human life, then, a misconception about the boundaries of "human"? Is it just that the advocates of this doctrine have got hold of a biological notion of what it is to be human, instead of a notion that defines the term as the dictionary suggests it should be defined, with regard to distinctively human characteristics?

We could, perhaps, try to save the doctrine by modifying it in this way. The suggested modification of the doctrine would place lethal experiments on the more developed nonhuman animals in the same category as experiments on severely retarded members of our own species. Similarly, if, as Jonathan Swift once suggested, human infants, boiled, roasted or fricasséed, make a tasty dish, then we would have to choose between ceasing to rear animals like pigs and cattle for food, or admitting that there is no moral objection to fattening retarded infants for the table. Clearly, this is not a position that many present advocates of the sanctity of human life would be prepared to embrace. In fact, it is so far from what present advocates of the doctrine mean, that it would be downright misleading to continue to use the same name for the doctrine. Whatever the proper or dictionary meaning of the word "human" is now, in popular usage, [it is] too closely identified with "member of the species *homo sapiens*" for us to apply it to chimpanzees, or deny it to retarded infants. I myself, in this paper, have used, and for reasons of convenience shall continue to use, the word in its popular, rather than dictionary, sense.

A further difficult question which any attempt to redraw the boundaries of the "human" community must face is: where do we place normal embryonic or infant members of our species, who have the potential, given normal development, to satisfy the criteria for membership, but do not satisfy them at present? Judged by the characteristics they actually possess, and excluding for the moment such indirect factors as the concerns of parents or others, an infant *homo sapiens* aged, say, 6 months, would seem to be much less of a "human" than an adult chimpanzee; and if we reduce the age of the infant to, say, one month, it compares unfavorably with those adult members of other species—pigs, cattle, sheep, rats, chickens, and mice—that we destroy by the million in our slaughterhouses and laboratories. Does the potential of these infants make a difference to the wrongness of killing them?

It is impossible for me to discuss this question adequately in the time I have available, so I will only point out that if we believe it is the potential of the infant that makes it wrong to kill it, we seem to be committed to the view that abortion, however soon after conception it may take place, is as seriously wrong as infanticide. Moreover, it is not easy to see on what grounds mere potential could give rise to a right to life, unless we valued what it was that the being had potential to become—in this case, a rational, self-conscious being. Now while we may think that a rational, self-conscious being has a right to life, relatively few of us, I think, value the existence of rational self-conscious beings in the sense that the more of them there are, the better we think it is. If we did value the existence of rational self-conscious beings in this way, we would be opposed to contraception, as well as abortion and infanticide, and even to abstinence or celibacy. But most of us think that there are enough rational self-conscious beings around already—in which case I find it hard to see why we should place great moral weight on every potentially rational, self-conscious being realizing its potential.

Assuming that we can settle the criteria for being "human" in the strict sense, and can settle this problem about potentially "human" beings, would this mean that we had settled the question of which lives are sacred, and which beings it is justifiable to kill for rather trivial reasons? Unfortunately, even then we would not have solved all our problems; for there is no necessary connection between what is characteristic of, or distinctive of, mankind, and what it is that makes it wrong to kill a being. To believe that this connection was automatic and followed immediately without further argument would only be a slightly more sophisticated form of speciesism than the crude biological basis of discrimination discussed earlier. While we might, in the end, decide that all and only those beings whose lives were sacred were those that possessed the characteristics distinctive of mankind, this would be a moral decision that could not be deduced simply from the definition of "human." We might, on reflection, decide the other way—for instance, we might hold that no sentient being should be killed if the probability is that its life will contain a favorable balance of pleasure or happiness over pain and suffering.

Although I have been unable to make up my own mind about the necessary criteria for a right to life—and I leave this question open in the hope that others will be able to help me decide—it is clear that we shall have to change our attitudes about killing so as to obliterate the sharp distinction that we currently make between beings that are members of our own species and beings that are not. How shall we do this?

There are three possibilities:

(1) While holding constant our attitudes to members of other species, we change our attitudes to members of our own species, so that we consider it legitimate to kill retarded human infants in painful ways for experimental purposes even when no immediately useful knowledge is likely to be derived from these experiments; and in addition we give up any moral objections we may have to rearing and killing these infants for food.

(2) While holding constant our attitudes to members of our own species, we change our attitudes to members of other species, so that we consider it wrong to kill them because we like the taste of their flesh, or for experimental purposes even when the experiment would result in immediately useful knowledge; and moreover we refuse to kill them even when they are suffering severe pain from some incurable disease, and are a burden to those who must look after them.

(3) We change our attitudes to both humans and non-humans, so that they come together at some point in between the present extremes.

None of these three positions makes an arbitrary discrimination on the basis of species, and all are consistent. So we cannot decide between them on these grounds; and accordingly, while I am quite certain that our present attitudes are wrong, I am a little more tentative about which of these possibilities is right. Still, if we look at what each implies, I think we can see that the third possibility has much in its favor—not surprisingly, in view of its median position. Thus, I doubt that anyone could seriously advocate performing an experiment like that I described earlier, on retarded infants of our own species; nor do I think that many of us could treat retarded infants as if they were purely means towards our gastronomic ends. I think that we can only carry on these practices with regard to other species because we have a huge prejudice in favor of the interests of our own species, and a corresponding tendency to neglect the interests of other species. If I am right about this, we are not likely to transfer this prejudice to members of our own species. Racist slave-owners, if forced to stop discriminating, would be unlikely to start enslaving whites.

As for the second possibility, while I advocate a very radical change in our attitudes towards other species, I do not think this change should go so far as to imply that we should eliminate all mercy-killing, or attempt to keep alive an animal which can only live in misery.

So we have to change our attitudes in both directions. We have to bring non-humans within the sphere of our moral concern, and cease to treat them purely as means to our ends. At the same time, once we realize that the fact that severely and irreparably retarded infants are members of the species *homo sapiens* is not in itself relevant to how we should treat them, we should be ready to reconsider current practices which cause suffering to all concerned and benefit nobody. As an example of such a practice, I shall consider, very briefly, the practice of allowing these infants to die by withholding treatment.

It quite often happens that a severely and irreparably retarded infant has, in addition to its retardation, a condition which, unless treated, will cause it to die in some foreseeable period—perhaps a day, perhaps a few months or a year. The condition may be one which doctors could, and in the case of a normal infant certainly would, cure; but sometimes, when the infant is severely and irreparably retarded, the doctor in charge will withhold this treatment and allow the infant to die. In general, we can only guess at how often this occurs; but a recent investigation of the Yale–New Haven special care nursery showed that over a 2 ½-year period, 43 deaths, or 14% of all deaths in the nursery, were related to withholding treatment. The decision to withhold treatment at this nursery was in each case made by parents and physicians together, on the basis that there was little or no chance for a meaningful life for the infant.[3] The investigators, Duff and Campbell, cautiously endorse this practice, and within the alternatives legally available to the doctors, it does seem to be the best that they can do; but if it is justifiable to withhold available forms of treatment, knowing that this will result in the death of the infant, what possible grounds can there be for refusing to kill the infant painlessly?

The idea that there is a significant moral distinction between an act and an omission, between killing and letting die, has already been attacked by philosophers. I accept their arguments, and I have nothing new to add to them, except for the reflection that we would never consider allowing a horse or dog to die in agony if it could be killed painlessly. Once we see that the case of a dying horse is really quite parallel to the case of a dying retarded infant, we may be more ready to drop the distinction between killing and letting die in the case of the infant too.

This is by no means an academic issue. Enormous, and in my view utterly needless, suffering is caused by our present attitudes. Take, for example, the condition known as *spina bifida*, in which the infant is born with its spinal cord exposed. Three out of every thousand babies have this condition, which adds up to a large number of babies. Although treatment is possible, with the more severe cases even immediate surgery and vigorous treatment will not result in successful rehabilitation. The children will grow up severely handicapped, both mentally and physically, and they will probably die in their teens. The burdens on the family can easily be imagined, and it is doubtful if the child's life is a benefit for him. But what is the alternative to surgery, under present medical ethics?

If surgery is not performed, the spina bifida baby will die—but not immediately. Some of them, perhaps a third, will last more than three months, and a few will survive for several years. One writer has described their condition in the following terms:

> Virtually all will be paralyzed from the waist down, and incontinent because of damage to their exposed nerves. Four out of five of these survivors will get hydrocephalus; their heads will swell out, some until they are too heavy to hold up. Severely retarded, often spastic and blind, they will spend their childhood in institutions that most of us

---

[3] R. S. Duff and A.G.M. Campbell, "Moral and Ethical Dilemmas in the Special Care Nursery," *New England Journal of Medicine*, vol. 289, no. 17 (1973).

do not care to think about, let alone visit. By adolescence virtually all will be dead.[4]

This kind of life is the alternative that parents must face if they hesitate to consent to surgery. It is a horrible, immoral choice to offer anyone, let alone parents immediately after the birth of their child. The obvious alternative to trying to bring up a severely retarded and handicapped child—a swift, painless death for the infant—is not available, because the law enforces the idea that the infant's life is sacred and cannot be directly terminated.

This, then, is one way in which our treatment of severely and irreparably retarded infants needs to be brought closer to our better forms of treatment of members of other species.

I said at the beginning of this paper that the doctor with an interest in medical ethics, and the moral philosopher, have different concerns, at least partly because of their different positions vis-à-vis the law. No doubt this applies to the practice of allowing infants to die while refusing to kill them. The law prohibits killing, but gives no clear directive about letting die; so doctors do what they can to relieve suffering within the boundaries of the law. For this, of course, they are to be commended; but there are indications that a policy which can be defended only in terms of making the best of a bad legal situation is also being thought of as embodying a significant moral distinction. Doctors can be heard sagely quoting Arthur Clough's lines: "Thou shalt not kill, but needst not strive officiously to keep alive," as if these lines were a piece of ancient wisdom—they seem to be unaware that the lines were written to satirize the moral position in support of which they are being quoted.[5] More seriously, the House of Delegates of the American Medical Association recently adopted a policy statement condemning "the intentional termination of the life of one human being by another" as "contrary to that for which the medical profession stands," although the same statement went on to allow the "cessation of the employment of extraordinary means to preserve the life of the body."[6] But what is the cessation of any form of life-sustaining treatment if it is not the intentional termination of the life of one human being by another? And what exactly is it for which the medical profession stands

---

[4] Gerald Leach, *The Biocrats* (Penguin, Middlesex, England, 1972), p. 197.
[5] I owe this point to Jonathan Glover.
[6] *New York Times*, Dec. 5, 1973.

that allows it to kill millions of sentient non-human beings, while prohib-iting it from releasing from suffering an infant *homo sapiens* with a lower potential for a meaningful life? While doctors may have to obey the law, they do not have to defend it.

I have suggested some ways in which, once we eliminate speciesist bias from our moral views, we might bring our attitudes to human and non-human animals closer together. I am well aware that I have not given any precise suggestions about when it is justifiable to kill either a retarded infant, or a non-human animal. I really have not made up my mind on this problem, and so I leave it open, in the hope that others will offer suggestions.

Peter Singer: Unsanctifying Human Life

1) What is *speciesism*? Why isn't it always speciesist to treat humans and dogs differently? Do you agree with Singer that speciesism is morally wrong?

2) Consider Singer's example of the baby born with Down's syndrome and a heart condition. Do you think it would be morally permissible to allow such a baby to die, rather than operating on it? Would it be mor-ally permissible to painlessly kill it? Why or why not?

3) Can animal experiments of the sort Singer discusses ever be morally justified? Why or why not?

4) Why does Singer think that some nonhuman animals (e.g., primates) deserve the same degree of moral consideration as some humans (e.g., the severely mentally disabled)? Do you find his argument convincing?

5) Singer mentions three possible ways that we could change our moral views so as to avoid speciesism. Which of these, if any, do you find most attractive? Why?

6) Singer compares cases of euthanasia in humans to the common prac-tice of "putting down" nonhuman animals. Is there any morally rel-evant difference between the two cases that would justify painlessly killing a terminally ill dog, but not a terminally ill baby?

26

People or Penguins: The Case for Optimal Pollution

William F. Baxter

....

Economist William Baxter (1929–1998) argues that we ought to seek solutions to all "problems of human organization" by utilizing four criteria: (1) people ought to be free to do as they please so long as they do not infringe the freedom of others; (2) waste is a bad thing; (3) every human being ought to be treated as an end, and not a mere means; and (4) any social policy should offer an incentive and opportunity to each person to increase his or her self-interest.

Relying on these criteria, Baxter addresses the issue of our environmental duties. He notes that the four criteria are "people-centered," or *anthropocentric*, as environmental philosophers would say. Social policies should be aimed exclusively at improving human well-being. For Baxter, the well-being of nonhumans has no value in its own right. He offers six reasons in support of such a claim. He then proceeds to explain why such a view is not as threatening to nonhumans as we might think. Many of our own interests are enhanced by taking care of the welfare of animals and the environment. But in cases of conflict, where we benefit only at their expense, we must place human interests first.

To those who say that we must respect nature for its own sake, and that we are under a moral duty to return the land to its "natural state," Baxter claims that there is no such state. He argues that the notion of a "natural" state is actually a disguised way of describing a situation that one thinks ought to be preserved. And yet, if he is correct, the situation that we ought to preserve is just the one that maximizes long-term human benefit. So, for example, we should not strive to create a "pure" world without any pollution at all. Instead, we ought to create a world that contains an optimal level of pollution—one that strikes the best cost-benefit balance among all human interests. It won't be easy to know what this balance is. But in principle, Baxter's approach can give us guidance for deciding how much respect we must extend to nonhumans—namely, just as much as will enable human beings to flourish.

I start with the modest proposition that, in dealing with pollution, or indeed with any problem, it is helpful to know what one is attempting to accomplish. Agreement on how and whether to pursue a particular objective, such as pollution control, is not possible unless some more general objective has been identified and stated with reasonable precision. We talk loosely of having clean air and clean water, of preserving our wilderness areas, and so forth. But none of these is a sufficiently general objective: each is more accurately viewed as a means rather than as an end.

With regard to clean air, for example, one may ask, "how clean?" and "what does clean mean?" It is even reasonable to ask, "why have clean air?" Each of these questions is an implicit demand that a more general community goal be stated—a goal sufficiently general in its scope and enjoying sufficiently general assent among the community of actors that such "why" questions no longer seem admissible with respect to that goal.

If, for example, one states as a goal the proposition that "every person should be free to do whatever he wishes in contexts where his actions do not interfere with the interests of other human beings," the speaker is unlikely to be met with a response of "why." The goal may be criticized as uncertain in its implications or difficult to implement, but it is so basic a tenet of our civilization—it reflects a cultural value so broadly shared, at least in the abstract—that the question "why" is seen as impertinent or imponderable or both.

I do not mean to suggest that everyone would agree with the "spheres of freedom" objective just stated. Still less do I mean to suggest that a society could subscribe to four or five such general objectives that would be adequate in their coverage to serve as testing criteria by which all other disagreements might be measured. One difficulty in the attempt to construct such a list is that each new goal added will conflict, in certain applications, with each prior goal listed; and thus each goal serves as a limited qualification on prior goals.

Without any expectation of obtaining unanimous consent to them, let me set forth four goals that I generally use as ultimate testing criteria in attempting to frame solutions to problems of human organization. My position regarding pollution stems from these four criteria. If the criteria appeal to you and any part of what appears hereafter does not, our disagreement will have a helpful focus: which of us is correct, analytically, in supposing that his position on pollution would better serve these general goals. If the criteria do not seem acceptable to you, then it is to be expected that our more particular judgments will differ, and the task will then be yours to identify the basic set of criteria upon which your particular judgments rest.

My criteria are as follows:

1. The spheres of freedom criterion stated above.

2. Waste is a bad thing. The dominant feature of human existence is scarcity—our available resources, our aggregate labors, and our skill in employing both have always been, and will continue for some time to be, inadequate to yield to every man all the tangible and intangible satisfactions he would like to have. Hence, none of those resources, or labors, or skills, should be wasted—that is, employed so as to yield less than they might yield in human satisfactions.

3. Every human being should be regarded as an end rather than as a means to be used for the betterment of another. Each should be afforded dignity and regarded as having an absolute claim to an even-handed application of such rules as the community may adopt for its governance.

4. Both the incentive and the opportunity to improve his share of satisfactions should be preserved to every individual. Preservation of incentive is dictated by the "no-waste" criterion and enjoins against the continuous, totally egalitarian redistribution of satisfactions, or wealth; but subject to that constraint, everyone should receive, by continuous redistribution if necessary, some minimal share of aggregate wealth so as to avoid a level of privation from which the opportunity to improve his situation becomes illusory.

The relationship of these highly general goals to the more specific environmental issues at hand may not be readily apparent, and I am not yet ready to demonstrate their pervasive implications. But let me give one indication of their implications. Recently scientists have informed us that use of DDT in food production is causing damage to the penguin population. For the present purposes let us accept that assertion as an indisputable scientific fact. The scientific fact is often asserted as if the correct implication—that we must stop agricultural use of DDT—followed from the mere statement of the fact of penguin damage. But plainly it does not follow if my criteria are employed.

My criteria are oriented to people, not penguins. Damage to penguins, or sugar pines, or geological marvels is, without more, simply irrelevant. One must go further, by my criteria, and say: Penguins are important because people enjoy seeing them walk about rocks; and furthermore, the well-being of people would be less impaired by halting use of DDT than by giving up penguins. In short, my observations about environmental problems will be people-oriented, as are my criteria. I have no interest in preserving penguins for their own sake.

It may be said by way of objection to this position, that it is very selfish of people to act as if each person represented one unit of importance and nothing else was of any importance. It is undeniably selfish. Nevertheless I think it is the only tenable starting place for analysis for several reasons. First, no other position corresponds to the way most people really think and act—i.e., corresponds to reality.

Second, this attitude does not portend any massive destruction of nonhuman flora and fauna, for people depend on them in many obvious ways, and they will be preserved because and to the degree that humans do depend on them.

Third, what is good for humans is, in many respects, good for penguins and pine trees—clean air for example. So that humans are, in these respects, surrogates for plant and animal life.

Fourth, I do not know how we could administer any other system. Our decisions are either private or collective. Insofar as Mr. Jones is free to act privately, he may give such preferences as he wishes to other forms of life: he may feed birds in winter and do with less himself, and he may even decline to resist an advancing polar bear on the ground that the bear's appetite is more important than those portions of himself that the bear may choose to eat. In short my basic premise does not rule out private altruism to competing life-forms. It does rule out, however, Mr. Jones' inclination to feed Mr. Smith to the bear, however hungry the bear, however despicable Mr. Smith.

Insofar as we act collectively on the other hand, only humans can be afforded an opportunity to participate in the collective decisions. Penguins cannot vote now and are unlikely subjects for the franchise—pine trees more unlikely still. Again each individual is free to cast his vote so as to benefit sugar pines if that is his inclination. But many of the more extreme assertions that one hears from some conservationists amount to tacit assertions that they are specially appointed representatives of sugar pines, and hence that their preferences should be weighted more heavily than the preferences of other humans who do not enjoy equal rapport with "nature." The simplistic assertion that agricultural use of DDT must stop at once because it is harmful to penguins is of that type.

Fifth, if polar bears or pine trees or penguins, like men, are to be regarded as ends rather than means, if they are to count in our calculus of social organization, someone must tell me how much each one counts, and someone must tell me how these life-forms are to be permitted to express their preferences, for I do not know either answer. If the answer is that certain people are to hold their proxies, then I want to know how those proxy-holders are to be selected: self-appointment does not seem workable to me.

Sixth, and by way of summary of all the foregoing, let me point out that the set of environmental issues under discussion—although they raise very complex technical questions of how to achieve any objective— ultimately raise a normative question: what *ought* we to do? Questions of *ought* are unique to the human mind and world—they are meaningless as applied to a nonhuman situation.

I reject the proposition that we *ought* to respect the "balance of nature" or to "preserve the environment" unless the reason for doing so, express or implied, is the benefit of man.

I reject the idea that there is a "right" or "morally correct" state of nature to which we should return. The word "nature" has no normative connotation. Was it "right" or "wrong" for the earth's crust to heave in contortion and create mountains and seas? Was it "right" for the first amphibian to crawl up out of the primordial ooze? Was it "wrong" for plants to reproduce themselves and alter the atmospheric composition in favor of oxygen? For animals to alter the atmosphere in favor of carbon dioxide both by breathing oxygen and eating plants? No answers can be given to these questions because they are meaningless questions.

All this may seem obvious to the point of being tedious, but much of the present controversy over environment and pollution rests on tacit normative assumptions about just such nonnormative phenomena: that it is "wrong" to impair penguins with DDT, but not to slaughter cattle for prime rib roasts. That it is wrong to kill stands of sugar pines with industrial fumes, but not to cut sugar pines and build housing for the poor. Every man is entitled to his own preferred definition of Walden Pond, but there is no definition that has any moral superiority over another, except by reference to the selfish needs of the human race.

From the fact that there is no normative definition of the natural state, it follows that there is no normative definition of clean air or pure water—hence no definition of polluted air—or of pollution—except by reference to the needs of man. The "right" composition of the atmosphere is one which has some dust in it and some lead in it and some hydrogen sulfide in it—just those amounts that attend a sensibly organized society thoughtfully and knowledgeably pursuing the greatest possible satisfaction for its human members.

The first and most fundamental step toward solution of our environmental problems is a clear recognition that our objective is not pure air or water but rather some optimal state of pollution. That step immediately suggests the question: How do we define and attain the level of pollution that will yield the maximum possible amount of human satisfaction?

Low levels of pollution contribute to human satisfaction but so do food and shelter and education and music. To attain ever lower levels of pollution, we must pay the cost of having less of these other things. I contrast that view of the cost of pollution control with the more popular statement that pollution control will "cost" very large numbers of dollars. The popular statement is true in some senses, false in others; sorting out the true and false senses is of some importance. The first step in that sorting process is to achieve a clear understanding of the difference between dollars and resources. Resources are the wealth of our nation; dollars are merely claim checks upon those resources. Resources are of vital importance; dollars are comparatively trivial.

Four categories of resources are sufficient for our purposes: At any given time a nation, or a planet if you prefer, has a stock of labor, of technological skill, of capital goods, and of natural resources (such as mineral deposits, timber, water, land, etc.). These resources can be used in various combinations to yield goods and services of all kinds—in some limited quantity. The quantity will be larger if they are combined efficiently, smaller if combined inefficiently. But in either event the resource stock is limited, the goods and services that they can be made to yield are limited; even the most efficient use of them will yield less than our population, in the aggregate, would like to have.

If one considers building a new dam, it is appropriate to say that it will be costly in the sense that it will require x hours of labor, y tons of steel and concrete, and z amount of capital goods. If these resources are devoted to the dam, then they cannot be used to build hospitals, fishing rods, schools, or electric can openers. That is the meaningful sense in which the dam is costly.

Quite apart from the very important question of how wisely we can combine our resources to produce goods and services, is the very different question of how they get distributed—who gets how many goods? Dollars constitute the claim checks which are distributed among people and which control their share of national output. Dollars are nearly valueless pieces of paper except to the extent that they do represent claim checks to some fraction of the output of goods and services. Viewed as claim checks, all the dollars outstanding during any period of time are worth, in the aggregate, the goods and services that are available to be claimed with them during that period—neither more nor less.

It is far easier to increase the supply of dollars than to increase the production of goods and services—printing dollars is easy. But printing more dollars doesn't help because each dollar then simply becomes a claim to fewer goods, i.e., becomes worth less.

The point is this: many people fall into error upon hearing the statement that the decision to build a dam, or to clean up a river, will cost $X million. It is regrettably easy to say: "It's only money. This is a wealthy country, and we have lots of money." But you cannot build a dam or clean a river with $X million—unless you also have a match, you can't even make a fire. One builds a dam or cleans a river by diverting labor and steel and trucks and factories from making one kind of goods to making another. The cost in dollars is merely a shorthand way of describing the extent of the diversion necessary. If we build a dam for $X million, then we must recognize that we will have $X million less housing and food and medical care and electric can openers as a result.

Similarly, the costs of controlling pollution are best expressed in terms of the other goods we will have to give up to do the job. This is not to say the job should not be done. Badly as we need more housing, more medical care, more can openers, and more symphony orchestras, we could do with somewhat less of them, in my judgment at least, in exchange for somewhat cleaner air and rivers. But that is the nature of the trade-off, and analysis of the problem is advanced if that unpleasant reality is kept in mind. Once the trade-off relationship is clearly perceived, it is possible to state in a very general way what the optimal level of pollution is. I would state it as follows:

People enjoy watching penguins. They enjoy relatively clean air and smog-free vistas. Their health is improved by relatively clean water and air. Each of these benefits is a type of good or service. As a society we would be well advised to give up one washing machine if the resources that would have gone into that washing machine can yield greater human satisfaction when diverted into pollution control. We should give up one hospital if the resources thereby freed would yield more human satisfaction when devoted to elimination of noise in our cities. And so on, trade-off by trade-off, we should divert our productive capacities from the production of existing goods and services to the production of a cleaner, quieter, more pastoral nation up to—and no further than—the point at which we value more highly the next washing machine or hospital that we would have to do without than we value the next unit of environmental improvement that the diverted resources would create.

Now this proposition seems to me unassailable but so general and abstract as to be unhelpful—at least unadministerable in the form stated. It assumes we can measure in some way the incremental units of human satisfaction yielded by very different types of goods....But I insist that the proposition stated describes the result for which we should be striving— and again, that it is always useful to know what your target is even if your weapons are too crude to score a bull's eye.

William F. Baxter: People or Penguins: The Case for Optimal Pollution

1) Baxter's first principle states that "every person should be free to do whatever he wishes in contexts where his actions do not interfere with the interests of other human beings." Do you find this principle attractive? How might Baxter respond to the objection that all of our actions have effects on people other than ourselves?

2) According to Baxter, it is wrong to use resources "so as to yield less than they might yield in human satisfactions." Are we ever justified in allocating resources in this way? Why or why not?

3) Baxter argues for a "people-centered" approach to environmental issues on the grounds that such an approach "corresponds to the way most people really think and act." Is this a good reason for adopting the approach?

4) Another of Baxter's arguments for the people-centered approach notes that only humans can participate in collective decision-making. Is this a good reason for excluding nonhuman animals from our moral considerations? Why or why not?

5) Baxter seems to argue that since plants and animals are not capable of acting morally, we do not have any moral obligations to plants or animals. Is this a good argument?

6) Many people intuitively believe that the optimal amount of pollution is no pollution at all. Why does Baxter disagree? Do you think he is right about this?

27

A Defense of Abortion

Judith Jarvis Thomson

In this article, Judith Thomson does what very few pro-choice advocates have been willing to do—namely, to grant, for the purposes of argument, that the fetus is as much a moral person as you or I. Still, she argues, being a person does not, by itself, entitle you to use someone else's resources, even if those resources are needed in order to preserve your life. Thus even if we grant that the fetus is a person, that is not enough to show that the fetus is entitled to the continued use of the mother's "resources" (her body). A pregnant woman has a right to bodily autonomy, and that right, in many cases, morally prevails over any rights possessed by a fetus.

Thomson uses a number of thought experiments to defend this claim. The most famous of these involves a world-class violinist. Suppose that you wake up one morning and find yourself connected to a transfusion machine that is providing life support for this musician. He surely has a right to life. But Thomson says that you would be within your rights to remove yourself from the apparatus—even knowing that, by doing this, he will die. The violinist, of course, is meant to be a stand-in for the fetus. According to Thomson, although it would be awfully nice of pregnant women to continue carrying their fetuses to term, they are not usually morally required to do so.

Thomson anticipates a variety of objections to this example, and provides further examples to support her view that women usually have a moral right to seek and obtain an abortion.

Most opposition to abortion relies on the premise that the fetus is a human being, a person, from the moment of conception. The premise is argued for, but, as I think, not well. Take, for example, the most common argument. We are asked to notice that the development of a human being from conception through birth into childhood is continuous; then it is said that to draw a line, to choose a point in this development and say "before this point the thing is not a person, after this point it is a person" is to make an arbitrary choice, a choice for which in the nature of things no good reason can be given. It is concluded that the fetus is, or anyway that we had better say it is, a person from the moment of conception. But this conclusion does not follow. Similar things might be said about the development of an acorn into an oak tree, and it does not follow that acorns are oak trees, or that we had better say they are. Arguments of this form are sometimes called "slippery slope arguments"—the phrase is perhaps self-explanatory—and it is dismaying that opponents of abortion rely on them so heavily and uncritically.

I am inclined to agree, however, that the prospects for "drawing a line" in the development of the fetus look dim. I am inclined to think also that we shall probably have to agree that the fetus has already become a human person well before birth. Indeed, it comes as a surprise when one first learns how early in its life it begins to acquire human characteristics. By the tenth week, for example, it already has a face, arms and legs, fingers and toes; it has internal organs, and brain activity is detectable. On the other hand, I think that the premise is false, that the fetus is not a person from the moment of conception. A newly fertilized ovum, a newly implanted clump of cells, is no more a person than an acorn is an oak tree. But I shall not discuss any of this. For it seems to me to be of great interest to ask what happens if, for the sake of argument, we allow the premise. How, precisely, are we supposed to get from there to the conclusion that abortion is morally impermissible? Opponents of abortion commonly spend most of their time establishing that the fetus is a person, and hardly any time explaining the step from there to the impermissibility of abortion. Perhaps they think the step too simple and obvious to require much comment. Or perhaps instead they are simply being economical in argument. Many of those who defend abortion rely on the premise that the fetus is not a person, but only a bit of tissue that will become a person at birth; and why pay out more arguments than you have to? Whatever the explanation, I suggest that the step they take is neither easy nor obvious, that it calls for closer examination than it is commonly given, and that when we do give it this closer examination we shall feel inclined to reject it.

I propose, then, that we grant that the fetus is a person from the moment of conception. How does the argument go from here? Something like this, I take it. Every person has a right to life. So the fetus has a right to life. No doubt the mother has a right to decide what shall happen in and to her body; everyone would grant that. But surely a person's right to life is stronger and more stringent than the mother's right to decide what happens in and to her body, and so outweighs it. So the fetus may not be killed; an abortion may not be performed.

It sounds plausible. But now let me ask you to imagine this. You wake up in the morning and find yourself back to back in bed with an unconscious violinist. A famous unconscious violinist. He has been found to have a fatal kidney ailment, and the Society of Music Lovers has canvassed all the available medical records and found that you alone have the right blood type to help. They have therefore kidnapped you, and last night the violinist's circulatory system was plugged into yours, so that your kidneys can be used to extract poisons from his blood as well as your own. The director of the hospital now tells you, "Look, we're sorry the Society of Music Lovers did this to you—we would never have permitted it if we had known. But still, they did it, and the violinist now is plugged into you. To unplug you would be to kill him. But never mind, it's only for nine months. By then he will have recovered from his ailment, and can safely be unplugged from you." Is it morally incumbent on you to accede to this situation? No doubt it would be very nice of you if you did, a great kindness. But do you *have* to accede to it? What if it were not nine months, but nine years? Or longer still? What if the director of the hospital says, "Tough luck, I agree, but you've now got to stay in bed, with the violinist plugged into you, for the rest of your life. Because remember this. All persons have a right to life, and violinists are persons. Granted you have a right to decide what happens in and to your body, but a person's right to life outweighs your right to decide what happens in and to your body. So you cannot ever be unplugged from him." I imagine you would regard this as outrageous, which suggests that something really is wrong with that plausible-sounding argument I mentioned a moment ago.

In this case, of course, you were kidnapped; you didn't volunteer for the operation that plugged the violinist into your kidneys. Can those who oppose abortion on the ground I mentioned make an exception for a pregnancy due to rape? Certainly. They can say that persons have a right to life only if they didn't come into existence because of rape; or they can say that all persons have a right to life, but that some have less of a right to life than others, in particular, that those who came into existence because of rape have less. But these statements have a rather unpleasant sound. Surely the question of whether you have a right to life at all, or how much of it you have, shouldn't turn on the question of whether or not you are the product of a rape. And in fact the people who oppose abortion on the ground I mentioned do not make this distinction, and hence do not make an exception in case of rape.

Nor do they make an exception for a case in which the mother has to spend the nine months of her pregnancy in bed. They would agree that would be a great pity, and hard on the mother; but all the same, all persons have a right to life, the fetus is a person, and so on. I suspect, in fact, that they would not make an exception for a case in which, miraculously enough, the pregnancy went on for nine years, or even the rest of the mother's life.

Some won't even make an exception for a case in which continuation of the pregnancy is likely to shorten the mother's life; they regard abortion as impermissible even to save the mother's life. Such cases are nowadays very rare, and many opponents of abortion do not accept this extreme view. All the same, it is a good place to begin: a number of points of interest come out in respect to it.

1. Let us call the view that abortion is impermissible even to save the mother's life "the extreme view." I want to suggest first that it does not issue from the argument I mentioned earlier without the addition of some fairly powerful premises. Suppose a woman has become pregnant, and now learns that she has a cardiac condition such that she will die if she carries the baby to term. What may be done for her? The fetus, being a person, has a right to life, but as the mother is a person too, so has she a right to life. Presumably they have an equal right to life. How is it supposed to come out that an abortion may not be performed? If mother and child have an equal right to life, shouldn't we perhaps flip a coin? Or should we add to the mother's right to life her right to decide what happens in and to her body, which everybody seems to be ready to grant—the sum of her rights now outweighing the fetus' right to life?

The most familiar argument here is the following. We are told that performing the abortion would be directly killing[1] the child, whereas

---

[1] The term "direct" in the arguments I refer to is a technical one. Roughly, what is meant by "direct killing" is either killing as an end in itself, or killing as a means to some end, for example, the end of saving someone else's life.

doing nothing would not be killing the mother, but only letting her die. Moreover, in killing the child, one would be killing an innocent person, for the child has committed no crime, and is not aiming at his mother's death. And then there are a variety of ways in which this might be continued. (1) But as directly killing an innocent person is always and absolutely impermissible, an abortion may not be performed. Or, (2) as directly killing an innocent person is murder, and murder is always and absolutely impermissible, an abortion may not be performed. Or, (3) as one's duty to refrain from directly killing an innocent person is more stringent than one's duty to keep a person from dying, an abortion may not be performed. Or, (4) if one's only options are directly killing an innocent person or letting a person die, one must prefer letting the person die, and thus an abortion may not be performed.

Some people seem to have thought that these are not further premises which must be added if the conclusion is to be reached, but that they follow from the very fact that an innocent person has a right to life. But this seems to me to be a mistake, and perhaps the simplest way to show this is to bring out that while we must certainly grant that innocent persons have a right to life, the theses in (1) through (4) are all false. Take (2), for example. If directly killing an innocent person is murder, and thus is impermissible, then the mother's directly killing the innocent person inside her is murder, and thus is impermissible. But it cannot seriously be thought to be murder if the mother performs an abortion on herself to save her life. It cannot seriously be said that she *must* refrain, that she *must* sit passively by and wait for her death. Let us look again at the case of you and the violinist. There you are, in bed with the violinist, and the director of the hospital says to you, "It's all most distressing, and I deeply sympathize, but you see this is putting an additional strain on your kidneys, and you'll be dead within the month. But you *have* to stay where you are all the same. Because unplugging you would be directly killing an innocent violinist, and that's murder, and that's impermissible." If anything in the world is true, it is that you do not commit murder, you do not do what is impermissible, if you reach around to your back and unplug yourself from that violinist to save your life.

I should perhaps stop to say explicitly that I am not claiming that people have a right to do anything whatever to save their lives. I think, rather, that there are drastic limits to the right of self-defense. If someone threatens you with death unless you torture someone else to death, I think you have not the right, even to save your life, to do so. But the case under consideration here is very different. In our case there are only two people involved, one whose life is threatened, and one who threatens it. Both are innocent: the one who is threatened is not threatened because of any fault, the one who threatens does not threaten because of any fault. For this reason we may feel that we bystanders cannot intervene. But the person threatened can.

In sum, a woman surely can defend her life against the threat to it posed by the unborn child, even if doing so involves its death. And this shows not merely that the theses in (1) through (4) are false; it shows also that the extreme view of abortion is false, and so we need not canvass any other possible ways of arriving at it from the argument I mentioned at the outset.

2. The extreme view could of course be weakened to say that while abortion is permissible to save the mother's life, it may not be performed by a third party, but only by the mother herself. But this cannot be right either. For what we have to keep in mind is that the mother and the unborn child are not like two tenants in a small house which has, by an unfortunate mistake, been rented to both: the mother *owns* the house. The fact that she does adds to the offensiveness of deducing that the mother can do nothing from the supposition that third parties can do nothing. But it does more than this: it casts a bright light on the supposition that third parties can do nothing. Certainly it lets us see that a third party who says "I cannot choose between you" is fooling himself if he thinks this is impartiality. If Jones has found and fastened on a certain coat, which he needs to keep him from freezing, but which Smith also needs to keep him from freezing, then it is not impartiality that says "I cannot choose between you" when Smith owns the coat. Women have said again and again "This body is *my* body!" and they have reason to feel angry, reason to feel that it has been like shouting into the wind.

3. Where the mother's life is not at stake, the argument I mentioned at the outset seems to have a much stronger pull. "Everyone has a right to life, so the unborn person has a right to life." And isn't the child's right to life weightier than anything other than the mother's own right to life, which she might put forward as ground for an abortion?

This argument treats the right to life as if it were unproblematic. It is not, and this seems to me to be precisely the source of the mistake.

For we should now, at long last, ask what it comes to, to have a right to life. In some views having a right to life includes having a right to be given at least the bare minimum one needs for continued life. But suppose that what in fact *is* the bare minimum a man needs for continued life is something he has no right at all to be given? If I am sick unto death, and the only thing that will save my life is the touch of Henry Fonda's cool hand on my fevered brow, then all the same, I have no right to be given the touch of Henry Fonda's cool hand on my fevered brow. It would be frightfully nice of him to fly in from the West Coast to provide it. It would be less nice, though no doubt well meant, if my friends flew out to the West Coast and carried Henry Fonda back with them. But I have no right at all against anybody that he should do this for me. Or again, to return to the story I told earlier, the fact that for continued life that violinist needs the continued use of your kidneys does not establish that he has a right to be given the continued use of your kidneys. He certainly has no right against you that *you* should give him continued use of your kidneys. For nobody has any right to use your kidneys unless you give him such a right; and nobody has the right against you that you shall give him this right—if you do allow him to go on using your kidneys, this is a kindness on your part, and not something he can claim from you as his due. Nor has he any right against anybody else that *they* should give him continued use of your kidneys. Certainly he had no right against the Society of Music Lovers that they should plug him into you in the first place. And if you now start to unplug yourself, having learned that you will otherwise have to spend nine years in bed with him, there is nobody in the world who must try to prevent you, in order to see to it that he is given something he has a right to be given.

Some people are rather stricter about the right to life. In their view, it does not include the right to be given anything, but amounts to, and only to, the right not to be killed by anybody. But here a related difficulty arises. If everybody is to refrain from killing that violinist, then everybody must refrain from doing a great many different sorts of things. Everybody must refrain from slitting his throat, everybody must refrain from shooting him—and everybody must refrain from unplugging you from him. But does he have a right against everybody that they shall refrain from unplugging you from him? To refrain from doing this is to allow him to continue to use your kidneys. It could be argued that he has a right against us that *we* should allow him to continue to use your kidneys. That is, while he had no right against us that we should give him the use of your kidneys, it might be argued that he anyway has a right against us that we shall not now intervene and deprive him of the use of your kidneys. I shall come back to third-party interventions later. But certainly the violinist has no right against you that *you* shall allow him to continue to use your kidneys.

As I said, if you do allow him to use them, it is a kindness on your part, and not something you owe him.

The difficulty I point to here is not peculiar to the right to life. It reappears in connection with all the other natural rights; and it is something which an adequate account of rights must deal with. For present purposes it is enough just to draw attention to it. But I would stress that I am not arguing that people do not have a right to life—quite to the contrary, it seems to me that the primary control we must place on the acceptability of an account of rights is that it should turn out in that account to be a truth that all persons have a right to life. I am arguing only that having a right to life does not guarantee having either a right to be given the use of or a right to be allowed continued use of another person's body—even if one needs it for life itself. So the right to life will not serve the opponents of abortion in the very simple and clear way in which they seem to have thought it would.

4. There is another way to bring out the difficulty. In the most ordinary sort of case, to deprive someone of what he has a right to is to treat him unjustly. Suppose a boy and his small brother are jointly given a box of chocolates for Christmas. If the older boy takes the box and refuses to give his brother any of the chocolates, he is unjust to him, for the brother has been given a right to half of them. But suppose that, having learned that otherwise it means nine years in bed with that violinist, you unplug yourself from him. You surely are not being unjust to him, for you gave him no right to use your kidneys, and no one else can have given him any such right. But we have to notice that in unplugging yourself, you are killing him; and violinists, like everybody else, have a right to life, and thus in the view we were considering just now, the right not to be killed. So here you do what he supposedly has a right you shall not do, but you do not act unjustly to him in doing it.

The emendation which may be made at this point is this: the right to life consists not in the right not to be killed, but rather in the right not to be killed unjustly. This runs a risk of circularity, but never mind: it would enable us to square the fact that the violinist has a right to life with the fact that you do not act unjustly toward him in unplugging yourself, thereby killing him. For if you do not kill him unjustly, you do not violate his right to life, and so it is no wonder you do him no injustice.

But if this emendation is accepted, the gap in the argument against abortion stares us plainly in the face: it is by no means enough to show that the fetus is a person, and to remind us that all persons have a right to life – we need to be shown also that killing the fetus violates its right to life, i.e., that abortion is unjust killing. And is it?

I suppose we may take it as a datum that in a case of pregnancy due to rape the mother has not given the unborn person a right to the use of her body for food and shelter. Indeed, in what pregnancy could it be supposed that the mother has given the unborn person such a right? It is not as if there were unborn persons drifting about the world, to whom a woman who wants a child says "I invite you in."

But it might be argued that there are other ways one can have acquired a right to the use of another person's body than by having been invited to use it by that person. Suppose a woman voluntarily indulges in intercourse, knowing of the chance it will issue in pregnancy, and then she does become pregnant; is she not in part responsible for the presence, in fact the very existence, of the unborn person inside her? No doubt she did not invite it in. But doesn't her partial responsibility for its being there itself give it a right to the use of her body? If so, then her aborting it would be more like the boy's taking away the chocolates, and less like your unplugging yourself from the violinist—doing so would be depriving it of what it does have a right to, and thus would be doing it an injustice.

And then, too, it might be asked whether or not she can kill it even to save her own life: If she voluntarily called it into existence, how can she now kill it, even in self-defense?

The first thing to be said about this is that it is something new. Opponents of abortion have been so concerned to make out the independence of the fetus, in order to establish that it has a right to life, just as its mother does, that they have tended to overlook the possible support they might gain from making out that the fetus is *dependent* on the mother, in order to establish that she has a special kind of responsibility for it, a responsibility that gives it rights against her which are not possessed by any independent person—such as an ailing violinist who is a stranger to her.

On the other hand, this argument would give the unborn person a right to its mother's body only if her pregnancy resulted from a voluntary act, undertaken in full knowledge of the chance a pregnancy might result from it. It would leave out entirely the unborn person whose existence is due to rape. Pending the availability of some further argument, then, we would be left with the conclusion that unborn persons whose existence is due to rape have no right to the use of their mothers' bodies, and thus that aborting them is not depriving them of anything they have a right to and hence is not unjust killing.

And we should also notice that it is not at all plain that this argument really does go even as far as it purports to. For there are cases and cases, and the details make a difference. If the room is stuffy, and I therefore open a window to air it, and a burglar climbs in, it would be absurd to say, "Ah, now he can stay, she's given him a right to the use of her house—for she is partially responsible for his presence there, having voluntarily done what enabled him to get in, in full knowledge that there are such things as burglars, and that burglars burgle." It would be still more absurd to say this if I had had bars installed outside my windows, precisely to prevent burglars from getting in, and a burglar got in only because of a defect in the bars. It remains equally absurd if we imagine it is not a burglar who climbs in, but an innocent person who blunders or falls in. Again, suppose it were like this: people-seeds drift about in the air like pollen, and if you open your windows, one may drift in and take root in your carpets or upholstery. You don't want children, so you fix up your windows with fine mesh screens, the very best you can buy. As can happen, however, and on very, very rare occasions does happen, one of the screens is defective; and a seed drifts in and takes root. Does the person-plant who now develops have a right to the use of your house? Surely not—despite the fact that you voluntarily opened your windows, you knowingly kept carpets and upholstered furniture, and you knew that screens were sometimes defective. Someone may argue that you are responsible for its rooting, that it does have a right to your house, because after all you *could* have lived out your life with bare floors and furniture, or with sealed windows and doors. But this won't do—for by the same token anyone can avoid a pregnancy due to rape by having a hysterectomy, or anyway by never leaving home without a (reliable!) army.

It seems to me that the argument we are looking at can establish at most that there are *some* cases in which the unborn person has a right to the use of its mother's body, and therefore *some* cases in which abortion is unjust killing. There is room for much discussion and argument as to precisely which, if any. But I think we should sidestep this issue and leave it open, for at any rate the argument certainly does not establish that all abortion is unjust killing.

5. There is room for yet another argument here, however. We surely must all grant that there may be cases in which it would be morally indecent to detach a person from your body at the cost of his life. Suppose you learn that what the violinist needs is not nine years of your life, but only one hour: all you need do to save his life is to spend one hour in that bed with him. Suppose also that letting him use your kidneys for that one hour

would not affect your health in the slightest. Admittedly you were kidnapped. Admittedly you did not give anyone permission to plug him into you. Nevertheless it seems to me plain you *ought* to allow him to use your kidneys for that hour—it would be indecent to refuse.

Again, suppose pregnancy lasted only an hour, and constituted no threat to life or health. And suppose that a woman becomes pregnant as a result of rape. Admittedly she did not voluntarily do anything to bring about the existence of a child. Admittedly she did nothing at all which would give the unborn person a right to the use of her body. All the same it might well be said, as in the newly emended violinist story, that she *ought* to allow it to remain for that hour—that it would be indecent in her to refuse.

6. My argument will be found unsatisfactory on two counts by many of those who want to regard abortion as morally permissible. First, while I do argue that abortion is not impermissible, I do not argue that it is always permissible. There may well be cases in which carrying the child to term requires only Minimally Decent Samaritanism[2] of the mother, and this is a standard we must not fall below. I am inclined to think it a merit of my account precisely that it does *not* give a general yes or a general no. It allows for and supports our sense that, for example, a sick and desperately frightened fourteen-year-old schoolgirl, pregnant due to rape, may *of course* choose abortion, and that any law which rules this out is an insane law. And it also allows for and supports our sense that in other cases resort to abortion is even positively indecent. It would be indecent in the woman to request an abortion, and indecent in a doctor to perform it, if she is in her seventh month, and wants the abortion just to avoid the nuisance of postponing a trip abroad. The very fact that the arguments I have been drawing attention to treat all cases of abortion, or even all cases of abortion in which the mother's life is not at stake, as morally on a par ought to have made them suspect at the outset.

Secondly, while I am arguing for the permissibility of abortion in some cases, I am not arguing for the right to secure the death of the unborn child. It is easy to confuse these two things in that up to a certain point in the life of the fetus it is not able to survive outside the mother's body; hence removing it from her body guarantees its death. But they are importantly different. I have argued that you are not morally required to spend nine months in bed, sustaining the life of that violinist; but to say this is by

---

[2]   Meeting a standard of minimally decent treatment towards those in need.—Ed.

no means to say that if, when you unplug yourself, there is a miracle and he survives, you then have a right to turn round and slit his throat. You may detach yourself even if this costs him his life; you have no right to be guaranteed his death, by some other means, if unplugging yourself does not kill him. There are some people who will feel dissatisfied by this feature of my argument. A woman may be utterly devastated by the thought of a child, a bit of herself, put out for adoption and never seen or heard of again. She may therefore want not merely that the child be detached from her, but more, that it die. Some opponents of abortion are inclined to regard this as beneath contempt—thereby showing insensitivity to what is surely a powerful source of despair. All the same, I agree that the desire for the child's death is not one which anybody may gratify, should it turn out to be possible to detach the child alive.

At this place, however, it should be remembered that we have only been pretending throughout that the fetus is a human being from the moment of conception. A very early abortion is surely not the killing of a person, and so is not dealt with by anything I have said here.

Judith Jarvis Thomson: A Defense of Abortion

1) Thomson's first thought experiment is the case of the violinist. Do you agree that it would be permissible to unplug yourself from the violinist? What conclusions about abortion should we draw from this thought experiment?

2) What is the "extreme view"? What are Thomson's objections to the view? Do you find her objections compelling?

3) Thomson claims that the notion of a "right to life" cannot be interpreted as a right to "the bare minimum one needs for continued life." Why does she claim this? What, according to Thomson, does having a right to life amount to? Do you agree with her about this?

4) Why doesn't Thomson think that abortion always involves unjust killing? What does the justice of abortion depend on, according to Thomson?

5) Under what conditions (if any) do you think a woman grants a fetus the right to use her body?

28

Why Abortion Is Immoral

Don Marquis

In this article, Don Marquis argues, from entirely secular premises, to the conclusion that abortion is, in most circumstances, a form of murder. He does this by first trying to explain why it is immoral to kill people like you and me. After canvassing a few popular but mistaken options, he arrives at his answer. Such killing is immoral because it deprives us of a future of value.

Human fetuses—most of them, at least—also share this feature. And therefore it is ordinarily wrong to kill human fetuses. And so abortion is usually immoral. Marquis considers a variety of objections to his view, and concludes his article by trying to show how each of them can be met.

The view that abortion is, with rare exceptions, seriously immoral has received little support in the recent philosophical literature. No doubt most philosophers affiliated with secular institutions of higher education believe that the anti-abortion position is either a symptom of irrational religious dogma or a conclusion generated by seriously confused philosophical argument. The purpose of this essay is to undermine this general belief. This essay sets out an argument that purports to show, as well as any argument in ethics can

Used by permission of Don Marquis and *The Journal of Philosophy*.

show, that abortion is, except possibly in rare cases, seriously immoral, that it is in the same moral category as killing an innocent adult human being.

I.

A sketch of standard anti-abortion and pro-choice arguments exhibits how those arguments possess certain symmetries that explain why partisans of those positions are so convinced of the correctness of their own positions, why they are not successful in convincing their opponents, and why, to others, this issue seems to be unresolvable. An analysis of the nature of this standoff suggests a strategy for surmounting it.

Consider the way a typical anti-abortionist argues. She will argue or assert that life is present from the moment of conception or that fetuses look like babies or that fetuses possess a characteristic such as a genetic code that is both necessary and sufficient for being human. Anti – abortionists seem to believe that (1) the truth of all of these claims is quite obvious, and (2) establishing any of these claims is sufficient to show that abortion is morally akin to murder.

A standard pro-choice strategy exhibits similarities. The pro-choicer will argue or assert that fetuses are not persons or that fetuses are not rational agents or that fetuses are not social beings. Pro-choicers seem to believe that (1) the truth of any of these claims is quite obvious, and (2) establishing any of these claims is sufficient to show that an abortion is not a wrongful killing.

In fact, both the pro-choice and the anti-abortion claims do seem to be true, although the "it looks like a baby" claim is more difficult to establish the earlier the pregnancy. We seem to have a standoff. How can it be resolved?

As everyone who has taken a bit of logic knows, if any of these arguments concerning abortion is a good argument, it requires not only some claim characterizing fetuses, but also some general moral principle that ties a characteristic of fetuses to having or not having the right to life or to some other moral characteristic that will generate the obligation or the lack of obligation not to end the life of a fetus. Accordingly, the arguments of the anti-abortionist and the pro-choicer need a bit of filling in to be regarded as adequate.

Note what each partisan will say. The anti-abortionist will claim that her position is supported by such generally accepted moral principles as "It is always prima facie seriously wrong to take a human life" or "It is always prima facie seriously wrong to end the life of a baby." Since these are generally accepted moral principles, her position is certainly not obviously wrong. The pro-choicer will claim that her position is supported by such plausible moral principles as "Being a person is what gives an individual intrinsic moral worth" or "It is only seriously prima facie wrong to take the life of a member of the human community." Since these are generally accepted moral principles, the pro-choice position is certainly not obviously wrong. Unfortunately, we have again arrived at a standoff.

Now, how might one deal with this standoff? The standard approach is to try to show how the moral principles of one's opponent lose their plausibility under analysis. It is easy to see how this is possible. On the one hand, the anti-abortionist will defend a moral principle concerning the wrongness of killing which tends to be broad in scope in order that even fetuses at an early stage of pregnancy will fall under it. The problem with broad principles is that they often embrace too much. In this particular instance, the principle "It is always prima facie wrong to take a human life" seems to entail that it is wrong to end the existence of a living human cancer-cell culture, on the grounds that the culture is both living and human. Therefore, it seems that the anti-abortionist's favored principle is too broad.

On the other hand, the pro-choicer wants to find a moral principle concerning the wrongness of killing which tends to be narrow in scope in order that fetuses will *not* fall under it. The problem with narrow principles is that they often do not embrace enough. Hence, the needed principles such as "It is prima facie seriously wrong to kill only persons" or "It is prima facie wrong to kill only rational agents" do not explain why it is wrong to kill infants or young children or the severely retarded or even perhaps the severely mentally ill. Therefore, we seem again to have a standoff. The anti-abortionist charges, not unreasonably, that pro-choice principles concerning killing are too narrow to be acceptable; the pro-choicer charges, not unreasonably, that anti-abortionist principles concerning killing are too broad to be acceptable.

All this suggests that a necessary condition of resolving the abortion controversy is a more theoretical account of the wrongness of killing. After all, if we merely believe, but do not understand, why killing adult human beings such as ourselves is wrong, how could we conceivably show that abortion is either immoral or permissible?

II.

In order to develop such an account, we can start from the following unproblematic assumption concerning our own case: it is wrong to kill *us*. Why is it wrong? Some answers can be easily eliminated. It might be said that what makes killing us wrong is that a killing brutalizes the one who kills. But the brutalization consists of being inured to the performance of an act that is hideously immoral; hence, the brutalization does not explain the immorality. It might be said that what makes killing us wrong is the great loss others would experience due to our absence. Although such hubris is understandable, such an explanation does not account for the wrongness of killing hermits, or those whose lives are relatively indepen- dent and whose friends find it easy to make new friends.

A more obvious answer is better. What primarily makes killing wrong is neither its effect on the murderer nor its effect on the victim's friends and relatives, but its effect on the victim. The loss of one's life is one of the greatest losses one can suffer. The loss of one's life deprives one of all the experiences, activities, projects, and enjoyments that would other- wise have constituted one's future. Therefore, killing someone is wrong, primarily because the killing inflicts (one of) the greatest possible losses on the victim. To describe this as the loss of life can be misleading, how- ever. The change in my biological state does not by itself make killing me wrong. The effect of the loss of my biological life is the loss to me of all those activities, projects, experiences, and enjoyments which would oth- erwise have constituted my future personal life. These activities, projects, experiences, and enjoyments are either valuable for their own sakes or are means to something else that is valuable for its own sake. Some parts of my future are not valued by me now, but will come to be valued by me as I grow older and as my values and capacities change. When I am killed, I am deprived both of what I now value which would have been part of my future personal life, but also what I would come to value. Therefore, when I die, I am deprived of all of the value of my future. Inflicting this loss on me is ultimately what makes killing me wrong. This being the case, it would seem that what makes killing *any* adult human being prima facie seriously wrong is the loss of his or her future.[1]

---

[1] I have been most influenced on this matter by Jonathan Glover, *Causing Death and Saving Lives* (New York: Penguin, 1977), ch. 3; and Robert Young, "What Is So Wrong with Killing People?" *Philosophy*, LIV, 210 (1979): 515–528.

How should this rudimentary theory of the wrongness of killing be evaluated? It cannot be faulted for deriving an 'ought' from an 'is', for it does not. The analysis assumes that killing me (or you, reader) is prima facie seriously wrong. The point of the analysis is to establish which natural property ultimately explains the wrongness of the killing, given that it is wrong. A natural property will ultimately explain the wrongness of killing, only if (1) the explanation fits with our intuitions about the matter and (2) there is no other natural property that provides the basis for a better explanation of the wrongness of killing. This analysis rests on the intuition that what makes killing a particular human or animal wrong is what it does to that particular human or animal. What makes killing wrong is some natural effect or other of the killing. Some would deny this. For instance, a divine-command theorist in ethics would deny it. Surely this denial is, however, one of those features of divine-command theory which renders it so implausible.

The claim that what makes killing wrong is the loss of the victim's future is directly supported by two considerations. In the first place, this theory explains why we regard killing as one of the worst of crimes. Killing is especially wrong, because it deprives the victim of more than perhaps any other crime. In the second place, people with AIDS or cancer who know they are dying believe, of course, that dying is a very bad thing for them. They believe that the loss of a future to them that they would otherwise have experienced is what makes their premature death a very bad thing for them. A better theory of the wrongness of killing would require a different natural property associated with killing which better fits with the attitudes of the dying. What could it be?

The view that what makes killing wrong is the loss to the victim of the value of the victim's future gains additional support when some of its implications are examined. In the first place, it is incompatible with the view that it is wrong to kill only beings who are biologically human. It is possible that there exists a different species from another planet whose members have a future like ours. Since having a future like that is what makes killing someone wrong, this theory entails that it would be wrong to kill members of such a species. Hence, this theory is opposed to the claim that only life that is biologically human has great moral worth, a claim which many anti-abortionists have seemed to adopt. This opposition, which this theory has in common with personhood theories, seems to be a merit of the theory.

In the second place, the claim that the loss of one's future is the wrong-making feature of one's being killed entails the possibility that the futures of some actual nonhuman mammals on our own planet are sufficiently like ours that it is seriously wrong to kill them also. Whether some animals do have the same right to life as human beings depends on adding to the account of the wrongness of killing some additional account of just what it is about my future or the futures of other adult human beings which makes it wrong to kill us. No such additional account will be offered in this essay. Undoubtedly, the provision of such an account would be a very difficult matter. Undoubtedly, any such account would be quite controversial. Hence, it surely should not reflect badly on this sketch of an elementary theory of the wrongness of killing that it is indeterminate with respect to some very difficult issues regarding animal rights.

In the third place, the claim that the loss of one's future is the wrong-making feature of one's being killed does not entail, as sanctity of human life theories do, that active euthanasia is wrong. Persons who are severely and incurably ill, who face a future of pain and despair, and who wish to die will not have suffered a loss if they are killed. It is, strictly speaking, the value of a human's future which makes killing wrong in this theory. This being so, killing does not necessarily wrong some persons who are sick and dying. Of course, there may be other reasons for a prohibition of active euthanasia, but that is another matter. Sanctity-of-human-life theories seem to hold that active euthanasia is seriously wrong even in an individual case where there seems to be good reason for it independently of public policy considerations. This consequence is most implausible, and it is a plus for the claim that the loss of a future of value is what makes killing wrong that it does not share this consequence.

In the fourth place, the account of the wrongness of killing defended in this essay does straightforwardly entail that it is prima facie seriously wrong to kill children and infants, for we do presume that they have futures of value. Since we do believe that it is wrong to kill defenseless little babies, it is important that a theory of the wrongness of killing easily account for this. Personhood theories of the wrongness of killing, on the other hand, cannot straightforwardly account for the wrongness of killing infants and young children. Hence, such theories must add special ad hoc accounts of the wrongness of killing the young. The plausibility of such ad hoc theories seems to be a function of how desperately one wants such theories to work. The claim that the primary wrong-making feature of a killing is the loss to the victim of the value of its future accounts for the wrongness of killing young children and infants directly; it makes the wrongness of such acts as obvious as we actually think it is. This is a further merit of this theory. Accordingly, it seems that this value of a future-like-ours theory of the wrongness of killing shares strengths of both sanctity-of-life and personhood accounts while avoiding weaknesses of both. In addition, it meshes with a central intuition concerning what makes killing wrong.

The claim that the primary wrong-making feature of a killing is the loss to the victim of the value of its future has obvious consequences for the ethics of abortion. The future of a standard fetus includes a set of experiences, projects, activities, and such which are identical with the futures of adult human beings and are identical with the futures of young children. Since the reason that is sufficient to explain why it is wrong to kill human beings after the time of birth is a reason that also applies to fetuses, it follows that abortion is prima facie seriously morally wrong.

This argument does not rely on the invalid inference that, since it is wrong to kill persons, it is wrong to kill potential persons also. The category that is morally central to this analysis is the category of having a valuable future like ours; it is not the category of personhood. The argument to the conclusion that abortion is prima facie seriously morally wrong proceeded independently of the notion of person or potential person or any equivalent. Someone may wish to start with this analysis in terms of the value of a human future, conclude that abortion is, except perhaps in rare circumstances, seriously morally wrong, infer that fetuses have the right to life, and then call fetuses "persons" as a result of their having the right to life. Clearly, in this case, the category of person is being used to state the *conclusion* of the analysis rather than to generate the *argument* of the analysis.

Of course, this value of a future-like-ours argument, if sound, shows only that abortion is prima facie wrong, not that it is wrong in any and all circumstances. Since the loss of the future to a standard fetus, if killed, is, however, at least as great a loss as the loss of the future to a standard adult human being who is killed, abortion, like ordinary killing, could be justified only by the most compelling reasons. The loss of one's life is almost the greatest misfortune that can happen to one. Presumably abortion could be justified in some circumstances, only if the loss consequent on failing to abort would be at least as great. Accordingly, morally permissible abortions will be rare indeed unless, perhaps, they occur so early in pregnancy that a fetus is not yet definitely an individual. Hence, this argument should be taken as showing that abortion is presumptively very seriously wrong, where the presumption is very strong—as strong as the presumption that killing another adult human being is wrong.

III.

How complete an account of the wrongness of killing does the value of a future-like-ours account have to be in order that the wrongness of abortion is a consequence? This account does not have to be an account of the necessary conditions for the wrongness of killing. Some persons in nursing homes may lack valuable human futures, yet it may be wrong to kill them for other reasons. Furthermore, this account does not obviously have to be the sole reason killing is wrong where the victim did have a valuable future. This analysis claims only that, for any killing where the victim did have a valuable future like ours, having that future by itself is sufficient to create the strong presumption that the killing is seriously wrong.

One way to overturn the value of a future-like-ours argument would be to find some account of the wrongness of killing which is at least as intelligible and which has different implications for the ethics of abortion.

One move of this sort is based upon the claim that a necessary condition of one's future being valuable is that one values it. Value implies a valuer. Given this one might argue that, since fetuses cannot value their futures, their futures are not valuable to them. Hence, it does not seriously wrong them deliberately to end their lives.

This move fails, however, because of some ambiguities. Let us assume that something cannot be of value unless it is valued by someone. This does not entail that my life is of no value unless it is valued by me. I may think, in a period of despair, that my future is of no worth whatsoever, but I may be wrong because others rightly see value—even great value—in it. Furthermore, my future can be valuable to me even if I do not value it. This is the case when a young person attempts suicide, but is rescued and goes on to significant human achievements. Such young people's futures are ultimately valuable to them, even though such futures do not seem to be valuable to them at the moment of attempted suicide. A fetus's future can be valuable to it in the same way. Accordingly, this attempt to limit the anti-abortion argument fails.

Another similar attempt to reject the anti-abortion position is based on Tooley's claim that an entity cannot possess the right to life unless it has the capacity to desire its continued existence. It follows that, since fetuses lack the conceptual capacity to desire to continue to live, they lack the right to life. Accordingly, Tooley concludes that abortion cannot be seriously prima facie wrong.[2]

One might attempt to defend Tooley's basic claim on the grounds that, because a fetus cannot apprehend continued life as a benefit, its continued life cannot be a benefit or cannot be something it has a right to or cannot be something that is in its interest. This might be defended in terms of the general proposition that, if an individual is literally incapable of caring about or taking an interest in some X, then one does not have a right to X or X is not a benefit or X is not something that is in one's interest.

Each member of this family of claims seems to be open to objections. As John C. Stevens[3] has pointed out, one may have a right to be treated with a certain medical procedure (because of a health insurance policy one has purchased), even though one cannot conceive of the nature of the procedure. And, as Tooley himself has pointed out, persons who have been indoctrinated, or drugged, or rendered temporarily unconscious may be literally incapable of caring about or taking an interest in something that is in their interest or is something to which they have a right, or is something that benefits them. Hence, the Tooley claim that would restrict the scope of the value of a future-like-ours argument is undermined by counterexamples.[4]

IV.

In this essay, it has been argued that the correct ethic of the wrongness of killing can be extended to fetal life and used to show that there is a strong presumption that any abortion is morally impermissible. If the ethic of killing adopted here entails, however, that contraception is also seriously immoral, then there would appear to be a difficulty with the analysis of this essay.

But this analysis does not entail that contraception is wrong. Of course, contraception prevents the actualization of a possible future of value. Hence, it follows from the claim that futures of value should be maximized that contraception is prima facie immoral. This obligation to

---

[2] Michael Tooley, *"Abortion and Infanticide."* (NY: Oxford University Press, 1984), pp. 46–7.

[3] "Must the Bearer of a Right Have the Concept of That to Which He Has a Right?" *Ethics*, xcv, 1 (1984): 68–74.

[4] See Tooley again in "Abortion and Infanticide," pp. 47–49.

maximize does not exist, however; furthermore, nothing in the ethics of killing in this paper entails that it does. The ethics of killing in this essay would entail that contraception is wrong only if something were denied a human future of value by contraception. Nothing at all is denied such a future by contraception, however.

Candidates for a subject of harm by contraception fall into four categories: (1) some sperm or other, (2) some ovum or other, (3) a sperm and an ovum separately, and (4) a sperm and an ovum together. Assigning the harm to some sperm is utterly arbitrary, for no reason can be given for making a sperm the subject of harm rather than an ovum. Assigning the harm to some ovum is utterly arbitrary, for no reason can be given for making an ovum the subject of harm rather than a sperm. One might attempt to avoid these problems by insisting that contraception deprives both the sperm and the ovum separately of a valuable future like ours. On this alternative, too many futures are lost. Contraception was supposed to be wrong, because it deprived us of one future of value, not two. One might attempt to avoid this problem by holding that contraception deprives the combination of sperm and ovum of a valuable future like ours. But here the definite article misleads. At the time of contraception, there are hundreds of millions of sperm, one (released) ovum and millions of possible combinations of all of these. There is no actual combination at all. Is the subject of the loss to be a merely possible combination? Which one? This alternative does not yield an actual subject of harm either. Accordingly, the immorality of contraception is not entailed by the loss of a future-like-ours argument simply because there is no nonarbitrarily identifiable subject of the loss in the case of contraception.

Don Marquis: Why Abortion Is Immoral

1) Marquis begins by criticizing some common arguments on both sides of the abortion issue. Do his criticisms succeed in refuting the common arguments? Why or why not?

2) What, according to Marquis, is wrong with killing adult humans? Is his theory the best account of what is wrong with such killing?

3) Marquis claims that abortion is wrong for the same reason that killing adult humans is wrong. Are there any differences between the two that would justify abortion?

4) One might object to Marquis's claim that fetuses have a valuable future by pointing out that fetuses do not have the cognitive capacities to

value anything. How does Marquis respond to this objection? Do you find his response convincing?

5) Marquis admits that his theory would be problematic if it led to the view that contraception is seriously morally wrong. How does he argue that his theory does not do this? Do you think he succeeds?

29

The Conscience of Huckleberry Finn
Jonathan Bennett

One ethical ideal is that of the person with integrity. Such a person is clear about what she stands for, and reliably guides her conduct by her chosen principles. So understood, integrity is a kind of conscientiousness, which most of us regard as a very important virtue.

But what should we say about cases in which one's conscience tells us to do things that are, unbeknownst to us, very seriously immoral? Jonathan Bennett invites us to think more deeply about the value of conscientiousness, by offering three cases studies for our consideration. In each, the relevant character (Huck Finn, the eighteenth-century religious thinker Jonathan Edwards, and the Nazi Heinrich Himmler) provides a different perspective on the importance of staying true to our moral ideals. Huck Finn, for instance, strayed from what he thought of as the path of virtue. In his eyes, morality required him to turn in the runaway slave who was accompanying him down the Mississippi. His failure to do so cost him sleepless nights. But we applaud his lack of integrity.

Bennett examines his case studies with a special interest in considering the tensions between integrity, on the one hand, and sympathy for others, on the other. Huck's sympathy for Jim, the runaway slave, was what caused him to break with his moral ideals. It would be nice if we were always required to resolve conflicts between sympathy and conscientiousness in the same way. But we aren't. Sometimes it is best

---

"The Conscience of Huckleberry Finn" from *Philosophy* 49 (1974). Reprinted with the permission of Cambridge University Press.

to indulge our sympathies. Had Himmler and other Nazi leaders done this, the Holocaust might never have happened. And yet our sympathies are not always reliable moral guidelines. Bennett does not try to offer a simple solution for such conflicts, but instead prompts us to think more deeply about the role of sympathy and conscientiousness in moral thinking.

....

I n this paper I shall present not just the conscience of Huckleberry Finn but two others as well. One of them is the conscience of Heinrich Himmler. He became a Nazi in 1923; he served drably and quietly, but well, and was rewarded with increasing responsibility and power. At the peak of his career he held many offices and commands, of which the most powerful was that of leader of the S.S.—the principal police force of the Nazi regime. In this capacity, Himmler commanded the whole concentration-camp system, and was responsible for the execution of the so-called 'final solution of the Jewish problem'. It is important for my purposes that this piece of social engineering should be thought of not abstractly but in concrete terms of Jewish families being marched to what they think are bathhouses, to the accompaniment of loud-speaker renditions of extracts from *The Merry Widow* and *Tales of Hoffman*, there to be choked to death by poisonous gases. Altogether, Himmler succeeded in murdering about four and a half million of them, as well as several million gentiles, mainly Poles and Russians.

The other conscience to be discussed is that of the Calvinist theologian and philosopher Jonathan Edwards. He lived in the first half of the eighteenth century, and has a good claim to be considered America's first serious and considerable philosophical thinker. He was for many years a widely-renowned preacher and Congregationalist minister in New England; in 1748 a dispute with his congregation led him to resign (he couldn't accept their view that unbelievers should be admitted to the Lord's Supper in the hope that it would convert them); for some years after that he worked as a missionary, preaching to Indians through an interpreter; then in 1758 he accepted the presidency of what is now Princeton University, and within two months died from a smallpox inoculation. Along the way he wrote some first-rate philosophy: his book attacking the notion of free will is still sometimes read. Why I should be interested in Edwards' conscience will be explained in due course. I shall use Heinrich Himmler, Jonathan Edwards and Huckleberry Finn to illustrate different aspects of a single theme, namely the relationship between *sympathy* on the one hand and *bad morality* on the other.

All that I can mean by a 'bad morality' is a morality whose principles I deeply disapprove of. When I call a morality bad, I cannot prove that mine is better; but when I here call any morality bad, I think you will agree with me that it is bad; and that is all I need.

There could be dispute as to whether the springs of someone's actions constitute a morality. I think, though, that we must admit that someone who acts in ways which conflict grossly with our morality may nevertheless have a morality of his own—a set of principles of action which he sincerely assents to, so that for him the problem of acting well or rightly or in obedience to conscience is the problem of conforming to those principles. The problem of conscientiousness can arise as acutely for a bad morality as for any other: rotten principles may be as difficult to keep as decent ones.

As for 'sympathy': I use this term to cover every sort of fellow-feeling, as when one feels pity over someone's loneliness, or horrified compassion over his pain, or when one feels a shrinking reluctance to act in a way which will bring misfortune to someone else. These feelings must not be confused with moral judgments. My sympathy for someone in distress may lead me to help him, or even to think that I ought to help him; but in itself it is not a judgment about what I ought to do, but just a feeling for him in his plight. We shall get some light on the difference between feelings and moral judgments when we consider Huckleberry Finn.

Obviously, feelings can impel one to action, and so can moral judgments; and in a particular case sympathy and morality may push in opposite directions. This can happen not just with bad moralities, but also with good ones like yours and mine. For example, a small child, sick and miserable, clings tightly to his mother and screams in terror when she tries to pass him over to the doctor to be examined. If the mother gave way to her sympathy, that is, to her feeling for the child's misery and fright, she would hold it close and not let the doctor come near; but don't we agree that it might be wrong for her to act on such a feeling? Quite generally, then, anyone's moral principles may apply to a particular situation in a way which runs contrary to the particular thrusts of fellow-feeling that he has in that situation. My immediate concern is with sympathy in relation to bad morality, but not because such conflicts occur only when the morality is bad.

Now, suppose that someone who accepts a bad morality is struggling to make himself act in accordance with it in a particular situation where his sympathies pull him another way. He sees the struggle as one between doing the right, conscientious thing, and acting wrongly and weakly, like the mother who won't let the doctor come near her sick, frightened baby. Since we don't accept this person's morality, we may see the situation very differently, thoroughly disapproving of the action he regards as the right one, and endorsing the action which from his point of view constitutes weakness and backsliding.

Conflicts between sympathy and bad morality won't always be like this, for we won't disagree with every single dictate of a bad morality. Still, it can happen in the way I have described, with the agent's right action being our wrong one, and vice versa. That is just what happens in a certain episode in chapter 16 of *The Adventures of Huckleberry Finn*, an episode which brilliantly illustrates how fiction can be instructive about real life.

Huck Finn has been helping his slave friend Jim to run away from Miss Watson, who is Jim's owner. In their raft-journey down the Mississippi River, they are near to the place at which Jim will become legally free. Now let Huck take over the story:

> Jim said it made him all over trembly and feverish to be so close to freedom. Well, I can tell you it made me all over trembly and feverish, too, to hear him, because I begun to get it through my head that he was most free—and who was to blame for it? Why, me. I couldn't get that out of my conscience, no how nor no way.... It hadn't ever come home to me, before, what this thing was that I was doing. But now it did; and it stayed with me, and scorched me more and more. I tried to make out to myself that I warn't to blame, because I didn't run Jim off from his rightful owner; but it warn't no use, conscience up and say, every time: 'But you knowed he was running for his freedom, and you could a paddled ashore and told somebody.' That was so—I couldn't get around that, no way. That was where it pinched. Conscience says to me: 'What had poor Miss Watson done to you, that you could see her nigger go off right under your eyes and never say one single word? What did that poor old woman do to you, that you could treat her so mean?...' I got to feeling so mean and so miserable I most wished I was dead.

Jim speaks of his plan to save up to buy his wife, and then his children, out of slavery; and he adds that if the children cannot be bought he will arrange to steal them. Huck is horrified:

Thinks I, this is what comes of my not thinking. Here was this nigger which I had as good as helped to run away, coming right out flat-footed and saying he would steal his children—children that belonged to a man I didn't even know; a man that hadn't ever done me no harm.

I was sorry to hear Jim say that, it was such a lowering of him. My conscience got to stirring me up hotter than ever, until at last I says to it: 'Let up on me—it ain't too late, yet—I'll paddle ashore at first light, and tell.' I felt easy, and happy, and light as a feather, right off. All my troubles was gone.

This is bad morality all right. In his earliest years Huck wasn't taught any principles, and the only ones he has encountered since then are those of rural Missouri, in which slave-owning is just one kind of ownership and is not subject to critical pressure. It hasn't occurred to Huck to question those principles. So the action, to us abhorrent, of turning Jim in to the authorities presents itself clearly to Huck as the right thing to do.

For us, morality and sympathy would both dictate helping Jim to escape. If we felt any conflict, it would have both of these on one side and something else on the other - greed for a reward, or fear of punishment. But Huck's morality conflicts with his sympathy, that is, with his unargued, natural feeling for his friend. The conflict starts when Huck sets off in the canoe towards the shore, pretending that he is going to reconnoitre, but really planning to turn Jim in:

As I shoved off, [Jim] says: 'Pooty soon I'll be a-shout'n for joy, en I'll say, it's all on accounts o' Huck I's a free man ... Jim won't ever forget you, Huck; you's de bes' fren' Jim ever had; en you's de only fren' old Jim's got now.'

I was paddling off, all in a sweat to tell on him; but when he says this, it seemed to kind of take the tuck all out of me. I went along slow then, and I warn't right down certain whether I was glad I started or whether I warn't. When I was fifty yards off, Jim says:

'Dah you goes, de ole true Huck; de on'y white genlman dat ever kep' his promise to ole Jim.' Well, I just felt sick. But I says, I *got* to do it—I can't get *out* of it.

In the upshot, sympathy wins over morality. Huck hasn't the strength of will to do what he sincerely thinks he ought to do. Two men hunting for runaway slaves ask him whether the man on his raft is black or white:

I didn't answer up prompt. I tried to, but the words wouldn't come. I tried, for a second or two, to brace up and out with it, but I warn't man enough—hadn't the spunk of a rabbit. I see I was weakening; so I just give up trying, and up and says: 'He's white.'

So Huck enables Jim to escape, thus acting weakly and wickedly—he thinks. In this conflict between sympathy and morality, sympathy wins.

One critic has cited this episode in support of the statement that Huck suffers 'excruciating moments of wavering between honesty and respectability'. That is hopelessly wrong, and I agree with the perceptive comment on it by another critic, who says:

> The conflict waged in Huck is much more serious: he scarcely cares for respectability and never hesitates to relinquish it, but he does care for honesty and gratitude—and both honesty and gratitude require that he should give Jim up. It is not, in Huck, honesty at war with respectability but love and compassion for Jim struggling against his conscience. His decision is for Jim and hell; a right decision made in the mental chains that Huck never breaks. His concern for Jim is and remains irrational. Huck finds many reasons for giving Jim up and none for stealing him. To the end Huck sees his compassion for Jim as a weak, ignorant, and wicked felony.[1]

That is precisely correct—and it can have that virtue only because Mark Twain wrote the episode with such unerring precision. The crucial point concerns *reasons*, which all occur on one side of the conflict. On the side of conscience we have principles, arguments, considerations, ways of looking at things:

'It hadn't ever come home to me before what I was doing'
'I tried to make out that I warn't to blame'
'Conscience said "But you knowed..."—I couldn't get around that'
'What had poor Miss Watson done to you?'
'This is what comes of my not thinking'
'...children that belonged to a man I didn't even know'.

On the other side, the side of feeling, we get nothing like that. When Jim rejoices in Huck, as his only friend, Huck doesn't consider the claims of friendship or have the situation 'come home' to him in a different light. All that happens is: 'When he says this, it seemed to kind of take the tuck all out of me. I went along slow then, and I warn't right down certain whether I was glad I started or whether I warn't.' Again, Jim's words about

---

[1] M. J. Sidnell, 'Huck Finn and Jim', *The Cambridge Quarterly* 2, pp. 205–206.

Huck's 'promise' to him don't give Huck any reason for changing his plan: in his morality promises to slaves probably don't count. Their effect on him is of a different kind: 'Well, I just felt sick.' And when the moment for final decision comes, Huck doesn't weigh up pros and cons: he simply *fails* to do what he believes to be right—he isn't strong enough, hasn't 'the spunk of a rabbit'. This passage in the novel is notable not just for its finely wrought irony, with Huck's weakness of will leading him to do the right thing, but also for its masterly handling of the difference between general moral principles and particular unreasoned emotional pulls.

Consider now another case of bad morality in conflict with human sympathy, the case of the odious Himmler. Here, from a speech he made to some S.S. generals, is an indication of the content of his morality:

> What happens to a Russian, to a Czech, does not interest me in the slightest. What the nations can offer in the way of good blood of our type, we will take, if necessary by kidnapping their children and raising them here with us. Whether nations live in prosperity or starve to death like cattle interests me only in so far as we need them as slaves to our *Kultur*; otherwise it is of no interest to me. Whether 10,000 Russian females fall down from exhaustion while digging an antitank ditch interests me only in so far as the antitank ditch for Germany is finished.[2]

But has this a moral basis at all? And if it has, was there in Himmler's own mind any conflict between morality and sympathy? Yes there was. Here is more from the same speech:

> ...I also want to talk to you quite frankly on a very grave matter... I mean...the extermination of the Jewish race....Most of you must know what it means when 100 corpses are lying side by side, or 500, or 1,000. To have stuck it out and at the same time—apart from exceptions caused by human weakness—to have remained decent fellows, that is what has made us hard. This is a page of glory in our history which has never been written and is never to be written.

Himmler saw his policies as being hard to implement while still retaining one's human sympathies—while still remaining a 'decent fellow'.

---

[2] Quoted in William L. Shirer, *The Rise and Fall of the Third Reich* (New York, 1960), pp. 937–938. Next quotation: ibid., p. 966. All further quotations relating to Himmler are from Roger Manvell and Heinrich Fraenkel, *Heinrich Himmlcr* (London, 1965), pp. 132, 197, 184 (twice), 187.

He is saying that only the weak take the easy way out and just squelch their sympathies, and is praising the stronger and more glorious course of retaining one's sympathies while acting in violation of them. In the same spirit, he ordered that when executions were carried out in concentration camps, those responsible 'are to be influenced in such a way as to suffer no ill effect in their character and mental attitude'. A year later he boasted that the S.S. had wiped out the Jews

> without our leaders and their men suffering any damage in their minds and souls. The danger was considerable, for there was only a narrow path between the Scylla of their becoming heartless ruffians unable any longer to treasure life, and the Charybdis of their becoming soft and suffering nervous breakdowns.

And there really can't be any doubt that the basis of Himmler's policies was a set of principles which constituted his morality—a sick, bad, wicked morality. He described himself as caught in 'the old tragic conflict between will and obligation'. And when his physician Kersten protested at the intention to destroy the Jews, saying that the suffering involved was 'not to be contemplated', Kersten reports that Himmler replied:

> He knew that it would mean much suffering for the Jews.... 'It is the curse of greatness that it must step over dead bodies to create new life. Yet we must...cleanse the soil or it will never bear fruit. It will be a great burden for me to bear.'

This, I submit, is the language of morality.

So in this case, tragically, bad morality won out over sympathy. I am sure that many of Himmler's killers did extinguish their sympathies, becoming 'heartless ruffians' rather than 'decent fellows'; but not Himmler himself. Although his policies ran against the human grain to a horrible degree, he did not sandpaper down his emotional surfaces so that there was no grain there, allowing his actions to slide along smoothly and easily. He did, after all, bear his hideous burden, and even paid a price for it. He suffered a variety of nervous and physical disabilities, including nausea and stomach-convulsions, and Kersten was doubtless right in saying that these were 'the expression of a psychic division which extended over his whole life'.

This same division must have been present in some of those officials of the Church who ordered heretics to be tortured so as to change their theological opinions. Along with the brutes and the cold careerists, there must have been some who cared, and who suffered from the conflict between their sympathies and their bad morality.

In the conflict between sympathy and bad morality, then, the victory may go to sympathy as in the case of Huck Finn, or to morality as in the case of Himmler.

Another possibility is that the conflict may be avoided by giving up, or not ever having, those sympathies which might interfere with one's principles. That seems to have been the case with Jonathan Edwards. I am afraid that I shall be doing an injustice to Edwards' many virtues, and to his great intellectual energy and inventiveness; for my concern is only with the worst thing about him— namely his morality, which was worse than Himmler's. According to Edwards, God condemns some men to an eternity of unimaginably awful pain, though he arbitrarily spares others—'arbitrarily' because none deserve to be spared:

> Natural men are held in the hand of God over the pit of hell; they have deserved the fiery pit, and are already sentenced to it; and God is dreadfully provoked, his anger is as great towards them as to those that are actually suffering the executions of the fierceness of his wrath in hell...; the devil is waiting for them, hell is gaping for them, the flames gather and flash about them, and would fain lay hold on them...; and...there are no means within reach that can be any security to them.... All that preserves them is the mere arbitrary will, and uncovenanted unobliged forbearance of an incensed God.[3]

Notice that he says 'they have deserved the fiery pit.' Edwards insists that men *ought* to be condemned to eternal pain; and his position isn't that this is right because God wants it, but rather that God wants it because it is right. For him, moral standards exist independently of God, and God can be assessed in the light of them (and of course found to be perfect). For example, he says:

> They deserve to be cast into hell; so that...justice never stands in the way, it makes no objection against God's using his power at any moment to destroy them. Yea, on the contrary, justice calls aloud for an infinite punishment of their sins.

Elsewhere, he gives elaborate arguments to show that God is acting justly in damning sinners. For example, he argues that a punishment

---

[3] Vergilius Ferm (ed.), *Puritan Sage: Collected Writings of Jonathan Edwards* (New York, 1953), p. 370. Next three quotations: ibid., p. 366, p. 294 ('no more than infinite'), p. 372.

should be exactly as bad as the crime being punished: God is infinitely excellent; so any crime against him is infinitely bad; and so eternal damnation is exactly right as a punishment—it is infinite, but, as Edwards is careful also to say, it is 'no more than infinite.'

Of course, Edwards himself didn't torment the damned; but the question still arises of whether his sympathies didn't conflict with his *approval* of eternal torment. Didn't he find it painful to contemplate any fellow-human's being tortured for ever? Apparently not:

> The God that holds you over the pit of hell, much as one holds a spider or some loathsome insect over the fire, abhors you, and is dreadfully provoked;...he is of purer eyes than to bear to have you in his sight; you are ten thousand times so abominable in his eyes as the most hateful venomous serpent is in ours.

When God is presented as being as misanthropic as that, one suspects misanthropy in the theologian. This suspicion is increased when Edwards claims that 'the saints in glory will...understand how terrible the sufferings of the damned are; yet...will not be sorry for [them].'[4] He bases this partly on a view of human nature whose ugliness he seems not to notice:

> The seeing of the calamities of others tends to heighten the sense of our own enjoyments. When the saints in glory, therefore, shall see the doleful state of the damned, how will this heighten their sense of the blessedness of their own state....When they shall see how miserable others of their fellow-creatures are...; when they shall see the smoke of their torment,...and hear their dolorous shrieks and cries, and consider that they in the mean time are in the most blissful state, and shall surely be in it to all eternity; how they will rejoice!

I hope this is less than the whole truth! His other main point about why the saints will rejoice to see the torments of the damned is that it is *right* that they should do so:

> The heavenly inhabitants...will have no love nor pity to the damned....[This will not show] a want of a spirit of love in them...; for the heavenly inhabitants will know that it is not fit that they should

---

[4] This and the next two quotations are from 'The End of the Wicked Contemplated by the Righteous: or, The Torments of the Wicked in Hell, no Occasion of Grief to the Saints in Heaven', from *The Works of President Edwards* (London, 1817), vol. IV, pp. 507–508, 511–512, and 509 respectively.

love [the damned] because they will know then, that God has no love
to them, nor pity for them.

The implication that of course one can adjust one's feelings of pity so
that they conform to the dictates of some authority—doesn't this suggest
that ordinary human sympathies played only a small part in Edwards' life?

Huck Finn, whose sympathies are wide and deep, could never avoid the
conflict in that way; but he is determined to avoid it, and so he opts for the only
other alternative he can see—to give up morality altogether. After he has tricked
the slave-hunters, he returns to the raft and undergoes a peculiar crisis:

> I got aboard the raft, feeling bad and low, because I knowed very well
> I had done wrong, and I see it warn't no use for me to try to learn to
> do right; a body that don't get *started* right when he's little, ain't got no
> show—when the pinch comes there ain't nothing to back him up and
> keep him to his work, and so he gets beat. Then I thought a minute,
> and says to myself, hold on—s'pose you'd a done right and give Jim
> up; would you feel better than what you do now? No, says I, I'd feel
> bad—I'd feel just the same way I do now. Well, then, says I, what's the
> use you learning to do right, when it's troublesome to do right and ain't
> no trouble to do wrong, and the wages is just the same? I was stuck.
> I couldn't answer that. So I reckoned I wouldn't bother no more about
> it, but after this always do whichever come handiest at the time.

Huck clearly cannot conceive of having any morality except the one
he has learned—too late, he thinks—from his society. He is not entirely a
prisoner of that morality, because he does after all reject it; but for him that
is a decision to relinquish morality as such; he cannot envisage revising his
morality, altering its content in face of the various pressures to which it is
subject, including pressures from his sympathies. For example, he does not
begin to approach the thought that slavery should be rejected on moral
grounds, or the thought that what he is doing is not theft because a person
cannot be owned and therefore cannot be stolen.

The basic trouble is that he cannot or will not engage in abstract intellectual operations of any sort. In chapter 33 he finds himself 'feeling to
blame, somehow' for something he knows he had no hand in; he assumes
that this feeling is a deliverance of conscience; and this confirms him in his
belief that conscience shouldn't be listened to:

> It don't make no difference whether you do right or wrong, a person's
> conscience ain't got no sense, and just goes for him *anyway*. If I had a
> yaller dog that didn't know no more than a person's conscience does,

I would pison him. It takes up more room than all the rest of a person's insides, and yet ain't no good, nohow.

That brisk, incurious dismissiveness fits well with the comprehensive rejection of morality back on the raft. But this is a digression.

On the raft, Huck decides not to live by principles, but just to do whatever 'comes handiest at the time'—always acting according to the mood of the moment. Since the morality he is rejecting is narrow and cruel, and his sympathies are broad and kind, the results will be good. But moral principles are good to have, because they help to protect one from acting badly at moments when one's sympathies happen to be in abeyance. On the highest possible estimate of the role one's sympathies should have, one can still allow for principles as embodiments of one's best feelings, one's broadest and keenest sympathies. On that view, principles can help one across intervals when one's feelings are at less than their best, i.e. through periods of misanthropy or meanness or self-centredness or depression or anger.

What Huck didn't see is that one can live by principles and yet have ultimate control over their content. And one way such control can be exercised is by checking of one's principles in the light of one's sympathies. This is sometimes a pretty straightforward matter. It can happen that a certain moral principle becomes untenable—meaning literally that one cannot hold it any longer—because it conflicts intolerably with the pity or revulsion or whatever that one feels when one sees what the principle leads to. One's experience may play a large part here: experiences evoke feelings, and feelings force one to modify principles. Something like this happened to the English poet Wilfred Owen, whose experiences in the First World War transformed him from an enthusiastic soldier into a virtual pacifist. I can't document his change of conscience in detail; but I want to present something which he wrote about the way experience can put pressure on morality.[5]

The Latin poet Horace wrote that it is sweet and fitting (or right) to die for one's country—*dulce et decorum est pro patria mori*—and Owen wrote a fine poem about how experience could lead one to relinquish that particular moral principle. He describes a man who is too slow donning his gas mask during a gas attack—'As under a green sea, I saw him drowning,' Owen says. The poem ends like this:

---

[5] Extracts from 'Dulce et Decorum Est' and 'Insensibility' are from *The Collected Poems of Wilfred Owen*, edited by C. Day Lewis. Copyright Chatto & Windus Ltd. 1946, copyright 1963. Reprinted by permission of The Owen Estate, Chatto & Windus Ltd., and New Directions Publishing Corporation.

In all my dreams, before my helpless sight
He plunges at me, guttering, choking, drowning.
If in some smothering dreams you too could pace
Behind the wagon that we flung him in,
And watch the white eyes writhing in his face,
His hanging face, like a devil's sick of sin;
If you could hear, at every jolt, the blood
Come gargling from the froth-erupted lungs,
Obscene as cancer, bitter as the cud
Of vile, incurable sores on innocent tongues,
My friend, you would not tell with such high zest
To children ardent for some desperate glory,
The old Lie: Dulce et decorum est
Pro patria mori.

There is a difficulty about drawing from all this a moral for ourselves. I imagine that we agree in our rejection of slavery, eternal damnation, genocide, and uncritical patriotic self-abnegation; so we shall agree that Huck Finn, Jonathan Edwards, Heinrich Himmler, and the poet Horace would all have done well to bring certain of their principles under severe pressure from ordinary human sympathies. But then we can say this because we can say that all those are bad moralities, whereas we cannot look at our own moralities and declare them bad. This is not arrogance: it is obviously incoherent for someone to declare the system of moral principles that he accepts to be *bad*, just as one cannot coherently say of anything that one believes it but it is *false*.

Still, although I can't point to any of my beliefs and say 'That is false', I don't doubt that some of my beliefs are false; and so I should try to remain open to correction. Similarly, I accept every single item in my morality—that is inevitable—but I am sure that my morality could be improved, which is to say that it could undergo changes which I should be glad of once I had made them. So I must try to keep my morality open to revision, exposing it to whatever valid pressures there are—including pressures from my sympathies.

I don't give my sympathies a blank cheque in advance. In a conflict between principle and sympathy, principles ought sometimes to win. For example, I think it was right to take part in the Second World War on the Allied side; there were many ghastly individual incidents which might have led someone to doubt the rightness of his participation in that war; and I think it would have been right for such a person to keep his sympathies in a subordinate place on those occasions, not allowing them to modify his principles in such a way as to make a pacifist of him. Still, one's sympathies should be kept as sharp and sensitive and aware as possible, and not only because they can sometimes affect one's principles or one's conduct or both. Owen, at any rate, says that feelings and sympathies are vital even when they can do nothing but bring pain and distress. In another poem he speaks of the blessings of being numb in one's feelings: 'Happy are the men who yet before they are killed / Can let their veins run cold', he says. These are the ones who do not suffer from any compassion which, as Owen puts it, 'makes their feet / Sore on the alleys cobbled with their brothers'. He contrasts these 'happy' ones, who 'lose imagination', with himself and others 'who with a thought besmirch / Blood over all our soul.' Yet the poem's verdict goes against the 'happy' ones. Owen does not say that they will act worse than the others whose souls are besmirched with blood because of their keen awareness of human suffering. He merely says that they are the losers because they have cut themselves off from the human condition:

> By choice they made themselves immune
> To pity and whatever moans in man
> Before the last sea and the hapless stars;
> Whatever mourns when many leave these shores;
> Whatever shares
> The eternal reciprocity of tears.

Jonathan Bennett: The Conscience of Huckleberry Finn

1) What does Bennett mean by "morality"? What does he mean by "sympathy"? How can the two come into conflict?
2) What conflict does Huck face? What lessons, if any, do you think we should take away from the case of Huck?
3) Many people would be inclined to claim that Himmler had neither any morality nor any significant sense of sympathy. Why does Bennett think that it would be a mistake to think this? Do you agree with him?
4) How did Jonathan Edwards resolve the conflict between morality and sympathy, according to Bennett? Why does Bennett object to this way of resolving the conflict?
5) What conclusions does Bennett draw from these cases? What role does he think that morality and sympathy ought to play in determining how we act? Do you think he is correct?

30

Terrorism: A Critique of Excuses

Michael Walzer

....

Terrorists target innocent people to further their own political agenda. Michael Walzer thinks that terrorism can never be justified: it can never be shown to be, in the end, the morally right thing to do. But can terrorism ever be excused? Can terrorists, while doing something very wrong, nonetheless be freed of any moral blame for their actions?

Walzer defends a negative answer to this question by considering the four most prominent excuses for terrorism. These excuses include the claim (1) that terrorism is a last resort, chosen when all else fails; (2) that nothing but terrorism is possible for weak insurgency movements; (3) that terrorism works, and whatever works for a good cause is itself morally acceptable; and (4) that all politics involves terrorism, and all political groups practice it. Walzer argues that each of these excuses fails.

How should we combat terrorism? While Walzer does not offer anything like a simple solution to this question, he identifies some constraints that must be met. We must avoid repeating the wrongs of terrorists when we fight against them. We must not target people indiscriminately. If we must engage in repression and retaliation, it must be directed at the terrorists themselves, and never at the people in whose name the terrorists are acting.

Terrorism is often a response to oppression. While Walzer rejects the idea that this ever justifies or excuses terrorism, he insists that the oppression should be reduced or (ideally) eliminated. Not all terrorism

Michael Walzer, "Terrorism: A Critique of Excuses" from *Problems of International Justice.* S. Luper-Foy, ed. (Westview Press, 1988), pp. 237–247. Reprinted with the permission of Michael Walzer.

stems from oppression. And when terror is a response to oppression, it can be very tempting to do nothing about the oppression, or even to increase one's iron grip. But Walzer rejects such responses. Justice requires that we relieve oppression, even when one's enemies are using it to justify terroristic attacks.

....

N o one these days advocates terrorism, not even those who regularly practice it. The practice is indefensible now that it has been recognized, like rape and murder, as an attack upon the innocent. In a sense, indeed, terrorism is worse than rape and murder commonly are, for in the latter cases the victim has been chosen for a purpose; he or she is the direct object of attack, and the attack has some reason, however twisted or ugly it may be. The victims of a terrorist attack are third parties, innocent bystanders; there is no special reason for attacking them; anyone else within a large class of (unrelated) people will do as well. The attack is directed indiscriminately against the entire class. Terrorists are like killers on a rampage, except that their rampage is not just expressive of rage or madness; the rage is purposeful and programmatic. It aims at a general vulnerability: Kill these people in order to terrify those. A relatively small number of dead victims makes for a very large number of living and frightened hostages.

This, then, is the peculiar evil of terrorism—not only the killing of innocent people but also the intrusion of fear into everyday life, the violation of private purposes, the insecurity of public spaces, the endless coerciveness of precaution. A crime wave might, I suppose, produce similar effects, but no one plans a crime wave; it is the work of a thousand individual decision-makers, each one independent of the others, brought together only by the invisible hand. Terrorism is the work of visible hands; it is an organizational project, a strategic choice, a conspiracy to murder and intimidate...you and me. No wonder the conspirators have difficulty defending, in public, the strategy they have chosen.

The moral difficulty is the same, obviously, when the conspiracy is directed not against you and me but against *them*—Protestants, say, not Catholics; Israelis, not Italians or Germans; blacks, not whites. These "limits" rarely hold for long; the logic of terrorism steadily expands the range of vulnerability. The more hostages they hold, the stronger the terrorists are. No one is safe once whole populations have been put at risk. Even if the risk were contained, however, the evil would be no different. So far as individual Protestants or Israelis or blacks are concerned, terrorism is random, degrading, and frightening. That is its hallmark, and that, again, is why it cannot be defended.

But when moral justification is ruled out, the way is opened for ideological excuse and apology. We live today in a political culture of excuses. This is far better than a political culture in which terrorism is openly defended and justified, for the excuse at least acknowledges the evil. But the improvement is precarious, hard won, and difficult to sustain. It is not the case, even in this better world, that terrorist organizations are without supporters. The support is indirect but by no means ineffective. It takes the form of apologetic descriptions and explanations, a litany of excuses that steadily undercuts our knowledge of the evil. Today that knowledge is insufficient unless it is supplemented and reinforced by a systematic critique of excuses. That is my purpose here. I take the principle for granted: that every act of terrorism is a wrongful act. The wrongfulness of the excuses, however, cannot be taken for granted; it has to be argued. The excuses themselves are familiar enough, the stuff of contemporary political debate. I shall state them in stereotypical form. There is no need to attribute them to this or that writer, publicist, or commentator; my readers can make their own attributions.

The most common excuse for terrorism is that it is a last resort, chosen only when all else fails. The image is of people who have literally run out of options. One by one, they have tried every legitimate form of political and military action, exhausted every possibility, failed everywhere, until no alternative remains but the evil of terrorism. They must be terrorists or do nothing at all. The easy response is to insist that, given this description of their case, they should do nothing at all; they have indeed exhausted their possibilities. But this response simply reaffirms the principle, ignores the excuse; this response does not attend to the terrorists' desperation. Whatever the cause to which they are committed, we have to recognize that, given the commitment, the one thing they cannot do is "nothing at all."

But the case is badly described. It is not so easy to reach the "last resort." To get there, one must indeed try everything (which is a lot of things) and not just once, as if a political party might organize a single demonstration, fail to win immediate victory, and claim that it was now justified in moving on to murder. Politics is an art of repetition. Activists and citizens learn from experience, that is, by doing the same thing over and over again. It is by no means clear when they run out of options, but even under conditions of oppression and war, citizens have a good run short of that. The same argument applies to state officials who claim that they have tried "everything" and are now compelled to kill hostages or bomb peasant villages. Imagine such people called before a judicial tribunal and required to answer the question, What exactly did you try? Does anyone believe that they could come up with a plausible list? "Last resort" has only a notional finality; the resort to terror is ideologically last, not last in an actual series of actions, just last for the sake of the excuse. In fact, most state officials and movement militants who recommend a policy of terrorism recommend it as a first resort; they are for it from the beginning, although they may not get their way at the beginning. If they are honest, then, they must make other excuses and give up the pretense of the last resort.

[Would terrorism be justified in a "supreme emergency" as that condition is described in "Emergency Ethics" (Chapter 3)*? It might be, but only if the oppression to which the terrorists claimed to be responding was genocidal in character. Against the imminent threat of political and physical extinction, extreme measures can be defended, assuming that they have some chance of success. But this kind of a threat has not been present in any of the recent cases of terrorist activity. Terrorism has not been a means of avoiding disaster but of reaching for political success.]

The second excuse is designed for national liberation movements struggling against established and powerful states. Now the claim is that nothing else is possible, that no other strategy is available except terrorism. This is different from the first excuse because it does not require would-be terrorists to run through all the available options. Or, the second excuse requires terrorists to run through all the options in their heads, not in the world; notional finality is enough. Movement strategists consider their options and conclude that they have no alternative to terrorism. They think that they do not have the political strength to try anything else, and thus they do not try anything else. Weakness is their excuse.

But two very different kinds of weakness are commonly confused here: the weakness of the movement vis-à-vis the opposing state and the movement's weakness vis-à-vis its own people. This second kind of weakness, the inability of the movement to mobilize the nation, makes terrorism the "only"

---

* In an earlier chapter, omitted here, Walzer defines a supreme emergency as a situation in which a group is faced with a serious risk of annihilation from a dedicated enemy.—Ed.

option because it effectively rules out all the others: nonviolent resistance, general strikes, mass demonstrations, unconventional warfare, and so on.

These options are only rarely ruled out by the sheer power of the state, by the pervasiveness and intensity of oppression. Totalitarian states may be immune to nonviolent or guerrilla resistance, but all the evidence suggests that they are also immune to terrorism. Or, more exactly, in totalitarian states state terror dominates every other sort. Where terrorism is a possible strategy for the oppositional movement (in liberal and democratic states, most obviously), other strategies are also possible if the movement has some significant degree of popular support. In the absence of popular support, terrorism may indeed be the one available strategy, but it is hard to see how its evils can then be excused. For it is not weakness alone that makes the excuse, but the claim of the terrorists to represent the weak; and the particular form of weakness that makes terrorism the only option calls that claim into question.

One might avoid this difficulty with a stronger insistence on the actual effectiveness of terrorism. The third excuse is simply that terrorism works (and nothing else does); it achieves the ends of the oppressed even without their participation. "When the act accuses, the result excuses." This is a consequentialist argument, and given a strict understanding of consequentialism, this argument amounts to a justification rather than an excuse. In practice, however, the argument is rarely pushed so far. More often, the argument begins with an acknowledgment of the terrorists' wrongdoing. Their hands are dirty, but we must make a kind of peace with them because they have acted effectively for the sake of people who could not act for themselves. But, in fact, have the terrorists' actions been effective? I doubt that terrorism has ever achieved national liberation—no nation that I know of owes its freedom to a campaign of random murder—although terrorism undoubtedly increases the power of the terrorists within the national liberation movement. Perhaps terrorism is also conducive to the survival and notoriety (the two go together) of the movement, which is now dominated by terrorists. But even if we were to grant some means-end relationship between terror and national liberation, the third excuse does not work unless it can meet the further requirements of a consequentialist argument. It must be possible to say that the desired end could not have been achieved through any other, less wrongful, means. The third excuse depends, then, on the success of the first or second, and neither of these look likely to be successful.

The fourth excuse avoids this crippling dependency. This excuse does not require the apologist to defend either of the improbable claims that terrorism is the last resort or that it is the only possible resort. The fourth excuse is simply that terrorism is the universal resort. All politics is (really) terrorism. The appearance of innocence and decency is always a piece of deception, more or less convincing in accordance with the relative power of the deceivers. The terrorist who does not bother with appearances is only doing openly what everyone else does secretly.

This argument has the same form as the maxim "All's fair in love and war." Love is always fraudulent, war is always brutal, and political action is always terrorist in character. Political action works (as Thomas Hobbes long ago argued) only by generating fear in innocent men and women. Terrorism is the politics of state officials and movement militants alike. This argument does not justify either the officials or the militants, but it does excuse them all. We hardly can be harsh with people who act the way everyone else acts. Only saints are likely to act differently, and sainthood in politics is supererogatory, a matter of grace, not obligation.

But this fourth excuse relies too heavily on our cynicism about political life, and cynicism only sometimes answers well to experience. In fact, legitimate states do not need to terrorize their citizens, and strongly based movements do not need to terrorize their opponents. Officials and militants who live, as it were, on the margins of legitimacy and strength sometimes choose terrorism and sometimes do not. Living in terror is not a universal experience. The world the terrorists create has its entrances and exits.

If we want to understand the choice of terror, the choice that forces the rest of us through the door, we have to imagine what in fact always occurs, although we often have no satisfactory record of the occurrence: A group of men and women, officials or militants, sits around a table and argues about whether or not to adopt a terrorist strategy. Later on, the litany of excuses obscures the argument. But at the time, around the table, it would have been no use for defenders of terrorism to say, "Everybody does it," because there they would be face to face with people proposing to do something else. Nor is it historically the case that the members of this last group, the opponents of terrorism, always lose the argument. They can win, however, and still not be able to prevent a terrorist campaign; the would-be terrorists (it does not take very many) can always split the movement and go their own way. Or, they can split the bureaucracy or the police or officer corps and act in the shadow of state power. Indeed, terrorism often has its origin in such splits. The first victims are the terrorists' former comrades or colleagues. What reason can we possibly have, then, for equating the two? If we value the politics of the men and women who oppose terrorism, we must reject the excuses of their murderers. Cynicism at such a time is unfair to the victims.

The fourth excuse can also take, often does take, a more restricted form. Oppression, rather than political rule more generally, is always terroristic in character, and thus, we must always excuse the opponents of oppression. When they choose terrorism, they are only reacting to someone else's previous choice, repaying in kind the treatment they have long received. Of course, their terrorism repeats the evil—innocent people are killed, who were never themselves oppressors—but repetition is not the same as initiation. The oppressors set the terms of the struggle. But if the struggle is fought on the oppressors' terms, then the oppressors are likely to win. Or, at least, oppression is likely to win, even if it takes on a new face. The whole point of a liberation movement or a popular mobilization is to change the terms. We have no reason to excuse the terrorism reactively adopted by opponents of oppression unless we are confident of the sincerity of their opposition, the seriousness of their commitment to a nonoppressive politics. But the choice of terrorism undermines that confidence.

We are often asked to distinguish the terrorism of the oppressed from the terrorism of the oppressors. What is it, however, that makes the difference? The message of the terrorist is the same in both cases: a denial of the peoplehood and humanity of the groups among whom he or she finds victims. Terrorism anticipates, when it does not actually enforce, political domination. Does it matter if one dominated group is replaced by another? Imagine a slave revolt whose protagonists dream only of enslaving in their turn the children of their masters. The dream is understandable, but the fervent desire of the children that the revolt be repressed is equally understandable. In neither case does understanding make for excuse – not, at least, after a politics of universal freedom has become possible. Nor does an understanding of oppression excuse the terrorism of the oppressed, once we have grasped the meaning of "liberation."

These are the four general excuses for terror, and each of them fails. They depend upon statements about the world that are false, historical arguments for which there is no evidence, moral claims that turn out to be hollow or dishonest. This is not to say that there might not be more particular excuses that have greater plausibility, extenuating circumstances in particular cases that we would feel compelled to recognize. As with murder, we can tell a story (like the story that Richard Wright tells in *Native Son*, for example) that might lead us, not to justify terrorism, but to excuse this or that individual terrorist. We can provide a personal history, a psychological study, of compassion destroyed by fear, moral reason by hatred and rage, social inhibition by unending violence—the product, an individual driven to kill or readily set on a killing course by his or her political leaders. But the force of this story will not depend on any of the four general excuses, all of which grant what the storyteller will have to deny: that terrorism is the deliberate choice of rational men and women. Whether they conceive it to be one option among others or the only one available, they nevertheless argue and choose. Whether they are acting or reacting, they have made a decision. The human instruments they subsequently find to plant the bomb or shoot the gun may act under some psychological compulsion, but the men and women who choose terror as a policy act "freely." They could not act in any other way, or accept any other description of their action, and still pretend to be the leaders of the movement or the state. We ought never to excuse such leaders.

What follows from the critique of excuses? There is still a great deal of room for argument about the best way of responding to terrorism. Certainly, terrorists should be resisted, and it is not likely that a purely defensive resistance will ever be sufficient. In this sort of struggle, the offense is always ahead. The technology of terror is simple; the weapons are readily produced and easy to deliver. It is virtually impossible to protect people against random and indiscriminate attack. Thus, resistance will have to be supplemented by some combination of repression and retaliation. This is a dangerous business because repression and retaliation so often take terroristic forms and there are a host of apologists ready with excuses that sound remarkably like those of the terrorists themselves. It should be clear by now, however, that counterterrorism cannot be excused merely because it is reactive. Every new actor, terrorist or counterterrorist, claims to be reacting to someone else, standing in a circle and just passing the evil along. But the circle is ideological in character; in fact, every actor is a moral agent and makes an independent decision.

Therefore, repression and retaliation must not repeat the wrongs of terrorism, which is to say that repression and retaliation must be aimed systematically at the terrorists themselves, never at the people for whom the terrorists claim to be acting. That claim is in any case doubtful, even when it is honestly made. The people do not authorize the terrorists to act in their name. Only a tiny number actually participate in terrorist activities; they are far more likely to suffer than to benefit from the terrorist program. Even if they supported the program and hoped to benefit from it, however, they would still be immune from attack—exactly as civilians in time of war who support the war effort but are not themselves part of it are subject to the same immunity. Civilians may be put at risk by attacks on military targets, as by attacks on terrorist targets, but the risk must be kept to a minimum, even at some cost to the attackers. The refusal to make ordinary people into targets, whatever their nationality or even their politics, is the only way to say no to terrorism. Every act of repression and retaliation has to be measured by this standard.

But what if the "only way" to defeat the terrorists is to intimidate their actual or potential supporters? It is important to deny the premise of this question: that terrorism is a politics dependent on mass support. In fact, it is always the politics of an elite, whose members are dedicated and fanatical and more than ready to endure, or to watch others endure, the devastations of a counter-terrorist campaign. Indeed, terrorists will welcome counterterrorism; it makes the terrorists' excuses more plausible and is sure to bring them, however many people are killed or wounded, however many are terrorized, the small number of recruits needed to sustain the terrorist activities.

Repression and retaliation are legitimate responses to terrorism only when they are constrained by the same moral principles that rule out terrorism itself. But there is an alternative response that seeks to avoid the violence that these two entail. The alternative is to address directly, ourselves, the oppression the terrorists claim to oppose. Oppression, they say, is the cause of terrorism. But that is merely one more excuse. The real cause of terrorism is the decision to launch a terrorist campaign, a decision made by that group of people sitting around a table whose deliberations I have already described. However, terrorists do exploit oppression, injustice, and human misery generally and look to these at least for their excuses. There can hardly be any doubt that oppression strengthens their hand. Is that a reason for us to come to the defense of the oppressed? It seems to me that we have our own reasons to do that, and do not need this one, or should not, to prod us into action. We might imitate those movement militants who argue against the adoption of a terrorist strategy—although not, as the terrorists say, because these militants are prepared to tolerate oppression. They already are opposed to oppression and now add to that opposition, perhaps for the same reasons, a refusal of terror. So should we have been opposed before, and we should now make the same addition.

But there is an argument, put with some insistence these days, that we should refuse to acknowledge any link at all between terrorism and oppression—as if any defense of oppressed men and women, once a terrorist campaign has been launched, would concede the effectiveness of the campaign. Or, at least, the defense would give terrorism the appearance of effectiveness and so increase the likelihood of terrorist campaigns in the future. Here we have the reverse side of the litany of excuses; we have turned over the record. First oppression is made into an excuse for terrorism, and then terrorism is made into an excuse for oppression. The first is the excuse of the far left; the second is the excuse of the neoconservative right. I doubt that genuine conservatives would think it a good reason for defending the status quo that it is under terrorist attack; they would have independent reasons and would be prepared to defend the status quo against any attack. Similarly, those of us who think that the status quo urgently requires change have our own reasons for thinking so and need not be intimidated by terrorists or, for that matter, anti-terrorists.

If one criticizes the first excuse, one should not neglect the second. But I need to state the second more precisely. It is not so much an excuse for oppression as an excuse for doing nothing (now) about oppression. The claim is that the campaign against terrorism has priority over every other political activity. If the people who take the lead in this campaign are the old oppressors, then we must make a kind of peace with them—temporarily, of course, until the terrorists have been beaten. This is a strategy that denies the possibility of a two-front war. So long as the men and women who pretend to lead the fight against oppression are terrorists, we can concede nothing to their demands. Nor can we oppose their opponents.

But why not? It is not likely in any case that terrorists would claim victory in the face of a serious effort to deal with the oppression of the people they claim to be defending. The effort would merely expose the hollowness of their claim, and the nearer it came to success, the more they would escalate their terrorism. They would still have to be defeated, for what they are after is not a solution to the problem but rather the power to impose their own solution. No decent end to the conflict in Ireland, say, or in Lebanon, or in the Middle East generally, is going to look like a victory for terrorism—if only because the different groups of terrorists are each committed, by the strategy they have adopted, to an indecent end. By working for our own ends, we expose the indecency.

Michael Walzer: Terrorism: A Critique of Excuses

1) Although many people talk of "terrorism" today, the term is seldom explicitly defined. What exactly is terrorism? Are all terrorist acts committed by individuals and private organizations, or can states also engage in terrorism?

2) What is the difference between "advocating" and "excusing" terrorism? Do you agree with Walzer that no one advocates terrorism today?

3) How does Walzer respond to the excuse that terrorism is a last resort, to be chosen only when all else fails or when no other strategies are possible? Do you find his criticisms of this excuse convincing?

4) Some people claim that while terrorism is distasteful, it is sometimes justified because it can attain desirable results. How does Walzer respond to this argument? Do you agree with his response?

5) Should we ever comply with the demands of terrorists? If so, under what conditions? If not, why not?

6) What constraints does Walzer place on responding to terrorism? Should we accept such constraints? Why or why not?

31

Liberalism, Torture, and the Ticking Bomb

David Luban

Legal philosopher David Luban opens this selection with a question: Why do we regard torture, of the sort that has been perpetrated in Abu Ghraib or Guantanamo, with such deep abhorrence? The answer, says Luban, is that torture is designed to strip its victim of dignity. It is inherently cruel. Luban claims that none of the four primary historical motives for torture—pleasing the victors in a military campaign, terrorizing a population into submission, punishing criminals, or extracting confessions from prisoners—is morally acceptable. Is there any other basis for torture that might justify this practice?

Luban asks this in the context of political liberalism, which is the view that individual liberty is vitally important, and that the state must respect the dignity of all of its citizens. A number of liberals have argued that torture can be morally acceptable, though only under very restricted circumstances. They point to the ticking bomb terrorist, one who may have knowledge of a powerful bomb that is about to explode in a crowded civilian area. Luban argues that even here, torture would be unacceptable.

He offers two reasons for his rejection of torture. First, the argument that supports it would authorize government officials to perpetrate any conceivable evil, so long as we have some reason to think that it is needed to prevent yet greater evil. Second, in the real world, once we authorize torture, a bureaucratic culture of torture is bound to take over, and torture will be inflicted in an ever-larger number of cases, leading to great abuse.

David Luban, "Liberalism, Torture and the Ticking Bomb" from *Harper's Magazine*, April (2006), pp. 11–16. Reprinted with permission of the publisher.

Torture used to be thought incompatible with American values. This was true across the political divide, because for the most part, American conservatives belong no less than progressives to liberal culture in the broad sense of "liberalism" that began with John Stuart Mill, a culture that stresses limited government, human dignity, and individual rights. Liberalism incorporates a vision of engaged, active human beings possessing an inherent dignity regardless of their social station. The victim of torture is in every respect the opposite of this vision. The torture victim is isolated instead of engaged, terrified instead of active, humiliated instead of dignified.

Only in the weeks and months after 9/11, when a number of surveys revealed unprecedented support for torturing terror suspects, were the extraordinarily shallow roots of our abhorrence of torture exposed. It quickly became clear that there is a liberal ideology of torture that can be used to justify interrogational torture in the face of danger.

The modern liberal revulsion toward torture is, in fact, unusual. As Nietzsche and Foucault remind us, through most of human history there was no taboo on torture in military and judicial contexts. Indeed, cruelty did not seem to figure in classical moral thought as an important vice, as political scientist Judith Shklar notes: "One looks in vain for a Platonic dialogue on cruelty. Aristotle discusses only pathological bestiality, not cruelty. Cruelty is not one of the seven deadly sins.... The many manifestations of cupidity seem, to Saint Augustine, more important than cruelty." It is only in relatively modern times that we have come to regard cruelty as the most vicious of all vices. Shklar points out that Montaigne and Montesquieu, both of them proto-liberals, were the first political philosophers to think this way; and, more generally, that "hating cruelty, and putting it first [among vices], remains a powerful part of the liberal consciousness."

What makes torture, the deliberate infliction of suffering and pain, especially abhorrent to liberals? This may seem like a bizarre question, because the answer seems self-evident: making people suffer is a horrible thing. But let me pose the question in different terms. Realistically, the abuses of detainees at Abu Ghraib, Baghram, and Guantánamo pale by comparison with the death, maiming, and suffering in collateral damage during the Afghan and Iraq wars. Bombs crush limbs and burn people's faces off; nothing even remotely as horrifying has been reported in American prisoner-abuse cases. Yet as much as we may regret or in some cases decry the wartime suffering of innocents, we do not regard it with the special abhorrence with which we regard torture. This seems hypocritical and irrational, almost fetishistic; why should torture be more illiberal than bombing and killing?

The answer lies in the relationship between torturer and victim. Torture aims to strip away from its victim all the qualities of human dignity that liberalism prizes. Torture is a microcosm, raised to the highest level of intensity, of the tyrannical political relationships that liberalism hates most. In both ancient Greece and Rome, for example, slaves were permitted to testify in a court of law only under torture, which, according to classicist Moses Finley, served to mark off the absolute difference in status between slaves and even the lowliest freemen.

The mechanism of cruelty is making the victim the audience of your own mastery, so it makes sense that the predominant setting for torture has always been military victory. I recently saw some spectacular Mayan murals depicting defeated enemies from a rival city-state having their fingernails torn out before being executed in a ritual reenactment of the battle. In the torment of defeated captives, liberals perceive the living embodiment of their worst nightmare: tyrannical rulers who take their pleasure from the degradation of those unfortunate enough to be subject to their will.

Besides victor's cruelty, there are three other historically significant illiberal motives for torture. First, there is torture for the purpose of terrorizing people into submission. Genghis Khan's conquests were made easier because his reputation for cruelty against those who resisted him led cities to surrender without a fight. Hitler, Pinochet, and Saddam Hussein tortured their political prisoners so that their enemies would be afraid to oppose them.

Second, torture was used until quite recently as a form of criminal punishment. It was torture as a form of punishment that drew Montaigne's condemnation, and it is noteworthy that the Eighth Amendment to the U.S. Constitution prohibits cruel and unusual punishments, rather than cruelty more generally. The abolition of punitive torture, according to Foucault, had to do with a change in the distribution of crime in Western Europe: as the West grew more prosperous, property crimes eclipsed crimes of passion as a social problem, leading to calls for a milder but more certain system of punishments. It seems equally clear that punitive torture had no place in liberal polities. Torture, Foucault claims, was a ritual of royal dominance, acted out in a public spectacle to shock and awe the multitude. With the growth of liberal democracy, the ideology of popular sovereignty deflated the purpose of punitive torture: if the people rule, then the responsibility of torture would fall on the people, and the need for a spectacle of suffering by which the people could impress themselves seemed pointless.

The third historically significant use of torture, distinct from punishment, is torture used to extract confessions from criminal suspects. The French language distinguishes between the two: *la supplice*, torture as punishment, and *la question*, torture to extract confessions. As legal historian John Langbein observes, premodern legal rules required either multiple eyewitnesses or confessions for criminal convictions. At first glance, these are important rights of the accused, but they had the perverse effect of legitimating judicial torture in order to make convictions possible. Once it was accepted that the criminal justice system could base guilty verdicts on evidence that rationally establishes the fact, without insisting on the ritual of confession, then the need for torture to secure convictions vanished. Furthermore, the only crimes for which the primary evidence is the perpetrator's own words are crimes of heretical of seditious belief—and liberalism rejects the criminalization of belief.

These, then, are the four illiberal motives for torture: victor's pleasure, terror, punishment, and extracting confessions. That leaves only one rationale for torture that might conceivably be acceptable to a liberal: torture as a technique of intelligence gathering from captives who will not talk. This may seem indistinguishable from torture to extract confessions, but there is a crucial difference in the fact that confession aims to document and ratify the past for purposes of retribution, whereas intelligence gathering aims to forestall future evils. In a somewhat perverse and paradoxical way, liberalism's insistence on limited government that exercises its power only for pragmatic purposes creates the possibility of seeing torture as a civilized, not an atavistic, practice, provided that its sole aim is preventing future harm. Now, for the first time, it becomes possible to think of the torturer as a conscientious public servant, heroic in the way that the New York firefighters were heroic, willing to do desperate things only because so many innocent lives weigh in the balance. Even though prohibition remains liberalism's primary position regarding torture, and the basic liberal stance is empathy for the torture victim, a more permissive stance remains a possibility, and in response to a catastrophe like 9/11, liberals may cautiously conclude that, in the words of a well-known *Newsweek* article, it is "Time to Think About Torture."

But the pressure of liberalism will compel them to think about torture in a highly stylized and artificial way, creating what I call the "liberal ideology of torture." This ideology insists that the sole purpose of torture must be intelligence gathering to prevent a catastrophe; that torture is necessary to prevent the catastrophe; that torture is the exception, not the rule, so that it has nothing to do with state tyranny; that those who inflict the torture are motivated solely by the looming catastrophe, with no tincture of cruelty; that torture in such circumstances is, in fact, little more than self-defense; and that, because of the associations of torture with the horrors of yesteryear, perhaps one should not even call harsh interrogation "torture." And the liberal ideology will crystallize all of these ideas in a single, mesmerizing example: the ticking bomb.

Everyone argues the pros and cons of torture through the ticking bomb. Senator Charles Schumer and Professor Alan Dershowitz, the Israeli Supreme Court, and indeed every journalist exploring the unpleasant question of torture, begins with the ticking bomb and ends there as well. The Schlesinger Report on Abu Ghraib notes that "for the U.S., most cases for permitting harsh treatment of detainees on moral grounds begin with variants of the 'ticking time-bomb' scenario." Disarm the ticking bomb, and the liberal ideology of torture begins to unravel.

Of course, the ticking-bomb scenario is not completely unreal. In 1995, an Al Qaeda plot to bomb eleven U.S. airliners and assassinate the Pope was thwarted by information tortured out of a Pakistani bomb maker by the Philippine police. According to journalists Marites Danguilan Vitug and Glenda M. Gloria, the police had received word of possible threats against the Pope. They went to work. "For weeks, agents hit him with a chair and a long piece of wood, forced water into his mouth, and crushed lighted cigarettes into his private parts...His ribs were almost totally broken...His captors were surprised he survived." Grisly, to be sure; but if they hadn't done it, thousands of innocent travelers might have died horrible deaths.

But look at the example one more time. The authorities know there may be a bomb plot in the offing, and they have captured a man who may know something about it but may not. Torture him? How much? For how long? How likely does it have to be that he knows something important? Fifty-fifty? A one percent chance of saving a thousand lives yields ten statistical lives. Does that mean that you can torture up to nine people? If suspects will not break under torture, why not torture their loved ones in front of them? Of course, you won't know until you try whether torturing his child will break the suspect. But that just changes the odds; it does not alter the argument. Once you accept that only the numbers count, then anything, no matter how gruesome, becomes possible. As philosopher Bernard Williams points out, "There are certain situations so monstrous that the idea that the processes of moral rationality could yield an answer in them is insane" and "to spend time thinking what one would decide if one were in such a situation is also insane, if not merely frivolous."

A second, insidious, error built into the ticking-bomb hypothesis is that it assumes a single, ad hoc decision about whether to torture, by officials who ordinarily would only do so in a desperate emergency. But the real world is a world of policies, guidelines, and directives, not of ad hoc emergency measures. We would much rather talk about the ticking bomb than about torture as an organized social practice, which would mean asking questions like these: Should we create a professional cadre of trained torturers? Do we want federal grants for research to devise new and better techniques? Patents issued on high-tech torture devices? Trade conventions in Las Vegas? Should there be a medical sub-specialty of torture doctors, who ensure that captives do not die before they talk? The fiction must also presume that the interrogator operates only under the strictest supervision, in a chain of command where his every move is vetted and controlled by superiors who are actually doing the deliberating. This assumption flies in the face of everything we know about how organizations work. The basic rule in every bureaucratic organization is that operational details and the guilty knowledge that goes with them get pushed down the chain of command as far as possible. We saw this phenomenon at Abu Ghraib, where military-intelligence officers gave military police vague orders like: "Loosen this guy up for us"; "Make sure he has a bad night"; "Make sure he gets the treatment."

Who guarantees that case-hardened torturers, inured to levels of violence and pain that would make ordinary people vomit at the sight, will know where to draw the line on when torture should be used? They rarely have in the past. They didn't in Algeria. They didn't in Israel, where, in 1999, the Supreme Court backpedaled from an earlier consent to harsh interrogation practices because the interrogators were running amok and torturing two thirds of their Palestinian captives. Mark Osiel, who studied the Argentine military in the Dirty War, reports that many of the torturers had qualms about what they were doing until priests reassured them that they were fighting God's fight. By the end of the Dirty War, the qualms were gone, and, as John Simpson and Jana Bennett report, officers were placing bets on who could kidnap the prettiest girl to rape and torture. Escalation is the rule, not the aberration. Abu Ghraib is the fully predictable image of what a torture culture looks like. You cannot reasonably expect that interrogators in a torture culture will be the fastidious and well meaning torturers that the liberal ideology fantasizes.

For all these reasons, the ticking-bomb scenario is an intellectual fraud. In its place, we must address the real questions about torture—questions about uncertainty, questions about the morality of consequences, and questions about what it does to a culture and the torturers themselves to introduce the practice. Once we do so, I suspect that few Americans will be willing to accept the ticking-bomb scenario as a serious argument.

A skeptic might respond that my dire warnings about a torture culture are exaggerated, overwrought, and (above all) hypothetical. Would that it were so. The secret memorandums by lawyers in President George W. Bush's administration that came close to legitimizing torture for interrogation purposes illustrate the ease with which arguments that pretend that torture can exist in a liberal society, but only as an exception, quickly lead to erecting a torture culture, a network of institutions and practices, such as extraordinary rendition, that regularize the exception and make it standard operating procedure.

The liberal ideology of torture, which assumes that torture can be neatly confined to exceptional ticking-bomb cases and surgically severed from cruelty and tyranny, represents a dangerous delusion. It becomes more dangerous still when coupled with an endless war on terror, a permanent emergency in which the White House insists that its emergency powers rise above the limiting power of statutes and treaties. Claims to long-term emergency powers that entail the power to torture should send chills through liberals of the right as well as the left, and no one should still think that liberal torture has nothing to do with tyranny.

David Luban: Liberalism, Torture, and the Ticking Bomb

1) Luban points out that the harms imposed by torture seem to be no worse than the harms imposed by wartime "collateral damage" (that is, the accidental harms imposed on innocent civilians in war). What leads him to conclude that torture is more morally problematic than such collateral damage? Do you agree with his reasoning?

2) Why might a liberal support torture in some cases, according to Luban? How does such a justification of torture differ from the "illiberal" justifications of torture Luban mentions?

3) What is the "ticking time-bomb" case? Could torture ever be justified in such circumstances? Why or why not?

4) Luban objects to the "liberal ideology of torture." He writes that "Once you accept that only the numbers count, then anything, no matter how gruesome, becomes possible." Do you agree with his suggestion that some acts are morally impermissible, no matter the circumstances?

5) In the end, Luban claims that "the ticking-bomb scenario is an intellectual fraud" and the liberal ideology of torture is "a dangerous delusion." What reasons does he give for these claims? Do you find his arguments persuasive?

=== ✒ ===

32

Letter from Birmingham City Jail

Martin Luther King, Jr.

Martin Luther King, Jr. (1929–1968), was the most prominent leader of the U.S. civil rights movement. During one of the many times that he was imprisoned for his activities, he penned this letter to his fellow clergymen, offering his justifications for the policy of nonviolent civil disobedience that he championed. He argues that such a policy does not unreasonably precipitate violence, does not lead to anarchy, is not objectionably extremist, and does not exhibit disrespect for the law. Further, this policy will minimize harm in the long run, and is supported by considerations of natural law.

This reading is not your typical sober, linear philosophical essay, but rather as much an impassioned and eloquent plea as it is a sustained argument. King here appeals to the hearts and minds of his readership, in an effort to justify the peaceful efforts of the social movement he so ably led prior to his assassination.

16 April 1963

My Dear Fellow Clergymen:

While confined here in the Birmingham city jail, I came across your recent statement calling my present activities "unwise and untimely." Seldom do I pause to answer criticism of my work and ideas. If I sought to answer all the criticisms that cross my desk, my secretaries would have little time for anything other than such correspondence in the course of the day, and I would have no time for constructive work. But since I feel that you are men of genuine good will and that your criticisms are sincerely set forth, I want to try to answer your statement in what I hope will be patient and reasonable terms....

You deplore the demonstrations taking place in Birmingham. But your statement, I am sorry to say, fails to express a similar concern for the conditions that brought about the demonstrations. I am sure that none of you would want to rest content with the superficial kind of social analysis that deals merely with effects and does not grapple with underlying causes. It is unfortunate that demonstrations are taking place in Birmingham, but it is even more unfortunate that the city's white power structure left the Negro community with no alternative.

In any nonviolent campaign there are four basic steps: collection of the facts to determine whether injustices exist; negotiation; self purification; and direct action. We have gone through all these steps in Birmingham. There can be no gainsaying the fact that racial injustice engulfs this community. Birmingham is probably the most thoroughly segregated city in the United States. Its ugly record of brutality is widely known. Negroes have experienced grossly unjust treatment in the courts. There have been more unsolved bombings of Negro homes and churches in Birmingham than in any other city in the nation. These are the hard, brutal facts of the case. On the basis of these conditions, Negro leaders sought to negotiate with the city fathers. But the latter consistently refused to engage in good faith negotiation....

You may well ask: "Why direct action? Why sit ins, marches and so forth? Isn't negotiation a better path?" You are quite right in calling for negotiation. Indeed, this is the very purpose of direct action. Nonviolent direct action seeks to create such a crisis and foster such a tension that a community which has constantly refused to negotiate is forced to confront the issue. It seeks so to dramatize the issue that it can no longer be ignored. My citing the creation of tension as part of the work of the nonviolent resister may sound rather shocking. But I must confess that I am not afraid of the word "tension." I have earnestly opposed violent tension, but there is a type of constructive, nonviolent tension which is necessary for growth. Just as Socrates felt that it was necessary to create a tension in the mind so that individuals could rise from the bondage of myths and half truths to the unfettered realm of creative analysis and objective appraisal, so must we see the need for nonviolent gadflies to create the kind of tension in society that will help men rise from the dark depths of prejudice and racism to the majestic heights of understanding and brotherhood. The purpose of our direct action program is to create a situation so crisis packed that it will inevitably open the door to negotiation. I therefore concur with you in your call for negotiation. Too long has our beloved Southland been bogged down in a tragic effort to live in monologue rather than dialogue....

We know through painful experience that freedom is never voluntarily given by the oppressor; it must be demanded by the oppressed. Frankly, I have yet to engage in a direct action campaign that was "well timed" in the view of those who have not suffered unduly from the disease of segregation. For years now I have heard the word "Wait!" It rings in the ear of every Negro with piercing familiarity. This "Wait" has almost always meant "Never." We must come to see, with one of our distinguished jurists, that "justice too long delayed is justice denied."

We have waited for more than 340 years for our constitutional and God given rights. The nations of Asia and Africa are moving with jetlike speed toward gaining political independence, but we still creep at horse and buggy pace toward gaining a cup of coffee at a lunch counter. Perhaps it is easy for those who have never felt the stinging darts of segregation to say, "Wait." But when you have seen vicious mobs lynch your mothers and fathers at will and drown your sisters and brothers at whim; when you have seen hate filled policemen curse, kick and even kill your black brothers and sisters; when you see the vast majority of your twenty-million Negro brothers smothering in an airtight cage of poverty in the midst of an affluent society; when you suddenly find your tongue twisted and your speech stammering as you seek to explain to your six-year-old daughter why she can't go to the public amusement park that has just been advertised on television, and see tears welling up in her eyes when she is told that Funtown is closed to colored children, and see ominous clouds of inferiority beginning to form in her little mental sky, and see her beginning to distort her personality by developing an unconscious bitterness toward white people; when you have to concoct an answer for a five-year-old son who is asking: "Daddy, why do white people treat colored people so mean?"; when you take a cross county drive and find it necessary to sleep night after night in the uncomfortable corners of your automobile because no motel will accept you; when you are humiliated day in and day out by nagging signs reading "white" and "colored"; when your first name becomes "nigger," your middle name becomes "boy" (however old you are) and your last name becomes "John," and your wife and mother are never given the respected title "Mrs."; when you are harried by day and haunted by night by the fact that you are a Negro, living constantly at tiptoe stance, never quite knowing what to expect next, and are plagued with inner fears and outer resentments; when you are forever fighting a degenerating sense of "nobodiness"—then you will understand why we find it difficult to wait. There comes a time when the cup of endurance runs over, and men are no longer willing to be plunged into the abyss of despair. I hope, sirs, you can understand our legitimate and unavoidable impatience.

You express a great deal of anxiety over our willingness to break laws. This is certainly a legitimate concern. Since we so diligently urge people to obey the Supreme Court's decision of 1954 outlawing segregation in the public schools, at first glance it may seem rather paradoxical for us consciously to break laws. One may well ask: "How can you advocate breaking some laws and obeying others?" The answer lies in the fact that there are two types of laws: just and unjust. I would be the first to advocate obeying just laws. One has not only a legal but a moral responsibility to obey just laws. Conversely, one has a moral responsibility to disobey unjust laws. I would agree with St. Augustine that "an unjust law is no law at all."

Now, what is the difference between the two? How does one determine whether a law is just or unjust? A just law is a man made code that squares with the moral law or the law of God. An unjust law is a code that is out of harmony with the moral law. To put it in the terms of St. Thomas Aquinas: An unjust law is a human law that is not rooted in eternal law and natural law. Any law that uplifts human personality is just. Any law that degrades human personality is unjust. All segregation statutes are unjust because segregation distorts the soul and damages the personality. It gives the segregator a false sense of superiority and the segregated a false sense of inferiority. Segregation, to use the terminology of the Jewish philosopher Martin Buber, substitutes an "I it" relationship for an "I thou" relationship and ends up relegating persons to the status of things. Hence segregation is not only politically, economically and sociologically unsound, it is morally wrong and sinful. Paul Tillich has said that sin is separation. Is not segregation an existential expression of man's tragic separation, his awful estrangement, his terrible sinfulness? Thus it is that I can urge men to obey the 1954 decision of the Supreme Court, for it is morally right; and I can urge them to disobey segregation ordinances, for they are morally wrong.

Let us consider a more concrete example of just and unjust laws. An unjust law is a code that a numerical or power majority group compels a minority group to obey but does not make binding on itself. This is difference made legal. By the same token, a just law is a code that a majority compels a minority to follow and that it is willing to follow itself. This is sameness made legal.

Let me give another explanation. A law is unjust if it is inflicted on a minority that, as a result of being denied the right to vote, had no part in enacting or devising the law. Who can say that the legislature of Alabama which set up that state's segregation laws was democratically elected? Throughout Alabama all sorts of devious methods are used to prevent Negroes from becoming registered voters, and there are some counties in which, even though Negroes constitute a majority of the population, not a single Negro is registered. Can any law enacted under such circumstances be considered democratically structured?

Sometimes a law is just on its face and unjust in its application. For instance, I have been arrested on a charge of parading without a permit. Now, there is nothing wrong in having an ordinance which requires a permit for a parade. But such an ordinance becomes unjust when it is used to maintain segregation and to deny citizens the First-Amendment privilege of peaceful assembly and protest.

I hope you are able to see the distinction I am trying to point out. In no sense do I advocate evading or defying the law, as would the rabid segregationist. That would lead to anarchy. One who breaks an unjust law must do so openly, lovingly, and with a willingness to accept the penalty. I submit that an individual who breaks a law that conscience tells him is unjust, and who willingly accepts the penalty of imprisonment in order to arouse the conscience of the community over its injustice, is in reality expressing the highest respect for law.

Of course, there is nothing new about this kind of civil disobedience. It was evidenced sublimely in the refusal of Shadrach, Meshach and Abednego to obey the laws of Nebuchadnezzar, on the ground that a higher moral law was at stake. It was practiced superbly by the early Christians, who were willing to face hungry lions and the excruciating pain of chopping blocks rather than submit to certain unjust laws of the Roman Empire. To a degree, academic freedom is a reality today because Socrates practiced civil disobedience. In our own nation, the Boston Tea Party represented a massive act of civil disobedience.

We should never forget that everything Adolf Hitler did in Germany was "legal" and everything the Hungarian freedom fighters did in Hungary was "illegal." It was "illegal" to aid and comfort a Jew in Hitler's Germany. Even so, I am sure that, had I lived in Germany at the time, I would have aided and comforted my Jewish brothers. If today I lived in a Communist country where certain principles dear to the Christian faith are suppressed, I would openly advocate disobeying that country's antireligious laws.

I must make two honest confessions to you, my Christian and Jewish brothers. First, I must confess that over the past few years I have been gravely disappointed with the white moderate. I have almost reached the regrettable conclusion that the Negro's great stumbling block in his stride toward freedom is not the White Citizen's Counciler or the Ku Klux Klanner, but the white moderate, who is more devoted to "order" than to justice; who prefers a negative peace which is the absence of tension to a positive peace which is the presence of justice; who constantly says: "I agree with you in the goal you seek, but I cannot agree with your methods of direct action"; who paternalistically believes he can set the timetable for another man's freedom; who lives by a mythical concept of time and who constantly advises the Negro to wait for a "more convenient season." Shallow understanding from people of good will is more frustrating than absolute misunderstanding from people of ill will. Lukewarm acceptance is much more bewildering than outright rejection.

I had hoped that the white moderate would understand that law and order exist for the purpose of establishing justice and that when they fail in this purpose they become the dangerously structured dams that block the flow of social progress. I had hoped that the white moderate would understand that the present tension in the South is a necessary phase of the transition from an obnoxious negative peace, in which the Negro passively accepted his unjust plight, to a substantive and positive peace, in which all men will respect the dignity and worth of human personality. Actually, we who engage in nonviolent direct action are not the creators of tension. We merely bring to the surface the hidden tension that is already alive. We bring it out in the open, where it can be seen and dealt with. Like a boil that can never be cured so long as it is covered up but must be opened with all its ugliness to the natural medicines of air and light, injustice must be exposed, with all the tension its exposure creates, to the light of human conscience and the air of national opinion before it can be cured.

In your statement you assert that our actions, even though peaceful, must be condemned because they precipitate violence. But is this a logical assertion? Isn't this like condemning a robbed man because his possession of money precipitated the evil act of robbery? Isn't this like condemning Socrates because his unswerving commitment to truth and his philosophical inquiries precipitated the act by the misguided populace in which they made him drink hemlock? Isn't this like condemning Jesus because his unique God consciousness and never ceasing devotion to God's will precipitated the evil act of crucifixion? We must come to see that, as the federal courts have consistently affirmed, it is wrong to urge an individual to cease his efforts to gain his basic constitutional rights because the quest may precipitate violence. Society must protect the robbed and punish the robber.

I had also hoped that the white moderate would reject the myth concerning time in relation to the struggle for freedom. I have just received a letter from a white brother in Texas. He writes: "All Christians know that the colored people will receive equal rights eventually, but it is possible that you are in too great a religious hurry. It has taken Christianity almost two thousand years to accomplish what it has. The teachings of Christ take time to come to earth." Such an attitude stems from a tragic misconception of time, from the strangely irrational notion that there is something in the very flow of time that will inevitably cure all ills. Actually, time itself is neutral; it can be used either destructively or constructively. More and more I feel that the people of ill will have used time much more effectively than have the people of good will. We will have to repent in this generation not merely for the hateful words and actions of the bad people but for the appalling silence of the good people. Human progress never rolls in on wheels of inevitability; it comes through the tireless efforts of men willing to be co workers with God, and without this hard work, time itself becomes an ally of the forces of social stagnation. We must use time creatively, in the knowledge that the time is always ripe to do right. Now is the time to make real the promise of democracy and transform our pending national elegy into a creative psalm of brotherhood. Now is the time to lift our national policy from the quicksand of racial injustice to the solid rock of human dignity.

You speak of our activity in Birmingham as extreme. At first I was rather disappointed that fellow clergymen would see my nonviolent efforts as those of an extremist. I began thinking about the fact that I stand in the middle of two opposing forces in the Negro community. One is a force of complacency, made up in part of Negroes who, as a result of long years of oppression, are so drained of self respect and a sense of "somebodiness" that they have adjusted to segregation; and in part of a few middle-class Negroes who, because of a degree of academic and economic security and because in some ways they profit by segregation, have become insensitive to the problems of the masses. The other force is one of bitterness and hatred, and it comes perilously close to advocating violence. It is expressed in the various black nationalist groups that are springing up across the nation, the largest and best known being Elijah Muhammad's Muslim movement. Nourished by the Negro's frustration over the continued existence of racial discrimination, this movement is made up of people who have lost faith in America, who have absolutely repudiated Christianity, and who have concluded that the white man is an incorrigible "devil."

I have tried to stand between these two forces, saying that we need emulate neither the "do nothingism" of the complacent nor the hatred and despair of the black nationalist. For there is the more excellent way of love and nonviolent protest. I am grateful to God that, through the influence of the Negro church, the way of nonviolence became an integral part of our struggle. If this philosophy had not emerged, by now many streets of the South would, I am convinced, be flowing with blood. And I am further convinced that if our white brothers dismiss as "rabble rousers" and "outside agitators" those of us who employ nonviolent direct action, and if they refuse to support our nonviolent efforts, millions of Negroes will, out of frustration and despair, seek solace and security in black nationalist ideologies—a development that would inevitably lead to a frightening racial nightmare.

Oppressed people cannot remain oppressed forever. The yearning for freedom eventually manifests itself, and that is what has happened to the American Negro. Something within has reminded him of his birthright of freedom, and something without has reminded him that it can be gained. Consciously or unconsciously, he has been caught up by the Zeitgeist, and with his black brothers of Africa and his brown and yellow brothers of Asia, South America and the Caribbean, the United States Negro is moving with a sense of great urgency toward the promised land of racial justice. Recognizing this vital urge that has engulfed the Negro community, one should readily understand why public demonstrations are taking place. The Negro has many pent up resentments and latent frustrations, and he must release them. So let him march; let him have his prayer pilgrimages to the city hall; understand why he must have sit-ins and freedom rides. If his repressed emotions are not released in nonviolent ways, they will seek expression through violence; this is not a threat but a fact of history. So I have not said to my people: "Get rid of your discontent." Rather, I have tried to say that this normal and healthy discontent can be channeled into the creative outlet of nonviolent direct action. And now this approach is being dismissed as extremist.

But though I was initially disappointed at being categorized as an extremist, as I continued to think about the matter I gradually gained a measure of satisfaction from the label. Was not Jesus an extremist for love: "Love your enemies, bless them that curse you, do good to them that hate you, and pray for them which despitefully use you, and persecute you." Was not Amos an extremist for justice: "Let justice roll down like waters and righteousness like an ever flowing stream." Was not Paul an extremist for the Christian gospel: "I bear in my body the marks of the Lord Jesus." Was not Martin Luther an extremist: "Here I stand; I cannot do otherwise, so help me God." And John Bunyan: "I will stay in jail to the end of my days before I make a butchery of my conscience." And Abraham Lincoln: "This nation cannot survive half slave and half free." And Thomas Jefferson: "We hold these truths to be self evident, that all men are created equal..." So the question is not whether we will be extremists, but what kind of extremists we will be. Will we be extremists for hate or for love? Will we be extremists for the preservation of injustice or for the extension of justice? In that dramatic scene on Calvary's hill three men were crucified. We must never forget that all three were crucified for the same crime— the crime of extremism. Two were extremists for immorality, and thus fell below their environment. The other, Jesus Christ, was an extremist for love, truth and goodness, and thereby rose above his environment. Perhaps the South, the nation and the world are in dire need of creative extremists....

Before closing I feel impelled to mention one other point in your statement that has troubled me profoundly. You warmly commended the Birmingham police force for keeping "order" and "preventing violence." I doubt that you would have so warmly commended the police force if you had seen its dogs sinking their teeth into unarmed, nonviolent Negroes. I doubt that you would so quickly commend the policemen if you were to observe their ugly and inhumane treatment of Negroes here in the city jail; if you were to watch them push and curse old Negro women and young Negro girls; if you were to see them slap and kick old Negro men and young boys; if you were to observe them, as they did on two occasions, refuse to give us food because we wanted to sing our grace together. I cannot join you in your praise of the Birmingham police department.

It is true that the police have exercised a degree of discipline in handling the demonstrators. In this sense they have conducted themselves rather "nonviolently" in public. But for what purpose? To preserve the evil system of segregation. Over the past few years I have consistently preached that nonviolence demands that the means we use must be as pure as the ends we seek. I have tried to make clear that it is wrong to use immoral means to attain moral ends. But now I must affirm that it is just as wrong, or perhaps even more so, to use moral means to preserve immoral ends. Perhaps Mr. Connor and his policemen have been rather nonviolent in public, as was Chief Pritchett in Albany, Georgia, but they have used the moral means of nonviolence to maintain the immoral end of racial injustice. As T. S. Eliot has said: "The last temptation is the greatest treason: To do the right deed for the wrong reason."

I wish you had commended the Negro sit inners and demonstrators of Birmingham for their sublime courage, their willingness to suffer and their amazing discipline in the midst of great provocation. One day the South will recognize its real heroes. They will be the James Merediths, with the noble sense of purpose that enables them to face jeering and hostile mobs, and with the agonizing loneliness that characterizes the life of the pioneer. They will be old, oppressed, battered Negro women, symbolized in a seventy-two-year-old woman in Montgomery, Alabama, who rose up with a sense of dignity and with her people decided not to ride segregated buses, and who responded with ungrammatical profundity to one who inquired about her weariness: "My feets is tired, but my soul is at rest." They will be the young high school and college students, the young ministers of the gospel and a host of their elders, courageously and nonviolently sitting in at lunch counters and willingly going to jail for conscience's sake. One day the South will know that when these disinherited children of God sat down at lunch counters, they were in reality standing up for what is best in the American dream and for the most sacred values in our Judaeo Christian heritage, thereby bringing our nation back to those great wells of democracy which were dug deep by the founding fathers in their formulation of the Constitution and the Declaration of Independence.

Never before have I written so long a letter. I'm afraid it is much too long to take your precious time. I can assure you that it would have been much shorter if I had been writing from a comfortable desk, but what else can one do when he is alone in a narrow jail cell, other than write long letters, think long thoughts and pray long prayers?

If I have said anything in this letter that overstates the truth and indicates an unreasonable impatience, I beg you to forgive me. If I have said anything that understates the truth and indicates my having a patience that allows me to settle for anything less than brotherhood, I beg God to forgive me.

I hope this letter finds you strong in the faith. I also hope that circumstances will soon make it possible for me to meet each of you, not as an integrationist or a civil-rights leader but as a fellow clergyman and a Christian brother. Let us all hope that the dark clouds of racial prejudice will soon pass away and the deep fog of misunderstanding will be lifted from our fear drenched communities, and in some not too distant tomorrow the radiant stars of love and brotherhood will shine over our great nation with all their scintillating beauty.

Yours for the cause of Peace and Brotherhood, Martin Luther King, Jr.

Martin Luther King, Jr.: Letter from Birmingham City Jail

1) Do you agree with King that it is sometimes morally permissible to break the law? Why or why not?
2) How does King think that we can distinguish just laws from unjust laws? Do you agree with him about this?
3) King claims that the "white moderate" is nearly as big a stumbling block to the pursuit of civil rights as the overt racist. What objections does King have to the white moderate?
4) How does King respond to the charge that he is an extremist? Do you agree with his claim that "the nation and the world are in dire need of creative extremists"?
5) King condemns violent forms of resistance, claiming that "it is wrong to use immoral means to attain moral ends." Do you agree with him on this? Are there times when the ends justify distasteful means?

33

Justifying Legal Punishment

Igor Primoratz

In this excerpt from his book *Justifying Legal Punishment* (1989), Igor Primoratz defends the retributivist idea that a punishment is justified only if it gives a criminal his just deserts. But what do criminals deserve? Primoratz argues for the following principle: criminals deserve to be deprived of the same value that they deprived their victims of. Primoratz regards all human beings as possessed of lives of equal moral worth, and also believes that nothing is as valuable as human life. So criminals deserve to die. Since justice is a matter of giving people what they deserve, it follows that justice demands that murderers be executed.

Primoratz considers the most popular arguments of the opposing camp, and finds problems for each of them. Opponents claim that capital punishment violates a murderer's right to life; that killing murderers is contradictory; that capital punishment is disproportionally harsh; that the innocent are inevitably going to be executed; and that systematic discrimination undermines any chance at moral legitimacy. Primoratz carefully considers each objection and offers his replies. In the end, he thinks that justice requires the death penalty, that justice is the supreme legal virtue, and that none of the objections is strong enough to undermine the case for capital punishment. Therefore the state ought to execute convicted murderers.

...According to the retributive theory, consequences of punishment, however important from the practical point of view, are irrelevant when it comes to its justification; *the* moral consideration is its justice. Punishment is morally justified insofar as it is meted out as retribution for the offense committed. When someone has committed an offense, he deserves to be punished: it is just, and consequently justified, that he be punished. The offense is the sole ground of the state's right and duty to punish. It is also the measure of legitimate punishment: the two ought to be proportionate. So the issue of capital punishment within the retributive approach comes down to the question, Is this punishment ever proportionate retribution for the offense committed, and thus deserved, just, and justified?

The classic representatives of retributivism believed that it was, and that it was the only proportionate and hence appropriate punishment, if the offense was *murder*—that is, criminal homicide perpetrated voluntarily and intentionally or in wanton disregard of human life. In other cases, the demand for proportionality between offense and punishment can be satisfied by fines or prison terms; the crime of murder, however, is an exception in this respect, and calls for the literal interpretation of the *lex talionis*. The uniqueness of this crime has to do with the uniqueness of the value which has been deliberately or recklessly destroyed. We come across this idea as early as the original formulation of the retributive view—the biblical teaching on punishment: "You shall accept no ransom for the life of a murderer who is guilty of death; but he shall be put to death."[1] The rationale of this command—one that clearly distinguishes the biblical conception of the criminal law from contemporaneous criminal law systems in the Middle East—is that man was not only created *by* God, like every other creature, but also, alone among all the creatures, *in the image of God*:

> That man was made in the image of God ... is expressive of the peculiar and supreme worth of man. Of all creatures, Genesis I relates, he alone possesses this attribute, bringing him into closer relation to God than all the rest and conferring upon him the highest value. ... This view of the uniqueness and supremacy of human life ... places life beyond the reach of other values. The idea that life may be measured in terms of money or other property ... is excluded. Compensation of any kind is ruled out. The guilt of the murderer is infinite because the murdered life is invaluable; the kinsmen of the slain man are not competent to say when he has been paid for. An absolute wrong has been committed, a

---

[1] Numbers 35.31 (R.S.V.).

sin against God which is not subject to human discussion.... Because human life is invaluable, to take it entails the death penalty.[2]

This view that the value of human life is not commensurable with other values, and that consequently there is only one truly equivalent punishment for murder, namely death, does not necessarily presuppose a theistic outlook. It can be claimed that, simply because we have to be alive if we are to experience and realize any other value at all, there is nothing equivalent to the murderous destruction of a human life except the destruction of the life of the murderer. Any other retribution, no matter how severe, would still be less than what is proportionate, deserved, and just. As long as the murderer is alive, no matter how bad the conditions of his life may be, there are always at least *some* values he can experience and realize. This provides a plausible interpretation of what the classical representatives of retributivism as a philosophical theory of punishment, such as Kant and Hegel, had to say on the subject.[3]

It seems to me that this is essentially correct. With respect to the larger question of the justification of punishment in general, it is the retributive theory that gives the right answer. Accordingly, capital punishment ought to be retained where it obtains, and reintroduced in those jurisdictions that have abolished it, although we have no reason to believe that, as a means of deterrence, it is any better than a very long prison term. It ought to be retained, or reintroduced, for one simple reason: that justice be done in cases of murder, that murderers be punished according to their deserts.

There are a number of arguments that have been advanced against this rationale of capital punishment....

[One] abolitionist argument... simply says that capital punishment is illegitimate because it violates the right to life, which is a fundamental,

---

[2] M. Greenberg, "Some Postulates of Biblical Criminal Law," in J. Goldin (ed.), *The Jewish Expression* (New York: Bantam, 1970), pp. 25–26. (Post-biblical Jewish law evolved toward the virtual abolition of the death penalty, but that is of no concern here.)

[3] "There is no *parallel* between death and even the most miserable life, so that there is no equality of crime and retribution [in the case of murder] unless the perpetrator is judicially put to death" (I. Kant, "The Metaphysics of Morals," *Kant's Political Writings*, ed. H. Reiss, trans. H. B. Nisbet [Cambridge: Cambridge University Press, 1970], p. 156). "Since life is the full compass of a man's existence, the punishment [for murder] cannot simply consist in a 'value', for none is great enough, but can consist only in taking away a second life" (G. W. F. Hegel, *Philosophy of Right*, trans. T. M. Knox [Oxford: Oxford University Press, 1965], p. 247).

absolute, sacred right belonging to each and every human being, and therefore ought to be respected even in a murderer.

If any rights are fundamental, the right to life is certainly one of them; but to claim that it is absolute, inviolable under any circumstances and for any reason, is a different matter. If an abolitionist wants to argue his case by asserting an absolute right to life, she will also have to deny moral legitimacy to taking human life in war, revolution, and self-defense. This kind of pacifism is a consistent but farfetched and hence implausible position.

I do not believe that the right to life (nor, for that matter, any other right) is absolute. I have no general theory of rights to fall back upon here; instead, let me pose a question. Would we take seriously the claim to an absolute, sacred, inviolable right to life—coming from the mouth of a *confessed murderer*? I submit that we would not, for the obvious reason that it is being put forward by the person who confessedly denied another human being this very right. But if the murderer cannot plausibly claim such a right for himself, neither can *anyone else* do that in his behalf. This suggests that there is an element of reciprocity in our general rights, such as the right to life or property. I can convincingly claim these rights only so long as I acknowledge and respect the same rights of others. If I violate the rights of others, I thereby lose the same rights. If I am a murderer, I have no *right* to live.

Some opponents of capital punishment claim that a criminal law system which includes this punishment is contradictory, in that it prohibits murder and at the same time provides for its perpetration: "It is one and the same legal regulation which prohibits the individual from murdering, while allowing the state to murder.... This is obviously a terrible irony, an abnormal and immoral logic, against which everything in us revolts."[4]

This seems to be one of the more popular arguments against the death penalty, but it is not a good one. If it were valid, it would prove too much. Exactly the same might be claimed of other kinds of punishment: of prison terms, that they are "contradictory" to the legal protection of liberty; of fines, that they are "contradictory" to the legal protection of property. Fortunately enough, it is not valid, for it begs the question at issue. In order to be able to talk of the state as "murdering" the person it executes, and to claim that there is "an abnormal and immoral logic" at work here,

---

[4] S. V. Vulović, *Problem smrtne kazne* (Belgrade: Geca Kon, 1925), pp. 23–24.

which thrives on a "contradiction," one has to use the word "murder" in the very same sense—that is, in the usual sense, which implies the idea of the *wrongful* taking the life of another—both when speaking of what the murderer has done to the victim and of what the state is doing to him by way of punishment. But this is precisely the question at issue: whether capital punishment *is* "murder," whether it is wrongful or morally justified and right.

The next two arguments attack the retributive rationale of capital punishment by questioning the claim that it is only this punishment that satisfies the demand for proportion between offense and punishment in the case of murder. The first points out that any two human lives are different in many important respects, such as age, health, physical and mental capability, so that it does not make much sense to consider them equally valuable. What if the murdered person was very old, practically at the very end of her natural life, while the murderer is young, with most of his life still ahead of him, for instance? Or if the victim was gravely and incurably ill, and thus doomed to live her life in suffering and hopelessness, without being able to experience almost anything that makes a human life worth living, while the murderer is in every respect capable of experiencing and enjoying things life has to offer? Or the other way round? Would not the death penalty in such cases amount either to taking a more valuable life as a punishment for destroying a less valuable one, or *vice versa*? Would it not be either too much, or too little, and in both cases disproportionate, and thus unjust and wrong, from the standpoint of the retributive theory itself?

Any plausibility this argument might appear to have is the result of a conflation of differences between, and value of, human lives. No doubt, any two human lives are *different* in innumerable ways, but this does not entail that they are not *equally valuable*. I have no worked-out general theory of equality to refer to here, but I do not think that one is necessary in order to do away with this argument. The modern humanistic and democratic tradition in ethical, social, and political thought is based on the idea that all human beings are equal. This finds its legal expression in the principle of equality of people under the law. If we are not willing to give up this principle, we have to stick to the assumption that, all differences notwithstanding, any two human lives, *qua* human lives, are equally valuable. If, on the other hand, we allow that, on the basis of such criteria as age, health, or mental or physical ability, it can be claimed that the life of one person is more or less valuable than the life of another, and we admit such claims in the sphere of law, including criminal law, we shall thereby give up the principle of equality of people under the law. In all consistency, we shall not be able to demand that property, physical and personal integrity, and all other rights and interests of individuals be given equal consideration in courts of law either—that is, we shall have to accept systematic discrimination between individuals on the basis of the same criteria across the whole field. I do not think anyone would seriously contemplate an overhaul of the whole legal system along these lines.

The second argument having to do with the issue of proportionality between murder and capital punishment draws our attention to the fact that the law normally provides for a certain period of time to elapse between the passing of a death sentence and its execution. It is a period of several weeks or months; in some cases it extends to years. This period is bound to be one of constant mental anguish for the condemned. And thus, all things considered, what is inflicted on him is disproportionately hard and hence unjust. It would be proportionate and just only in the case of "a criminal who had warned his victim of the date at which he would inflict a horrible death on him and who, from that moment onward, had confined him at his mercy for months."[5]

The first thing to note about this argument is that it does not support a full-fledged abolitionist stand; if it were valid, it would not show that capital punishment is *never* proportionate and just, but only that it is *very rarely* so. Consequently, the conclusion would not be that it ought to be abolished outright, but only that it ought to be restricted to those cases that would satisfy the condition cited above. Such cases do happen, although, to be sure, not very often; the murder of Aldo Moro, for instance, was of this kind. But this is not the main point. The main point is that the argument actually does not hit at capital punishment itself, although it is presented with that aim in view. It hits at something else: a particular way of carrying out this punishment, which is widely adopted in our time. Some hundred years ago and more, in the Wild West, they frequently hanged the man convicted to die almost immediately after pronouncing the sentence. I am not arguing here that we should follow this example today; I mention this piece of historical fact only in order to show that the interval between sentencing someone to death and carrying out the sentence is not a *part* of capital punishment itself. However unpalatable we

[5] A. Camus, "Reflections on the Guillotine," *Resistance, Rebellion and Death*, trans. J. O'Brien (London: Hamish Hamilton, 1961), p. 143.

might find those Wild West hangings, whatever objections we might want to voice against the speed with which they followed the sentencing, surely we shall not deny them the *description* of "executions." So the implication of the argument is not that we ought to do away with capital punishment altogether, nor that we ought to restrict it to those cases of murder where the murderer had warned the victim weeks or months in advance of what he was going to do to her, but that we ought to reexamine the procedure of carrying out this kind of punishment. We ought to weigh the reasons for having this interval between the sentencing and executing, against the moral and human significance of the repercussions such an interval inevitably carries with it.

These reasons, in part, have to do with the possibility of miscarriages of justice and the need to rectify them. Thus we come to the argument against capital punishment which, historically, has been the most effective of all: many advances of the abolitionist movement have been connected with discoveries of cases of judicial errors. Judges and jurors are only human, and consequently some of their beliefs and decisions are bound to be mistaken. Some of their mistakes can be corrected upon discovery; but precisely those with most disastrous repercussions—those which result in innocent people being executed—can never be rectified. In all other cases of mistaken sentencing we can revoke the punishment, either completely or in part, or at least extend compensation. In addition, by exonerating the accused we give moral satisfaction. None of this is possible after an innocent person has been executed; capital punishment is essentially different from all other penalties by being completely irrevocable and irreparable. Therefore, it ought to be abolished.

A part of my reply to this argument goes along the same lines as what I had to say on the previous one. It is not so far-reaching as abolitionists assume; for it would be quite implausible, even fanciful, to claim that there have *never* been cases of murder which left no room whatever for reasonable doubt as to the guilt and full responsibility of the accused. Such cases may not be more frequent than those others, but they do happen. Why not retain the death penalty at least for them?

Actually, this argument, just as the preceding one, does not speak out against capital punishment itself, but against the existing procedures for trying capital cases. Miscarriages of justice result in innocent people being sentenced to death and executed, even in the criminal-law systems in which greatest care is taken to ensure that it never comes to that. But this does not stem from the intrinsic nature of the institution of capital punishment; it results from deficiencies, limitations, and imperfections of the criminal law procedures in which this punishment is meted out. Errors of justice do not demonstrate the need to do away with capital punishment; they simply make it incumbent on us to do everything possible to improve even further procedures of meting it out.

To be sure, this conclusion will not find favor with a diehard abolitionist. "I shall ask for the abolition of Capital Punishment until I have the infallibility of human judgement demonstrated to me," that is, as long as there is even the slightest possibility that innocent people may be executed because of judicial errors, Lafayette said in his day.[6] Many an opponent of this kind of punishment will say the same today. The demand to do away with capital punishment altogether, so as to eliminate even the smallest chance of that ever happening—the chance which, admittedly, would remain even after everything humanly possible has been done to perfect the procedure, although then it would be very slight indeed—is actually a demand to give a privileged position to murderers as against all other offenders, big and small. For if we acted on this demand, we would bring about a situation in which proportionate penalties would be meted out for all offenses, *except* for murder. Murderers would not be receiving the only punishment truly proportionate to their crimes, the punishment of death, but some other, lighter, and thus disproportionate penalty. All other offenders would be punished according to their deserts; only murderers would be receiving less than *they* deserve. In all other cases justice would be done in full; only in cases of the gravest of offenses, the crime of murder, justice would not be carried out in full measure. It is a great and tragic miscarriage of justice when an innocent person is mistakenly sentenced to death and executed, but systematically giving murderers advantage over all other offenders would also be a grave injustice. Is the fact that, as long as capital punishment is retained, there is a possibility that over a number of years, or even decades, an injustice of the first kind may be committed, unintentionally and unconsciously, reason enough to abolish it altogether, and thus end up with a system of punishments in which injustices of the second kind are perpetrated daily, consciously, and inevitably?

There is still another abolitionist argument that actually does not hit out against capital punishment itself, but against something else. Figures

---

[6] Quoted in E. R. Calvert, *Capital Punishment in the Twentieth Century* (London: G. P. Putnam's Sons, 1927), p. 132.

are sometimes quoted which show that this punishment is much more often meted out to the uneducated and poor than to the educated, rich, and influential people; in the United States, much more often to blacks than to whites. These figures are adduced as a proof of the inherent injustice of this kind of punishment. On account of them, it is claimed that capital punishment is not a way of doing justice by meting out deserved punishment to murderers, but rather a means of social discrimination and perpetuation of social injustice.

I shall not question these findings, which are quite convincing, and anyway, there is no need to do that in order to defend the institution of capital punishment. For there seems to be a certain amount of discrimination and injustice not only in sentencing people to death and executing them, but also in meting out other penalties. The social structure of the death rows in American prisons, for instance, does not seem to be basically different from the general social structure of American penitentiaries. If this argument were valid, it would call not only for abolition of the penalty of death, but for doing away with other penalties as well. But it is not valid; as Burton Leiser has pointed out,

> ...this is not an argument, either against the death penalty or against any other form of punishment. It is an argument against the unjust and inequitable distribution of penalties. If the trials of wealthy men are less likely to result in convictions than those of poor men, then something must be done to reform the procedure in criminal courts. If those who have money and standing in the community are less likely to be charged with serious offenses than their less affluent fellow citizens, then there should be a major overhaul of the entire system of criminal justice. ... But the maldistribution of penalties is no argument against any particular form of penalty.[7]

Igor Primoratz: Justifying Legal Punishment

1) Retributivists such as Primoratz hold that the punishment of a crime ought to be proportional to the offense. Do you find such a view plausible? Are there any other morally relevant considerations when considering how someone should be punished?

---

[7] B. M. Leiser, *Liberty, Justice and Morals: Contemporary Value Conflicts* (New York: Macmillan, 1973), p. 225.

2) Primoratz argues that the only punishment proportional to the offense of murder is the death penalty. What reasons does he give for thinking this? Do you think he is correct?

3) Some argue that capital punishment violates the right to life. Primoratz responds that the right to life is not "absolute." What does he mean by this, and how does he argue for it? Do you agree with him?

4) How does Primoratz respond to the objection that the death penalty is hypocritical because it involves killing people for the offense of killing other people? Do you find his response convincing?

5) Many people object to the death penalty on the grounds that it sometimes results in innocent people being executed, and is often applied in a discriminatory way. Why doesn't Primoratz think these concerns justify abolishing the death penalty? Do you agree?

34

An Eye for an Eye?

Stephen Nathanson

....

In this excerpt from his book *An Eye for an Eye?* (1987), Stephen
Nathanson argues against the classic retributivist principle of punishment: lex talionis. This principle tells us to treat criminals just as they
treated their victims—an eye for an eye, a tooth for a tooth. Nathanson
finds two major problems for lex talionis. First, it advises us to commit
highly immoral actions—raping a rapist, for instance, or torturing a
torturer. Second, it is impossible to apply in many cases of deserved
punishment—for instance, the principle offers no advice about what to
do with drunk drivers, air polluters, embezzlers, or spies.

Retributivists might replace lex talionis with a principle of proportional punishment, according to which increasingly bad crimes
must be met with increasingly harsher punishment. This proposal is
plausible, says Nathanson, but it offers no justification for the death
penalty. All it tells us is that the worst crimes ought to be met with
the harshest punishments. But it says nothing about how harsh those
punishments should be.

Nathanson concludes by discussing the symbolism of abolishing
the death penalty, and claims that we express a respect for each person's
inalienable rights by refraining from depriving a murderer of his life.

....

"An Eye for an Eye?" from *An Eye for an Eye?* by Steven Nathanson (1987). Reprinted with
permission of Rowman & Littlefield.

Suppose we ... try to determine what people deserve from a strictly moral point of view. How shall we proceed?

The most usual suggestion is that we look at a person's actions because what someone deserves would appear to depend on what he or she does. A person's actions, it seems, provide not only a basis for a moral appraisal of the person but also a guide to how he should be treated. According to the lex talionis or principle of "an eye for an eye," we ought to treat people as they have treated others. What people deserve as recipients of rewards or punishments is determined by what they do as agents.

This is a powerful and attractive view, one that appears to be backed not only by moral common sense but also by tradition and philosophical thought. The most famous statement of philosophical support for this view comes from Immanuel Kant, who linked it directly with an argument for the death penalty. Discussing the problem of punishment, Kant writes,

> What kind and what degree of punishment does legal justice adopt as its principle and standard? None other than the principle of equality ... the principle of not treating one side more favorably than the other. Accordingly, any undeserved evil that you inflict on someone else among the people is one that you do to yourself. If you vilify, you vilify yourself; if you steal from him, you steal from yourself; if you kill him, you kill yourself. Only the law of retribution (*jus talionis*) can determine exactly the kind and degree of punishment.[1]

Kant's view is attractive for a number of reasons. First, it accords with our belief that what a person deserves is related to what he does. Second, it appeals to a moral standard and does not seem to rely on any particular legal or political institutions. Third, it seems to provides a measure of appropriate punishment that can be used as a guide to creating laws and instituting punishments. It tells us that the punishment is to be identical with the crime. Whatever the criminal did to the victim is to be done in turn to the criminal.

In spite of the attractions of Kant's view, it is deeply flawed. When we see why, it will be clear that the whole "eye for an eye" perspective must be rejected.

---

[1] Kant, *Metaphysical Elements of Justice*, translated by John Ladd (Indianapolis: Bobbs-Merrill, 1965), p. 101.

Problems with the Equal Punishment Principle

[Kant's view] does not provide an adequate criterion for determining appropriate levels of punishment.

We can see this, first, by noting that for certain crimes, Kant's view recommends punishments that are not morally acceptable. Applied strictly, it would require that we rape rapists, torture torturers, and burn arsonists whose acts have led to deaths. In general, where a particular crime involves barbaric and inhuman treatment, Kant's principle tells us to act barbarically and inhumanly in return. So, in some cases, the principle generates unacceptable answers to the question of what constitutes appropriate punishment.

This is not its only defect. In many other cases, the principle tells us nothing at all about how to punish. While Kant thought it obvious how to apply his principle in the case of murder, his principle cannot serve as a general rule because it does not tell us how to punish many crimes. Using the Kantian version or the more common "eye for an eye" standard, what would we decide to do to embezzlers, spies, drunken drivers, airline hijackers, drug users, prostitutes, air polluters, or persons who practice medicine without a license? If one reflects on this question, it becomes clear that there is simply no answer to it. We could not in fact design a system of punishment simply on the basis of the "eye for an eye" principle.

In order to justify using the "eye for an eye" principle to answer our question about murder and the death penalty, we would first have to show that it worked for a whole range of cases, giving acceptable answers to questions about amounts of punishment. Then, having established it as a satisfactory general principle, we could apply it to the case of murder. It turns out, however, that when we try to apply the principle generally, we find that it either gives wrong answers or no answers at all. Indeed, I suspect that the principle of "an eye for an eye" is no longer even a principle. Instead, it is simply a metaphorical disguise for expressing belief in the death penalty. People who cite it do not take it seriously. They do not believe in a kidnapping for a kidnapping, a theft for a theft, and so on. Perhaps "an eye for an eye" once was a genuine principle, but now it is merely a slogan. Therefore, it gives us no guidance in deciding whether murderers deserve to die.

In reply to these objections, one might defend the principle by saying that it does not require that punishments be strictly identical with crimes.

Rather, it requires only that a punishment produce an amount of suffering in the criminal which is equal to the amount suffered by the victim. Thus, we don't have to hijack airplanes belonging to airline hijackers, spy on spies, etc. We simply have to reproduce in them the harm done to others.

Unfortunately, this reply really does not solve the problem. It provides no answer to the first objection, since it would still require us to behave barbarically in our treatment of those who are guilty of barbaric crimes. Even if we do not reproduce their actions exactly, any action which caused equal suffering would itself be barbaric. Second, in trying to produce equal amounts of suffering, we run into many problems. Just how much suffering is produced by an airline hijacker or a spy? And how do we apply this principle to prostitutes or drug users, who may not produce any suffering at all? We have rough ideas about how serious various crimes are, but this may not correlate with any clear sense of just how much harm is done.

Furthermore, the same problem arises in determining how much suffering a particular punishment would produce for a particular criminal. People vary in their tolerance of pain and in the amount of unhappiness that a fine or a jail sentence would cause them. Recluses will be less disturbed by banishment than extroverts. Nature lovers will suffer more in prison than people who are indifferent to natural beauty. A literal application of the principle would require that we tailor punishments to individual sensitivities, yet this is at best impractical. To a large extent, the legal system must work with standardized and rather crude estimates of the negative impact that punishments have on people.

The move from calling for a punishment that is identical to the crime to favoring one that is equal in the harm done is no help to us or to the defense of the principle. "An eye for an eye" tells us neither what people deserve nor how we should treat them when they have done wrong.

Proportional Retributivism

The view we have been considering can be called "equality retributivism," since it proposes that we repay criminals with punishments equal to their crimes. In the light of problems like those I have cited, some people have proposed a variation on this view, calling not for equal punishments but rather for punishments which are *proportional* to the crime. In defending such a view as a guide for setting criminal punishments, Andrew von Hirsch writes:

If one asks how severely a wrongdoer deserves to be punished, a familiar principle comes to mind: Severity of punishment should be commensurate with the seriousness of the wrong. Only grave wrongs merit severe penalties; minor misdeeds deserve lenient punishments. Disproportionate penalties are undeserved—severe sanctions for minor wrongs or vice versa. This principle has variously been called a principle of "proportionality" or "just deserts"; we prefer to call it commensurate deserts.[2]

Like Kant, von Hirsch makes the punishment which a person deserves depend on that person's actions, but he departs from Kant in substituting proportionality for equality as the criterion for setting the amount of punishment.

In implementing a punishment system based on the proportionality view, one would first make a list of crimes, ranking them in order of seriousness. At one end would be quite trivial offenses like parking meter violations, while very serious crimes such as murder would occupy the other. In between, other crimes would be ranked according to their relative gravity. Then a corresponding scale of punishments would be constructed, and the two would be correlated. Punishments would be proportionate to crimes so long as we could say that the more serious the crime was, the higher on the punishment scale was the punishment administered.

This system does not have the defects of equality retributivism. It does not require that we treat those guilty of barbaric crimes barbarically. This is because we can set the upper limit of the punishment scale so as to exclude truly barbaric punishments. Second, unlike the equality principle, the proportionality view is genuinely general, providing a way of handling all crimes. Finally, it does justice to our ordinary belief that certain punishments are unjust because they are too severe or too lenient for the crime committed.

The proportionality principle does, I think, play a legitimate role in our thinking about punishments. Nonetheless, it is no help to death penalty advocates, because it does not require that murderers be executed. All that it requires is that if murder is the most serious crime, then murder should be punished by the most severe punishment on the scale. The principle does not

---

[2] *Doing Justice* (New York: Hill & Wang, 1976), p. 66; reprinted in *Sentencing*, edited by H. Gross and A. von Hirsch (Oxford University Press, 1981), p. 243. For a more recent discussion and further defense by von Hirsch, see his *Past or Future Crimes* (New Brunswick, N.J.: Rutgers University Press, 1985).

tell us what this punishment should be, however, and it is quite compatible with the view that the most severe punishment should be a long prison term.

This failure of the theory to provide a basis for supporting the death penalty reveals an important gap in proportional retributivism. It shows that while the theory is general in scope, it does not yield any *specific* recommendations regarding punishment. It tells us, for example, that armed robbery should be punished more severely than embezzling and less severely than murder, but it does not tell us how much to punish any of these. This weakness is, in effect, conceded by von Hirsch, who admits that if we want to implement the "commensurate deserts" principle, we must supplement it with information about what level of punishment is needed to deter crimes.[3] In a later discussion of how to "anchor" the punishment system, he deals with this problem in more depth, but the factors he cites as relevant to making specific judgments (such as available prison space) have nothing to do with what people deserve. He also seems to suggest that a range of punishments may be appropriate for a particular crime. This runs counter to the death penalty supporter's sense that death alone is appropriate for some murderers.[4]

Neither of these retributive views, then, provides support for the death penalty. The equality principle fails because it is not in general true that the appropriate punishment for a crime is to do to the criminal what he has done to others. In some cases this is immoral, while in others it is impossible. The proportionality principle may be correct, but by itself it cannot determine specific punishments for specific crimes. Because of its flexibility and open-endedness, it is compatible with a great range of different punishments for murder.[5] ...

The Symbolism of Abolishing the Death Penalty

What is the symbolic message that we would convey by deciding to renounce the death penalty and to abolish its use?

---

[3] Von Hirsch, *Doing Justice*, pp. 93–94. My criticisms of proportional retributivism are not novel. For helpful discussions of the view, see Hugo Bedau, "Concessions to Retribution in Punishment," in *Justice and Punishment*, edited by J. Cederblom and W. Blizek (Cambridge, Mass.: Ballinger, 1977), and M. Golding, *Philosophy of Law* (Englewood Cliffs, N.J.: Prentice Hall, 1975), pp. 98–99.
[4] See von Hirsch, *Past or Future Crimes*, ch. 8.
[5] For more positive assessments of these theories, see Jeffrey Reiman, "Justice, Civilization, and the Death Penalty," *Philosophy and Public Affairs* 14 (1985): 115–48; and Michael Davis, "How to Make the Punishment Fit the Crime," *Ethics* 93 (1983).

I think that there are two primary messages. The first is the most frequently emphasized and is usually expressed in terms of the sanctity of human life, although I think we could better express it in terms of respect for human dignity. One way we express our respect for the dignity of human beings is by abstaining from depriving them of their lives, even if they have done terrible deeds. In defense of human well-being, we may punish people for their crimes, but we ought not to deprive them of everything, which is what the death penalty does.

If we take the life of a criminal, we convey the idea that by his deeds he has made himself worthless and totally without human value. I do not believe that we are in a position to affirm that of anyone. We may hate such a person and feel the deepest anger against him, but when he no longer poses a threat to anyone, we ought not to take his life.

But, one might ask, hasn't the murderer forfeited whatever rights he might have had to our respect? Hasn't he, by his deeds, given up any rights that he had to decent treatment? Aren't we morally free to kill him if we wish?

These questions express important doubts about the obligation to accord any respect to those who have acted so deplorably, but I do not think that they prove that any such forfeiture has occurred. Certainly, when people murder or commit other crimes, they do forfeit some of the rights that are possessed by the law-abiding. They lose a certain right to be left alone. It becomes permissible to bring them to trial and, if they are convicted, to impose an appropriate—even a dreadful—punishment on them.

Nonetheless, they do not forfeit all their rights. It does not follow from the vileness of their actions that we can do anything whatsoever to them. This is part of the moral meaning of the constitutional ban on cruel and unusual punishments. No matter how terrible a person's deeds, we may not punish him in a cruel and unusual way. We may not torture him, for example. His right not to be tortured has not been forfeited. Why do these limits hold? Because this person remains a human being, and we think that there is something in him that we must continue to respect in spite of his terrible acts.

One way of seeing why those who murder still deserve some consideration and respect is by reflecting again on the idea of what it is to *deserve* something. In most contexts, we think that what people deserve depends on what they have done, intended, or tried to do. It depends on features that are qualities of individuals. The best person for the job deserves to be hired. The person who worked especially hard deserves our gratitude. We can call the concept that applies in these cases *personal* desert.

There is another kind of desert, however, that belongs to people by virtue of their humanity itself and does not depend on their individual efforts or achievements. I will call this impersonal kind of desert *human* desert. We appeal to this concept when we think that everyone deserves a certain level of treatment no matter what their individual qualities are. When the signers of the Declaration of Independence affirmed that people had inalienable rights to "life, liberty, and the pursuit of happiness," they were appealing to such an idea. These rights do not have to be earned by people. They are possessed "naturally," and everyone is bound to respect them.

According to the view that I am defending, people do not lose all of their rights when they commit terrible crimes. They still deserve some level of decent treatment simply because they remain living, functioning human beings. This level of moral desert need not be earned, and it cannot be forfeited. This view may sound controversial, but in fact everyone who believes that cruel and unusual punishment should be forbidden implicitly agrees with it. That is, they agree that even after someone has committed a terrible crime, we do not have the right to do anything whatsoever to him.

What I am suggesting is that by renouncing the use of death as a punishment, we express and reaffirm our belief in the inalienable, unforfeitable core of human dignity.

Why is this a worthwhile message to convey? It is worth conveying because this belief is both important and precarious. Throughout history, people have found innumerable reasons to degrade the humanity of one another. They have found qualities in others that they hated or feared, and even when they were not threatened by these people, they have sought to harm them, deprive them of their liberty, or take their lives from them. They have often felt that they had good reasons to do these things, and they have invoked divine commands, racial purity, and state security to support their deeds.

These actions and attitudes are not relics of the past. They remain an awful feature of the contemporary world. By renouncing the death penalty, we show our determination to accord at least minimal respect even to those whom we believe to be personally vile or morally vicious. This is, perhaps, why we speak of the *sanctity* of human life rather than its value or worth. That which is sacred remains, in some sense, untouchable, and its value is not dependent on its worth or usefulness to us. Kant expressed this ideal of respect in the famous second version of the Categorical Imperative: "So act as to treat humanity, whether in thine own person or in that of any other, in every case as an end withal, never as a means only."

When the state has a murderer in its power and could execute him but does not, this conveys the idea that even though this person has done wrong and even though we may be angry, outraged, and indignant with him, we will nonetheless control ourselves in a way that he did not. We will not kill him, even though we could do so and even though we are angry and indignant. We will exercise restraint, sanctioning killing only when it serves a protective function.

Why should we do this? Partly out of a respect for human dignity. But also because we want the state to set an example of proper behavior. We do not want to encourage people to resort to violence to settle conflicts when there are other ways available. We want to avoid the cycle of violence that can come from retaliation and counter-retaliation. Violence is a contagion that arouses hatred and anger, and if unchecked, it simply leads to still more violence. The state can convey the message that the contagion must be stopped, and the most effective principle for stopping it is the idea that only defensive violence is justifiable. Since the death penalty is not an instance of defensive violence, it ought to be renounced.

We show our respect for life best by restraining ourselves and allowing murderers to live, rather than by following a policy of a life for a life. Respect for life and restraint of violence are aspects of the same ideal. The renunciation of the death penalty would symbolize our support of that ideal.

Stephen Nathanson: An Eye for an Eye?

1) Nathanson rejects the principle of lex talionis, according to which we ought to treat criminals as they have treated others. What reasons does he give for rejecting this principle? Do you find his reasons convincing?

2) Nathanson considers the following modification of the principle of lex talionis: "a punishment should produce an amount of suffering in the criminal which is equal to the amount suffered by the victim." Do you think this is a plausible principle? What objections does Nathanson offer to the principle?

3) What is the principle of proportional retributivism? Why doesn't Nathanson think that this principle supports the death penalty? Do you agree with him?
4) What symbolic message does Nathanson think that abolishing the death penalty would convey? Is this a good reason to abolish the death penalty?
5) Are the any reasons for supporting the death penalty that Nathanson does not consider? If so, are these reasons ever strong enough to justify sentencing someone to death?

35

America's Unjust Drug War

Michael Huemer

Michael Huemer argues that the recreational use of drugs, including cocaine and heroin, ought to be legal, and that the long-standing U.S. policy of criminalizing their possession and sale is morally unjustified. He presents, and then seeks to rebut, what he regards as the two most prominent arguments for their criminalization.

These arguments are, first, that drugs are very harmful to those who use them, and the prevention of such harm justifies the state in criminalizing drug use. The second argument is that drug use reliably causes harm to third parties, and since the state's mission is to prevent such harm, the state is again justified in outlawing drug use. Huemer agrees that there are some cases in which drug use does threaten others (such as when one drives while under the influence), and agrees that such activity ought to be prohibited. But, he argues, this represents a small minority of cases—in all other situations, drug use ought to be legally permitted.

Huemer then turns from criticizing prohibitionist arguments, and offers a positive argument for decriminalization. This argument claims that we have a natural moral right—i.e., one that exists independently of its recognition by society—to use our bodies as we please, so long as we do not violate the rights of others in doing so. Unusual exceptions aside, we do not violate another's rights when we use drugs. Therefore we have a moral right use drugs. Huemer thinks that the government thus violates our moral rights when it prohibits most drug use.

Michael Huemer "America's Unjust Drug War" from *The New Prohibition*. ed. Bill Masters, (Accurate Press, 2004) pp. 133–144. Reprinted with the permission of Michael Huemer.

Should the recreational use of drugs such as marijuana, cocaine, heroin, and LSD, be prohibited by law? *Prohibitionists* answer yes. They usually argue that drug use is extremely harmful both to drug users and to society in general, and possibly even immoral, and they believe that these facts provide sufficient reasons for prohibition. *Legalizers* answer no. They usually give one or more of three arguments: First, some argue that drug use is not as harmful as prohibitionists believe, and even that it is sometimes beneficial. Second, some argue that drug prohibition "does not work," in other words, it is not very successful in preventing drug use and/ or has a number of very bad consequences. Lastly, some argue that drug prohibition is unjust or violates rights.

I won't attempt to discuss all these arguments here. Instead, I will focus on what seem to me the three most prominent arguments in the drug legalization debate: first, the argument that drugs should be outlawed because of the harm they cause to drug users; second, the argument that they should be outlawed because they harm people other than the user; and third, the argument that drugs should be legalized because drug prohibition violates rights. I shall focus on the moral/philosophical issues that these arguments raise, rather than medical or sociological issues. I shall show that the two arguments for prohibition fail, while the third argument, for legalization, succeeds.

I. Drugs and Harm to Users

The first major argument for prohibition holds that drugs should be prohibited because drug use is extremely harmful to the users themselves, and prohibition decreases the rate of drug abuse. This argument assumes that the proper function of government includes preventing people from harming themselves. Thus, the argument is something like this:

1. Drug use is very harmful to users.
2. The government should prohibit people from doing things that harm themselves.
3. Therefore, the government should prohibit drug use.

Obviously, the second premise is essential to the argument; if I believed that drug use was very harmful, but I did *not* think that the government should prohibit people from harming themselves, then I would not take this as a reason for prohibiting drug use. But premise (2), if taken without qualification, is extremely implausible. Consider some examples of things people do that are harmful (or entail a risk of harm) to themselves: smoking tobacco, drinking alcohol, eating too much, riding motorcycles, having unprotected or promiscuous sex, maintaining relationships with inconsiderate or abusive boyfriends and girlfriends, maxing out their credit cards, working in dead-end jobs, dropping out of college, moving to New Jersey, and being rude to their bosses. Should the government prohibit all of these things?[1] Most of us would agree that the government should not prohibit *any* of these things, let alone all of them. And this is not merely for logistical or practical reasons; rather, we think that controlling those activities is not the business of government.

Perhaps the prohibitionist will argue, not that the government should prohibit *all* activities that are harmful to oneself, but that it should prohibit activities that harm oneself in a certain way, or to a certain degree, or that also have some other characteristic. It would then be up to the prohibitionist to explain how the self-inflicted harm of drug use differs from the self-inflicted harms of the other activities mentioned above. Let us consider three possibilities.

(1) One suggestion would be that drug use also harms people other than the user; we will discuss this harm to others in section II. If, as I will contend, neither the harm to drug users nor the harm to others justifies prohibition, then there will be little plausibility in the suggestion that the combination of harms justifies prohibition. Of course, one could hold that a certain threshold level of total harm must be reached before prohibition of an activity is justified, and that the combination of the harm of drugs to users and their harm to others passes that threshold even though neither kind of harm does so by itself. But if, as I will contend, the "harm to users" and "harm to others" arguments both fail because it is not the government's business to apply criminal sanctions to prevent the kinds of harms in question, *then* the combination of the two harms will not make a convincing case for prohibition.

(2) A second suggestion is that drug use is generally *more* harmful than the other activities listed above. But there seems to be no reason to believe this. As one (admittedly limited) measure of harmfulness, consider the mortality statistics. In the year 2000, illicit drug use directly or indirectly caused an estimated 17,000 deaths in the

---

[1] Douglas Husak (*Legalize This! The Case for Decriminalizing Drugs*, London: Verso, 2002, pages 7, 101–103) makes this sort of argument. I have added my own examples of harmful activities to his list.

United States.[2] By contrast, tobacco caused an estimated 435,000 deaths.[3] Of course, more people use tobacco than use illegal drugs,[4] so let us divide by the number of users: tobacco kills 4.5 people per 1000 at-risk persons per year; illegal drugs kill 0.66 people per 1000 at-risk persons per year.[5] Yet almost no one favors outlawing tobacco and putting smokers in prison. On a similar note, obesity caused an estimated 112,000 deaths in the same year (due to increased incidence of heart disease, strokes, and so on), or 1.8 per 1000 at-risk persons.[6]

---

[2] Ali Mokdad, James Marks, Donna Stroup, and Julie Gerberding, "Actual Causes of Death in the United States, 2000," *Journal of the American Medical Association* 291, no. 10, 2004: 1238–45, p. 1242. The statistic includes estimated contributions of drug use to such causes of death as suicide, homicide, motor vehicle accidents, and HIV infection.

[3] Mokdad et al., p. 1239; the statistic includes estimated effects of secondhand smoke. The Centers for Disease Control provides an estimate of 440,000 ("Annual Smoking-Attributable Mortality, Years of Potential Life Lost, and Economic Costs—United States, 1995–1999," *Morbidity and Mortality Weekly Report* 51, 2002: 300–303, http://www.cdc.gov/mmwr/PDF/wk/mm5114. pdf, page 300).

[4] James Inciardi ("Against Legalization of Drugs" in Arnold Trebach and James Inciardi, *Legalize It? Debating American Drug Policy*, Washington, D.C.: American University Press, 1993, pp. 161, 165) makes this point, accusing drug legalizers of "sophism." He does not go on to calculate the number of deaths per user, however.

[5] I include both current and former smokers among "at risk persons." The calculation for tobacco is based on Mokdad et al.'s report (p. 1239) that 22.2% of the adult population were smokers and 24.4% were former smokers in 2000, and the U.S. Census Bureau's estimate of an adult population of 209 million in the year 2000 ("Table 2: Annual Estimates of the Population by Sex and Selected Age Groups for the United States: April 1, 2000 to July 1, 2007 [NC-EST2007-02]," release date May 1, 2008, http://www.census.gov/popest/national/asrh/NC-EST2007/NC-EST2007-02.xls). The calculation for illicit drugs is based on the report of the Office of National Drug Control Policy (hereafter, ONDCP) that, in the year 2000, 11% of persons aged 12 and older had used illegal drugs in the previous year ("Drug Use Trends," October 2002, http://www.whitehousedrugpolicy.gov/publications/factsht/druguse/), and the U.S. Census Bureau's report of a population of about 233 million Americans aged 12 and over in 2000 ("Table 1: Annual Estimates of the Population by Sex and Five-Year Age Groups for the United States: April 1, 2000 to July 1, 2007 [NC-EST2007-01])," release date May 1, 2008, http://www.census.gov/popest/national/asrh/NC-EST2007/NC-EST2007-02.xls). Interpolation was applied to the Census Bureau's "10 to 14" age category to estimate the number of persons aged 12 to 14. In the case of drugs, if "at risk persons" are considered to include only those who admit to having used illegal drugs in the past month, then the death rate is 1.2 per 1000 at-risk persons.

[6] Based on 112,000 premature deaths caused by obesity in 2000 (Katherine Flegal, Barry Graubard, David Williamson, and Mitchell Gail, "Excess Deaths Associated With Underweight, Overweight, and Obesity," *Journal of the American Medical Association* 293, no. 15, 2005: 1861–7), a 30.5% obesity rate among U.S. adults in 2000 (Allison Hedley, Cynthia Ogden, Clifford Johnson, Margaret Carroll, Lester Curtin, and Katherine Flegal, "Prevalence of Overweight and Obesity Among U.S. Children, Adolescents, and Adults, 1999–2002," *Journal of the*

Health professionals have warned about the pandemic of obesity, but no one has yet called for imprisoning obese people.

There are less tangible harms of drug use—harms to one's general quality of life. These are difficult to quantify. But compare the magnitude of the harm to one's quality of life that one can bring about by, say, dropping out of high school, working in a dead-end job for several years, or marrying a jerk—these things can cause extreme and lasting detriment to one's well-being. And yet no one proposes jailing those who drop out, work in bad jobs, or make poor marriage decisions. The idea of doing so would seem ridiculous, clearly beyond the state's prerogatives.

(3) Another suggestion is that drug use harms users *in a different way* than the other listed activities. What sorts of harms do drugs cause? First, illicit drugs may worsen users' health and, in some cases, entail a risk of death. But many other activities—including the consumption of alcohol, tobacco, and fatty foods; sex; and (on a broad construal of "health") automobiles—entail health risks, and yet almost no one believes those activities should be criminalized.

Second, drugs may damage users' relationships with others—particularly family, friends, and lovers—and prevent one from developing more satisfying personal relationships.[7] Being rude to others can also have this effect, yet no one believes you should be put in jail for being rude. Moreover, it is very implausible to suppose that people should be subject to criminal sanctions for ruining their personal relationships. I have no general theory of what sort of things people should be punished for, but consider the following example: suppose that I decide to break up with my girlfriend, stop calling my family, and push away all my friends. I do this for no good reason—I just feel like it. This would damage my personal relationships as much as anything could. Should the police now arrest me and put me in jail? If not, then why should they arrest me for doing something that only has a *chance* of indirectly bringing about a similar result? The following seems like a reasonable political principle: If it would be wrong (because not part of the government's legitimate functions) to punish people for *directly bringing about* some result, then it would also be wrong to punish people for doing some other action on the grounds that the action has a *chance* of bringing about that result indirectly. If the state may not

---

American Medical Association 291, no. 23, 2004: 2847–2850) and a U.S. adult population of 209 million in 2000 (U.S. Census Bureau, "Table 2," *op. cit.*).

[7] Inciardi, pp. 167, 172.

prohibit me from *directly cutting off* my relationships with others, then the fact that my drug use *might have the result* of damaging those relationships does not provide a good reason to prohibit me from using drugs.

Third, drugs may harm users' financial lives, costing them money, causing them to lose their jobs or not find jobs, and preventing them from getting promotions. The same principle applies here: if it would be an abuse of government power to prohibit me from directly bringing about those sorts of negative financial consequences, then surely the fact that drug use might indirectly bring them about is not a good reason to prohibit drug use. Suppose that I decide to quit my job and throw all my money out the window, for no reason. Should the police arrest me and put me in prison?

Fourth and finally, drugs may damage users' moral character, as James Q. Wilson believes:

> [I]f we believe—as I do—that dependency on certain mind-altering drugs *is* a moral issue and that their illegality rests in part on their immorality, then legalizing them undercuts, if it does not eliminate altogether, the moral message. That message is at the root of the distinction between nicotine and cocaine. Both are highly addictive; both have harmful physical effects. But we treat the two drugs differently not simply because nicotine is so widely used as to be beyond the reach of effective prohibition, but because its use does not destroy the user's essential humanity. Tobacco shortens one's life, cocaine debases it. Nicotine alters one's habits, cocaine alters one's soul. The heavy use of crack, unlike the heavy use of tobacco, corrodes those natural sentiments of sympathy and duty that constitute our human nature and make possible our social life.[8]

In this passage, Wilson claims that the use of cocaine (a) is immoral, (b) destroys one's humanity, (c) alters one's soul, and (d) corrodes one's sense of sympathy and duty. One problem with Wilson's argument is the lack of evidence supporting claims (a)-(d). Before we put people in prison for corrupting their souls, we should require some objective evidence that their souls are in fact being corrupted. Before we put people in prison for being immoral, we should require some argument showing that their actions are in fact immoral. Perhaps Wilson's charges of immorality and corruption all come down to the charge that drug users lose their sense

---

[8] James Q. Wilson, "Against the Legalization of Drugs," *Commentary* 89, 1990: 21–8, p. 26.

of sympathy and duty—that is, claims (a)-(c) all rest upon claim (d). It is plausible that *heavy* drug users experience a decreased sense of sympathy with others and a decreased sense of duty and responsibility. Does this provide a good reason to prohibit drug use?

Again, it seems that one should not prohibit an activity on the grounds that it may indirectly cause some result, unless it would be appropriate to prohibit the direct bringing about of that result. Would it be appropriate, and within the legitimate functions of the state, to punish people for being unsympathetic and undutiful, or for behaving in an unsympathetic and undutiful way? Suppose that Howard—though not a drug user—doesn't sympathize with others. When people try to tell Howard their problems, he just tells them to quit whining. Friends and coworkers who ask Howard for favors are rudely rebuffed. Furthermore—though he does not harm others in ways that would be against our current laws—Howard has a poor sense of duty. He doesn't bother to show up for work on time, nor does he take any pride in his work; he doesn't donate to charity; he doesn't try to improve his community. All around, Howard is an ignoble and unpleasant individual. Should he be put in jail?

If not, then why should someone be put in jail merely for doing something that would have a *chance* of causing them to become like Howard? If it would be an abuse of governmental power to punish people for being jerks, then the fact that drug use may cause one to become a jerk is not a good reason to prohibit drug use.

II. Drugs and Harm to Others

Some argue that drug use must be outlawed because drug use harms the user's family, friends, and coworkers, and/or society in general. A report produced by the Office of National Drug Control Policy states:

> Democracies can flourish only when their citizens value their freedom and embrace personal responsibility. Drug use erodes the individual's capacity to pursue both ideals. It diminishes the individual's capacity to operate effectively in many of life's spheres—as a student, a parent, a spouse, an employee—even as a coworker or fellow motorist. And, while some claim it represents an expression of individual autonomy, drug use is in fact inimical to personal freedom, producing a reduced capacity to participate in the life of the community and the promise of America.[9]

---

[9] ONDCP, *National Drug Control Strategy 2002*, Washington, D.C.: Government Printing Office, http://www.whitehousedrugpolicy.gov/publications/policy/03ndcs/, pp. 1–2.

At least one of these alleged harms—dangerous driving—*is* clearly the business of the state. For this reason, I entirely agree that people should be prohibited from driving while under the influence of drugs. But what about the rest of the alleged harms?

Return to our hypothetical citizen Howard. Imagine that Howard—again, for reasons having nothing to do with drugs—does not value freedom, nor does he embrace personal responsibility. It is unclear exactly what this means, but, for good measure, let us suppose that Howard embraces a totalitarian political ideology and denies the existence of free will. He constantly blames other people for his problems and tries to avoid making decisions. Howard is a college student with a part-time job. However, he is a terrible student and worker. He hardly ever studies and frequently misses assignments, as a result of which he gets poor grades. As mentioned earlier, Howard comes to work late and takes no pride in his work. Though he does nothing against our current laws, he is an inattentive and inconsiderate spouse and parent. Nor does he make any effort to participate in the life of his community, or the promise of America. He would rather lie around the house, watching television and cursing the rest of the world for his problems. In short, Howard does all the bad things to his family, friends, coworkers, and society that the ONDCP says *may* result from drug use. And most of this is voluntary.

Should Congress pass laws against what Howard is doing? Should the police then arrest him, and the district attorney prosecute him, for being a loser?

Once again, it seems absurd to suppose that we would arrest and jail someone for behaving in these ways, undesirable as they may be. Since drug use only has a *chance* of causing one to behave in each of these ways, it is even more absurd to suppose that we should arrest and jail people for drug use on the grounds that drug use has these potential effects.

III. The Injustice of Drug Prohibition

Philosopher Douglas Husak has characterized drug prohibition as the greatest injustice perpetrated in the United States since slavery.[10] This is no hyperbole. If the drug laws are unjust, then America has over half a million people unjustly imprisoned.[11]

---

[10] Husak, *Legalize This!*, p. 2.
[11] In 2006, there were approximately 553,000 people in American prisons and jails whose most serious offense was a drug offense. This included 93,751 federal inmates (U.S. Department of

Why think the drug laws are *unjust*? Husak's argument invokes a principle with which few could disagree: it is unjust for the state to punish people without having a good reason for doing so.[12] We have seen the failure of the most common proposed rationales for drug prohibition. If nothing better is forthcoming, then we must conclude that prohibitionists have no rational justification for punishing drug users. We have deprived hundreds of thousands of people of basic liberties and subjected them to severe hardship conditions, for no good reason.

This is bad enough. But I want to say something stronger: it is not merely that we are punishing people for no good reason. We are punishing people for exercising their natural rights. Individuals have a right to use drugs. This right is neither absolute nor exceptionless; suppose, for example, that there existed a drug which, once ingested, caused a significant proportion of users, without any further free choices on their part, to attack other people without provocation. I would think that stopping the use of this drug would be the business of the government. But no existing drug satisfies this description. Indeed, though I cannot take time to delve into the matter here, I think it is clear that the drug *laws* cause far more crime than drugs themselves do.

The idea of a right to use drugs derives from the idea that individuals own their own bodies. That is, a person has the right to exercise control over his own body—including the right to decide how it should be used, and to exclude others from using it—in a manner similar to the way one may exercise control over one's (other) property. This statement is somewhat vague; nevertheless, we can see the general idea embodied in common sense morality. Indeed, it seems that if there is *anything* one would have rights to, it would be one's own body. This explains why we think others may not physically attack you or kidnap you. It explains

---

Justice, "Prisoners in 2006," December 2007, http://www.ojp.usdoj.gov/bjs/pub/pdf/p06.pdf, p. 9). State prisons held another 269,596 drug inmates, based on the 2006 state prison population of 1,377,815 ("Prisoners in 2006," p. 2) and the 2004 rate of 19.57% of state prisoners held on drug charges ("Prisoners in 2006," p. 24). Local jails held another 189,204 drug inmates, based on the 2006 local jail population of 766,010 ("Prisoners in 2006," p. 3) and the 2002 rate of 24.7% of local inmates held on drug charges (U.S. Department of Justice, "Profile of Jail Inmates 2002," published July 2004, revised October 12, 2004, http://www.ojp.usdoj.gov/bjs/pub/pdf/pji02.pdf, p. 1). In all cases, I have used the latest statistics available as of this writing.

[12]   Husak, *Legalize This!*, p. 15. See his chapter 2 for an extended discussion of various proposed rationales for drug prohibition, including many issues that I lack space to discuss here.

why we do not accept the use of unwilling human subjects for medical experiments, even if the experiments are beneficial to society—the rest of society may not decide to use your body for its own purposes without your permission. It explains why some believe that women have a right to an abortion—and why some others do not. The former believe that a woman has the right to do what she wants with her own body; the latter believe that the fetus is a distinct person, and a woman does not have the right to harm *its* body. Virtually no one disputes that, *if* a fetus is merely a part of the woman's body, *then* a woman has a right to choose whether to have an abortion; just as virtually no one disputes that, *if* a fetus is a distinct person, then a woman lacks the right to destroy it. Almost no one disputes that persons have rights over their own bodies but not over others' bodies.

The right to control one's body cannot be interpreted as implying a right to use one's body in *every* conceivable way, any more than we have the right to use our property in every conceivable way. Most importantly, we may not use our bodies to harm others in certain ways, just as we may not use our property to harm others. But drug use seems to be a paradigm case of a legitimate exercise of the right to control one's own body. Drug consumption takes place in and immediately around the user's own body; the salient effects occur *inside* the user's body. If we consider drug use merely as altering the user's own body and mind, it is hard to see how anyone who believes in rights a t all could deny that it is protected by a right, for: (a) it is hard to see how anyone who believes in rights could deny that individuals have rights over their own bodies and minds, and (b) it is hard to see how anyone who believes in such rights could deny that drug use, considered merely as altering the user's body and mind, is an example of the exercise of one's rights over one's own body and mind.

Consider two ways a prohibitionist might object to this argument. First, a prohibitionist might argue that drug use does not *merely* alter the user's own body and mind, but also harms the user's family, friends, co-workers, and society. I responded to this sort of argument in section II. Not just *any* way in which an action might be said to "harm" other people makes the action worthy of criminal sanctions. Here we need not try to state a general criterion for what sorts of harms make an action worthy of criminalization; it is enough to note that there are some kinds of "harms" that virtually no one would take to warrant criminal sanctions, and that these include the "harms" I cause to others by being a poor student, an incompetent worker, or an apathetic citizen.[13] That said, I agree with the prohibitionists at least this far: no one should be permitted to drive or operate heavy machinery while under the influence of drugs that impair their ability to do those things; nor should pregnant mothers be permitted to ingest drugs, if it can be proven that those drugs cause substantial risks to their babies (I leave open the question of what the threshold level of risk should be, as well as the empirical questions concerning the actual level of risk created by illegal drugs). But, in the great majority of cases, drug use does not harm anyone in any *relevant* ways—that is, ways that we normally take to merit criminal penalties— and should not be outlawed.

Second, a prohibitionist might argue that drug use fails to qualify as an exercise of the user's rights over his own body, because the individual is not truly acting freely in deciding to use drugs. Perhaps individuals only use drugs because they have fallen prey to some sort of psychological compulsion, because drugs exercise a siren-like allure that distorts users' perceptions, because users don't realize how bad drugs are, or something of that sort. The exact form of this objection doesn't matter; in any case, the prohibitionist faces a dilemma. If users do not freely choose to use drugs, then it is unjust to *punish* them for using drugs. For if users do not choose freely, then they are not morally responsible for their decision, and it is unjust to punish a person for something he is not responsible for. But if users *do* choose freely in deciding to use drugs, then this choice is an exercise of their rights over their own bodies.

I have tried to think of the best arguments prohibitionists could give, but in fact prohibitionists have remained puzzlingly silent on this issue. When a country goes to war, it tends to focus on how to win, sparing little thought for the rights of the victims in the enemy country. Similarly, one effect of America's declaring "war" on drug users seems to have been that prohibitionists have given almost no thought to the rights of drug users. Most either ignore the issue or mention it briefly only to dismiss it without argument.[14] In an effort to discredit legalizers, the Office of National Drug Control Policy produced the following caricature—

---

[13] Husak (*Drugs and Rights*, Cambridge University Press, 1992, pp. 166–168), similarly, argues that no one has a *right* that I be a good neighbor, proficient student, and so on, and that only harms that violate rights can justify criminal sanctions.

[14] See Inciardi for an instance of ignoring and Daniel Lungren ("Legalization Would Be a Mistake" in Timothy Lynch, ed., *After Prohibition*, Washington, D.C.: Cato Institute, 2000,

The easy cynicism that has grown up around the drug issue is no accident. Sowing it has been the deliberate aim of a decades-long campaign by proponents of legalization, critics whose mantra is "nothing works," and whose central insight appears to be that they can avoid having to propose the unmentionable—a world where drugs are ubiquitous and where use and addiction would skyrocket—if they can hide behind the bland management critique that drug control efforts are "unworkable."[15]

—apparently denying the existence of the central issues I have discussed in this essay. It seems reasonable to assume that an account of the state's right to forcibly interfere with individuals' decisions regarding their own bodies is not forthcoming from these prohibitionists.

IV. Conclusion

Undoubtedly, the drug war has been disastrous in many ways that others can more ably describe—in terms of its effects on crime, on police corruption, and on other civil liberties, to name a few. But more than that, the drug war is morally outrageous in its very conception. If we are to call ours a free society, we cannot deploy force to deprive people of their liberty and property for whimsical reasons. The exercise of such coercion requires a powerful and clearly-stated rationale. Most of the reasons that have been proposed in the case of drug prohibition would be considered feeble if advanced in other contexts. Few would take seriously the suggestion that people should be imprisoned for harming their own health, being poor students, or failing to share in the American dream. It is still less credible that we should imprison people for an activity that only *may* lead to those consequences. Yet these and other, similarly weak arguments form the core of prohibition's defense.

Prohibitionists are likewise unable to answer the argument that individuals have a right to use drugs. Any such answer would have to deny either that persons have rights of control over their own bodies, or that consuming drugs constituted an exercise of those rights. We have seen that the sort of harms drug use allegedly causes to society do not make a case

---

Page 180 for an instance of unargued dismissal. Wilson (p. 24) addresses the issue, if at all, only by arguing that drug use makes users worse parents, spouses, employers, and co-workers. This fails to refute the contention that individuals have a right to use drugs.

[15] ONDCP, *National Drug Control Strategy 2002*, p. 3.

against its being an exercise of the user's rights over his own body. And the claim that drug users can't control their behavior or don't know what they are doing renders it even more mysterious why one would believe drug users deserve to be punished for what they are doing.

I will close by responding to a query posed by prohibition-advocate James Inciardi:

> The government of the United States is not going to legalize drugs anytime soon, if ever, and certainly not in this [the 20th] century. So why spend so much time, expense, and intellectual and emotional effort on a quixotic undertaking? ... [W]e should know by now that neither politicians nor the polity respond positively to abrupt and drastic strategy alterations.[16]

The United States presently has 553,000 people unjustly imprisoned. Inciardi may—tragically—be correct that our government has no intention of stopping its flagrant violations of the rights of its people any time soon. Nevertheless, it remains the duty of citizens and of political and social theorists to identify the injustice, and not to tacitly assent to it. Imagine a slavery advocate, decades before the Civil War, arguing that abolitionists were wasting their breath and should move on to more productive activities, such as arguing for incremental changes in the way slaves are treated, since the southern states had no intention of ending slavery any time soon. The institution of slavery is a black mark on our nation's history, but our history would be even more shameful if no one at the time had spoken against the injustice.

Is this comparison overdrawn? I don't think so. The harm of being unjustly imprisoned is qualitatively comparable (though it usually ends sooner) to the harm of being enslaved. The increasingly popular scapegoating and stereotyping of drug users and sellers on the part of our nation's leaders is comparable to the racial prejudices of previous generations. Yet very few seem willing to speak on behalf of drug users. Perhaps the unwillingness of those in public life to defend drug users' rights stems from the negative image we have of drug users and the fear of being associated with them. Yet these attitudes remain baffling. I have used illegal drugs myself. I know of many decent and successful individuals who have used illegal drugs. Nearly half of all Americans over the age of 11 have used illegal drugs—including at least two United States Presidents,

---

[16] Inciardi, p. 205.

one Vice-President, one Speaker of the House, and one Supreme Court Justice.[17] But now leave aside the absurdity of recommending criminal sanctions for all these people. My point is this: if we are convinced of the injustice of drug prohibition, then—even if our protests should fall on deaf ears—we can not remain silent in the face of such a large-scale injustice in our own country. And, fortunately, radical social reforms *have* occurred, more than once in our history, in response to moral arguments.

Michael Huemer: America's Unjust Drug War

1) Huemer admits that using drugs can be harmful to the user, but points out that alcohol, tobacco, unhealthy food, and unsafe sex can also be harmful. Is there any morally relevant difference between the harms caused by drugs and the harms caused by these other activities?
2) Huemer invokes the following principle: "if it would be wrong to punish people for *directly bringing about* some result, then it would also be wrong to punish people for doing some other action on the grounds that the action has a *chance* of bringing about that result indirectly." Do you find this principle plausible? Why or why not?
3) Consider Huemer's case involving Howard. Should Howard be punished for acting the way he does? If not, does it follow that we should not punish drug users?
4) Do individuals have a right to use drugs? What is Huemer's argument for thinking that they do? Do you find it convincing?
5) Suppose that we accept Huemer's contention that we ought to legalize recreational drug use. Does it follow that all of those currently in prison for drug-related offenses have been unjustly imprisoned?

---

[17] In 2006, 45% of Americans aged 12 and over reported having used at least one illegal drug (U.S. Department of Health and Human Services, "National Survey on Drug Use and Health," 2006, Table 1.1B, http://www.oas.samhsa.gov/NSDUH/2k6NSDUH/tabs/Sect1peTabs1to46.htm). Bill Clinton, Al Gore, Newt Gingrich and Clarence Thomas have all acknowledged past drug use (reported by David Phinney, "Dodging the Drug Question," ABC News, August 19, 1999, http://abcnews.go.com/sections/politics/DailyNews/prez_questions990819.html). George W. Bush has refused to state whether he has ever used illegal drugs. Barack Obama has admitted to cocaine and marijuana use (*Dreams from My Father*, New York: Random House, 2004, p. 93).

36

Why Shouldn't Tommy and Jimmy Have Sex?: A Defense of Homosexuality

John Corvino

. . . .

In this article, John Corvino considers and rejects each of the four most popular kinds of arguments that seek to establish the immorality of homosexuality. The first of these arguments claims that homosexuality is unnatural, and is therefore immoral. Corvino distinguishes five different senses in which things can be unnatural, and concludes, for each of these meanings, that homosexuality is either perfectly natural or, if unnatural, is not unnatural in a way that makes it immoral.

The second kind of argument against homosexuality is that it is harmful, either to homosexuals themselves or to third parties. Corvino thinks that the harm-to-others charge would be very serious if it could be sustained. But he argues that it fails, as does the claim that partners in homosexual relations are likelier to harm other people than those involved in heterosexual relations.

The third argument is one based on biblical teaching. The Hebrew scriptures appear to contain explicit condemnations of male homosexual conduct, and both Jewish and Christian traditions have long condemned homosexuality. Corvino argues that a plausible interpretive principle for ancient texts enables us to justify a position, within these religious frameworks, that puts these condemnations in context and enables believers, in good faith, to emerge with a view that finds homosexuality morally acceptable.

"Why Shouldn't Tommy and Jimmy Have Sex?" from *Same Sex: Debating the Ethics, Science and Culture of Homosexuality*, ed. John Corvino (1997). Reprinted with permission of Rowman & Littlefield.

The last argument takes the form of a slippery slope: If homo-sexuality is morally permitted, then so, too, is bestiality and polygamy. But these are immoral, and therefore so too is homosexuality. Corvino thinks that we can resist the slippery slope, because (as he argues) there are special reasons to condemn bestiality and polygamy that do not apply to the case of homosexuality.

....

Tommy and Jim are a homosexual couple I know. Tommy is an accountant; Jim is a botany professor. They are in their forties and have been together fourteen years, the last five of which they've lived in a Victorian house that they've lovingly restored. Although their relationship has had its challenges, each has made sacrifices for the sake of the other's happiness and the relationship's long-term success.

I assume that Tommy and Jim have sex with each other (although I've never bothered to ask). Furthermore, I contend that they probably *should* have sex with each other. For one thing, sex is pleasurable. But it is also much more than that: a sexual relationship can unite two people in a way that virtually nothing else can. It can be an avenue of growth, of commu-nication, and of lasting interpersonal fulfillment. These are reasons why most heterosexual couples have sex even if they don't want children, don't want children yet, or don't want additional children. And if these reasons are good enough for most heterosexual couples, then they should be good enough for Tommy and Jim.

Of course, having a reason to do something does not preclude there being an even better reason for not doing it. Tommy might have a good reason for drinking orange juice (it's tasty and nutritious) but an even bet-ter reason for not doing so (he's allergic). The point is that one would need a pretty good reason for denying a sexual relationship to Tommy and Jim, given the intense benefits widely associated with such relationships. The question I shall consider in this paper is thus quite simple: Why shouldn't Tommy and Jim have sex?

Homosexual Sex Is "Unnatural"

Many contend that homosexual sex is "unnatural." But what does that mean? Many things that people value—clothing, houses, medicine, and government, for example—are unnatural in some sense. On the other hand, many things that people detest—disease, suffering, and death, for example—are "natural" in the sense that they occur "in nature." If the unnaturalness charge is to be more than empty rhetorical flourish, those who levy it must specify what they mean. Borrowing from Burton Leiser, I will examine several possible meanings of "unnatural."[1]

What Is Unusual or Abnormal Is Unnatural

One meaning of "unnatural" refers to that which deviates from the norm, that is, from what most people do. Obviously, most people engage in heterosexual relationships. But does it follow that it is wrong to engage in homosexual relationships? Relatively few people read Sanskrit, pilot ships, play the mandolin, breed goats, or write with both hands, yet none of these activities is immoral simply because it is unusual. As the Ramsey Colloquium, a group of Jewish and Christian scholars who oppose homosexuality, writes, "The statistical frequency of an act does not determine its moral status."[2] So while homosexuality might be unnatural in the sense of being unusual, that fact is morally irrelevant.

What Is Not Practiced by Other Animals Is Unnatural

Some people argue, "Even animals know better than to behave homosexually; homosexuality must be wrong." This argument is doubly flawed. First it rests on a false premise. Numerous studies—including Anne Perkins's study of "gay" sheep and George and Molly Hunt's study of "lesbian" seagulls—have shown that some animals do form homosexual pair-bonds. Second, even if animals did not behave homosexually, that fact would not prove that homosexuality is immoral. After all, animals don't cook their food, brush their teeth, participate in religious worship, or attend college; human beings do all of these without moral censure. Indeed, the idea that animals could provide us with our standards—especially our sexual standards—is simply amusing.

What Does Not Proceed from Innate Desires Is Unnatural

Recent studies suggesting a biological basis for homosexuality have resulted in two popular positions. One side proposes that homosexual people are "born that way" and that it is therefore natural (and thus good) for them to

---

[1] Burton M. Leiser, *Liberty, Justice, and Morals: Contemporary Value Conflicts* (New York: Macmillan, 1986), pp. 51–57.
[2] The Ramsey Colloquium, "The Homosexual Movement," *First Things* (March 1994), pp. 15–20.

form homosexual relationships. The other side maintains that homosexuality is a lifestyle choice, which is therefore unnatural (and thus wrong). Both sides assume a connection between the origin of homosexual orientation, on the one hand, and the moral value of homosexual activity, on the other. And insofar as they share that assumption, both sides are wrong.

Consider first the pro-homosexual side: "They are born that way; therefore it's natural and good." This inference assumes that all innate desires are good ones (i.e., that they should be acted upon). Bur that assumption is clearly false. Research suggests that some people are born with a predisposition toward violence, but such people have no more right to strangle their neighbors than anyone else. So while people like Tommy and Jim may be born with homosexual tendencies, it doesn't follow that they ought to act on them. Nor does it follow that they ought *not* to act on them, even if the tendencies are not innate. I probably do not have any innate tendency to write with my left hand (since I, like everyone else in my family, have always been right-handed), but it doesn't follow that it would be immoral for me to do so. So simply asserting that homosexuality is a lifestyle choice will not show that it is an immoral lifestyle choice.

Do people "choose" to be homosexual? People certainly don't seem to choose their sexual *feelings*, at least not in any direct or obvious way. (Do you? Think about it.) Rather, they find certain people attractive and certain activities arousing, whether they "decide" to or not. Indeed, most people at some point in their lives wish that they could control their feelings more—for example, in situations of unrequited love—and find it frustrating that they cannot. What they *can* control to a considerable degree is how and when they act upon those feelings. In that sense, both homosexuality and heterosexuality involve lifestyle choices. But in either case, determining the origin of the feelings will not determine whether it is moral to act on them.

What Violates an Organ's Principal Purpose Is Unnatural

Perhaps when people claim that homosexual sex is unnatural they mean that it cannot result in procreation. The idea behind the argument is that human organs have various natural purposes: eyes are for seeing, ears are for hearing, genitals are for procreating. According to this argument, it is immoral to use an organ in a way that violates its particular purpose.

Many of our organs, however, have multiple purposes. Tommy can use his mouth for talking, eating, breathing, licking stamps, chewing gum, kissing women, or kissing Jim; and it seems rather arbitrary to claim that all but the last use are "natural." (And if we say that some of the other uses are "unnatural, but not immoral," we have failed to specify a morally relevant sense of the term "natural.")

Just because people can and do use their sexual organs to procreate, it does not follow that they should not use them for other purposes. Sexual organs seem very well suited for expressing love, for giving and receiving pleasure, and for celebrating, replenishing, and enhancing a relationship—even when procreation is not a factor. Unless opponents of homosexuality are prepared to condemn heterosexual couples who use contraception or individuals who masturbate, they must abandon this version of the unnaturalness argument. Indeed, even the Roman Catholic Church, which forbids contraception and masturbation, approves of sex for sterile couples and of sex during pregnancy, neither of which can lead to procreation. The Church concedes here that intimacy and pleasure are morally legitimate purposes for sex, even in cases where procreation is impossible. But since homosexual sex can achieve these purposes as well, it is inconsistent for the Church to condemn it on the grounds that it is not procreative.

One might object that sterile heterosexual couples do not *intentionally* turn away from procreation, whereas homosexual couples do. But this distinction doesn't hold. It is no more possible for Tommy to procreate with a woman whose uterus has been removed than it is for him to procreate with Jim. By having sex with either one, he is intentionally engaging in a non-procreative sexual act.

Yet one might press the objection further and insist that Tommy and the woman *could* produce children if the woman were fertile: whereas homosexual relationships are essentially infertile, heterosexual relationships are only incidentally so. But what does that prove? Granted, it might require less of a miracle for a woman without a uterus to become pregnant than for Jim to become pregnant, but it would require a miracle nonetheless. Thus it seems that the real difference here is not that one couple is fertile and the other not, nor that one couple "could" be fertile (with the help of a miracle) and the other not, but rather that one couple is male-female and the other male-male. In other words, sex between Tommy and Jim is wrong because it's male-male—i.e., because it's homosexual. But that, of course, is no argument at all.

What Is Disgusting or Offensive Is Unnatural

It often seems that when people call homosexuality "unnatural" they really just mean that it's disgusting. But plenty of morally neutral activities—handling snakes, eating snails, performing autopsies, cleaning toilets, and so on—disgust people. Indeed, for centuries, most people found interracial relationships disgusting, yet that feeling—which has by no means disappeared—hardly proves that such relationships are wrong. In sum, the charge that homosexuality is unnatural, at least in its most common forms, is longer on rhetorical flourish than on philosophical cogency. At best it expresses an aesthetic judgment, not a moral judgment.

Homosexual Sex Is Harmful

One might instead argue that homosexuality is harmful. The Ramsey Colloquium, for instance, argues that homosexuality leads to the breakdown of the family and, ultimately, of human society, and it points to the "alarming rates of sexual promiscuity, depression, and suicide and the ominous presence of AIDS within the homosexual subculture."[3] Thomas Schmidt marshals copious statistics to show that homosexual activity undermines physical and psychological health.[4] Such charges, if correct, would seem to provide strong evidence against homosexuality. But are the charges correct? And do they prove what they purport to prove?

One obvious (and obviously problematic) way to answer the first question is to ask people like Tommy and Jim. It would appear that no one is in a better position to judge the homosexual lifestyle than those who know it firsthand. Yet it is unlikely that critics would trust their testimony. Indeed, the more homosexual people try to explain their lives, the more critics accuse them of deceitfully promoting an agenda. (It's like trying to prove that you're not crazy. The more you object, the more people think, "That's exactly what a crazy person would say.")

One might instead turn to statistics. An obvious problem with this tack is that both sides of the debate bring forth extensive statistics and "expert" testimony, leaving the average observer confused. There is a more subtle problem as well. Because of widespread antigay sentiment, many homosexual people won't acknowledge their romantic feelings to themselves, much less to researchers. I have known a number of gay men who did not "come out" until their forties and fifties, and no amount of professional competence on the part of interviewers would have been likely to

---

[3] The Ramsey Colloquium, "Homosexual Movement," p. 19.
[4] Thomas Schmidt, "The Price of Love" in *Straight and Narrow? Compassion and Clarity in the Homosexuality Debate* (Downers Grove, IL: InterVarsity Press, 1995), chap. 6.

open their closets sooner. Such problems compound the usual difficulties of finding representative population samples for statistical study.

Yet even if the statistical claims of gay rights opponents were true, they would not prove what they purport to prove, for several reasons. First, as any good statistician realizes, correlation does not equal cause. Even if homosexual people were more likely to commit suicide, be promiscuous, or contract AIDS than the general population, it would not follow that their homosexuality causes them to do these things. An alternative—and very plausible—explanation is that these phenomena, like the disproportionately high crime rates among African Americans, are at least partly a function of society's treatment of the group in question. Suppose you were told from a very early age that the romantic feelings that you experienced were sick, unnatural, and disgusting. Suppose further that expressing these feelings put you at risk of social ostracism or, worse yet, physical violence. Is it not plausible that you would, for instance, be more inclined to depression than you would be without such obstacles? And that such depression could, in its extreme forms, lead to suicide or other self-destructive behaviors? (It is indeed remarkable that couples like Tommy and Jim continue to flourish in the face of such obstacles.)

A similar explanation can be given for the alleged promiscuity of homosexuals. The denial of legal marriage, the pressure to remain in the closet, and the overt hostility toward homosexual relationship are all more conducive to transient, clandestine encounters than they are to long-term unions. As a result, that which is challenging enough for heterosexual couples—settling down and building a life together—becomes far more challenging for homosexual couples.

But what about AIDS? Opponents of homosexuality sometimes claim that even if homosexual sex is not, strictly speaking, immoral, it is still a bad idea, since it puts people at risk for AIDS and other sexually transmitted diseases. But that claim is misleading: it is infinitely more risky for Tommy to have sex with a woman who is HIV-positive than with Jim, who is HIV-negative. Obviously, it's not homosexuality that's harmful, it's the virus; and the virus may be carried by both heterosexual and homosexual people.

Now it may be true (in the United States, at least) that homosexual males are statistically more likely to carry the virus than heterosexual females and thus that homosexual sex is *statistically* more risky than heterosexual sex (in cases where the partner's HIV status is unknown). But opponents of homosexuality need something stronger than this statistical claim. For if it is wrong for men to have sex with men because their doing so puts them at a higher AIDS risk than heterosexual sex, then it is also wrong for women to have sex with men because their doing so puts them at a higher AIDS risk than homosexual sex (lesbians as a group have the lowest incidence of AIDS). Purely from the standpoint of AIDS risk, women ought to prefer lesbian sex.

If this response seems silly, it is because there is obviously more to choosing a romantic or sexual partner than determining AIDS risk. And a major part of the decision, one that opponents of homosexuality consistently overlook, is considering whether one can have a mutually fulfilling relationship with the partner. For many people like Tommy and Jim, such fulfillment—which most heterosexuals recognize to be an important component of human flourishing—is only possible with members of the same sex.

In sum, there is nothing *inherently* risky about sex between persons of the same gender. It is only risky under certain conditions: for instance, if they exchange diseased bodily fluids or if they engage in certain "rough" forms of sex that could cause tearing of delicate tissue. Heterosexual sex is equally risky under such conditions. Thus, even if statistical claims like those of Schmidt and the Ramsey Colloquium were true, they would not prove that homosexuality is immoral. At best, they would prove that homosexual people—like everyone else—ought to take great care when deciding to become sexually active.

Of course, there's more to a flourishing life than avoiding harm. One might argue that even if Tommy and Jim are not harming each other by their relationship, they are still failing to achieve the higher level of fulfillment possible in a heterosexual relationship, which is rooted in the complementarity of male and female. But this argument just ignores the facts: Tommy and Jim are homosexual *precisely because* they find relationships with men (and, in particular, with each other) more fulfilling than relationships with women. Even evangelicals (who have long advocated "faith healing" for homosexuals) are beginning to acknowledge that the choice for most homosexual people is not between homosexual relationships and heterosexual relationships, but rather between homosexual relationships and celibacy. What the critics need to show, therefore, is that no matter how loving, committed, mutual, generous, and fulfilling the relationship may be, Tommy and Jim would flourish more if they were celibate. Given the evidence of their lives (and of others like them), this is a formidable task indeed.

Thus far I have focused on the allegation that homosexuality harms those who engage in it. But what about the allegation that homosexuality harms other, nonconsenting parties? Here I will briefly consider two claims: that homosexuality threatens children and that it threatens society.

Those who argue that homosexuality threatens children may mean one of two things. First, they may mean that homosexual people are child molesters. Statistically, the vast majority of reported cases of child sexual abuse involve young girls and their fathers, stepfathers, or other familiar (and presumably heterosexual) adult males. But opponents of homosexuality argue that when one adjusts for relative percentage in the population, homosexual males appear more likely than heterosexual males to be child molesters. As I argued above, the problems with obtaining reliable statistics on homosexuality render such calculations difficult. Fortunately, they are also unnecessary.

Child abuse is a terrible thing. But when a heterosexual male molests a child (or rapes a woman or commits assault), the act does not reflect upon all heterosexuals. Similarly, when a homosexual male molests a child, there is no reason why that act should reflect upon all homosexuals. Sex with adults of the same sex is one thing; sex with *children* of the same sex is quite another. Conflating the two not only slanders innocent people, it also misdirects resources intended to protect children. Furthermore, many men convicted of molesting young boys are sexually attracted to adult women and report no attraction to adult men. To call such men "homosexual," or even "bisexual," is probably to stretch such terms too far.

Alternatively, those who charge that homosexuality threatens children might mean that the increasing visibility of homosexual relationships makes children more likely to become homosexual. The argument for this view is patently circular. One cannot prove that doing X is bad by arguing that it causes other people to do X, which is bad. One must first establish independently that X is bad. That said, there is not a shred of evidence to demonstrate that exposure to homosexuality leads children to become homosexual.

But doesn't homosexuality threaten society? A Roman Catholic priest once put the argument to me as follows: "Of course homosexuality is bad for society. If everyone were homosexual, there would be no society." Perhaps it is true that if everyone were homosexual, there would be no society. But if everyone were a celibate priest, society would collapse just as surely, and my friend the priest didn't seem to think that he was doing anything wrong simply by failing to procreate.

I have argued that Tommy and Jim's sexual relationship harms neither them nor society. On the contrary, it benefits both. It benefits them because it makes them happier—not merely in a short-term, hedonistic sense, but in a long-term, "big picture" sort of way. And, in turn, it benefits society, since it makes Tommy and Jim more stable, more productive, and more generous than they would otherwise be. In short, their relationship—including its sexual component—provides the same kinds of benefits that infertile heterosexual relationships provide (and perhaps other benefits as well). Nor should we fear that accepting their relationship and others like it will cause people to flee in droves from the institution of heterosexual marriage. After all the usual response to a gay person is not "How come *he* gets to be gay and I don't?"

Homosexuality Violates Biblical Teaching

At this point in the discussion, many people turn to religion. "If the secular arguments fail to prove that homosexuality is wrong," they say, "so much the worse for secular ethics. This failure only proves that we need God for morality." Since people often justify their moral beliefs by appeal to religion, I will briefly consider the biblical position.

At first glance, the Bible's condemnation of homosexual activity seems unequivocal. Consider, for example, the following two passages, one from the "Old" Testament and one from the "New":

> You shall not lie with a male as with a woman; it is an abomination. (Lev. 18:22)
>
> For this reason God gave them up to degrading passions. Their women exchanged natural intercourse for unnatural, and in the same way also the men, giving up natural intercourse with women, were consumed with passion for one another. Men committed shameless acts with men and received in their own persons the due penalty for their error. (Rom. 1:26–27)

Note, however, that these passages are surrounded by other passages that relatively few people consider binding. For example, Leviticus also declares,

> The pig ... is unclean for you. Of their flesh you shall not eat, and their carcasses you shall not touch; they are unclean for you. (11:7–8)

Taken literally, this passage not only prohibits eating pork, but also playing football, since footballs are made of pigskin. (Can you believe that the University of Notre Dame so flagrantly violates Levitical teaching?) Similarly, St. Paul, author of the Romans passage, also writes, "Slaves, obey your earthly masters with fear and trembling, in singleness of heart, as you obey Christ" (Eph. 6:5)—morally problematic advice if there ever were any. Should we interpret this passage (as Southern plantation owners once did) as implying that it is immoral for slaves to escape? After all, God himself says in Leviticus,

> [Y]ou may acquire male and female slaves...from among the aliens residing with you, and from their families that are with you, who have been born in your land; and they may be your property. You may keep them as a possession for your children after you, for them to inherit as property. (25:44–46)

How can people maintain the inerrancy of the Bible in light of such passages? The answer, I think, is that they learn to interpret the passages *in their historical context*.

Consider the Bible's position on usury, the lending of money for interest (for *any* interest, not just excessive interest). The Bible condemns this practice in no uncertain terms. In Exodus God says that "if you lend money to my people, to the poor among you you shall not exact interest from them" (22:25). Psalm 15 says that those who lend at interest may not abide in the Lord's tent or dwell on his holy hill (1–5). Ezekiel calls usury "abominable"; compares it to adultery, robbery, idolatry, and bribery; and states that anyone who "takes advanced or accrued interest...shall surely die; his blood shall be upon himself" (18:13).

Should believers therefore close their savings accounts? Not necessarily. According to orthodox Christian teaching, the biblical prohibition against usury no longer applies. The reason is that economic conditions have changed substantially since biblical times, such that usury no longer has the same negative consequences it had when the prohibitions were issued. Thus, the practice that was condemned by the Bible differs from contemporary interest banking in morally relevant ways.

Yet are we not in a similar position regarding homosexuality? Virtually all scholars agree that homosexual relations during biblical times were vastly different from relationships like Tommy and Jim's. Often such relations were integral to pagan practices. In Greek society, they typically involved older men and younger boys. If those are the kinds of features that the biblical authors had in mind when they issued their condemnations, and such features are no longer typical, then the biblical condemnations no longer apply. As with usury, substantial changes in cultural context have altered the meaning and consequences—and thus the moral value—of the practice in question. Put another way, using the Bible's condemnations of

homosexuality against contemporary homosexuality is like using its condemnations of usury against contemporary banking.

Let me be clear about what I am *not* claiming here. First, I am not
claiming that the Bible has been wrong before and therefore may be wrong
this time. The Bible may indeed by wrong on some matters, but for the
purpose of this argument I am assuming its infallibility. Nor am I claiming
that the Bible's age renders it entirely inapplicable to today's issues. Rather,
I am claiming that when we do apply it, *we must pay attention to morally
relevant cultural differences between biblical times and today*. Such attention will help us distinguish between specific time-bound prohibitions (for
example, laws against usury or homosexual relations) and the enduring
moral values they represent (for example, generosity or respect for persons). And as the above argument shows, my claim is not very controversial. Indeed, to deny it is to commit oneself to some rather strange views
on slavery, usury, women's roles, astronomy, evolution, and the like.

Here, one might also make an appeal to religious pluralism. Given the
wide variety of religious beliefs (e.g., the Muslim belief that women should
cover their faces, the Orthodox Jewish belief against working on Saturday,
the Hindu belief that cows are sacred and should not be eaten), each of us
inevitably violates the religious beliefs of others. But we normally don't
view such violations as occasions for moral censure, since we distinguish
between beliefs that depend on particular revelations and beliefs that can
be justified independently (e.g., that stealing is wrong). Without an independent justification for condemning homosexuality, the best one can
say is, "My religion says so." But in a society that cherishes religious freedom, that reason alone does not normally provide grounds for moral or
legal sanctions. That people still fall back on that reason in discussions of
homosexuality suggests that they may not have much of a case otherwise.

Conclusion

As a last resort, opponents of homosexuality typically change the subject:
"But what about incest, polygamy, and bestiality? If we accept Tommy and
Jim's sexual relationship, why shouldn't we accept those as well?" Oppo-
nents of interracial marriage used a similar slippery-slope argument in
the 1960s when the Supreme Court struck down antimiscegenation laws.[5]
It was a bad argument then, and it is a bad argument now.

---

[5] *Loving v. Virginia*, 388 U.S. 1967.

Just because there are no good reasons to oppose interracial or homo-sexual relationships, it does not follow that there are no good reasons to oppose incestuous, polygamous, or bestial relationships. One might argue, for instance, that incestuous relationships threaten delicate famil-ial bonds, or that polygamous relationships result in unhealthy jealousies (and sexism), or that bestial relationships—do I need to say it?—aren't really "relationships" at all, at least not in the sense we've been discussing. Perhaps even better arguments could be offered (given much more space than I have here). The point is that there is no logical connection between homosexuality, on the one hand, and incest, polygamy, and bestiality, on the other.

Why, then, do critics continue to push this objection? Perhaps it's because accepting homosexuality requires them to give up one of their favorite arguments: "It's wrong because we've always been taught that it's wrong." This argument—call it the argument from tradition—has an obvi-ous appeal: people reasonably favor tried-and-true ideas over unfamiliar ones, and they recognize the foolishness of trying to invent morality from scratch. But the argument from tradition is also a dangerous argument, as any honest look at history will reveal.

I conclude that Tommy and Jim's relationship, far from being a moral abomination, is exactly what it appears to be to those who know them: a morally positive influence on their lives and on others. Accept-ing this conclusion takes courage, since it entails that our moral tra-ditions are fallible. But when these traditions interfere with people's happiness for no sound reason, they defeat what is arguably the very point of morality: promoting individual and communal well-being. To put the argument simply, Tommy and Jim's relationship makes them better people. And that's not just good for Tommy and Jim: that's good for everyone.

John Corvino: Why Shouldn't Tommy and Jim Have Sex?: A Defense of Homosexuality

1) What reasons do Tommy and Jim have for having sex? Do you agree with Corvino that these are the same reasons that many heterosexual couples have for having sex?
2) What does it mean to say that an activity is "unnatural"? Is the fact that something is unnatural ever a good reason for concluding that it is morally wrong?

3) Is homosexual sex harmful or risky to those who engage in it, in a way that heterosexual sex is not? If so, is this a good reason to think that it is morally wrong?

4) Some people argue that public acceptance of homosexual relationships would make children more likely to become homosexual. Why doesn't Corvino think this is a good argument against homosexual relationships? Do you agree with him?

5) How does Corvino respond to religious arguments against homosexuality? Do you find his responses convincing?

6) What is a "slippery slope" argument? Why does Corvino think that slippery slope arguments against homosexuality are bad arguments? Do you agree with him?

==== ❧ ====

37

Adultery

Bonnie Steinbock

Philosopher Bonnie Steinbock raises the question of whether there is anything immoral about adultery. If you are religious, and your religion (like most) criticizes adultery, then you'll have a quick answer to this question. But Steinbock wants us to think about whether there are grounds that both religious and nonreligious people can accept that will indict adultery. She thinks that there are.

In addition to the practical reasons against committing adultery, Steinbock claims that two moral reasons oppose it: adultery is a form of promise-breaking, and it is a form of deception. Yet as Steinbock admits, these reasons would disappear if we were to allow open marriages, in which there was no promise of an exclusive sexual relationship between spouses. She argues that such relations are not immoral, although she does believe that they stray from a valuable ideal of what a marriage should be.

Steinbock concludes with a discussion of love, marital fidelity, and sexual relations. She finds it hard to see the value in remaining sexually faithful to someone you no longer love. She also notes the possibility of emotionally betraying someone you are sexually faithful to. If she is correct, then the links between emotional and sexual fidelity, marriage, and love may be more complicated than we at first thought.

Bonnie Steinbock, "Adultery." In QQ: Report from the Center for Philosophy and Public Policy 6.1 (1986): 12–14.

According to a 1980 survey in *Cosmopolitan*, 54 percent of American wives have had extramarital affairs; a study of 100,000 married women by the considerably tamer *Redbook* magazine found that 40 percent of the wives over 40 had been unfaithful. While such surveys are, to some extent, self-selecting—those who do it are more likely to fill out questionnaires about it—sexual mores have clearly changed in recent years. Linda Wolfe, who reported the results of the *Cosmopolitan* survey, suggests that "this increase in infidelity among married women represents not so much a deviation from traditional standards of fidelity as a break with the old double standard." Studies show that men have always strayed in significant numbers.

Yet 80 percent of "*Cosmo* girls" did not approve of infidelity and wished their own husbands and lovers would be faithful. Eighty-eight percent of respondents to a poll taken in Iowa in 1983 viewed "coveting your neighbor's spouse" as a "major sin." It seems that while almost nobody approves of adultery, men have always done it, and women are catching up.

The increase in female adultery doubtless has to do with recent and radical changes in our attitudes toward sex and sexuality. We no longer feel guilty about enjoying sex; indeed, the capacity for sexual enjoyment is often regarded as a criterion of mental health. When sex itself is no longer intrinsically shameful, restraints on sexual behavior are loosened. In fact, we might question whether the abiding disapproval of infidelity merely gives lip service to an ancient taboo. Is there a rational justification for disapproving of adultery which will carry force with everyone, religious and nonreligious alike?

Trust and Deception

Note first that adultery, unlike murder, theft, and lying, is not universally forbidden. Traditional Eskimo culture, for example, regarded sharing one's wife with a visitor as a matter of courtesy. The difference can be explained by looking at the effects of these practices on social cohesiveness. Without rules protecting the lives, persons, and property of its members, no group could long endure. Indeed, rules against killing, assault, lying, and stealing seem fundamental to having a morality at all.

Not so with adultery. For adultery is a *private* matter, essentially concerning only the relationship between husband and wife. It is not essential to morality like these other prohibitions: there are stable societies with genuine moral codes which tolerate extra-marital sex. Although adultery remains a criminal offense in some jurisdictions, it is rarely prosecuted. Surely this is because it is widely regarded as a private matter: in the words of Billie Holiday, "Ain't nobody's business if I do."

However, even if adultery is a private matter, with which the state should not interfere, it is not a morally neutral issue. Our view of adultery is connected to our thoughts and feelings about love and marriage, sex and the family, the value of fidelity, sexual jealousy, and exclusivity. How we think about adultery will affect the quality of our relationships, the way we raise our children, the kind of society we have and want to have. So it is important to consider whether our attitudes toward adultery are justifiable.

Several practical considerations militate against adultery: pregnancy and genital herpes immediately spring to mind. However, unwanted pregnancies are a risk of all sexual intercourse, within or without marriage; venereal disease is a risk of all nonexclusive sex, not just adulterous sex. So these risks do not provide a reason for objecting specifically to adultery. In any event, they offer merely pragmatic, as opposed to moral, objections. If adultery is wrong, it does not become less so because one has been sterilized or inoculated against venereal disease.

Two main reasons support regarding adultery as seriously immoral. One is that adultery is an instance of promise-breaking, on the view that marriage involves, explicitly or implicitly, a promise of sexual fidelity: to forsake all others. That there is this attitude in our culture is clear. Mick Jagger, not noted for sexual puritanism, allegedly refused to marry Jerry Hall, the mother of his baby, because he had no intention of accepting an exclusive sexual relationship. While Jagger's willingness to become an unwed father is hardly mainstream morality, his refusal to marry, knowing that he did not wish to be faithful, respects the idea that *marriage* requires such a commitment. Moreover, the promise of sexual fidelity is regarded as a very serious and important one. To cheat on one's spouse indicates a lack of concern, a willingness to cause pain, and so a lack of love. Finally, one who breaks promises cannot be trusted. And trust is essential to the intimate partnership of marriage, which may be irreparably weakened by its betrayal.

The second reason for regarding adultery as immoral is that it involves deception, for example, lying about one's whereabouts and relations with others. Perhaps a marriage can withstand the occasional lie, but a pattern of lying will have irrevocable consequences for a marriage, if discovered, and probably even if not. Like breaking promises, lying is regarded as a fundamental kind of wrongdoing, a failure to take the one lied to seriously as a moral person entitled to respect.

Open Marriage

These two arguments suffice to make most cases of adultery wrong, given the attitudes and expectations of most people. But what if marriage did not involve any promise of sexual fidelity? What if there were no need for deception, because neither partner expected or wanted such fidelity? Objections to "open marriage" cannot focus on promise-breaking and deception, for the expectation of exclusivity is absent. If an open marriage has been freely chosen by both spouses, and not imposed by a dominant on a dependent partner, would such an arrangement be morally acceptable, even desirable?

The attractiveness of extramarital affairs, without dishonesty, disloyalty, or guilt, should not be downplayed. However satisfying sex between married people may be, it cannot have the excitement of a new relationship. ("Not *better*," a friend once said defensively to his wife, attempting to explain his infidelity, "just *different*.") Might we not be better off, our lives fuller and richer, if we allowed ourselves the thrill of new and different sexual encounters?

Perhaps the expectation of sexual exclusivity in marriage stems from emotions which are not admirable: jealousy and possessiveness. That most people experience these feelings is no reason for applauding or institutionalizing them. Independence in marriage is now generally regarded as a good thing: too much "togetherness" is boring and stifling. In a good marriage, the partners can enjoy different activities, travel apart, and have separate friends. Why draw the line at sexual activity?

The natural response to this question invokes a certain conception of love and sex: sex is an expression of affection and intimacy and so should be reserved for people who love each other. Further, it is assumed that one can and should have such feelings for only one other person at any time. To make love with someone else is to express feelings of affection and intimacy that should be reserved for one's spouse alone.

This rejection of adultery assumes the validity of a particular conception of love and sex, which can be attacked in two ways. We might divorce sex from love and regard sex as a pleasurable activity in its own right, comparable to the enjoyment of a good meal. In his article "Is Adultery Immoral?" Richard Wasserstrom suggests that the linkage of sex with love reflects a belief that unless it is purified by a higher emotion, such as love, sex is intrinsically bad or dirty.

But this is an overly simplistic view of the connection between sex and love. Feelings of love occur between people enjoying sexual intercourse, not out of a sense that sexual pleasure must be purified, but precisely because of the mutual pleasure they give one another. People naturally have feelings of affection for those who make them happy, and sex is a very good way of making someone extraordinarily happy. At the same time, sex is by its nature intimate, involving both physical and psychological exposure. This both requires and creates trust, which is closely allied to feelings of affection and love. This is not to say that sex necessarily requires or leads to love; but a conception of the relation between love and sex that ignores these factors is inadequate and superficial.

Alternatively, one might acknowledge the connection between sex and love, but attack the assumption of exclusivity. If parents can love all their children equally and if adults can have numerous close friends, why should it be impossible to love more than one sexual partner at a time? Perhaps we could learn to love more widely and to accept that a spouse's sexual involvement with another is not a sign of rejection or lack of love.

The logistics of multiple involvement are certainly daunting. Having an affair (as opposed to a roll in the hay) requires time and concentration; it will almost inevitably mean neglecting one's spouse, one's children, one's work. More important, however, exclusivity seems to be an intrinsic part of "true love." Imagine Romeo pouring out his heart to both Juliet *and* Rosalind! In our ideal of romantic love, one chooses to forgo pleasure with other partners in order to have a unique relationship with one's beloved. Such "renunciation" is natural in the first throes of romantic love; it is precisely because this stage does *not* last that we must promise to be faithful through the notoriously unromantic realities of married life.

Fidelity as an Ideal

On the view I have been defending, genuinely open marriages are not *immoral*, although they deviate from a valued ideal of what marriage should be. While this is not the only ideal, or incumbent on all rational agents, it is a moral view in that it embodies a claim about a good way for people to live. The prohibition of adultery, then, is neither arbitrary nor irrational. However, even if we are justified in accepting the ideal of fidelity, we know that people do not always live up to the ideals they accept and we recognize that some failures to do so are worse than others. We regard a brief affair, occasioned by a prolonged separation, as morally different from installing a mistress.

Further, sexual activity is not necessary for deviation from the ideal of marriage which lies behind the demand for fidelity. As John Heckler observed during his bitter and public divorce from former Health and Human Services Secretary Margaret Heckler, "In marriage, there are two partners. When one person starts contributing far less than the other person to the marriage, that's the original infidelity. You don't need any third party." While this statement was probably a justification of his own infidelities, the point is valid. To abandon one's spouse, whether to a career or to another person, is also a kind of betrayal.

If a man becomes deeply involved emotionally with another woman, it may be little comfort that he is able to assure his wife that "Nothing happened." Sexual infidelity has significance as a sign of a deeper betrayal—falling in love with someone else. It may be objected that we cannot control the way we feel, only the way we behave; that we should not be blamed for falling in love, but only for acting on the feeling. While we may not have direct control over our feelings, however, we are responsible for getting ourselves into situations in which certain feelings naturally arise. "It just happened" is rarely an accurate portrayal of an extramarital love affair.

If there can be betrayal without sex, can there be sex without betrayal? In the novel *Forfeit*, by Dick Francis, the hero is deeply in love with his wife, who was paralyzed by polio in the early days of their marriage. Her great unspoken fear is that he will leave her; instead, he tends to her devotedly. For several years, he forgoes sex, but eventually succumbs to an affair. While his adultery is hardly praiseworthy, it is understandable. He could divorce his wife and marry again, but it is precisely his refusal to abandon her, his continuing love and tender care, that makes us admire him.

People do fall in love with others and out of love with their spouses. Ought they to refrain from making love while still legally tied? I cannot see much, if any, moral value in remaining physically faithful, on principle, to a spouse one no longer loves. This will displease those who regard the wrongness of adultery as a moral absolute, but my account has nothing to do with absolutes and everything to do with what it means to love someone deeply and completely. It is the value of that sort of relationship that makes sexual fidelity an ideal worth the sacrifice.

Neither a mere religiously based taboo, nor a relic of a repressive view of sexuality, the prohibition against adultery expresses a particular conception of married love. It is one we can honor in our own lives and bequeath to our children with confidence in its value as a coherent and rational ideal.

Bonnie Steinbock: Adultery

1) What reasons does Steinbock give for thinking that adultery is seriously immoral? Do these reasons apply to all cases of adultery?

2) Steinbock claims that open marriages "deviate from a valued ideal of what marriage should be." Do you agree with her about this? Is it morally wrong for spouses to agree to an open marriage?

3) Is it morally permissible to have sex merely for pleasure, or should people have sex only with partners whom they love?

4) Steinbock suggests at the end of the article that adultery may be permissible in some circumstances. What circumstances are these, and what reasons does she give for thinking adultery is permissible in such cases? Do you agree with her?

38

Licensing Parents

Hugh LaFollette

Hugh LaFollette argues that potential parents ought to be required to obtain a license before they are permitted to raise a child. He recognizes, of course, that there are certain practical hurdles to doing this, but thinks that these can be either met directly or addressed over time. And in any event, as he sees it, matters of principle strongly support a licensing scheme.

LaFollette argues that if an activity stands a significant chance of causing substantial harm to others, then, if we allow it at all, we ought to require a license before letting people engage in it. Driving a car, performing surgery, dispensing prescription drugs—each rightly requires a license, even though the relevant tests for competence are not guaranteed to be one hundred percent accurate, and some people who very much want to do these things will be disqualified from doing them. If LaFollette is right, raising children falls into this same category. As a result, parents need to be licensed, and some will fail to pass the relevant tests. Such people, argues LaFollette, should not be allowed to become parents.

There is a natural reply to such an argument: adults have a right to raise children, and any licensing requirement violates that right. LaFollette carefully reviews the different ways in which one might understand and argue for such a right. He thinks that the best ways are compatible with, and even lend support to, his licensing idea.

In this essay I shall argue that the state should require all parents to be licensed. My main goal is to demonstrate that the licensing of parents is theoretically desirable, though I shall also argue that a workable and just licensing program actually could be established.

My strategy is simple. After developing the basic rationale for the licensing of parents, I shall consider several objections to the proposal and argue that these objections fail to undermine it. I shall then isolate some striking similarities between this licensing program and our present policies on the adoption of children. If we retain these adoption policies—as we surely should—then, I argue, a general licensing program should also be established. Finally, I shall briefly suggest that the reason many people object to licensing is that they think parents, particularly biological parents, own or have natural sovereignty over their children.

Regulating Potentially Harmful Activities

Our society normally regulates a certain range of activities; it is illegal to perform these activities unless one has received prior permission to do so. We require automobile operators to have licenses. We forbid people from practicing medicine, law, pharmacy, or psychiatry unless they have satisfied certain licensing requirements.

Society's decision to regulate just these activities is not ad hoc. The decision to restrict admission to certain vocations and to forbid some people from driving is based on an eminently plausible, though not often explicitly formulated, rationale. We require drivers to be licensed because driving an auto is an activity which is potentially harmful to others, safe performance of the activity requires a certain competence, and we have a moderately reliable procedure for determining that competence. The potential harm is obvious: incompetent drivers can and do maim and kill people. The best way we have of limiting this harm without sacrificing the benefits of automobile travel is to require that all drivers demonstrate at least minimal competence. We likewise license doctors, lawyers, and psychologists because they perform activities which can harm others. Obviously they must be proficient if they are to perform these activities properly, and we have moderately reliable procedures for determining proficiency. Imagine a world in which everyone could legally drive a car, in which everyone could legally perform surgery, prescribe medications, dispense drugs, or offer legal advice. Such a world would hardly be desirable.

Consequently, any activity that is potentially harmful to others and requires certain demonstrated competence for its safe performance, is subject to regulation—that is, it is theoretically desirable that we regulate it. If we also have a reliable procedure for determining whether someone has the requisite competence, then the action is not only subject to regulation but ought, all things considered, to be regulated.

It is particularly significant that we license these hazardous activities, even though denying a license to someone can severely inconvenience and even harm that person. Furthermore, available competency tests are not 100 percent accurate. Denying someone a driver's license in our society, for example, would inconvenience that person acutely. In effect that person would be prohibited from working, shopping, or visiting in places reachable only by car. Similarly, people denied vocational licenses are inconvenienced, even devastated. We have all heard of individuals who had the "life-long dream" of becoming physicians or lawyers, yet were denied that dream. However, the realization that some people are disappointed or inconvenienced does not diminish our conviction that we must regulate occupations or activities that are potentially dangerous to others. Innocent people must be protected even if it means that others cannot pursue activities they deem highly desirable.

Furthermore, we maintain licensing procedures even though our competency tests are sometimes inaccurate. Some people competent to perform the licensed activity (for example, driving a car) will be unable to demonstrate competence (they freeze up on the driver's test). Others may be incompetent, yet pass the test (they are lucky or certain aspects of competence—for example, the sense of responsibility—are not tested). We recognize clearly—or should recognize clearly—that no test will pick out all and only competent drivers, physicians, lawyers, and so on. Mistakes are inevitable. This does not mean we should forget that innocent people may be harmed by faulty regulatory procedures. In fact, if the procedures are sufficiently faulty, we should cease regulating that activity entirely until more reliable tests are available. I only want to emphasize here that tests need not be perfect. Where moderately reliable tests are available, licensing procedures should be used to protect innocent people from incompetents.

These general criteria for regulatory licensing can certainly be applied to parents. First, parenting is an activity potentially very harmful to children. The potential for harm is apparent: each year more than half a million children are physically abused or neglected by their parents. Many millions more are psychologically abused or neglected—not given love, respect, or a sense of self-worth. The results of this maltreatment are obvious. Abused children bear the physical and psychological scars of maltreatment throughout their lives. Far too often they turn to crime. They are far more likely than others to abuse their own children. Even if these maltreated children never harm anyone, they will probably never be well-adjusted, happy adults. Therefore, parenting clearly satisfies the first criterion of activities subject to regulation.

The second criterion is also incontestably satisfied. A parent must be competent if he is to avoid harming his children; even greater competence is required if he is to do the "job" well. But not everyone has this minimal competence. Many people lack the knowledge needed to rear children adequately. Many others lack the requisite energy, temperament, or stability. Therefore, child-rearing manifestly satisfies both criteria of activities subject to regulation. In fact, I dare say that parenting is a paradigm of such activities since the potential for harm is so great (both in the extent of harm any one person can suffer and in the number of people potentially harmed) and the need for competence is so evident. Consequently, there is good reason to believe that all parents should be licensed. The only ways to avoid this conclusion are to deny the need for licensing *any* potentially harmful activity; to deny that I have identified the standard criteria of activities which should be regulated; to deny that parenting satisfies the standard criteria; to show that even though parenting satisfies the standard criteria there are special reasons why licensing parents is not theoretically desirable; or to show that there is no reliable and just procedure for implementing this program.

While developing my argument for licensing I have already identified the standard criteria for activities that should be regulated, and I have shown that they can properly be applied to parenting. One could deny the legitimacy of regulation by licensing, but in doing so one would condemn not only the regulation of parenting, but also the regulation of drivers, physicians, druggists, and doctors. Furthermore, regulation of hazardous activities appears to be a fundamental task of any stable society.

Thus only two objections remain. In the next section I shall see if there are any special reasons why licensing parents is not theoretically desirable. Then, in the following section, I shall examine several practical objections designed to demonstrate that even if licensing were theoretically desirable, it could not be justly implemented.

Theoretical Objections to Licensing

Licensing is unacceptable, someone might say, since people have a right to have children, just as they have rights to free speech and free religious expression. They do not need a license to speak freely or to worship as they wish. Why? Because they have a right to engage in these activities.

Similarly, since people have a right to have children, any attempt to license parents would be unjust.

This is an important objection since many people find it plausible, if not self-evident. However, it is not as convincing as it appears. The specific rights appealed to in this analogy are not without limitations. Both slander and human sacrifice are prohibited by law; both could result from the unrestricted exercise of freedom of speech and freedom of religion. Thus, even if people have these rights, they may sometimes be limited in order to protect innocent people. Consequently, even if people had a right to have children, that right might also be limited in order to protect innocent people, in this case children. Secondly, the phrase "right to have children" is ambiguous; hence, it is important to isolate its most plausible meaning in this context. Two possible interpretations are not credible and can be dismissed summarily. It is implausible to claim either that infertile people have rights to be *given* children or that people have rights to intentionally create children biologically without incurring any subsequent responsibility to them.

A third interpretation, however, is more plausible, particularly when coupled with observations about the degree of intrusion into one's life that the licensing scheme represents. On this interpretation people have a right to rear children if they make good-faith efforts to rear procreated children the best way they see fit. One might defend this claim on the ground that licensing would require too much intrusion into the lives of sincere applicants.

Undoubtedly one should be wary of unnecessary governmental intervention into individuals' lives. In this case, though, the intrusion would not often be substantial, and when it is, it would be warranted. Those granted licenses would face merely minor intervention; only those denied licenses would encounter marked intrusion. This encroachment, however, is a necessary side-effect of licensing parents—just as it is for automobile and vocational licensing. In addition, as I shall argue in more detail later, the degree of intrusion arising from a general licensing program would be no more than, and probably less than, the present (and presumably justifiable) encroachment into the lives of people who apply to adopt children. Furthermore, since some people hold unacceptable views about what is best for children (they think children should be abused regularly), people do not automatically have rights to rear children just because they will rear them in a way they deem appropriate.

Consequently, we come to a somewhat weaker interpretation of this right claim: a person has a right to rear children if he meets certain minimal standards of child rearing. Parents must not abuse or neglect their children and must also provide for the basic needs of the children. This claim of right is certainly more credible than the previously canvassed alternatives, though some people might still reject this claim in situations where exercise of the right would lead to negative consequences, for example, to overpopulation. More to the point, though, this conditional right is compatible with licensing. On this interpretation one has a right to have children only if one is not going to abuse or neglect them. Of course the very purpose if licensing is just to determing whether people *are* going to abuse or neglect their children. If the determination is made that someone will maltreat children, then that person is subject to the limitations of the right to have children and can legitimately be denied a parenting license.

In fact, this conditional way of formulating the right to have children provides a model for formulating all alleged rights to engage in hazardous activities. Consider, for example, the right to drive a car. People do not have an unconditional right to drive, although they do have a right to drive if they are competent. Similarly, people do not have an unconditional right to practice medicine; they have a right only if they are demonstrably competent. Hence, denying a driver's or physician's license to someone who has not demonstrated the requisite competence does not deny that person's rights. Likewise, on this model, denying a parenting license to someone who is not competent does not violate that person's rights.

Of course someone might object that the right is conditional on actually being a person who will abuse or neglect children, whereas my proposal only picks out those we can reasonably predict will abuse children. Hence, this conditional right *would* be incompatible with licensing.

There are two ways to interpret this objection and it is important to distinguish these divergent formulations. First, the objection could be a way of questioning our ability to predict reasonably and accurately whether people would maltreat their own children. This is an important practical objection, but I will defer discussion of it until the next section. Second, this objection could be a way of expressing doubt about the moral propriety of the prior restraint licensing requires. A parental licensing program would deny licenses to applicants judged to be incompetent even though they had never maltreated any children. This practice would be in tension with our normal skepticism about the propriety of prior restraint.

Despite this healthy skepticism, we do sometimes use prior restraint. In extreme circumstances we may hospitalize or imprison people judged insane, even though they are not legally guilty of any crime, simply because we predict they are likely to harm others. More typically, though, prior restraint is used only if the restriction is not terribly onerous and the restricted activity is one which could lead easily to serious harm. Most types of licensing (for example, those for doctors, drivers, and druggists) fall into this latter category. They require prior restraint to prevent serious harm, and generally the restraint is minor—though it is important to remember that some individuals will find it oppressive. The same is true of parental licensing. The purpose of licensing is to prevent serious harm to children. Moreover, the prior restraint required by licensing would not be terribly onerous for many people. Certainly the restraint would be far less extensive than the presumably justifiable prior restraint of, say, insane criminals. Criminals preventively detained and mentally ill people forceably hospitalized are denied most basic liberties, while those denied parental licenses would be denied only that one specific opportunity. They could still vote, work for political candidates, speak on controversial topics, and so on. Doubtless some individuals would find the restraint onerous. But when compared to other types of restraint currently practiced, and when judged in light of the severity of harm maltreated children suffer, the restraint appears *relatively* minor.

Furthermore, we could make certain, as we do with most licensing programs, that individuals denied licenses are given the opportunity to reapply easily and repeatedly for a license. Thus, many people correctly denied licenses (because they are incompetent) would choose (perhaps it would be provided) to take counseling or therapy to improve their chances of passing the next test. On the other hand, most of those mistakenly denied licenses would probably be able to demonstrate in a later test that they would be competent parents.

Consequently, even though one needs to be wary of prior restraint, if the potential for harm is great and the restraint is minor relative to the harm we are trying to prevent—as it would be with parental licensing—then such restraint is justified. This objection, like all the theoretical objections reviewed, has failed.

Practical Objections to Licensing

I shall now consider five practical objections to licensing. Each objection focuses on the problems or difficulties of implementing this proposal. According to these objections, licensing is (or may be) theoretically desirable; nevertheless, it cannot be efficiently and justly implemented.

The first objection is that there may not be, or we may not be able to discover, adequate criteria of "a good parent." We simply do not have the knowledge, and it is unlikely that we could ever obtain the knowledge, that would enable us to distinguish adequate from inadequate parents.

Clearly there is some force to this objection. It is highly improbable that we can formulate criteria that would distinguish precisely between good and less than good parents. There is too much we do not know about child development and adult psychology. My proposal, however, does not demand that we make these fine distinctions. It does not demand that we license only the best parents; rather it is designed to exclude only the very bad ones. This is not just a semantic difference, but a substantive one. Although we do not have infallible criteria for picking out good parents, we undoubtedly can identify bad ones—those who will abuse or neglect their children. Even though we could have a lively debate about the range of freedom a child should be given or the appropriateness of corporal punishment, we do not wonder if a parent who severely beats or neglects a child is adequate. We know that person isn't. Consequently, we do have reliable and useable criteria for determining who is a bad parent; we have the criteria necessary to make a licensing program work.

The second practical objection to licensing is that there is no reliable way to predict who will maltreat their children. Without an accurate predictive test, licensing would be not only unjust, but also a waste of time. Now I recognize that as a philosopher (and not a psychologist, sociologist, or social worker), I am on shaky ground if I make sweeping claims about the present or future abilities of professionals to produce such predictive tests. Nevertheless, there are some relevant observations I can offer.

Initially, we need to be certain that the demands on predictive tests are not unreasonable. For example, it would be improper to require that tests be 100 percent accurate. Procedures for licensing drivers, physicians, lawyers, druggists, etc., plainly are not 100 percent (or anywhere near 100 percent) accurate. Presumably we recognize these deficiencies yet embrace the procedures anyway. Consequently, it would be imprudent to demand considerably more exacting standards for the tests used in licensing parents.

In addition, from what I can piece together, the practical possibilities for constructing a reliable predictive test are not all that gloomy. Since my proposal does not require that we make fine line distinctions between good and less than good parents, but rather that we weed out those who are potentially very bad, we can use existing tests that claim to isolate relevant predictive characteristics—whether a person is violence-prone, easily frustrated, or unduly self-centered. In fact, researchers at Nashville General Hospital have developed a brief interview questionnaire which seems to have significant predictive value. Based on their data, the researchers identified 20 percent of the interviewees as a "risk group"—those having great potential for serious problems. After one year they found "the incidence of major breakdown in parent-child interaction in the risk group was approximately four to five times as great as in the low risk group."[1] We also know that parents who maltreat children often have certain identifiable experiences, for example, most of them were themselves maltreated as children. Consequently, if we combined our information about these parents with certain psychological test results, we would probably be able to predict with reasonable accuracy which people will maltreat their children.

However, my point is not to argue about the precise reliability of present tests. I cannot say emphatically that we now have accurate predictive tests. Nevertheless, even if such tests are not available, we could undoubtedly develop them. For example, we could begin a longitudinal study in which all potential parents would be required to take a specified battery of tests. Then these parents could be "followed" to discover which ones abused or neglected their children. By correlating test scores with information on maltreatment, a usable, accurate test could be fashioned. Therefore, I do not think that the present unavailability of such tests (if they are unavailable) would count against the legitimacy of licensing parents.

The third practical objection is that even if a reliable test for ascertaining who would be an acceptable parent were available, administrators would unintentionally misuse that test. These unintentional mistakes would clearly harm innocent individuals. Therefore, so the argument goes, this proposal ought to be scrapped. This objection can be dispensed with fairly easily unless one assumes there is some special reason to believe that more mistakes will be made in administering parenting licenses than in other regulatory activities. No matter how reliable our proceedings are, there will always be mistakes. We may license a physician who, through incompetence, would cause the death of a patient; or we may mistakenly deny a physician's license to someone who would be competent. But the fact that mistakes are made does not and should not lead us to abandon attempts to determine competence. The harm done in these cases could be far worse than the harm of mistakenly denying a person a parenting license. As far as I can tell, there is no reason to believe that more mistakes will be made here than elsewhere.

The fourth proposed practical objection claims that any testing procedure will be intentionally abused. People administering the process will

---

[1] The research gathered by Altemeir was reported by Ray Helfer in "Review of the Concepts and a Sampling of the Research Relating to Screening for the Potential to Abuse and/or Neglect One's Child." Helfer's paper was presented at a workshop sponsored by the National Committee for the Prevention of Child Abuse, 3–6 December 1978.

disqualify people they dislike, or people who espouse views they dislike, from rearing children.

The response to this objection is parallel to the response to the previous objection, namely, that there is no reason to believe that the licensing of parents is more likely to be abused than driver's license tests or other regulatory procedures. In addition, individuals can be protected from prejudicial treatment by pursuing appeals available to them. Since the licensing test can be taken on numerous occasions, the likelihood of the applicant's working with different administrative personnel increases and therefore the likelihood decreases that intentional abuse could ultimately stop a qualified person from rearing children. Consequently, since the probability of such abuse is not more than, and may even be less than, the intentional abuse of judicial and other regulatory authority, this objection does not give us any reason to reject the licensing of parents.

The fifth objection is that we could never adequately, reasonably, and fairly enforce such a program. That is, even if we could establish a reasonable and fair way of determining which people would be inadequate parents, it would be difficult, if not impossible, to enforce the program. How would one deal with violators and what could we do with babies so conceived? There are difficult problems here, no doubt, but they are not insurmountable. We might not punish parents at all—we might just remove the children and put them up for adoption. However, even if we are presently uncertain about the precise way to establish a just and effective form of enforcement, I do not see why this should undermine my licensing proposal. If it is important enough to protect children from being maltreated by parents, then surely a reasonable enforcement procedure can be secured. At least we should assume one can be unless someone shows that it cannot.

An Analogy with Adoption

So far I have argued that parents should be licensed. Undoubtedly many readers find this claim extremely radical. It is revealing to notice, however, that this program is not as radical as it seems. Our moral and legal systems already recognize that not everyone is capable of rearing children well. In fact, well-entrenched laws require adoptive parents to be investigated—in much the same ways and for much the same reasons as in the general licensing program advocated here. For example, we do not allow just anyone to adopt a child; nor do we let someone adopt without first estimating the likelihood of the person's being a good parent. In fact, the adoptive process is far more rigorous than the general licensing procedures I envision. Prior to adoption the candidates must first formally apply to adopt a child. The applicants are then subjected to an exacting home study to determine whether they really want to have children and whether they are capable of caring for and rearing them adequately. No one is allowed to adopt a child until the administrators can reasonably predict that the person will be an adequate parent. The results of these procedures are impressive. Despite the trauma children often face before they are finally adopted, they are five times less likely to be abused than children reared by their biological parents.[2]

Nevertheless we recognize, or should recognize, that these demanding procedures exclude some people who would be adequate parents. The selection criteria may be inadequate; the testing procedures may be somewhat unreliable. We may make mistakes. Probably there is some intentional abuse of the system. Adoption procedures intrude directly in the applicants' lives. Yet we continue the present adoption policies because we think it better to mistakenly deny some people the opportunity to adopt than to let just anyone adopt.

Once these features of our adoption policies are clearly identified, it becomes quite apparent that there are striking parallels between the general licensing program I have advocated and our present adoption system. Both programs have the same aim—protecting children. Both have the same drawbacks and are subject to the same abuses. The only obvious dissimilarity is that the adoption requirements are *more* rigorous than those proposed for the general licensing program. Consequently, if we think it is so important to protect adopted children, even though people who want to adopt are less likely than biological parents to maltreat their children, then we should likewise afford the same protection to children reared by their biological parents.

I suspect, though, that many people will think the cases are not analogous. The cases are relevantly different, someone might retort, because biological parents have a natural affection for their children and the strength

---

[2] According to a study published by the Child Welfare League of America, at least 51 percent of the adopted children had suffered, prior to adoption, more than minimal emotional deprivation. See A *Follow-up Study of Adoptions: Post Placement Functioning of Adoption Families*, Elizabeth A. Lawder et al., New York 1969.

According to a study by David Gil (*Violence Against Children*, Cambridge: Harvard University Press, 1970) only .4 percent of abused children were abused by adoptive parents. Since at least 2 percent of the children in the United States are adopted (*Encyclopedia of Social Work*, National Association of Social Workers, New York, 1977), that means the rate of abuse by biological parents is five time that of adoptive parents.

of this affection makes it unlikely that parents would maltreat their biologically produced children.

Even if it were generally true that parents have special natural affections for their biological offspring, that does not mean that all parents have enough affection to keep them from maltreating their children. This should be apparent given the number of children abused each year by their biological parents. Therefore, even if there is generally such a bond, that does not explain why we should not have licensing procedures to protect children of parents who do not have a sufficiently strong bond. Consequently, if we continue our practice of regulating the adoption of children, and certainly we should, we are rationally compelled to establish a licensing program for all parents.

However, I am not wedded to a strict form of licensing. It may well be that there are alternative ways of regulating parents which would achieve the desired results—the protection of children—without strictly prohibiting nonlicensed people from rearing children. For example, a system of tax incentives for licensed parents, and protective services scrutiny of nonlicensed parents, might adequately protect children. If it would, I would endorse the less drastic measure. My principal concern is to protect children from maltreatment by parents. I begin by advocating the more strict form of licensing since that is the standard method of regulating hazardous activities. I have argued that all parents should be licensed by the state. This licensing program is attractive, not because state intrusion is inherently judicious and efficacious, but simply because it seems to be the best way to prevent children from being reared by incompetent parents. Nonetheless, even after considering the previous arguments, many people will find the proposal a useless academic exercise, probably silly, and possibly even morally perverse. But why? Why do most of us find this proposal unpalatable, particularly when the arguments supporting it are good and the objections to it are philosophically flimsy?

I suspect the answer is found in a long-held, deeply ingrained attitude toward children, repeatedly reaffirmed in recent court decisions, and present, at least to some degree, in almost all of us. The belief is that parents own, or at least have natural sovereignty over, their children. It does not matter precisely how this belief is described, since on both views parents legitimately exercise extensive and virtually unlimited control over their children. Others can properly interfere with or criticize parental decisions only in unusual and tightly prescribed circumstances—for example, when parents severely and repeatedly abuse their children. In all other cases, the parents reign supreme.

This belief is abhorrent and needs to be supplanted with a more child-centered view. Why? Briefly put, this attitude has adverse effects on children and on the adults these children will become. Parents who hold this view may well maltreat their children. If these parents happen to treat their children well, it is only because they want to, not because they think their children deserve or have a right to good treatment. Moreover, this belief is manifestly at odds with the conviction that parents should prepare children for life as adults. Children subject to parents who perceive children in this way are likely to be adequately prepared for adulthood. Hence, to prepare children for life as adults and to protect them from maltreatment, this attitude toward children must be dislodged. As I have argued, licensing is a viable way to protect children. Furthermore, it would increase the likelihood that more children will be adequately prepared for life as adults than is now the case.

Hugh LaFollette: Licensing Parents

1) LaFollette claims that "any activity that is potentially harmful to others and requires certain demonstrated competence for its safe performance, is subject to regulation." Do you find this principle to be plausible? Why or why not?
2) LaFollette argues that the above principle applies to parenting, since parenting is potentially harmful to children and requires competence to be done safely. Do you agree that parenting has these features? If so, does that justify licensing parents?
3) LaFollette compares licensing parents to licensing other activities, such as driving, practicing law, and being a doctor. Are there any morally relevant differences between these activities and parenting, such that we are justified in licensing the former but not the latter?
4) Do people have a *right* to have and raise children? If so, is it morally impermissible to require parents to be licensed?
5) Do you think that LaFollette's proposal could actually be applied in a way that was fair and nondiscriminatory? Why or why not?
6) LaFollette points out that we already require adoptive parents to be "licensed." Is it inconsistent of us to do this while allowing biological parents to go unlicensed?

39

What Do Grown Children Owe Their Parents?

Jane English

It may be tempting to think that adults owe their parents a debt of support. After all, most parents have provided for their children in a variety of ways, over the course of many years. Doesn't this effort and assistance generate a duty on the part of grown children to reciprocate—at least to some extent?

Jane English (1947–1978) says no. Adults owe their parents nothing. The sacrifices that parents make on their children's behalf are made voluntarily, and so the benefits that parents confer on their children do not generate any duties on the children's part. That doesn't mean, of course, that adults ought to disrespect their parents. English encourages good relations between parents and their adult children, but does not think that such relations are based on any special duty that adult children bear to their parents. Rather, such relationships ought to be based on a model of friendship, in which any sacrifices are made willingly, rather than from duty.

Friends give to one another based on their resources, abilities, and needs. Grown children should willingly give to their parents, provided that they are on friendly terms. But suppose they are not. It is tempting, in many cases, to argue that adults are still duty-bound to provide for their parents' needs, as a way of discharging a debt for "services rendered." English argues that this way of understanding an adult's relations with her parents is fundamentally flawed.

Jane English, "What Do Grown Children Owe Their Parents?" from *Having Children*, eds. Onora O'Neill and William Ruddick. (1979) pp. 174–178. By permission of Oxford University Press, Inc.

What do grown children owe their parents? I will contend that the answer is "nothing." Although I agree that there are many things that children ought to do for their parents, I will argue that it is inappropriate and misleading to describe them as things "owed." I will maintain that parents' voluntary sacrifices, rather than creating "debts" to be "repaid," tend to create love or "friendship." The duties of grown children are those of friends and result from love between them and their parents, rather than being things owed in repayment for the parents' earlier sacrifices. Thus, I will oppose those philosophers who use the word "owe" whenever a duty or obligation exists. Although the "debt" metaphor is appropriate in some moral circumstances, my argument is that a love relationship is not such a case.

Misunderstandings about the proper relationship between parents and their grown children have resulted from reliance on the "owing" terminology. For instance, we hear parents complain, "You owe it to us to write home (keep up your piano playing, not adopt a hippie lifestyle), because of all we sacrificed for you (paying for piano lessons, sending you to college)." The child is sometimes even heard to reply, "I didn't ask to be born (to be given piano lessons, to be sent to college)." This inappropriate idiom of ordinary language tends to obscure, or even to undermine, the love that is the correct ground of filial obligation.

1. Favors Create Debts

There are some cases, other than literal debts, in which talk of "owing," though metaphorical, is apt. New to the neighborhood, Max barely knows his neighbor, Nina, but he asks her if she will take in his mail while he is gone for a month's vacation. She agrees. If, subsequently, Nina asks Max to do the same for her, it seems that Max has a moral obligation to agree (greater than the one he would have had if Nina had not done the same for him), unless for some reason it would be a burden far out of proportion to the one Nina bore for him. I will call this a *favor*: when A, at B's request, bears some burden for B, then B incurs an obligation to reciprocate. Here the metaphor of Max's "owing" Nina is appropriate. It is not literally a debt, of course, nor can Nina pass this IOU on to heirs, demand payment in the form of Max's taking out her garbage, or sue Max. Nonetheless, since Max ought to perform one act of similar nature and amount of sacrifice in return, the term is suggestive. Once he reciprocates, the debt is "discharged"—that is, their obligations revert to the condition they were in before Max's initial request.

Contrast a situation in which Max simply goes on vacation and, to his surprise, finds upon his return that his neighbor has mowed his grass twice weekly in his absence. This is a voluntary sacrifice rather than a favor, and Max has no duty to reciprocate. It would be nice for him to volunteer to do so, but this would be supererogatory on his part. Rather than a favor, Nina's action is a friendly gesture. As a result, she might expect Max to chat over the back fence, help her catch her straying dog, or something similar—she might expect the development of a friendship. But Max would be chatting (or whatever) out of friendship, rather than in repayment for mown grass. If he did not return her gesture, she might feel rebuffed or miffed, but not unjustly treated or indignant, since Max has not failed to perform a duty. Talk of "owing" would be out of place in this case.

It is sometimes difficult to distinguish between favors and non-favors, because friends tend to do favors for each other, and those who exchange favors tend to become friends. But one test is to ask how Max is motivated. Is it "to be nice to Nina" or "because she did x for me"? Favors are frequently performed by total strangers without any friendship developing. Nevertheless, a temporary obligation is created, even if the chance for repayment never arises. For instance, suppose that Oscar and Matilda, total strangers, are waiting in a long checkout line at the supermarket. Oscar, having forgotten the oregano, asks Matilda to watch his cart for a second. She does. If Matilda now asks Oscar to return the favor while she picks up some tomato sauce, he is obliged to agree. Even if she had not watched his cart, it would be inconsiderate of him to refuse, claiming he was too busy reading the magazines. He may have a duty to help others, but he would not "owe" it to her. But if she had done the same for him, he incurs an additional obligation to help, and talk of "owing" is apt. It suggests an agreement to perform equal, reciprocal, canceling sacrifices.

2. The Duties of Friendship Versus Debts

The terms "owe" and "repay" are helpful in the case of favors, because the sameness of the amount of sacrifice on the two sides is important; the monetary metaphor suggests equal quantities of sacrifice. But friendship ought to be characterized by *mutuality* rather than reciprocity: friends offer what they can give and accept what they need, without regard for the total amounts of benefits exchanged. And friends are motivated by love rather than by the prospect of repayment. Hence, talk of "owing" is singularly out of place in friendship.

For example, suppose Alfred takes Beatrice out for an expensive dinner and a movie. Beatrice incurs no obligation to "repay" him with a goodnight kiss or a return engagement. If Alfred complains that she "owes" him something, he is operating under the assumption that she should repay a favor, but on the contrary his was a generous gesture done in the hopes of developing a friendship. We hope that he would not want her repayment in the form of sex or attention if this was done to discharge a debt rather than from friendship. Since, if Alfred is prone to reasoning in this way, Beatrice may well decline the invitation or request to pay for her own dinner, his attitude of expecting a "return" on his "investment" could hinder the development of a friendship. Beatrice should return the gesture only if she is motivated by friendship.

Another common misuse of the "owing" idiom occurs when the Smiths have dined at the Joneses' four times, but the Joneses at the Smiths' only once. People often say, "We owe them three dinners." This line of thinking may be appropriate between business acquaintances, but not between friends. After all, the Joneses invited the Smiths not in order to feed them or to be fed in turn, but because of the friendly contact presumably enjoyed by all on such occasions. If the Smiths do not feel friendship toward the Joneses, they can decline future invitations and not invite the Joneses; they owe them nothing. Of course, between friends of equal resources and needs, roughly equal sacrifices (though not necessarily roughly equal dinners) will typically occur. If the sacrifices are highly out of proportion to the resources, the relationship is closer to servility than to friendship.

Another difference between favors and friendship is that after a friendship ends, the duties of friendship end. The party that has sacrificed less owes the other nothing. For instance, suppose Elmer donated a pint of blood that his wife Doris needed during an operation. Years after their divorce, Elmer is in an accident and needs one pint of blood. His new wife, Cora, is also of the same blood type. It seems that Doris not only does not "owe" Elmer blood, but that she should actually refrain from coming forward if Cora has volunteered to donate. To insist on donating not only interferes with the newlyweds' friendship, but it belittles Doris and Elmer's former relationship by suggesting that Elmer gave blood in hopes of favors returned instead of simply out of love for Doris. It is one of the heartrending features of divorce that it attends to quantity in a relationship previously characterized by mutuality. If Cora could not donate, Doris's obligation is the same as that for any former spouse in need of blood; it is not increased by the fact that Elmer similarly aided her. It is affected by the degree to which they are still friends, which in turn may (or may not) have been influenced by Elmer's donation.

In short, unlike the debts created by favors, the duties of friendship do not require equal quantities of sacrifice. Performing equal sacrifices does not cancel the duties of friendship, as it does the debts of favors. Unrequested sacrifices do not themselves create debts, but friends have duties regardless of whether they requested or initiated the friendship. Those who perform favors may be motivated by mutual gain, whereas friends should be motivated by affection. These characteristics of the friendship relation are distorted by talk of "owing."

3. Parents and Children

The relationship between children and their parents should be one of friendship characterized by mutuality rather than one of reciprocal favors. The quantity of parental sacrifice is not relevant in determining what duties the grown child has. The medical assistance grown children ought to offer their ill mothers in old age depends upon the mothers' need, not upon whether they endured a difficult pregnancy, for example. Nor do one's duties to one's parents cease once an equal quantity of sacrifice has been performed, as the phrase "discharging a debt" may lead us to think.

Rather, what children ought to do for their parents (and parents for children) depends upon (1) their respective needs, abilities, and resources and (2) the extent to which there is an ongoing friendship between them. Thus, regardless of the quantity of childhood sacrifices, an able, wealthy child has an obligation to help his needy parents more than does a needy child. To illustrate, suppose sisters Cecile and Dana are equally loved by their parents, even though Cecile was an easy child to care for, seldom ill, while Dana was often sick and caused some trouble as a juvenile delinquent. As adults, Dana is a struggling artist living far away, while Cecile is a wealthy lawyer living nearby. When the parents need visits and financial aid, Cecile has an obligation to bear a higher proportion of these burdens than her sister. This results from her abilities, rather than from the quantities of sacrifice made by the parents earlier.

Sacrifices have an important causal role in creating an ongoing friendship, which may lead us to assume incorrectly that it is the sacrifices that are the source of the obligation. That the source is the friendship instead can be seen by examining cases in which the sacrifices occurred but the friendship, for some reason, did not develop or persist. For example, if a woman gives up her newborn child for adoption, and if no feelings of love ever develop on either side, it seems that the grown child does not have an obligation to "repay" her for her sacrifices in pregnancy. For that matter, if the adopted child has an unimpaired love relationship with the adoptive parents, he or she has the same obligations to help them as a natural child would have.

The filial obligations of grown children are a result of friendship, rather than owed for services rendered. Suppose that Vance married Lola despite his parents' strong wish that he marry within their religion, and that as a result, the parents refuse to speak to him again. As the years pass, the parents are unaware of Vance's problems, his accomplishments, the birth of his children. The love that once existed between them, let us suppose, has been completely destroyed by this event and thirty years of desuetude. At this point, it seems, Vance is under no obligation to pay his parents' medical bills in their old age, beyond his general duty to help those in need. An additional, filial obligation would only arise from whatever love he may still feel for them. It would be irrelevant for his parents to argue, "But look how much we sacrificed for you when you were young," for that sacrifice was not a favor but occurred as part of a friendship which existed at that time but is now, we have supposed, defunct. A more appropriate message would be, "We still love you, and we would like to renew our friendship."

I hope this helps to set the question of what children ought to do for their parents in a new light. The parental argument, "You ought to do x because we did y for you," should be replaced by, "We love you and you will be happier if you do x," or "We believe you love us, and anyone who loved us would do x." If the parents' sacrifice had been a favor, the child's reply, "I never asked you to do y for me," would have been relevant; to the revised parental remarks, this reply is clearly irrelevant. The child can either do x or dispute one of the parents' claims: by showing that a love relationship does not exist, or that love for someone does not motivate doing x, or that he or she will not be happier doing x.

Seen in this light, parental requests for children to write home, visit, and offer them a reasonable amount of emotional and financial support in life's crises are well founded, so long as a friendship still exists. Love for others does call for caring about and caring for them. Some other parental requests, such as for more sweeping changes in the child's lifestyle or life goals, can be seen to be insupportable, once we shift the justification from debts owed to love. The terminology of favors suggests the reasoning,

408 THE ETHICAL LIFE

"Since we paid for your college education, you owe it to us to make a career of engineering, rather than becoming a rock musician." This tends to alienate affection even further, since the tuition payments are depicted as investments for a return rather than done from love, as though the child's life goals could be "bought." Basing the argument on love leads to different reasoning patterns. The suppressed premise, "If A loves B, then A follows B's wishes as to A's lifelong career" is simply false. Love does not even dictate that the child adopt the parents' values as to the desirability of alternative life goals. So the parents' strongest available argument here is, "We love you, we are deeply concerned about your happiness, and in the long run you will be happier as an engineer." This makes it clear that an empirical claim is really the subject of the debate.

The function of these examples is to draw out our considered judgments as to the proper relation between parents and their grown children, and to show how poorly they fit the model of favors. What is relevant is the ongoing friendship that exists between parents and children. Although that relationship developed partly as a result of parental sacrifices for the child, the duties that grown children have to their parents result from the friendship rather than from the sacrifices. The idiom of owing favors to one's parents can actually be destructive if it undermines the role of mutuality and leads us to think in terms of quantitative reciprocal favors.

Jane English: What Do Grown Children Owe Their Parents?

1) What is the difference, according to English, between the duty to repay debts and the duties of friendship?
2) Do you agree with English that friends do not *owe* one another anything? Why or why not?
3) English claims that "the filial obligations of grown children are a result of friendship, rather than owed for services rendered." What reasons does she give for thinking this? Do you agree with her?
4) Consider the case of Vance. Does Vance have greater obligations to his elderly parents than he has to strangers? Why or why not?
5) What form should parents' requests to their children take, according to English? Do you find her account of such requests plausible?